Dancing Feat

One Man's Mission to Dance Like a Colombian

Neil Bennion

DANCING FEAT

Enquiries: contact@neilbennion.com

CONTENTS

Caribbean Sea
Tayrona National Natural Park
Taganga
Barranquilla
Cartagena
Ciudad Perdida
Santa Marta
Valledupar
San Basilio de Palenque
Tolú
San Antero
Magangué
Mompós
El Banco
PANAMA
River Cauca
Barrancabermeja
Medellín
San Gil
River Magdalena
Marmato
Tunja
Aquitania
Pereira
Zipaquirá
Pacific Ocean
BOGOTÁ
Filandia
Acacías
Puerto López
Villavicencio
Cali
Neiva
Colombia
Silvia
Popayán
Pasto
Túquerres
ECUADOR
PERU

VENEZUELA

BRAZIL

NORTH
AMERICA
CENTRAL
AMERICA
SOUTH
AMERICA

Foreword

This is a work of non-fiction. I have, however, made various alterations to the identities of people involved, changing names, descriptions and sometimes even blood types. This has been done partly to protect their privacy but mostly just because I'm awkward.

I mention money quite a bit. At the time of writing, the exchange rate was roughly 1 pound sterling = 3,000 Colombian pesos = 1.50 US dollars = 17 Lutherian wangdangs.

I'd like to say a big thanks to my family and friends for all their support and encouragement, and to everyone who put up with me saying "Yeah, it's nearly finished!" for so long that it couldn't possibly have been true the whole time.

Thanks also to the many Colombians who played a part in my journey, especially all those who were the unfortunate victims of my attempts at dancing along the way.

Thanks to Helena Drysdale, Frank Safford and David Knight, each of whom helped me overcome obstacles to publication. And also to Evan for help with the publishing side, Karol Gajda for the marketing side and Alejandro Silva, and various members of my own family, for test reading and sanity checking. Along with Mama and Papa Bennion for helping at pretty much every stage along the way.

Finally, a really big thanks to me, without whom none of this would have been possible.

For Mum and Dad

CHAPTER ONE

Danceless

"You dance like a twat."

I don't know what I was expecting to hear, but it definitely wasn't that. It was the morning after a night out in London's East End. We'd gone to a cool bar, had a few drinks and chucked a few shapes about. Except, according to my girlfriend of the time, mine looked like they'd been thrown by an amateur potter.

But that was all a long time ago now. And, besides, I solved the problem quite easily. Spurred on by my ex's comment, I went to dance classes and... no, wait: I just never danced with her again. Not for the entire remaining two years of the relationship.

Criticism is one of the great manipulators, and my dancing has been the subject of a lot of it over the years. The result has been that I've spent much of my adult life oscillating between someone who dances badly and someone who doesn't dance at all.

The thing is I came born with that natural English style, known as 'self-conscious, stiff-limbed awkwardness'. In this informal, well-adopted genre, changes to movement come with the same natural flow and spontaneity as the local-council planning permission process.

Legs aren't so bad: you can just do something repetitive with them, and they're mostly out of the line of sight. It's the arms that are the problem. The younger of my two sisters had a novel solution to this problem, appropriating some of the more emphatic and cooler-looking gestures she'd learnt in her sign language classes.

"There's a bomb! There's a bomb!" she would sign. "Get out! Get out!"

It's certainly a quick way of identifying all the deaf people in a club.

My own approach to dancing is to just tidy the arms away, where they can't do so much damage. This appears to be a common approach by rubbish dancers – store them permanently by the side, bent at the elbow. It's the same strategy adopted by the Tyrannosaurus Rex, a species which, incidentally, were also appalling dancers, and frequently mocked by the more able triceratops.

When it comes to dance, people will often say that you shouldn't care what people think; you should just get out there and enjoy yourself. This is great advice, especially if you have no desire to ever procreate. It's also the basis of one of the other styles of dance I subject the world to from time to time: over-expression. Lubricated by alcohol and enthusiasm, it's easy to get confused into thinking that because something feels good, it follows that it also looks good.

I've come to the conclusion that I must be like one of those talent show rejects that sings in unbridled joy, misreading the audience's reaction as an endorsement, with no-one having the heart to tell them that they're an object of derision. Unless they, too, have a brutally honest partner.

"You sing like a twat."

All four windows are wound-down partway, blasting me with lukewarm air. It dilutes the smells of the vehicle's interior: that of gasoline, aged-dustiness and the worn-out faux-leather seats that I'm sliding about on. I'm in Latin America alright – I could tell that with my eyes closed. Especially since I've just taken a flight there.

In the distance, a green chain of mountains rears up, corpulent and wrinkled; giant white loofahs in the sky for company. Somewhere between us and the mountains lies the city; behind us the airport is already just a memory.

We whistle along the concrete-sectioned highway, the radio filling the air with local rhythms. Some songs burst with rapid-fire beat clusters, whilst others are more lilting and gentle. Some sound bouncy and poppy, whilst others are slow and romantic. I can even tell some of them are cheesy, despite most of the lyrics being beyond the grasp of my so-so Spanish. What I can't tell about any of the tracks is what type of music they are. They all just sound 'Latin'.

I adore music, which makes it all the more frustrating not being able to dance. You hear some music you love, and you feel that deep urge within to just… do… something. But for me this is where it all falls apart. I lack even the most basic vocabulary required for the interaction – I'm like a Labrador trying to discuss semiotics. So the great music plays on, and I just standing there barking. No, really.

A major part of this problem is the style of dancing I've grown up with. My parents, and their parents before them, used to go out and dance 'with' each other, which translated to some kind of physical contact. But I've grown up with the idea that dancing 'with' somebody else really means dancing 'at' them.

I feel like my generation has been kind of cheated: the only chance you have of a developing a real connection is by copying each other's actions, which can only be done ironically, or perhaps throwing in the odd wrestling hold. Okay, you can also make eye contact, though strangely enough women don't tend to give me much of that when I'm dancing.

So it would be great to learn how to dance properly.

That said, if I never managed it, it wouldn't be the end of the world, would it? In fact, it's entirely possible that I could just carry through my life as many other Englishmen have done, without ever learning to distinguish myself in that respect.

But there's another issue – I don't drink. It's been four years since I stopped – a consequence of a health problem I developed.

At first it was hellish. It was only when it was taken away that I realised how deeply ingrained alcohol had been into my life. Parties, dates and dinners; Birthdays, weddings and barbecues; Bonding with my dad; Watching sport; Lying in the gutter mumbling incoherently – every social activity, big or small, had alcohol at its core. And every single one was now awkward.

Even the pub, so long an amber-toned refuge from the harshness of life, was transformed into a land of sodden beermats and shouty people. Whilst nightclubs suddenly seemed pointless.

But you can get used to pretty much anything given enough time. I became comfortable – happy even – going out at night, weaving non-judgementally around the pavement vomit of Manchester, giving the staggerers and fight-starters a respectful distance.

More than just getting used to it, I began to flourish. Not drinking forced me to seek out all sorts of alternatives to fill the vacated space. I learnt how to meditate and I learnt how to massage (well, how to pay for a massage). I took a greater interest in cultural events, cinema and scientific scepticism. I found myself seeking new and interesting things to do of an evening instead of always reaching for a glass. In short, it enriched me.

But despite all I've gained, there is still something missing from my evenings. Out-and-out, mind-blowing hedonism is probably always going to be out of reach, but I need something else. I need a way of letting go. I need fun, excitement and anticipation. I need a focus for the evening other than just the repeated pouring of liquids in the general direction of the oesophagus.

None of the alternatives I've tried have matched up. Joining language clubs, going bowling, stealing cars – they're all good social activities, but none of them quite hits the mark. And there are only so many games of naked Twister you can propose before people stop answering your calls.

And that's where we come back to dance. For here is an activity which allows people to reach great heights of self-expression and make them feel alive. An activity which, at its extreme, is nothing less than an exploration of ecstasy and a baring of the soul, yet which can be done casually with friends, too.

(You're right, that's begging for a joke.)

It's something that's actually good for you if you know what you're doing, and something which previous girlfriends have complained I couldn't do properly. Something that doing in a state of sobriety seems like madness (indeed there are those who claim they've never done it sober).

(Okay, I'll stop now.)

I need dance in my life.

There's another potential upside to this. Due to a mixture of incompetence, too much time at the writing desk and the side-effects of not drinking, I've somehow found myself in my mid-thirties and without a woman in my life to call my long-term partner. It's disappointing – I thought I'd have been trapped in a loveless marriage for years by now.

Dance seems like a great way for men to meet women. Not least because if we've agreed to clasp onto each other for three to five minutes then at least I've got some kind of a sales window. Actually forget meeting women – I'm just going to use it to sell conservatories to strangers.

Back in the here and now, the cityscape at the base of the mountains begins to loom, and soon we're on its fringes, joined at a distance by commercial new-builds and modern apartment blocks. The scent of cut grass blows in from well-maintained reservations – the smell of investment – and soon we've reached the outer limits of a spanking-new guided bus system.

Spanish is everywhere, streaming out of the radio, directing traffic and selling products. Not that it's always necessary: as the road changes from highway to street, shops appear with images of their wares hand-painted directly on the wall. Hardware stores have images of hammers and bed shops have images of beds. I wonder what they paint on the outside of brothels.

I saw a lot of this kind of thing (hand-painted signs more than brothels) on my previous journey to Latin America, so I know this is quite normal here.

I must admit, though, I'm still seduced by the idea we are sold in the UK of what Latin America, or at least Latin spirit, looks like. I'm thinking specifically of those white rum adverts with their compelling narratives of open-air partying and sultry Latin *chicas*. But then I've seen some of the reality of nights out in this part of the world, too, and it's still pretty impressive.

I've stood periscope-like on a dance floor full of Bolivians wondering how they all just seemed to know what to do – public information films, perhaps? I've been to bars in South America and seen even the stiffest-looking office worker soften their shoulders at the merest hint of Latin music and begin casually gyrating where they stood. And I've seen dancing on the Caribbean coast of Central America that looked closer to sex than, well, sex.

But some countries have stronger dance cultures than others. Indeed, there's one in particular that I've heard a lot about over the years – a country that would probably be famous for its dance and music were it not famous for other things first. It's a country whose reputation precedes it. It's also a country I've never been to. Until today, that is.

The taxi driver has his seat pushed right forward to compensate for his own lack of height, creating masses of space in front of me and making him look really eager. I'm willing to bet he could not only name every type of music coming out of his radio, but could also dance to each one of them without a second thought, too.

The traffic thickens and the buildings begin to close in and rise up. Some look only a few decades old, but are already beyond tired, whilst others, I'm guessing from the 1920s and 30s, have a semi-modern elegance, redolent of rolodexes and yellowing memos. They're not ancient, but they've certainly been around a while.

Not unlike myself, really. I'm still relatively young, but time is marching on. The years are speeding up. Blink and I'll be 40 (I don't know what'll happen if I wink). At some point you start to realise that all those things that you thought you would get round to at some point ... well you really might want to start getting round to them. And dance is one of those things.

I've put this off far too long already. I don't want to dance self-consciously anymore, nor over-expressively. I don't want to dance any variation on a theme of 'twat'. I want to dance well. I want people to look at me and say "He might be a twat in many and varied ways, but you wouldn't know it to watch him dance."

I want to be able to dance *with* a partner instead of *at* her; to share that thing; to connect in that way. I want to be able to say "Shall we dance" without an unsaid "individually, but relatively near" appended to the end.

I want women to be attracted to the way I dance; to find it appealing; to smile at me out of a sense of connection rather than pity. I don't want to be a solitary old man, sat all alone growing more and more right wing. I want to grow more and more right wing with someone I love.

I want a way of socialising with people beyond just a shared inability to form coherent sentences. I want something to look forward to at weekends; a reason to get out from behind my writing desk; a way of letting go and actually having some fun.

I want to have the guts to get on the dance floor at all, instead of having a dance confidence that's so brittle that I'd rather pretend to be deaf and charge out of the club under instruction from my younger sister than actually lay some moves down.

I want to be able to dance, dammit. That's where I'm at. Is that really too much to ask?

The rough green fabric of the mountains is closing in now, the city gently rising on its hem. We're nearly there. The driver takes a turn crosstown and the buildings take a turn for the historic. Squat, colonial-style edifices with rendered walls and red roof tiles suddenly dominate. They look like a mashed-up packet of crayons: bright green with pink mouldings; orange with blue mouldings; yellow with red mouldings. Back home, if you painted your house a bright colour you'd be considered an idiot. Here, you could be as expressive as you like and you'd be lucky if anyone noticed.

As for my own expressive shortcomings, if I'm going to address them then I want to do it properly. You can take dance classes everywhere these days. But I have a need for adventure to fulfil, too. Travel is in my blood (and, as a result, parasites are often in my intestines). I need to move, explore, discover; to go to places that excite me; to yield to that part of the soul that can only be sated by having one's photo taken in front of foreign landmarks.

The thought of taking the odd class once a week with – I don't know – 'Salsa Dave' doesn't inspire or motivate me. Forget the substitute: I want to go straight to the source.

I want a piece of the life that rum adverts push – a real slice of hot Latin action. I want to go where rhythm is in the blood, where the street is a dance floor, and where you can get into trouble for the ownership of powdered milk (like British politician Michael Fabricant).

I want to go to a place I've never been before, in search of something I've never had.

I want to dance like a Colombian.

CHAPTER TWO

Let Me Be Frank

For as long as I've known it it's been the place you don't go to. Don't even look at Colombia, people say. Don't even write the word down. If you so much as point to it on a map, men in balaclavas will burst into your room and, at the very least, find a very pointed manner of showing you the difference between gorillas and guerrillas (a particularly annoying ambiguity given they both hang out in jungles). But then it's precisely this kind of danger that means that, for me at least, Colombia has long been a tantalising country with a deep sense of intrigue.

It's the place where South America begins; where Central America's dwindling bough suddenly engorges into a full-on trunk; where the great mountainous spine of the Americas explodes into the swashbuckling horde of peaks, plateaus and volcanoes known as the Andes.

It's also the place that took on the name of that great explorer Christopher Columbus, the man who would have discovered the Americas had some other people (the Vikings) not discovered them first, and had there not also been a whole bunch of people living there already.

It's the place I've wanted to come to ever since I deliberately skipped it the first time round (I bravely flew over it in a plane some years ago), the place that might have been called 'Cristophia' if countries preferred being named after forenames rather than surnames and the place everyone misspells, regardless.

Most importantly, it's the place I've come to learn how to dance.

Earlier this very same morning, I was in England. Actually it may have been a different morning – I can never tell with time zones. But now I'm most definitely someplace else. I'm in Bogotá, Colombia's capital and its biggest city – home to about eight million people.

I walk about the historic centre admiring its frock-like prettiness, my jacket making a synthetic swishing sound as my arms pass it by. It's a little chilly here – not what most would expect of a South American city – and I've got the faint catch of altitude in my breath. On the famous Plaza de Bolívar the fussy cathedral rises up against a backdrop of green mountains – the ones I saw on the way in. Pigeons mill about the square, and birdseed sellers do likewise.

It's easy to like this part of town, but even the ugly areas adjacent have me enraptured. I skip along the sidewalks, through the street hustle of mixed architecture, just soaking it all up, past a handful of shoe-shiners sat on little stools, and a clutch of juice vendors with their trolleys of stacked oranges.

A man pushes a steaming hand-cart past and the scent of hot maize wafts out in a visible trail, mixing with the smell of under-combusted gasoline and the fragrance from passing locals. It all smells like perfume to me.

Everyday Bogotá folk walk by, their clothes neither dreary nor exuberant, being largely all jeans, t-shirts and hooded-tops in sensible colours. Coats are the order of the day, here, with the temperature plummeting from perfectly reasonable to decidedly chilly the moment the sun disappears behind clouds. As for the people inside the clothes, they're mostly *mestizo* – a racial mixture of Spanish and indigenous.

Old men hang about in clusters on the main drag seemingly not doing much at all. They look sharply dressed from a distance, but get up close and their trousers and shirts are made from cheap fabric, whilst their shoes are uninspiring lumps of black.

So this is what Colombia looks like – it's good to finally have some images to put to the name.

After all what do you think about when you think about Colombia? It would be nice to think the answer is Gabriel García Márquez, or Shakira, or even Carlos Valderrama. But more likely it conjures up images of bushy moustaches, drug mules and summary executions. Ransom demands, coca plantations and khaki-clad insurgents. Opulent palaces, machine guns, and high-grade Arabica. In short, variations on a theme of cocaine, coffee and kidnapping.

Whilst Colombia's bad reputation is not unfounded, the country is changing as rapidly and dramatically as a weather pattern on high mountains. Crime figures are well down on ten years ago, and the country appears to have stabilised in general. Colombia is finally opening up for tourism once again.

Not that any of this left my parents feeling any better about it when I was making my plans.

"Have you thought about going to Argentina and learning the tango?"

No, Dad, I haven't.

It doesn't matter how old I get, I'm still their son.

My mum was similarly troubled by my decision. She also appeared to have hacked into the UK Government's travel advice website, since when I went there, hoping to assess the reality of the situation, I was greeted by a litany of emboldened text calmly warning me "NOTHING AND NOWHERE IS SAFE! YOU'RE GOING TO DIE! YOU'RE GOING TO DIE!"

I spent much of the build-up giving them (my parents and the UK Government) words of comfort, trying to help them to rationalise the situation by sharing things I'd heard through less official sources. But it's hard not to be affected by other people's worries. What if they were right? What if this really was a bad idea?

A lot of the time, travel is just treating the world as your own personal cultural playground (wheeeee!), but when you start talking about potential kidnap, it's a lot more serious (booooo!). Before leaving, I found myself daydreaming about what I would do if I got kidnapped. I decided I'd lie about the existence of my family to avoid dragging others into my mess. And perhaps, as I got bundled into a car, I'd follow the example of Alan Johnson of the BBC and throw a business card on the floor, or whatever else I had to hand – a credit card or something.

"It was nice of that man to think of us while he was being kidnapped, wasn't it Fernanda? That new dress looks lovely on you. Switch the home cinema on, would you?"

But now I'm here this all seems over thetop. I sit in a café off the main drag eating a *tamal* – a steaming mush of maize and pork amidst layers of banana leaf which unfurl like a big, green carnation – washed down with a weak black coffee. Outside, people walk past. They're not kidnapping people, not killing each other and not exporting drugs. Or if they're doing any of those things, they're doing them surreptitiously.

In the absence of any obvious and immediate threat, the part of my brain that's a scaredy-cat has mostly shut up. In fact, after less than a day here, I feel like Colombia is saying to me "What took you so long?"

Bogotá railway station is a grand old stone building capped with a massive bird of prey. The man in charge of proceedings inside is similarly imposing – girthy, with a gruff voice – and he's telling the crowd of Colombians congregated around him how trains work. Most of the things he says are obvious: get on the carriage specified by your ticket; sit in the seats allotted to you; don't put your head on the track in front of any of the wheels, at least whilst they're moving.

But then trains must be something of a novelty here. In Colombia, as in so much of Latin America, they've been almost completely usurped by the coach, and this steam train is the country's last remaining regular passenger service. It's a great shame considering that the country is still criss-crossed with steel tracks and has such a rich heritage of banditry.

With my demise somewhat less imminent than first anticipated, I've turned my attention to why I'm out here in the first place. The plan 'go to Colombia and learn to dance' is more than a little vague, and I have no idea where to start. So, whilst I get a handle on things, I've decided to go on this excursion.

In a yard adjacent to the platform, grass encroaches upon the peaceful corpses of old locomotives; remnants of a more gentrified time. Their paint is all but gone, their parts are terminally seized up and their open boiler hatches make them look like duffed-in top hats.

Our own steed (all train metaphors involve horses, for some reason) is very much alive: a living, breathing steam engine in regal green with yellow detailing, and sporting a big old brass bell on top (between its ears). The healthy aroma of hot grease and engine oil hangs in the air as we board the rake of red carriages that trail back from it.

I was quite into trains when I was in my early teens, entranced as I was by the romance of travel (and apparently also of writing numbers in notebooks), and put an unhealthy amount of time and effort into watching them. Time that might have been better served learning something more socially relevant like – picking something entirely at random here – learning to dance.

I've always been rubbish at dancing. My first memory of doing it was to the first record I ever owned – Adam and the Ants' Stand and Deliver. This took the form of high speed random movements of the feet, which I performed whilst staring down, amazed at my own skill and precision. I don't think I did anything with my arms bar preventing myself colliding with furniture, adults and other obstacles.

Come my primary school years, the cool kids were into rudimentary break-dancing and bad robotics. I remember one of them claiming that when you got to high school, the kids said things like "Dance some 'breakie' or we'll flush your bag down the toilet." But I never experienced this when I got there, and more's the pity because fear is an excellent motivator.

In fact the only real dance opportunities in my high school years came at the occasional school disco, where dancing was this thing that you had to do in the vicinity of people you found attractive. Which was unfortunate, since the majority of us boys were about as accomplished at dancing as we were at growing moustaches. The girls, meanwhile, looked like they'd been practising in their bedrooms for years, and probably had.

With my late teens came long hair, parent-confusing clothes and alternative music. For a brief, halcyon period, I knew all the styles: indie shoe-gazing, hard-rock hair-throwing, gothic faux-mystical hand-waving and so on.

However, when I finally got a serious haircut and packed away my penchant for frivolous teenage sub-cultures, I was in trouble. My circle of friends widened to encompass something other than people in a permanent state of readiness for a Halloween party, and none of the styles I'd learnt had any value. I was cast adrift, like someone who had prepared for a canoeing expedition by learning to play the flute. At least a guitar would have made a serviceable paddle.

I've reached my current state via my own particular route, but I don't think I'm alone in the resulting dance inability. You can see the evidence all over the UK, especially in the habit of what I call bar dancing. This is where you lean on a bar, and move some minor part of your body in time with the music.

"I can actually dance," you're saying. "I just choose not to at this point."

In Bogotá's railway station, the horse gives a long shrieking whistle of steam and the train jolts into action. Soon we're rattling along in carriages that are rickety but charming, like a well-mannered old man with no incontinence issues.

Despite our early morning departure time, plenty of folk have made it out to see us pass through the city. People stand on balconies, sit on grassy mounds in couples and generally point and wave, presumably hoping the thing might wave a mechanical arm back. Like I said, they don't have many trains in Colombia.

I don't really know what to make of the locals at the moment, though historical evidence suggests that at least some of them must have 'a bit of a temper'. Colombia is a country that has been ravaged by years of retribution and counter-retribution, like an argument where everyone demands the last word, despite having long since forgotten who had the first.

One of my favourite alternative bands in my teen years, Big Black, had a song called 'Colombian Necktie'. I never gave the name a second thought at the time, but years later I found out that this wasn't a smart piece of male apparel, but a novel method of killing someone. Popularised in the 1950s, it involved slitting the victim's throat and pulling their tongue out through the hole. Imagine trying to find a shirt to match that.

This was during La Violencia (The Violence) – a barbaric period of Colombian history triggered off by a political assassination. Or maybe it was caused by somebody flicking a bit of paper at someone else – you know how these things can escalate. Fortunately, it all petered out into one of those harmless bloody civil conflicts.

Despite, or perhaps because of, this history of bloodshed, my few interactions with Colombians so far (admittedly mainly just to buy stuff) have been marked with an overwhelming torrent of civility. "*¡Con gusto!*" (With pleasure!), people say, "*¡A la orden!*" (At your service!), or even "*¡Siempre a la orden!*" (Always at your service!), which seems unlikely, though I appreciate the sentiment.

I've got it – they plan to charm me to death. These people are animals.

The family I'm sharing opposing bench seats with certainly

doesn't appear to want to slit my throat and pull my tongue out through it. In fact they're keen to share their grapes with me from their family lunchbox, which makes our socially peculiar interleaving of limbs seem less of an issue. Perhaps they're being nice to me now to make the cruelty seem even greater when it does occur.

There are three of them in the group: A middle-aged lady, an older woman – who I take to be her mother – and a young lad who is the nephew of the first. The train is packed with similar Colombian families on a day out, and chatter fills the old carriages.

As we trundle out through Bogotá's suburbs, the middle-aged lady starts pointing things out.

"*Esto es un centro comercial,*" she says, "*y esto es una piscina nueva.*" This is a mall, and this is a new swimming pool.

In this manner, she introduces me to all sorts of things: a police training academy (just looks like horses in a field), new housing developments, and a whole bunch of places which only have relevance to her and her family. It's about as interesting as the list of ingredients on the side of a bag of sugar, but I appreciate the sentiment.

The level of development is quite surprising, but the lady explains that this is because we're going through the moneyed north of the city, and the poor barrios are mainly in the South. The rough spots that she does point out are communities of rough shacks that scurry up the mountainside some distance away.

By now, we're hammering through flat open countryside, with fields of corn, grasslands and the occasional red-roofed house. The green, hilly, Andean ridge keeping us company the whole time on our right side, with another distant on our left – we're on a high-altitude plain nestling with the mountains.

At one point, a thick, choking blast of engine smoke finds its way in through the open windows.

"It's a type of dry cleaning," says the lady opposite. "*¡Agua con vapor!*" Water with steam!

A small brass band complete with portable amp wanders in drawing a big cheer from the passengers. The band members, all men, stand in the cramped aisle and start playing, trying to orientate themselves in such a way as not to give anyone trumpet-ear. Plenty of people on the train, my new friends included, clap along to the brassy music, which to me sounds vaguely Mexican.

Once these guys are done they move on, replaced by another group playing another type of music that everyone is familiar with except for me. This new band consists of a guy with a drum, another with a rasp, and a third with an accordion and melancholic eyes, though I suspect the final element isn't essential to the genre.

The love for the music is clear – I can hear the progress of each band down the train by the distant cheers.

As well as the various bands, there's an ebb and flow of people selling home-made food and drink. In fact it's a lot like a Women's Institute fundraiser, except with men present. And on a train. And with no fairy cakes.

I buy a coffee in a plastic cup, but this just turns out to be a highly efficient way of scalding my hand – not the original intention but I make a mental note just in case it ever is in the future.

All this time the music continues, and when a band takes too long a break between songs, the passengers make their displeasure instantly clear.

"*¡Mú – si – ca!*" shouts the grandmother, delivering the word itself in a rhythmic manner. Music!

But where my fellow passengers recognise individual songs to the point where they often join in with the singing, I can't even identify the basic genres. Indeed, the only band that prompts any kind of recognition in me is one with a guy playing the *zampoña* (panpipes). I'm taken back to my previous visit to Latin America, and hearing a panpipe version of Hotel California. It was the first time I'd ever experienced such a rendition outside of a lift.

Even when we're in a gap between bands, the rhythm doesn't stop: The train delivers a constant clattering beat as it hustles its way through satellite towns with its own running accompaniment: the sliding door that repeatedly squeaks and bangs closed and open; the bells that ring out from each of the many level crossings; the steam whistle that shrieks out like a punctuating cymbal crash.

Meanwhile the whole carriage rocks from side to side in time with the ensemble, forcing anyone walking down the aisle into an unseemly dance of lurching missteps.

If nothing else, just based on their love of music, it would seem I've come to the right country.

Back in Bogotá, a guy called Frank from the USA is trying to persuade me to come to a club with him and a group of other foreigners – I've based myself in a hostel to start with, whilst I get my bearings.

Their original plan was to go to a kind of party-on-a-hill at a place called La Calera. This would have been perfect – I could have met local people and told them in my rusty Spanish how I was there to dance, safe in the knowledge that I wouldn't actually have to do any. Unfortunately, the venue has changed from a place that doesn't feature dancing to one that probably does: a salsa club.

Frank's invitation is a pivotal moment, or at least it would be if pivoting wasn't some kind of dance skill. I can picture myself now, strolling confidently onto the dance floor, local girls fighting each other just for the right to teach me how to dance. I pick up moves at a rate of knots whilst casually slicking my hair back with my free hand. Even though I wear my hair messy with wax in it and that would just make it look strange, not to mention cover my hand in goo.

Still, here it is: here's my big chance to get out there on the dance floor and show everyone what I'm made of.

"Nah, I'll leave it I think."

That's right – custard.

I explain that I can't dance and, somewhat oddly considering I've come here purely for that reason, that I don't want to either. Fear has got the better of me. I want to stay as far away from the dance floor as possible.

"Come on," says Frank, "I reckon it will be sink or swim."

I agree. In fact this is the perfect metaphor. If you throw a non-swimmer in deep water, it's not 50/50 as to whether they'll discover they can do a passable front crawl: they'll either drown or be rescued by dolphins. The only dolphins in Colombia are the Amazonian pink river dolphins, and I'm guessing they don't frequent the dance floors of Bogotá. Not that I'm ever likely to find out.

It's not just fear though – there's a certain amount of reason (or post-hoc justification). Salsa isn't like other dances – you can't just wing it. It has specific steps, I know that much. But that's all I know. Well, that and the knowledge that if I were to go, I'd spend the whole evening in a place specifically designed for dancing, all the while trying desperately not to.

Frank doesn't know any salsa, either, but then he has a distinctly unfair advantage due to his education.

"It's a big southern thing called Cotillion," he says.

Cotillion is best known as the tradition of introducing debutantes to society, but it has another meaning, too.

"It's learning how to be a gentleman and everything. They teach you how to dance, when to call girls, how to eat. It's basic manners – when to hold doors..."

As a result, Frank learnt the foxtrot, the square-step, swing and other things, though apparently not salsa. I prattle on again about wishing I could dance, too, so I could join them in going out, but Frank's not buying it.

"I think you only really need to know how to keep a beat and how to hold a girl."

I want to be Frank.

A couple of years ago, I was flirting with a woman in an Après-Ski club in Austria. Things were going quite nicely, at least until some random drunkard came up, barged into our conversation, and asked her for a dance. She hesitated, seemingly not wanting to dance with him, but nor wanting to appear unreasonable.

What I should have done at this point is clear – I should have just said "Actually, *we're* going to dance," and whisked her away. Or whisked him away, instead, just for the laugh. Certainly Frank would have done something like that. Or offered him a duel – one of the two. But I couldn't whisk her away, because I couldn't dance, not unless we were going to do that Adam and the ants thing together. And I could hardly say "I can't dance – so you're not allowed to either!"

So instead she went off and danced with him whilst I watched uselessly from the sidelines. What he was doing was nothing special – just some generic man-holding-woman type stuff – but it was enough.

The story doesn't end there, though, as the dynamic changed – he blew it by putting his hands in places that he didn't have permission for. In one clean movement she disposed of him and yanked me over to join her.

At this point you're probably expecting a moment of triumph. But it wasn't – not really. All that happened was that I held her hands and circled round with her awkwardly, our feet colliding, our bodies swaying out of time. It was a bit of a mess.

Still, that brief physical interaction – that moment of bodily communication with someone – left me wanting more. It was like eating an amazing slice of cake for the first time. It gave me the taste for more cake – even if I did get crumbs all down me – and it made me determined that no man would ever take cake out from under my nose ever again, or at least not solely for a lack of knowing how to eat it.

I love cake.

But I'm never going to reach that stage at this rate. I'm the one guy in the hostel who's come here specifically to learn how to dance, yet it's me who has chosen to stay in. I seriously need to address this.

Morning arrives in Bogotá, the sunlight smudging the bright colours of La Candelaria together in a warm cast. Once my fellow hostel dwellers make it out of bed, the hostel is buzzing with talk of the previous night. Everyone I speak to has had a great time, Frank included, whereas I just stayed indoors, tapping away on my laptop.

This is not good. Before I came here, I pictured myself dancing my way around the country, entirely reprogramming the dance part of my brain, and leaving as some kind of expert. But unless I plan to do all of this by visualisation, telepathy or osmosis, something inside me is going to have to change quite radically.

CHAPTER THREE

Hot in the City

Everyone's had a salsa lesson at some point in their lives. There are even Magellanic penguins that have had a single, awkward, never-to-be-repeated attempt at learning the dance.

Cali is known as the salsa capital of the world. It's a somewhat self-appointed title, but then maybe it's fair enough, because Cali isn't just about salsa, Cali is salsa. Cut Cali and it bleeds salsa. Get Cali drunk and it vomits salsa. Inflate Cali and stamp on it and… oh you get the point.

Regardless of any debate over the whole 'salsa capital' business, there's one thing that's indisputable – Cali is the best place in the world to learn Cali-style salsa. And I'm on a coach headed in that very direction.

"*¡Solo éxitos!*" proclaims a husky, bearded voice. Just hits!

I recline in one of the coach's comfortable seats as we head out through Bogotá's suburbs, Latin music in a variety of still-unidentifiable styles pulsing gently through the vehicle from the radio.

Inter-city travel in Colombia was still a risky activity even just a few years ago, and night travel in particular was considered a no-no, which must have made travel in general a tad tricky considering that some point-to-point coach journeys take in excess of twenty hours. This one is only due to last ten, but I've cleverly waited until midday to leave to increase the thrill.

Soon we're carving up into the hills, my ears popping as we wind up through wispy clouds that drift in from empty space and tease the asphalt. Big US-style trucks – from the old and grizzly to the modern and gleaming – strain and grunt their way up with the rest of the traffic, causing long convoys and inviting the kind of overtaking which is best done with eyes closed.

Occasional spates of buildings huddle together in the high altitude chill, occupying the narrow hem between the road and the drop-off. Scratchy little open-fronted garages offer running repairs whilst open-air cafes with a few plastic tables and chairs provide fabulous vistas back onto to the traffic procession itself.

There's also a peculiar abundance of places selling hand-made furniture.

"Here you go, sweetheart – a raffia chair!"

"You've been over the mountains again, haven't you?"

Colombia is a country with some fairly serious terrain, with the most obvious feature being the Andes. They dominate the country, surging up from Ecuador in the South and splaying out into three separate cordilleras. Two of these peter out as they near the coast, whilst the third, showing more of a backpacker mentality, thinks "What the hell – while I'm in the area I may as well go to Venezuela." The three ranges create two notable valleys – the Cauca and the Magdalena – each bearing a river of the same name.

The journey from Bogotá to Cali has started with us hauling ourselves out of the cradle of the easternmost Andean chain, and this is our current endeavour. Next, we'll drop down into the Magdalena valley, sprint across, then scale the central chain, before collapsing, beaten, in the Cauca valley and dragging our twitching corpses southwards.

I'm probably over-dramatising it. In reality the driver will turn the steering wheel and operate some foot pedals for a while and then we'll be there. It's certainly a lot quicker and more comfortable than in colonial times, when such journeys involved traversing treacherous mountain paths by mule. Some sections were so bad that the transport of choice was literally a chair attached to someone else's back. The piggy-back fights alone must have been horrendous.

After the promised period of sanity and respite in the valley, it's time to get mountainous again. My ears pop, pop and pop again as we make our final ascent, circling upwards in a long, slow train of vehicles, the trucks revealing novelty light arrays as darkness sets in. The altitude is making me feel a touch queasy, so I open my water bottle and the liquid practically sprays out from the pressure change.

Finally, and with some relief, we breach the high point of the pass and begin our descent to the valley floor below. We hammer down the final straight of the Cauca valley in total darkness, the passenger-facing LED speed indicator bleating out '*ALERTA*' as though in warning to the unknown trials that await.

This is the dance school? I'm confused. It just looks like someone's house. I look to the driver of the little yellow taxi who points at the number above the door.

Yep – this is the place.

I press the buzzer and wait.

Some part of me doesn't want to learn salsa at all. It's too obvious; too faddish; too much something that everyone was into ten or more years ago. In some ways it's almost too English. But I don't really know where else to start: I flew out here with the minimal amount of research and expected it all to fall into place. Yet in a way, it makes it the perfect starting point – here's an early opportunity to exorcise some baggage (not to mention unpack some demons).

Mind you, from the video clips I've seen, Cali's brand of salsa bears little resemblance to the lovey-dovey dance I've seen before. Rather than romantic, it's actually quite funky, being crazy-fast with nimble footwork, like Fred Astaire and Ginger Rogers doing a hip-hop routine. I'm not entirely sure that this is what I'm looking for, but then perhaps what I'm actually looking for is any excuse not to.

A woman who looks in her late thirties or early forties, with dark hair pulled back from her face and strong eyebrows, lets me in. Her name is Marta and she's going to be my dance teacher. And my first lesson is due to start any minute now.

She leads me up several flights of stairs, my nerves ratcheting up with each turn. We emerge back outside on a tiled rooftop patio. A perimeter wall stops people from falling off and dying, whilst a sloping canopy takes the brunt of the sun's efforts. The view out is one of peaceful treetops, and the soundtrack is the gentle twitter of birds.

It's a serene spot, but it clearly has another purpose: mirrors lean against the low wall on one side whilst on the other there's a big amplifier, with impressive-looking trophies of couples in dramatic dance clinches sat atop it. There's only one thing you do up here, and it's not your laundry. Although it would dry quite quickly, to be fair.

The place feels like a hide, which is rather appropriate given my feelings about learning to dance in public. In fact, the whole thought of dance classes in general fills me with a strange, unfocussed anxiety, like something genuinely bad is about to happen. My instincts shout out "YOU REALLY DON'T NEED TO DO THIS." It's a bit like when I'm about to chat up a girl, except with less simpering.

Marta has a confident smile and walks about with an innate sense of balance. To the accompaniment of string music we start some slow, elegant stretching. Or rather Marta starts with some slow elegant stretching whilst I wobble about on one foot trying to match her pretend-flying position, putting myself in grave danger of featuring in an episode of Air Crash Investigations.

She's dressed sensibly for the occasion, in stretchy leotardy-type stuff, whereas I've come in jeans. I should have just gone the whole hog and starched them. Still, the one good thing about doing stretching exercises, even in restrictive clothing, is that we're not dancing. In fact, I could quite happily do stretching exercises for the entire two hours duration of the class.

Marta switches the music on the CD player to something more appropriate; something more Latin; something that I would just about recognise as salsa if the person putting it on said "here you go – here's some salsa".

"*Uno, dos, tres,*" says Marta, in time with the music, "*cinco, seis, siete.*" One, two, three. Five, six, seven.

I've done counting before, and I can tell you that this sequence is incomplete. It turns out that the fourth and eighth beats are like rest beats. I do actually have a decent sense of rhythm – I used to play drums in the school band – I just don't know what to do with it.

Marta starts going forwards and then backwards in time with the music, prompting me to copy. That's it, now I remember: salsa is the forwards and backwards dance. Memories of my previous attempts at the dance flash through my mind; of my forays into salsa hell.

Salsa hell, as I define it, is the group lesson where your view of the teacher is totally obscured by other equally shit dancers. The result is that you spend your whole time copying other people, who themselves are copying other people, who are doing it wrong. This isn't salsa – it's that whisper-down-the-line game.

Despite my first attempt being of this ilk, I found the courage to have another go, this time whilst travelling in Bolivia. Here, the dance teacher approached me through the crowd and suggested that, as I didn't have a dance partner, I should dance with my thumbs in my belt.

A fellow gringo glanced over at me. "You look gay," he said.

This shouldn't have had any impact on me. After all, what's wrong with looking gay? Or even camp for that matter, which is what I guess he really meant. But it did. Because instead of thinking "He's only saying that to relieve his own insecurity," I went for "Do I really look gay?" And thus spent the rest of the lesson scrutising the minutiae of my own movements. It's not really anything to do with sexuality, it's just self-consciousness, and it's immobilising.

Come the third opportunity to learn salsa – in a nightclub in Eastern Europe – I looked at the teacher, or rather the obscure part of him that was actually visible, and bailed.

This is why I'm having a one-on-one class, and why I'm happy to be doing it in a suburban location. There's nobody around to see my mistakes and, unless Marta deliberately hires a load of misstepping extras to stand between us, I actually stand a chance of making it to a second lesson.

So here I am, going forwards on the *uno* and then backwards on the *cinco* in a continuing cycle. It's not the same as walking though, as the front of your foot touches the ground first. Also because you don't actually go anywhere.

It's only now that the full, true extent of my stiffness becomes horribly apparent. I doubt very much I look like I'm dancing, as I certainly don't feel like I am. I feel like an android, and an indecisive one at that. I'm the awkward guy who everyone is glad they don't dance like. I'm all pressed trousers and tucked-in shirt. I'm your dad. No really – sorry to break it to you like that.

This is just one of a number of basic *pasos* (steps) that we work our way through. Others include one where we go from side to side, and another where we spin away backwards to alternate sides, which feels like it should be accompanied by us saying "ta-da!"

each time.

This latter move appears to be one of the hallmarks of Cali-style salsa, whilst another is giving a little kick forward with a foot whenever you're about to put it backwards – a little fancy flourish to fill the empty beat. It's a bit like Rosa Klebb in From Russia with Love, except without the spring-loaded poison-tipped shoe-dagger. Although I suppose that last bit depends which part of town you're in.

We're making progress, but it's hard work in the heat. We might be in the shade but I sweat my way through the whole first hour, the droplets forming and trickling down underneath my damnable jeans. And it's not just hydration I'm losing; my concentration is dropping, too – every single movement of every limb requires intense thought.

All the while, Marta makes it look so easy, prowling around the dance floor with a poise that gives her a semblance of the feline. She doesn't start chasing herself in the mirrors, though.

With the basics stuck down with chewing gum, if not exactly nailed, Marta decides it's time for us to start dancing together. She invites me to reach my right hand behind her and onto her shoulder blade, then rests her arm atop mine, and prompts me to clasp her free hand with my own.

"*Así,*" says Marta. Like this.

We're suddenly a lot closer. Almost improperly close, in fact. This can't be right, can it?

"*¡Buenos días!*" says her husband, appearing with some home-made fruit juice, and giving us both a cheery smile. Good morning!

Ah, okay. I guess it is right, then – I've just got to get used to it. Either that or use special fake arms to extend the distance between us. But then, as the two hours finally come to an end, there are many things I'm going to have to get used to. There's quite a lot to this dancing lark, isn't there?

With my first lesson done, I leave the security cage surrounding the ground-floor patio and walk out into the sunshine. Wow, I think I may have just got through that.

Out on the streets of my local *barrio,* the day has done its stretching exercises and is now fully warmed up. I take to the narrow pavement to seek out the narrow band of shade, the multiple layers I was wearing in Bogotá jettisoned as useless in the breezeless valley heat.

With salt encrusted on my temples, I head back to the guest house for a shower – something of a misnomer given that it's just a cold-water pipe that happens to be high up. It's a cruel experience first thing in the morning but close to heavenly after being out in the sun.

The world seems a better place now I've taken my first steps on the dance road. And I'm not going to have to wait long to get some practice – a local girl has approached me via the internet asking if I'd like to go out to a club with her and some friends.

Well why not? It's an early opportunity to put the Bogotá experience behind me. Besides, it'll be a useful cultural exchange – they can teach me about salsa, and I can teach them how to stand around in bars looking awkward. So despite part of my brain squealing with anguish, I do that thing where you force yourself to click 'send', then spend the rest of the day wondering why the hell you did.

I've set up base in the historic quarter of San Antonio – all wooden shutters, gaily-painted render and terracotta roof tiles. Ornate metal grills muzzle every window and door of the low buildings, whilst telegraph cables sally by overhead, creating an intertwined mesh. If you fell on San Antonio from a height, you'd probably just sproing back up into the air (the usual disclaimers apply).

Some buildings are in a state of elegant decline, whilst others have been spruced up into bohemian cafes and restaurants. But the *barrio* still feels lived in: corner shops sell detergent and toilet roll from behind glass-fronted counters, and lampposts are tattooed with the remnants of fly posters advertising plumbers and the like.

It's a nice place; a calm place. It's also a hilly place: Cali snuggles up into the eaves of the Andes, with San Antonio rising up on one of the mountain's foothills. Its grid-system streets battle uphill, reaching a precipitous edge before spilling away into the adjacent *barrios*. On-street parking in these parts is only a faulty handbrake away from a game of skittles, and my thighs are in a near-constant state of tension as I walk about.

The location of many modern-day Colombian cities was determined by the Spanish conquistadors. Following the 'discovery' of the Americas, they arrived on the continent in large numbers, charging about like a load of drunken Erasmus students, and founding a bunch of cities en route.

In the 1530s, some of them forged expeditions through Colombia as part of the hunt to find El Dorado (The Golden One), which was not a city, as myth held it, but in fact a tribal chief with a penchant for getting covered in gold and going out on a raft on a sacred lake. The conquistador Sebastian de Belalcázar headed such a group, coming in from Peru in the South and casually founding the city of Santiago de Cali on the way.

The heat of the city doesn't seem to bother the Caleños, who rarely seem bothered by anything much, and tend to slink about their city in a relaxed state. Dress is pretty casual here, too: the men wear polo shirts and the ubiquitous baseball cap, whilst the women combine strappy tops with jeans and keep their hair tied back out the way.

The skin tone of the locals is generally darker here than I witnessed in Bogotá. In general, Afro-Colombian communities tend to be congregated along the country's coasts, with Cali being close enough to be an honorary part of that, despite being separated from the Pacific by a mountain range.

Mind you, there's actually a bit of everything here in racial terms. Colombians' origins fall (mainly) into three distinct groups – African, European and indigenous – and they're all well represented in this city, with racial mixing having created a broad spread of skin tones.

But then my reason for being here isn't to perform an ethnographic study of the place – I've come here to dance. Although with the evening getting ever nearer, I'd happily do a swap.

I'm not quite sure what I'm expecting the nightclub to be – perhaps some upmarket hyper-disco; all neon lights and razzamatazz. Instead it's an intimate little place with a couple of small dance floors and a parade of small tables and chairs that chase each other around the outside. It would feel a bit like some little indie club in a provincial English town if the music wasn't almost entirely salsa.

Not many people are up and dancing when I arrive, but there's still a clear difference with the clubs back home. This is nothing like Wigan Pier nightclub where I (mis)spent my youth, throwing my long hair (and long limbs) around to the Pixies. There I, and everybody else, danced apart. Here everyone is dancing in couples. If you danced on your own here you'd look like an idiot.

The venue's low ceilings seem to compact the tonking percussion and jazzy instrumentation, making it even denser. Walls are painted in bold splashes of blue and yellow, with prints referencing Cuba, New York and FANIA records. There are also black and white headshots of some cool-looking people, who I presume to be famous salsa musicians. It's either that or I've wandered into a hairdresser's.

Salsa music was developed in the 1960s and 1970s by Cuban and Puerto Rican immigrants in New York. It took its inspiration from a number of Cuban genres, themselves a mixture of European and African styles, and generated a huge following right across Latin America. It has since spread all over the world, splintering into subgenres and spawning a global dance scene that everyone has participated in at least once, Magellanic penguins included.

I join my new companions at a table by the dance floor – they're a quiet bunch, and conversation seems hard to come by.

All the way to the club, I'd been thinking "*Uno, dos, tres...*" and picturing myself dancing for fear of forgetting the moves, the memory of which seemed extremely delicate. But now I'm here it looks like I needn't have worried – no-one in our group is doing any dancing. I suspect this is because all three men in the group are foreigners, and the girls think (well, know) that we'll be rubbish. This is fine by me – I sip from a bottle of water and watch as the casual shoes and trainers smudge the floor-space in time with the music.

At least any sense of footwear stress I might have had has been resolved. In preparation for the trip, I bought a pair of suede-soled dance shoes. Wearing these for a lesson was obviously going to be okay, but what about nights out? If you're going to a dance club, were you meant to wear dance shoes?

I couldn't just wear them on the way – I've not come here to de-lint the streets of Cali – but nor did I want to carry them with me and thus have to lace them up, grandly, on the edge of the dance floor before dancing like an idiot. In the end, I decided to just leave them. It was the right decision – my well-worn old-school trainers make a good match with most of the other footwear on parade.

My grandad on my dad's side had a similar call to make during the Second World War. Based in Richmond for his duties in the armed forces, he liked to frequent the nearby Hammersmith Palais for a bit of dance-floor action. In that era, it was obligatory to carry your gas mask with you at all times, so he'd duly go out with his holder slung about his neck. Then, on arrival, he'd pop it open and pull out his dance shoes. It's hard to fault his dedication, although he'd have looked well breathing heavily into a shoe had there been a gas attack.

"Now's not the time for that kind of thing!"

Back in Cali, I'm staying safely in the bunker with my head down. Becoming increasingly self-conscious at my own lack of action, I start talking to the US ex-pat next to me. I tell him why I'm here and he has a fairly obvious question for me in response – why don't I just get up there and dance?

The honesty of my response takes even me by surprise.

"I'm terrified."

It's true – I am. I don't know exactly what it is I'm terrified of. I mean, how wrong can it go? It's not like I'm doing a Bedouin sword dance, where I could accidentally slay everyone in my vicinity just through basic ineptitude.

"Sorry!"

I sit watching a gyrating couple on the dance floor, kidding myself that I'm studying their technique. The longer I leave it, the harder it's going to get. Another ten minutes passes, and the very real danger begins to emerge that I'll leave the club not having attempted a single dance.

Damn it. I've just got to go for it, haven't I?

A freshly-spun track starts up. I steady myself, take a couple of breaths, and go over to the girl who invited me out.

"¿Quieres bailar conmigo?" Do you want to dance with me?

It's the point of no return – you can't really add "Only joking!" and bail out. Not least because it makes no sense as a joke.

"Yes, why not?"

The walk is mercifully short. Within moments, I'm standing opposite her, unmoving, with one hand on her back and the other clasping her own hand. A few moments later, I'm still standing opposite her. I'm trying to mentally fit the numbers to the music, and my feet to the numbers. Okay, right – I've got it. Now all I need to do is push off on 'one', and here it comes.

Oops, missed it.

It's okay – here it comes again!

Oops, missed it again.

Finally, just when it seems like we might end up spending the whole song stood still, I catch it, and we're away. Forwards and backwards we go. Then again. And then again. It might be repetitive, but I'm dancing, dammit. Well, if you can call repeated changes of direction dancing.

I've just decided – you can.

"*Otro paso,*" says my partner, gazing off into space. Another step.

Changing step as a novice dancer is a bit like changing gear as a novice driver. You can't just go ahead and do it – it requires advanced planning, maybe even a short meeting. But, cumbersome as I am, and with a few bars preparation, I eventually manage it. I successfully grind out the whole song in this awkward, rudimentary way.

"You did it!" says the ex-pat as I arrive heroically back at my seat.

He's right. I danced salsa and it was just really boring rather than embarrassing. I didn't decapitate anyone, and whilst I probably still dance like a twat, there are surely bigger ones.

If I keep racking up the milestones like this, I'll have delivered a baby and performed an unaccompanied spacewalk by the end of the week.

Nice one.

Cali is a hot city and a sticky city, but more than anything else it's a noisy city. Day and night, the nearby dual carriageway hums with battered old sedans, brand new 4x4s and swarms of little yellow taxis. Cars whump across its concrete sections and *busetas* (microbuses) battle their way up and down the thoroughfare.

Even on the back streets, there's a constant buzz: televisions broadcast out onto the streets through the ubiquitous window grills, incessant chatter fills cheap cafes, and ice-cream handcarts tour the neighbourhood emitting a version of Beethoven's Für Elise that maddeningly never breaks out of the piece's first movement.

Then there's the Latin music, which infuses itself everywhere. It's the soundtrack to every taxi you take, it accompanies you as you walk round the supermarket and it provides a natural rhythm to your chewing in cafes.

Come night time, the heat of the day has gone and the noise has pretty much gone with it. The netting in my room blows gently inwards, else gets sucked back against the window bars, and the silence of darkness is broken only by the pea-whistle of a *vigilante* (security guard) patrolling his beat.

Vigilantes are easy to recognise. Invariably men, they generally hang about on street corners – perhaps sat on a chair – wielding some formidable piece of wood. They don't dress like Batman, but they can still look quite menacing and some of them are quite unkempt. In fact the first time I saw one I thought he was a mugger and skirted around him at a distance.

Kidnap and murder rates may be down but street crime is still commonplace and hence so are the *vigilantes*, who are paid for by local residents and business-owners. In one part of Cali I even spot an *academía de vigilantes* (security guard school), which surprises me as the job doesn't seem all that varied.

"This morning we're going to be looking at how to hit someone repeatedly with a wooden baton. Any questions?"

"What do we do with the whistle?"

"We'll look at that in the afternoon."

I ask one *vigilante* what Cali is like for thieves. He tells me that they're everywhere, before launching into a list of synonyms: "*Ladrones... muchachos de la calle... gérmenes...*" (Thieves... street boys... germs...). I think he said *gérmenes*, though it could have been *gamines* (street urchins). Either way, I don't think he likes them.

I wouldn't make a good *vigilante*: I sleep right through a big kerfuffle with a burglar at a nearby property. A fellow guest-house dweller tells me they heard weeping and assumed it was the owner, but that it turned out to be the burglar himself – the owner had caught him and given him something to think about.

Even with *vigilantes* about I know I have to be careful: in a city like Cali the safety levels can vary dramatically from *barrio* to *barrio*. But whilst this might bother me back home, I'm not actually thinking about it too much – I'm more preoccupied with my dance mission.

Marta has told me that when I've finished with the five classes that I've arranged, I'm expected to do a *clausura*. Which is fine, except… what's a *clausura*?

It's a graduation dance, she tells me, and it's obligatory.

I don't like the sound of this – why can't I just learn some stuff quietly, on my own, and then go away again? Besides, it seems a bit rich to be allowed to graduate having attended such a meagre number of classes. Mind you, they gave me an IT degree so I probably shouldn't complain.

In order to see what I've let myself in for, Marta has invited me to witness a *clausura* taking place at the main studio of her dance school. The place consists of one main room that opens up straight off the street, with only a wooden counter preventing pedestrians and stray animals from wandering onto the dance floor.

I walked past the school during the day and decided it was the street-est thing I'd ever seen. People in mismatched clothes practised opposite wall-mounted mirrors, fans blowing down from above. There was clearly no messing about here; no pretence; no "let's chat about dance over a skinny latte". You come here? You graft; you sweat; you dance. It was how I'd imagine some rough-ass boxing gym in New York to be.

Indeed, it was this atmosphere that made me choose Marta's school in the first place: I watched from the street, impressed, and decided that this was exactly what I wanted. Then promptly booked my set of special, secret classes based miles away.

Now, on the evening of the *clausura*, the venue has taken on more of a show-time feel. We're part of an audience of about ten or fifteen people sat on a chorus-line of chairs with our backs to the street, a palm tree gently bowing in the sultry night sky behind us. There's a slight rumble of traffic from the main thoroughfare and salsa is *uno-dos-tres*-ing its way out of the PA system.

"They play the music faster here," says the man sat next to me. "This isn't meant to be played at this speed."

He's from Buenaventura – a city that played an important role in Cali's musical development. By 1917, two important new trade infrastructures were complete: the Panama Canal, linking the Pacific to the Atlantic, and a local railway linking Cali to the Pacific coast at Buenaventura. Suddenly Cali was something of a global trading hub.

The regular influx of sailors meant there was also an influx of stuff from the places they'd visited along the way, with records, and even exotic dance moves, amongst them. This exciting foreign music first appeared in the bars and brothels of Buenaventura's red-light district, spreading from there to Cali and mainstream society.

Cuban music was a particular favourite amongst Caleños, so when salsa appeared it gained a strong hold and the city took it on as its own. It's perhaps not unlike the influence of black US soul music in the early 1970s on my home town of Wigan, and the north of England in general, where a whole 'northern soul' scene sprang up, with a funky style of dancing to boot.

Come the 1990s, a prospering drug industry helped to bankroll the appearance in Cali of salsa's biggest names, cementing the genre's appeal. Not that Cali doesn't have its own, local flavour – they like it fast here, even if that means speeding it up themselves.

"It sounds like Donald Duck!"

I think he actually means Mickey Mouse, which is just as well: learning salsa is stressful enough without someone quacking at you in high-speed Spanish.

Several couples are due to perform tonight. The women are dressed in leotards with skin-coloured cut-outs, and the kind of sparkly makeup that you wouldn't wear to work. Well, unless you work as an actor in a science fiction series. The men also look pretty dandy – all stretchy trousers and shirts with over-sized sequined collars.

The first couple present themselves to the audience in a self-assured 'we're going to dance for you' kind of way. Then the music begins and, without even waiting several bars to find where 'one' is, they commence: feet kicking charged air; arms going over heads; bodies spinning.

The speed and intricacy of their movements is mesmerising, as is the audacity: one minute the woman is engaging in a dizzying sequence of pirouettes, the next the man's twirling her effortlessly about his head. It's flashy and elaborate, but delivered with total control. At one point, she goes round and round his body like it's a helter-skelter, eventually surfacing at ground level between his legs. She doesn't say "Wheeeeeee!", but she should.

Marta gets everyone clapping to build up the excitement and atmosphere, but it's almost unnecessary. How could you not be wowed by this? I'd like to say they're much better than me, but it doesn't even feel like we're engaged in the same pursuit.

"*Te toca la próxima*," someone leans over to tell me. Your turn next.

"You are capable."

Marta is calling out the different *pasos* from the sidelines and I have to switch between them without stopping. The reason for her reassurance is because I keep getting it wrong. I either mess up, or I screw up or I simply do it badly. This is clearly simple stuff, yet my standard couldn't be further from the *clausura* if I took it on a plane with me and flew home.

I mean, it's good that I've got this test ahead of me to focus my mind, but it means that I actually really need to learn how to dance salsa, and fast. In both senses. Especially as I've only got three classes left after this one. The pressure is definitely on.

At least I've come dressed more comfortably this time, although my limited wardrobe means I'm sporting a combination of khaki shorts and dainty black dance shoes. I'm only a cap away from looking like a 1950s schoolboy.

We press on with the *pasos*, with Marta noting that I keep dropping my hands by my side as I dance. She has a ready-made solution – a white plastic rod I have to hold in front of me as I dance. It quickly takes on the sense of a flotation device in a swimming pool – the worse I do, the more tightly I grip on to it – but I'm floundering even with it. This is ridiculous. I'm not even close.

Even if I could get it right, it's not exactly something you could showcase at a *clausura*.

"Just wait until you see this guy going forwards and backwards in a line!"

The frustration mounts, and I start blurting out excuses every time I screw up. It would seem that I can happily come to dance classes looking like an idiot, but I can't accept a mistake in my footwork without stopping and explaining why it happened.

Marta takes me to one side – or rather she would do if I wasn't already stood to one side (that's a sideways *paso* joke). Getting it wrong is okay, she says – I'll make mistakes all the time on the dance floor. The most important thing is that I just carry on.

The problems certainly aren't letting up, and they continue

apace when we come together to practise as a couple, meaning Marta has to issue a stream of verbal corrections as we go.

"*¡Firme el brazo!*" she tells me. Firm up your arm!

Don't lift your foot! Stand up straight! Look at me, not the floor! Stop grinding your teeth!

Despite the problems, we keep pressing over onwards, with Marta deciding it's time to add some simple *vueltas* (turns) to my repertoire. If we can call it that.

This comes with the added element of the whole male-lead thing. Not only do I have to dance for myself, Marta explains, I also have to coordinate my partner. This translates to giving her signals and giving her a gentle shove at the appropriate moment. I'm musician and conductor all at the same time – as if there wasn't enough going on.

Putting Marta through a turn is easy: I just direct her with my hands and away she goes, turning with perfect equilibrium. But every time I try to do a turn myself, I lose my balance and career off wildly in the direction of the balcony.

"This is your partner," Marta says, pointing to a nearby satellite dish, "– look for your partner."

She doesn't tell me to wink at it, but then there are some things a man just knows to do instinctively.

For a long time it seems like I'm wasting my time, uselessly buffing the tiles with my suede soles whilst the birds all chirp insults. But finally, a long way in, things start coming together. The mistakes grow fewer and the corrections naturally follow. It all comes together in time for us to put together a tricky sequence in which we both turning successively, one after the other.

"Not good," says Marta with a smile. "Really good!"

I walk up the hilly backstreets full of endorphins, the rhythms still skipping through my mind. I went and did that thing I was scared of – again! – and I'm feeling impervious. I'm also feeling hungry.

Fortunately, lunch is the main meal of the day in Colombia, and quantity is never a problem. I sit in one of my local tiled-floor cafes whilst steam wafts up from the bowl in front of me – a broth-like soup with potatoes and sweet corn. Outside, the sound of Für Elise rises in volume then gradually dissipates back to nothing.

Like I said, lunch is big. As well as the soup, you get a drink and a main dish, consisting of a centrepiece of meat surrounded by rice, potatoes and beans. It's also good value, rarely costing more than 5,000 pesos (US$2.50; £1.67). But there's a problem, and it's quite a simple one – it just doesn't have much flavour. It's not like it's bad food or anything – the ingredients are good quality – it's just that they just cook it, and then it's cooked and that's that. Chicken, for instance, is just chicken, cooked on hotplate. It's then served up surrounded by the regular staples.

Staple foods are so called because you might as well staple them to your hard palate since they're all you're likely to be tasting for the duration of your stay in a country. The food they eat here is certainly traditional – the diet of modern Colombians is similar to that of their pre-Columbian ancestors – and if I ate it once or twice a week it would be fine. But it's inescapable, and eating it on a daily basis is wearing. I mean, I like Für Elise, too, in theory.

I'm seriously considering sneaking in my own herbs and spices. As it is, I settle for clinking about with a spoon in the little glass bowl of *ají*, heaping on as much of the thin, chilli-based *salsa* as I can reasonably get away with. If I can't have flavour, I'll have to go for heat.

"Foreigners always love the chilli!" says the café owner.

Yeah, why is that?

Also, the whole issue in general would be that bit easier to digest if it weren't for the question that so often follows.

"*¿Le gusta?*" Do you like it?

I've very quickly become familiar with Colombian game of 'compliment the food' having had to play it nearly every day. This is where someone asks you about the food with a big expectant smile. Replying with anything other than praise is like running over their puppy with your monster truck – great fun, but you just know you'll never hear the end of it.

"*¡Sí! ¡sí!*"

It's funny in an 'I think I'm going to cry' kind of way.

They're proud people, and they want you to like their stuff. And to them, having grown up with it, it's nothing short of delicious. But I can see already that there's an awful lot to like about Colombia, so I feel I can make an exception for the food. And I plan to be here for a while – perhaps it will grow on me over time.

I feel like I've barely arrived here, yet I already have a morning routine in place. I get up from under polyester sheets, 'shower' then stagger-dance about on the wooden boards putting my clothes on. After a trip to the local bakery to pick up some breakfast, I take controlled strides down the hill to one of the City's main arteries – Calle Quinta – taking swigs of sugary coffee whilst trying to avoid wearing it.

Down on Quinta, street traders cluster round the bases of tired pedestrian bridges. Polite graffiti murals cover walls and underpasses, spreading messages about being nice to animals and saving the planet, and the air is thickened with the sweet scent of *churros* (deep-fried pastry rings).

I walk along the scarred pavements and bitten kerbs and head for the Mío – a brand-new dedicated-carriageway bus network similar to the one I saw in Bogotá. It's a dash of slick modernity between grey, boxy buildings that lifts everywhere it touches and makes the whole city feel newer and more progressive.

It's also a great place to observe Colombian etiquette. Getting on and off between the sliding doors isn't so much 'after you' as 'chee-arge!', but once on board everyone suddenly takes a turn for the genteel. Priority seats are set aside for the pregnant, the elderly and so on, and everyone respects them. It goes further: men naturally defer to women and, at any given point, far more of the former are stood up than the latter.

You ignore the rules at the risk of social discontent. On one occasion I get dark looks and pointed mutterings from a bunch of schoolchildren for not giving up my seat for some bloke on crutches who I'd failed to notice.

Ultimately, I end up deferring to everyone, just in case. I'm not the only one who takes this strategy: seats frequently remain vacant, seemingly because people would rather stand the whole way than perch in a state of permanent alertness for someone higher on the list of deservingness, which, if you're a healthy man under the age of 60, is everyone.

Finally, after leaving the Mío behind and engaging in some suburban trekking, my morning routine ends with me at Marta's house, where I spend two hours alternating between dancing and whinging.

But given the way the last class ended, the class I'm arriving for today should be different. That's how it works, right? You keep doing something: you keep improving.

Ha – if only! We start by trying to recap the *vueltas*, clacking about on the hard tiles, but when I'm unexpectedly shit at those we drop our sights to the basic footwork. But then even that falls apart. Suddenly I can't do a thing. It's no joke: my dancing ability regresses right back to zero.

Marta is on my case more than ever: I'm still lifting my feet; my front leg isn't straight when the weight is on it; I'm lifting my whole foot instead of just the heel. I spot myself doing the last one in the mirror and it looks like I'm doing the Sailor's frigging Hornpipe. And when I correct one thing, something else starts going wrong.

The daily juice break can't come soon enough. I mentally collapse into it, slumping on the plastic chair and pressing the cold glass against my forehead awhile, before stirring it with the straw to loosen the pulp. I take it off my face before I do this.

In contrast to my lunch-time experiences, the juices are heavenly. Along with the familiar varieties of papaya, banana and mango, there's a whole raft of others which are completely new to me. My favourite quickly becomes a citric fruit called *lulo*, whose flavour sits somewhere between orange and passion fruit, with a tang that cuts deep into the crevasses of your mouth. I can't get enough of it, and I'm trying pretty hard.

Despite my best attempts at fruit juice-based stalling, we can't put it off the second half forever and soon we're off again. It quickly feels like we shouldn't have bothered – once more it's just a succession of failed attempts at things I thought I had mastered. It's hot and my hair is guarding a nest of moisture on my head. Why am I doing this, anyway? I mean, so what if I can't dance? I can't skin goats either, but it's never been an impediment in my life.

Marta comes to stand opposite me, holding the rod and doing the mirror image of what I should be doing, but the only thing flowing smoothly is the stream of errors and the associated river of excuses. It's a load of rubbish. I can't do it. I get so hacked off with it all that I simply let go of the rod, leaving her holding it alone.

She looks at me, unimpressed.

"Neil, I think you're a perfectionist."

Well, you know, maybe. But if I were to perform at my *clausura* right this moment, I somehow doubt anyone would be saying "This guy's a perfectionist". A few might think I was some kind of comic interlude, but that's all.

I mean how can we even be serious about doing this? It feels like there's a big, red-LED doomsday clock on the wall, constantly counting down with a *tweep-tweep-tweep* sound. To stand any chance of it not being a disaster. I need to be improving in great big reduced-gravity leaps. Instead I'm going backwards, and even then in a clumsy, knocking-shit-over kind of way.

The lesson ends and I leave quietly. I don't do many things quietly, so this is significant. I arrive at the bus stop for the journey home and joke to myself that at least I've made it there without first getting it wrong, then stopping to explain why, then having another two goes and failing again both times.

The bus arrives, and I attempt to board it, but I can't get through the payment turnstile. With all the other passengers watching on, I have to stand and wait for the driver to get up and help me through. I sit staring out the window, wondering if respiration will be the next thing I've been taking for granted that I become crap at.

My visit to the shopping mall comes as a welcome respite from all this talk of *clausuras.* It also has a hint of mystery about it – I think I might be on a date, but I'm not quite sure. It's not meant to be one – we're meeting for a language exchange – but it somehow kind of feels like one.

Isabela, an elegant and softly spoken Caleña, has invited me out to Chipichape; a shopping mall in the north of the city which is pronounced far too much like 'cheeky chappy' for me to comfortably ignore. We lean in towards each other, our bare arms resting on the plastic surface and our conversation rattling about the hard surfaces.

Is a mall a place for a date? It's certainly calm and relaxed here. People sit chatting in cafes set in the little open-air plazas where fountains splash the afternoon away. We're completely removed from the reality of the city. But then maybe that's the point: Colombians can come here and have a pleasant stroll around and meet with friends without any of the street hassle or thieves, or even the need to actually buy anything.

And this is the odd thing about the place: despite there being plenty of people about, the shops are almost empty. It's not hard to see why, either: many of the goods here are imported and prices are similar to – or even higher than – back home. But with a reasonable salary for a young, middle-class person in Cali being about 1 million pesos (500 US dollars; 333 pounds sterling), they represent extravagant luxury for all but the richest.

Class does seem to be directly related to wealth. The upper-class saunter about the smarter districts dressed like something from a pop video, whilst the lower classes try and scratch a living on the street. The middle classes, meanwhile, go to university to study sensible things like architecture and software engineering, and drink their coffee in places like this.

I'm learning new things about Colombia all the time, even in shopping malls. I'm just not sure if I've just been on a date or not.

The final couple of salsa lessons consist of more of what's come before: practising footwork, professing love for telecommunications equipment and trying to avoid hurling myself off a second floor balcony, either out of incompetence or frustration. However, there's a light at the end of the tunnel, and it's not a modern, guided bus.

I don't know what happened, but I've actually started showing some glimpses of competence. For a start, I find myself finally able to do the footwork without looking like a sailor. On top of that, the turns have suddenly clicked to the point where we're able to complete flowing sequences. I must have been sleep-dancing or something.

There's even time to try some new moves. Marta has me doing some flashy pieces of footwork like I saw in the video, including one where you slip your feet forwards and backwards alternately at high speed, like the Ali shuffle. I pick them up without even half the fuss afforded to the basic *pasos*.

You might think this would reduce my fear of the *clausura*, but you'd be wrong. The only difference is that before it was justified, whereas now it's just of the regular, irrational variety. Fear is still fear, and I simply can't envisage me standing up and dancing for a crowd of people.

The classes are done, but the performance isn't for a few days yet, so I've got a little bit of time to pretend it doesn't exist. Marta tells me I need to head to the main studio, where they'll arrange for a partner for me. But I'm mentally entrenched in my position – I do not want to do this.

"*¿Cómo te sientes?*" asks Marta. How do you feel?

"*Bien... muy bien.*" Good... very good.

I should steeple my fingers as I'm saying it, really. You see, when it comes to obtaining creative solutions, the motivational effects of fear should never be underestimated. In this instance they've helped me develop a foolproof way of side-stepping the *clausura.*

I've already told Marta about my intention to go round Colombia learning an as-yet-undetermined list of dances. Well how about, I suggest, I come back in several months' time and put together a proper dance show, consisting of everything I've learnt?

It actually makes a lot of sense for me to do such a show: it will help keep me motivated, provide a focus for the journey and mean that the whole thing ends with something of a punctuation mark. This last point is particularly relevant given that I plan to write a book about my experiences – if you're going to humiliate yourself on a grand scale, you may as well document it.

But none of this is behind why I'm suggesting it to Marta. The real outcome I've got in mind here is not getting on a stage until a long, long way into the future, and even then only if I don't think there's any way of avoiding it.

Marta embraces my proposal wholeheartedly. It's a great idea – we can turn it into a big Neil-orientated extravaganza!

Great! Let's all pretend to do that! I'm still mentally doing a jig when Marta casually mentions that we're still going do the original *clausura.* I mean why wouldn't we? After all, it's already scheduled

Arrgh, what have I done? Before I only had to do a one-dance-and-I'm-outta-here *clausura* – I've somehow managed to add to that some kind of multi-faceted super-show in which I'm the main man.

I just hope I turn out better at performing dances than I am at avoiding them.

Did you know that there is additional material to accompany this book? There are photos, videos and all sorts of other stuff related to the journey, and you can dip in as you read. All the music I mention is in there too – it's pretty much a soundtrack accompanying the whole journey.

To get access, simply sign up for my author mailing list - you can unsubscribe at any time.

http://neilbennion.com/dancingfeatsignup

CHAPTER FOUR

Forwards and Backwards

I've got it!

If I sign up for more lessons, then I won't have to do the *clausura*! You can't graduate if you're still studying – how much sense would that make? I'll be able to put it off until the next opportunity, which could be easily be another two weeks away. And, hey, maybe I'll just neglect to mention that I'll be gone by then.

"What a shame," I'll say. "I'm sooooooo sorry. I've got to catch a bus to the other side of the country!" Then leave, sniggering like a naughty – yet clearly brilliant – schoolboy.

I send Marta an email to this effect. Excluding the 'dastardly plan' elements, obviously – experience has taught me that this reduces the chance of success.

Her response is an agreed set of dates for my new lessons. And an email not to forget the *clausura*, which still stands. Forget dance footwear: running shoes would have made a better investment. Also, I think I need to read the Art of War.

Then the horrible possibility dawns on me that Marta will expect me to do a further *clausura* after my second set of lessons. In trying to weasel my way out of a single *clausura*, I may well have ended up creating three. The damn things are breeding.

There's no use – I'm going to have to roll out the big guns. I'm going to have to go into denial.

The sun is in free fall towards the Andes, glinting off the three crosses that guard over the city and anointing the buildings with its golden glow. I'm out with Isabela, who I may or may not be dating, along with a group of her friends.

We sit together, imprinting grassy outlines onto our palms. It feels like we're up in the heavens rather than just the steep grassy park which rises out of San Antonio. At this height, aided by the convex shape of the hill, we're mixing it with the upper reaches of the city's skyscrapers, way up above all the street grime.

The park is open and free; somewhere you can breathe. Couples cuddle up and look out over the skyline whilst groups of young people sit in circles drinking, smoking and stroking their guitars. The air is thick with the smell of *arepas* – unleavened cornmeal patties which vendors grill on the street – and the occasional waft of something stronger.

I've wandered up here before and there's always something going on. Halfway up the hill is a tiny amphitheatre with concrete steps where comics ply their trade. At the top of it is a paved plateau where people murmur in and out of a little church and a concrete driveway down which children toboggan on plastic crates.

On a previous occasion, I saw a small crowd gathered round a performance of some kind. Getting closer, I could see a man with a guitar serenading someone, presumably a dancer. Intrigued, I pressed right up to the edge of the crowd – it was a dog in a dress and hat, dancing on its hind legs. It's a shame it's not there today – I'd ask it how much it wanted to appear as a ringer for me in the *clausura*. Mind you, people would probably click on.

"This guy's improved too much."

We start heading down off the hill as a group, Isabela's hand in mine.

"Where are we going?" I ask her.

"*¡A bailar!*" To dance!

The more time I spend here the more I realise how lightly I got off on my first night out. These people are obsessed.

As we walk down, people are discussing alcohol, and money is changing hands. One of the group goes on a mission then returns with a bottle of colourless liquor. A couple of little plastic cups, like oversized thimbles (or undersized buckets) are splashed full – tinting the air with aniseed – then passed on and knocked back. This is *aguardiente* (meaning 'fiery water') – the spirit of choice in these parts.

The girls seem to get off lightly, getting less than a full cup, whilst I get let off completely, though only after I've dealt with the initial disbelief at my non-drinking. This takes the form of my being quizzed about each drink specifically in turn.

"Beer?"

"No."

"Whisky?"

"No."

"Rum?"

"No."

We could be in for a long night...

"Schwarzwälder Zwetschgenwasser?"

"No."

"Eau-de-vie de vin originaire de Franche-Comté?"

"No."

I'm used to this kind of thing by now, having fielded variations on a theme of "Why don't you drink?" for the last five years of my life.

I gave up drinking alcohol following a serious health problem that put me in hospital for three weeks, and put my life on hold for well over a year. Still, I'm alive, and I'm very grateful for that. Especially given that they thought I might even have cancer of the bile duct, and that's about as healthy as an argument with a Colombian truck.

It turned out I had a rare condition you've almost certainly never heard of, which is great because we all love to feel special. And although alcohol wasn't the cause, it certainly wasn't helping – my spleen would let out howls of protest every time I so much as went near a drink– so I decided to call time on my drinking.

Nowadays, I could probably drink in moderation, but I choose not to, chiefly because I like provoking arguments with people at bars, which I do with deliberately confrontational language like "What soft drinks have you got?"

With the switch from day to night, the jugglers that perform at traffic lights have switched from simple balls to fiery torches which light up their faces and sear the night air. Perhaps there's a problem with bears in these parts. Together, our little group crosses the small, forgotten river that demarks the historic centre from the fashionable and affluent north of the city, and we eventually arrive on La Sexta – an avenue of big, open-fronted bars that thump out

Latin beats from behind shouty neon facades.

This is the so-called *zona rosa* (pink zone) – the party district, and something which is apparently common to every city in Colombia. It's a bit like Blackpool except with fewer 'kiss me quick' hats and more 'no guns' signs. The venues are much brighter and brasher than the little salsa club, and the clientele looks different, too – the men more serious and the women more pouty.

Actually, there's something strange going on here with the women – they cast big shadows. You, know, in profile. At the top. No, no – below the head.

Breasts, you idiot, they've got big breasts.

However, unlike Darwinian selection, or the urge to walk out of time with music you dislike, it's not a natural phenomenon: Cali is a renowned centre of plastic surgery. In fact, there's such a high concentration of it that it's just as well silicone doesn't have a critical mass.

The scene is parted down the middle by flurries of little yellow taxis, else the movable feast of whoops and cheers of a passing *chiva* – a brightly-painted, open-sided party bus with people dancing and spirits being liberally splashed around. Back in the day, these vehicles used to serve rural communities, carrying all manner of wares, even livestock. Nowadays they're more commonly associated with party animals.

I look at each of the pulsating venues in turn trying to work out if this is the one we're headed for, but we pass each one by without stopping. Eventually, we leave the *zona rosa* altogether and take a turn back towards the river. At which point I discover there was no need to look for the action after all – the action has come out to us.

Revellers spill out from a tiny standalone bar and into the sizzling night air. Some are just stood talking, but many are dancing, caught up in the eddying currents of music; drawn dizzyingly about and washed this way and that by the irresistible and increasingly familiar *ring-a-ting-ting* of salsa cowbells. Laughter and chatter floats over the top and little beer bottles clatter about on the floor. A fountain on a nearby traffic island tries to compete, but it's wasting its time.

My God, this is it. Somehow, without warning, I've walked straight into that rum advert – people are literally dancing on the street. Okay, so strictly speaking they're actually dancing on the pavement, but that's good enough for me: I don't expect people to risk death by little yellow taxi just to feed my fantasy. They gyrate in the bar's entrance, between the propped-up motorbikes and even on the road between the parked cars: anywhere there's space.

However, there was something important missing from my mental images of these places. Me. I never pictured myself dancing there. As we start to squeeze through the movement, I feel the burn of anxiety – they're going to expect me to dance, aren't they?

Quite why this should be a problem, I don't know. I'm out here to learn – that's the whole point of the trip – and I've got more *clausuras* than I know what to do with, so I should be taking every opportunity I can to practise. But the reality is that I feel almost as scared as the first time. So I just stand there, watching; quietly hoping no-one else notices that I'm not dancing. I should be pretty safe though, as I get the impression it's the bloke's role to ask.

"*¿Quieres bailar?*" Isabela asks. Do you want to dance?

"*No.*"

My brain has already generated a whole pack of excuses for me. I just don't feel like it. And being English, I'm not made for this kind of thing. And without Marta here to prompt me, I can't remember the different moves. And... well give me twenty minutes and I'll have twenty more excuses. They'd all be irrelevant, though: Isabela takes my hands with her own gentle, persuasive ones and starts dancing with me regardless.

Checkmate.

Aware that it would probably look rude if I shouted "Taxi!" I instead try to take us through some of the basic *pasos*. However, we hit a problem straight away: instead of mirroring what I'm doing, she stays where she is, shuffling about in her gentle, elegant manner. I guess my leading isn't up to much. I compensate by making my *pasos* so small that I can dance without really shifting location.

Isabela is not the only one who dances like this – there are many round and about who are dancing in a similar way. In fact, it's pretty much the dominant mode. This bothers me: I go to a salsa school to learn to dance like the locals, but many of the locals do something else entirely, in this case a whole load of this foot shuffling with the odd twirl thrown in.

The strange thing is that they can still read each other's

intentions, so they're clearly not winging it. It looks simple, but this is deceptive, as I can't seem to figure it out, let alone copy it – it's so fuzzily indistinct as to be impenetrable. It seems to be second nature; like they have a deep, ingrained feel for the music and how your body connects with it. I suppose it's like how when two people speak a language they can just mumble, and they both understand exactly what each other is saying, or at least pretend to.

These are the people who never went to classes; they just know it. If so, this is arguably the purest example of the Latin dance culture. They're the old guy down the boozer who can rattle off Roll Out The Barrel or any number of other tunes, but couldn't tell you what key they're playing in. Or what instrument they're doing it on. Or their own name.

Whilst I was doing my solo Adam and the Ants thing, they were occupied with something more useful – learning how to dance with other human beings. If this is what it means to truly dance like a Colombian, then I'll need to be here for a long time, ideally starting about 30 years ago.

But not all the locals dance like this. Others – I'm guessing those who've had lessons – combine this instinctive feel with polished technique, performing bold sequences of turns, filling in with flourishes of clever footwork. But it never looks like they're executing a sequence of manoeuvres - it look as natural as breathing. This has got to be the standard I'm aiming at.

That still leaves one last category – the rarest of all, in fact.

"I can't dance salsa," says one young bloke.

He's more into emo, he tells me.

"Salsa sucks!" adds his friend.

Finally – some people to challenge the idea that every Caleño and his dog can dance. It must take guts to live in the salsa capital of the world and not be able to dance to it. I'm a rebel just like you guys.

With my 'no' stance broken for the evening, I find I now have the courage to dance with a couple of other girls. These two do respond to my *pasos* and I'm even able to do a couple of turns with them. However, my L-plates are well-known throughout the community and this causes its own problem: if my style differs from theirs, they assume I'm doing it wrong.

With the first partner, the fact I'm trying to keep my arms firm, as drilled into me by Marta, is causing some consternation.

"Are you tense?"

No, I'm holding you firmly – can't you tell the near-imperceptible difference?

With another, I'm holding her with my hand around the shoulder blade area, but she thinks it should be on her lower back. Marta has specifically told me you don't put it that low because that's a signal you're going to spin someone, and also it means you lack the control required to lead effectively.

Gaaaaahhh! Am I the only person who knows how to dance round here?

Amidst all the muddled shuffling and sweeping precision, a filthy tramp wanders towards us, his skin ingrained with dirt. Here we go, here's about to put his hand out for cash. But no – instead he starts dancing salsa, solo on the pavement in front of us. He executes his moves with a gleeful, carefree verve, quickly gaining the attention of the party crowd.

It's now that the hand comes out – to offer a girl a dance. To her total credit, she shows no signs of prissiness, and accepts. Together they shimmy in front of us on the street, a venue which ironically doubles as his home. Finally, he's done, and his hand does come out for the more expected reason, to which I and others gladly oblige. Someone pipes up that we shouldn't as he'll only spend it on alcohol, but this seems like a difficult stance to maintain given that we're stood at a bar.

I feel a sense of wonder at the relationship this city has with dance, but at the same time I feel somewhat dejected – the beggar is just the latest in a long line of people, animals and inanimate objects that can dance better than me. But then, unless I can learn to grasp the nettle (I'd say cactus, but I don't think the grasping thing works with those), it will never be any different.

A mere two days before the *clausura* is due to occur, I finally resign myself to the beyond-all-control happening-ness of this event. I head off down to the dance school academy, hoping that it's not too late to find someone willing to bask in my reflected ineptitude.

I wander in off the street carrying my dance shoes and a nervous smile. I don't want to do this. I've left it very late – perhaps too late – and even then I feel like I shouldn't have come.

My throat tightens whenever I think about it. I've got to stand up and dance in front of 15 or 20 people. This is so much worse than dancing in a club, as these people will have come specifically to watch us dance – that's the whole point.

The beggar incident illustrates a further problem: I'll be dancing in front of a crowd of people all of whom will likely be better dancers than me. Whatever I do I can't actually impress them.

The one unfortunate enough to have to partner me is a short *mestiza* woman in her twenties called Laura – one of the in-house dance teachers. She has an easy familiarity that convinces me I'm in good hands. But I'm the lead, of course, and whether or not she's in good hands is quite another matter.

We start by running through all the various *pasos* and *vueltas* in my dance vocabulary, trying to link some things together in a way that will be visually appealing. People stroll past outside, and I feel a touch exposed, but self-consciousness has now become a luxury: I just have to go for it. Our task is quite simple – we need to choreograph an audience-facing routine to music which we will then perform step-for-step on the night.

The reality, however, is less straightforward.

Despite the sequences being fairly basic, executing them competently proves surprisingly difficult. Whilst Laura's moves are tidy and pin-sharp, mine are nowhere near. I'm the weak link, every single time.

On top of this, you can only perform the moves in sequence if you can remember that sequence. As it stands, it's just a litany of 'er...' moments, where we hesitate in unison whilst the music blithely continues. I jot some notes down on the fly, but unless we plan to adopt a parking-attendant theme, I'm not going to be able to hold this whilst we dance – It's just going to have to go in by sheer force of repetition.

A further complication comes with sharing the area with other dancers. This means there's a constant negotiation for space on the dance floor, and also for the chance to play one's chosen music through the PA system. Something else gnaws at me, too: why are so many dancers preparing? This can't be for the same show as me, can it?

The positive in all this is that I get to see all sorts of elegant physical conversations occurring all about us. A group of kids around the 12-year-old mark are doing what Laura tells me is mambo. One young lad amongst them spins a stick-thin girl all about his body, like a hand twirling a pencil. He's about a third of my age, and I'm in awe of him. Meanwhile, some other guy works solo on a seamless melange of deft kicks and flicks that leave sparkling traces behind them.

I ask Laura how long it took him to get to that level.

"Three months, four months."

And there's the rub: I don't have that kind of time. I barely have any time at all.

The next day is the last full day before the *clausura*, and Laura and I are back at work in the devilish heat.

It can get quite oppressive in the city at times – rarely scorching, just persistent – and even the locals need to escape now and then. It was for this reason that Isabela and I went to a favourite Caleño escape a few days ago – a site high up in the city's backdrop of mountains known as Kilometro 18. This is a place named after how far up the road it is, presumably because everybody was too busy dancing to have time for inconsequential stuff like fancy appellations.

We'd agreed to go there for sunset, although it begged the question "Which one?" since it was already dark when Isabela and a couple of her friends come to pick me up. Out here, my own traditional fifteen minutes of habitual tardiness looks almost gentlemanly and doesn't even necessitate an apology.

The chill quickly encroached into the car we gained altitude, the city twisting about below us in a whirlpool of yellow lights. Our destination was a little strip of bars and cafes forked off the main road, where well wrapped-up vendors stood on waste ground caramelising corn.

Caleños walked about clad in hats and scarves – a peculiar site – some with a cotton neckerchief poking up out of their jackets, bandit-style. A shivering mist hung in the air reducing visibility, softening the edges of everything and making the place look like an indistinct fragment of memory.

Some 10 years ago, 70 people were kidnapped from this area by an armed group – it's easy to forget how recently such things were an issue.

We shuddered our way to a cosy little restaurant on a hillside from which a rich scent of candle wax emanated, a big hanging bowl of hot coals serving up a warm welcome to all those who, like us, had suddenly decided that they actually quite liked the heat after all.

There we sat, with our jackets still on, warming our hands on big bowl-like mugs of *chocolate con queso* (hot chocolate and cheese) – or rather, splattering it onto the paper tablecloth by dropping squeaky, feta-like depth charges into the cocoa. We stayed there for quite a while in the restaurant's cosy dimness, hidden up in a dream, the *clausura* just some imaginary thing way down, beyond the mist, in the city below.

But now the dream is that spot up in the mountains, and the city heat is the reality once more. Into battle we go, pressing on amidst the constant veneer of moisture on skin, the musty sweetness of day-old sweat on clothes and the on-off breeze of swivelling fans.

I find myself wiping my hands on my shorts a lot to ensure a solid contact we can both trust – I'd rather not accidently fling Laura out of the dance school if I can help it.

For Laura, the moves continue to come easily and naturally – after all, it's her job, and she's just putting in a shift. For me, however, it's a long and drawn out personal struggle with the forces of technique.

The relative difference in heights is just one of those technical aspects, and something I've already encountered with a few different partners. It's especially noticeable when I'm the one doing the turn, and I can feel a short partner over-extending. Obviously, I don't want to rip their arms out of their sockets – it wouldn't be very visually appealing for a start – but nor do I want to dance hunched over. There must be some middle ground here. Perhaps I can rip their arms out whilst dancing hunched over – that way we're both giving something.

Laura gives me some guidance – when she's doing the turn, I need to position our conjoined hands in the right place, just above her head. If it's me doing the turn, I have to give a brief dip as her hands come over the top. Either that or do the whole thing on my knees with a pair of shoes strapped to them to fool the audience. That last one's my idea, not hers.

After so many repetitions, the music has become ingrained in my head. It starts abruptly with skinny, squealing trumpets, then comes the pots-and-pans percussion and finally a rhythmic piano with that entrancingly discordant Latin flavour.

It's been another long, hard day of slogging away; of making excuses to take breaks; of forcing myself to get up and carry on again. The reward is that we actually have an end product. It's got a bit of everything, too – turns, footwork and even special, complicated bits that I'm bound to fuck up.

Seven hours of work have yielded two minutes of joined-up dance. It seems slightly pathetic when I put it like that, but hey – they're long minutes. Or they sure as hell will be for anyone watching.

There is a slight problem in that we've got twenty seconds more music than choreography. Laura wants us to extend the routine to fit, but I flatly refuse –it's hard enough to remember as it is. I'll stop and just smile at the audience for the last twenty seconds if need be. In fact I quite like that idea. Perhaps realising I'm not going to budge, Laura arranges for someone technical to cut the extra time out the middle, and we're done.

I still feel on edge with the thought of dancing in front of all those people, all staring intently at me, but for now I've done all I can. It's time to relax.

That evening I go out to the little salsa club with Isabela, who I do now appear to be dating but who shows no inclination to actually want to kiss. We'd been holding hands an awful lot, but when I thought the time had come and I went for it, I got the subtle yet crushing rejection that comes with the slight turn of a woman's head at a crucial moment.

Back in the UK, if you've not kissed by the end of the third date, then you probably don't have mouths. Yet we were on something like the fifth. Maybe I'd read the signals all wrong. Perhaps she just wasn't into me. In which case no problem. But then why were we dating?

"Do you like me?" I asked her.

"*¡Sí!*"

Then what was going on? I mean, a certain amount of reticence is understandable, after all, I'm just some itinerant dance student who'll be gone again in a flash, but it would nice to know where I stood.

Isabela thought a while about how to put it, finally settling on three words.

"*Poco a poco.*" Little by little.

I've already decided when I go out that evening that I'm not going to dance. I've had three hours of practice and two hours of class with Marta, and tomorrow is the *clausura*. The last thing I want is more dance. Forget the Latin party culture – I just want to sit there and relax in the company of friends. Yes, I have always got an excuse but, just out of sheer novelty value, this time it's actually a valid one.

"*¿Quieres bailar?*" asks Isabela. Do you want to dance?

It's all about technique in this game – you've got to be strong, confident and show you mean business. Oh, and you improve with practice.

"No."

"Why won't you dance?"

"Because I don't want to."

I'm sat down this time, so it's not like she can even just grab me again. Instead, she snubs me and heads off to find another partner. This is not a good result: I might have got away with not dancing, but it's created an issue between us. And now she's dancing I've got no-one to talk to. And if I go up and talk to other people, someone will expect me to dance with them. And if I relent and do so, then it'll look like it's Isabela I've got the problem with.

I'm told I over-complicate things.

Fifteen minutes later, I've been reduced to making crumpling sounds with a plastic bottle of water. To make matters worse, there's a distinct lack of men out tonight, meaning that those that are here are needed up on the dance floor. In fact, one of Isabela's friends, a guy in his late twenties, is helping to make up for the shortfall by dancing with two girls at a time – one off each hand.

I've met the double-dancer before – he has a kind of relaxed gravitas and speaks plainly and to the point. He also dances practically all the time, so when I see him approaching, I know there's probably a good reason.

"Why won't you dance?"

Well, you know, just because.

"Are you angry?"

A perplexed expression settles on his face as he tries to understand this anomaly.

I don't like being expected to justify myself – I get it enough in life as a non-drinker – but my breaking of a cultural norm here is now causing issues, and after all, this guy is just looking out for his friend. So I concede and tell him about what I'm feeling. I don't tell him that I'm an inveterate dance-avoider, but then that's probably self-evident.

"Okay," he says, "but next time you have to dance."

Isabela comes back up to me, and we make our peace.

"Here, if you go to the disco," she tells me, "you go to dance."

Yeah, I get that now. You can get away with not drinking, and you can even get away with not washing (I'm talking about the vagrant now, not me), but nothing short of a leg in plaster will serve as an excuse for not getting up when there is salsa playing. And whilst kissing might be optional on a date, dancing is obligatory.

My work (of making a mess of things) done for the evening, I decide I may as well leave. As I head outside, Isabela follows me to say goodbye. She gives me her regular peck, only this time she presses it gently onto my lips.

Poco a poco.

I'm concerned. I mean I've spent most of my time in Cali concerned, but now I'm really concerned. It's the morning of the big day – well, big night – and the school is packed with practising dancers.

"Tonight, it will be full," says Laura.

Well it's pretty jammed as it is. Oh wait – does she mean with spectators? I've got a horrible feeling about this.

As the music coming through the PA system shifts in bewildering fits between up-tempo salsa, down-tempo Bolero and a whole lot of other stuff in between, we run through our sequence again and again, trying perfect it.

We might have a routine, but we're far from ready: my memory fails me repeatedly, and so do my motor skills. The transitions are jerky, and some of the individual moves are simply beyond me, despite all the hours we've put in.

Indeed, there's one element that forever eludes me, no matter how many times I do it: a kind of shoulder shimmy where you throw each shoulder forward alternately, in a quick, fluid sequence.

"Look at me!" It says. Or more specifically, "Look at my shoulders!"

When Laura does it, she looks jazzy. When I do it, I look like I'm having a seizure. I've been rubbish at it right from the start, and I'm still no closer to getting it right.

There are other things to think about now, though. I spy numerous other dancers trying on hats to see which best finishes their outfit, and it suddenly strikes me that I don't have an outfit in the first place, let alone one to finish.

From what I can work out, dance apparel has its own special set of requirements. It needs to be stretchy, so as to allow freedom of movement; to be close-fitting, so it doesn't snag, and to be embossed with half a metric ton of sequins, so nobody can confuse you with a regular human being. Surprisingly, I don't seem to have packed anything that meets these requirements.

It's not unusual for me to lack the appropriate attire. I once went to a wedding reception in jeans and blazer during the great suit shortage of the mid-2000s (I think may only have affected me). Friends reassured me that I'd be fine just like that, and that it was going to be quite a casual affair.

The venue turned out to be a location of great opulence, and all 150 or so invited guests were immaculately suited, the vast majority of my friends having decided to go that way at the last minute. I might as well have come dressed as a massive crab. The good news is that the couple have since divorced, which also annuls any *faux pas* that occurred that day.

If the city has a very centre, then it's probably Plaza Caicedo – a big square of pathways and grass, with palm trees that soar skywards, dwarfing the ornate candelabra streetlamps and making the place seem like a prehistoric garden.

It's an area with the feel of run-down civility, everyday life occurring in front of the pristine, wedding cake-esque Palacio Nacional. Vendors push about ambulant stalls, shaded by tired multicolour parasols. Old men with cured skin sit around in chinos, shirts and shoes, sharing jokes with each other as the day strolls by. Folk mill about selling hot coffee from flasks, mobile phone calls by the minute and other street wares. Pigeons scratch around the centrepiece statue, occasionally crapping on it when they get bored.

The streets that spread out from the square form the discount shopping district – this is where working class (and even many middle class) people come to buy their clothes, having left slobber marks on the shop windows in the mall. It's where t-shirted motorbike riders hustle between street stalls piled up with cheap footwear, and where outdated remote controls sit in cracked glass cabinets, waiting for owners. It's also where I hope to acquire something suitable for the *clausura*.

I charge about, aware of the shortage of time, looking for something that will serve my needs. It's probably too late to find anything specialist, so I just set my sights on something smart. Even then I know that finding trousers that are long enough is likely to be a problem in this part of the world.

Men stand out on chairs, microphone in hand, barking out prices, trying to entice customers inside shops. Entire labyrinthine mini-malls open up off the street, places you might never find your way out of, each one containing a mayhem of clothes shops, each one of those a noisy argument of shapes and colours. It feels like the inside of my head: all sorts of stuff is swishing round in there, and I can't tell the junk from the treasure.

"It's madness!" says one of the microphone men.

I leave the hassle behind and head back to a business-clothes place I spotted on the way in. It turns out to be a good choice – the trousers here are unfinished in length and they tailor them to fit. The pair I pick are neither spangly nor figure-hugging but matched up with a shirt at least they'll look presentable. There are about four hours to go and I'm finally ready.

Scratch that – I've just got an outfit. It's really not the same thing.

The academy looks very different. Balloons and flags festoon the place whilst a multi-tiered stand of trophies rises up one corner. Suddenly the previous *clausura* looks like some casual get together.

Oh my God, will you just look at the number of seats? Row upon row of white plastic chairs stretch back towards the entrance where I stand. If they fill them, there'll be something like four times the number of the previous event. It's only a small place, but the whole setup screams out "BIG SHOW!"

I get a panicky urge to practise some more, to suddenly make it perfect somehow. But there's no longer room in the school given all the bustle and seating and preparatory work. So instead I head outside onto the pavement. There, under the darkening sky, I run through the routine, toning down my movements out of self-consciousness and keeping an eye out for passers-by in case I need to break into some emergency casual whistling.

Then audience members start arriving, greeted by Marta, and I realise that the game's up. Soon the room will be reverberating with the chatter of people and the judder of chairs. I'll just have to make do with what I've got. I head backstage to the area set aside for performers, feeling somewhat like a circus rookie seeking sanctuary in a cannon.

The next time I emerge will be to dance.

I arrive into a buzz of activity. It's a small space, and we're all wedged in amidst piled-up boxes, dangling clothes and a forest of foam trees. Nearly every conceivable piece of floor is taken up by people. Women and girls sit crossed legged with their make-up box for company, whilst other dancers tip-toe through, seeking gaps with their feet. Mascara is applied and stretchy dancewear is readjusted and snapped into place.

Laura hasn't gone for stretchy: she's wearing tiny white shorts and a matching tight, short-sleeved blouse, with a pink sash acting as a belt. The look is finished off with a pair of little silver heels. Girls tell me that it's easier to dance salsa in heels, but I've decided to give it a miss.

With or without them, I'm still completely out of place. There are familiar faces all around me – I've been watching these people practise all week – but I don't belong here. I feel like an embedded journalist posing with a soldier's gun, despite not having the first idea which way to point one. I'm a complete fraud.

Face-glitter is everywhere and makeup is being applied, reapplied and re-reapplied. I take a pasting to the face at the order of Marta, presumably because, despite all the Cauca Valley sun, I still resemble a French mime artist, albeit without the superior motor control. I expect I'll still make people laugh, though.

The nervousness I've walled in at the back of my mind starts seeping round the sides and welling at the front. This is really going to happen, and there's nothing I can do to stop it. Maybe I could seek refuge in the foam trees until the show is over – hide out like a rainforest man, with a plastic machete.

I think back to times when I've felt confident; successful; on top form: I'm giving the best man's speech at my friend's wedding; pulling off a sequence of great saves in a five-a-side game; winning imperiously at Game of Life ("In your face, vicar!"). I'm not sure it helps but it gives me something to do with my brain.

The audience is growing in size – I can hear their murmurings. I decide to take a peek through a gap in the screens. Bad idea – not only are all the seats taken but so is the floor space between them. Worse still, yet more people are massing behind them, spilling out into the dark night. Cameras poke out everywhere, like gun barrels preparing to take down frightened deer.

I walk away, shaking my head and laughing. This is so messed up.

"Shhhhhh!"

We need to be quiet – they can hear us out front and the show is about to begin.

An amplified voice cuts through the chatter: Marta is addressing the audience. The performers for the first act all stand expectantly. Moments later, they are calmly filing out to a soundtrack of whistles and cheers. Then music begins to paint the air with colour, followed by whoops from the crowd: the show is underway.

A list taped to one wall shows the order of play. I run my eyes down the list, like a passenger on a runaway train counting the stops until the end of the line. We're an agonising tenth – about halfway through.

Some part of me wants to postpone this indefinitely. Another part wants to get out there right this very second. The remaining part just wishes I had valid tranquiliser prescription. It would help if things were a little less surreal: I'm surrounded by kids with painted faces and men with bare muscular chests and bow ties. It's like being in a David Lynch film.

Laura is in a different state entirely: calm but focussed, absorbed by her preparation. Her dark hair is now slicked back into a high ponytail that feeds forward over one shoulder, her face adorned by streaks of glittery lilac eye-shadow and smouldering red lipstick. She's done this kind of thing so many times before, and she'll be up twice more tonight to do routines in *pachanga* and cha-cha-cha, whatever the hell they are.

One by one, the acts troop out, Marta's voice introduces,

people applaud and music plays. Then the acts return again, looking unfazed.

The nerves in the last few seconds are near overwhelming. My breath feels like it's too high up in my lungs as we wait in the airlock of screens that demarks the backstage area. Laura has one last piece of advice for me – if we *equivocamos* (make a mistake) I should just follow her lead.

Time's up.

Out we go, into the blazing lights, the applause, the whistling. There are so many faces in front of me that I can't focus on any. It's just a wall of expectancy hemming me in and blocking the exit.

Marta introduces me as "Ne-ul" and asks what I'll be dancing to.

"Ramona," I say, "by Ismael Rivera."

Whatever else happens this evening – even if I violently spin off and tear down the lighting and screens, smashing through the trophies like a bowling ball – at least people will say I got that bit right.

"His trousers were nice, too."

Marta and I share a brief exchange in Spanish. I don't really hear what she says, or what I say. I just blather out some words into the hot night. It's excruciating. I just want to dance. And/or run away.

Laura and I lean into each other, adopting the starting pose. We wait. And wait. And wait.

The speakers burst into life with the quacking of skinny trumpets. I've heard this intro scores of times before. Somehow this time it sounds unexpected and unfamiliar. I push off and we're away, straight in a couple of sets of the basic "ta-da!" *pasos*. We throw our free hands up in the air each time in showmanship. The crowd responds immediately with whoops of encouragement.

My hands feel cold and clammy, but I'm settling in now, finding my stride. We charge into a move called *hablar y contestar* (speak and answer) where we do successive turns – her, then me, then me, then her – during a simple forwards-and-backwards *paso*. I make some slight slips-ups as I turn simply through being too eager. Or perhaps it's Laura's fault for not having a face like a satellite dish.

It's not a show-stopper, though, and the audience don't seem to have noticed. In fact, they're cheering and whistling our every move. I'd stop and check my flies if there were time.

We switch into the detested – by me, anyway – shoulder thrusts, opening up to face the audience. It's now that the first cracks begin to show. Under pressure they're more spasmodic than ever. Everyone still cheers, though. They must be thinking "I like this bit where he pretends to have temporal lobe epilepsy". I could probably draw a face on my hand and pretend to talk with it and they'd still love it. What can I say – they're a good crowd.

"People don't care here if you dance badly," one of the dance school regulars previously told me, "they just like to see you enjoying yourself when you're dancing."

But there's no time for other people's quotes – the routine is racing by. In fact it's going too quickly: my timing goes as we launch into a trip-hazard of sideways cross-legged quicksteps and very nearly drop it. I've just about recovered when I lose it in a bigger way going into some face-to-face controlled footwork. It takes a whole two bars to whip it back in line.

I'm playing catch up all the time now. It's like when you're running and you begin to fall headlong, and with each step you're desperately trying to squeeze another foot underneath. The whole dance is teetering on the brink.

Then comes the fall.

Presumably thrown by all my own errors, Laura has a slip of memory and goes into the Ali-shuffle at the wrong time. I can't really blame her. It must be like trying to do a piano duet with Les Dawson.

"No!"

We come to a complete halt. We stand there, whilst the music plays and the audience watches, showing each other what we think we should be doing. Every second is a disaster; a humiliation. I'm sure I'm right, so I just take control, guiding her into a later *paso*, and we continue.

We're still going somehow, but now the mistakes are outnumbering the steps. It's a mess. We enter into a scrappy 'Kentucky' *vuelta*, then a frenetic and rushed sequence of U-turns, before careering into the final sequence. The finish line's in sight. We pull apart then elastically spring back together and into the closing figure: the *pistola* (pistol).

Laura propels herself onto my waist from the side and BANG – we're done.

Cue a cacophony of whistles and applause. Somehow – somehow – we've ended in perfect synchronicity with the end of the music; ruffled, shaken, but on time. It's like we've both emerged from vaulting fences and diving under hedgerows in some kind of back-garden race, emerging in perfect time to walk straight onto a bus, which we casually board with torn clothing, messy hair, and cuts and bruises.

"Two for backstage, please."

But we can't go just yet – there are still the formalities, starting with the obligatory bow. It feels like framing bad art, but it's customary, and the audience responds with yet more appreciation. I feel embarrassed, but I can only respect their sense of irony. Marta concludes by explaining to the audience that I'm "a little nervous", although "a little rubbish" might be more accurate.

"*Es un proceso,*" she tells them. It's a process.

In the intermission follows, an unfeasible number of people come up to me to congratulate me. Marta, the great motivator, rummages around in a hat for positives and pulls one out by the ears: it was great that I took control when things started to go awry.

"The best thing about you is that you're an obstinate fucker," she's basically telling me.

And even that gives me mixed emotions, because I agreed I'd follow Laura if anything went wrong, and I didn't.

Some ex-pat from the US tells me he's been here for 12 years and not accomplished what I have. He must be truly awful. These people are all really kind, but I'm not deceived. I know it was a poor performance; a belief backed up by Marta's having made excuses on my behalf. What was it she said? It's a process. Boy does that burn.

When the show resumes, I sit out with the audience to see what I was missing when I was backstage. And what I see just serves to highlight the gulf between me and everyone else. Each and every individual, couple or group performs a routine much more complex than mine and with far greater aplomb. Some huge guy shows great changes of tempo to slide about the place with proficient ease – he owns the dance floor. In her other routines, Laura demonstrates a level of smoothness and confidence I didn't come near to eliciting from her. Even some random bloke, pulled out of the audience by Marta to give an award, performs a great little ad-hoc routine with his partner on a whim. By the time the last act walks off, my hands smart from clapping.

It's not quite all over, though: all the dancers that have been involved are expected to take part in some kind of chorus line finale. I reluctantly join them in a big semi-circle in front of the audience as we perform a set of synchronised salsa *pasos.* "Look at us!" is the message. "We're all about the dancing!"

Heaven only knows what I'm doing up there.

I do feel exhilaration at having done it and also tremendous relief that it's out the way. But the overriding emotion, the one that I keep returning to, is one of disappointment.

I smile out towards the audience, but it's a lie. All those hours of preparation, just for it to go so badly. The idea that I could come here and just casually assimilate a whole bunch of different dances seems hopelessly arrogant. I've only just begun and yet it already feels like it's all over.

CHAPTER FIVE

Back on the Horse

I've heard it said that when you wrap your car round a tree, the last thing you should do is avoid driving. What you need to do is get out there again. Wrap it round a bunch more trees. Really get over the whole 'wrapping the car round trees' thing. Maybe start by wrapping your car round the same tree a few times, then move on to progressively larger and scarier-looking trees; haunted trees even.

Truly experienced drivers can wrap their cars round all sorts of natural hazards, roadside paraphernalia and even other vehicles without it affecting their journey times.

"Yeah, you've got to get back on the horse," says a fellow guest–house dweller.

She's right. After the sinking disappointment of the weekend, I've just got to get back on the dance floor and get on with it, despite the obvious hazard of... okay, there are no hazards. There are no excuses.

Of course, a lack of excuses doesn't automatically translate to a surfeit of enthusiasm. Some part of me is still back there in the *clausura.* In fact, the whole 'it's a process' thing is repeating on me like the cow lung that I mistakenly ordered a few nights ago. I don't want to dance so badly that people make excuses for me – I'd rather not dance at all.

And so it is that on the sweaty balcony in suburban Cali, I'm dancing. Or rather I'm 'dancing' – my body might be moving with the music, but I have a complete lack of engagement with what I'm doing. Even coming here at all feels like a waste of my time – it's an act of obligation rather than one of desire.

I try to snap out of the mood, but fail. I don't want to be here and I can't convince myself otherwise. Marta tries to motivate me with praise for what little I achieve, but it makes no difference. It's like someone praising my ability to knit: I don't actually care if I'm any good at it.

With relief that it's over, I head back home in the face-slap air con of the guided bus. Why am I even doing this? I don't mean this set of classes, or even the salsa: I mean the whole exercise in dance learning. Perhaps this journey is too much about what I think I should be doing, rather than what I really want to.

But whilst I might be not getting on with dance, the people are a different matter. The most immediate thing I noticed was how warm and accepting people were towards me. Now I'm finding that it goes even further – you have to be careful expressing any kind of wish or desire because there's a good chance someone will try to help you fulfil it.

It's exactly this that occurs in the dance school when I casually reveal to one of the women there that I don't have many photos of Cali. In fact, I haven't seen much of Cali at all, outside of the spheres of a few small localities. Her instant reponse is to invite me to go and see some more.

The very next day I'm in the passenger seat of her husband's car. Straight from work in a shirt and tie, Felipe is giving me a quick tour of the town en route to their house. He's an enthusiastic guide, telling me a lot about Cali and the surrounding Cauca Valley. Felipe has a fondness for self-questioning, and also declarative statements that start with "Does it..." as though they were questions.

"What is a valley?" he asks. "Does it have a plain between two mountain ranges and a river."

The Cauca valley, he explains, is a major producer of sugarcane, and the source of both *aguardiente* (the aniseed liquor) and a rough, toffee-like sugar-concentrate called *panela*, which you see in shops everywhere.

It's probably no coincidence that these are the two fuels that keep the Cali dance fires burning. The *aguardiente* I've already seen in action, whilst the *panela*, according to Marta, is nibbled on by professional salsa dancers to help keep up their energy levels during tournaments.

The tour continues with Felipe pointing out a white-washed building complex which dominates one side of the road.

"This is a war hospital," says Felipe. "Why? Because we are in a war."

He's not the first person I've heard expressing the current situation in such terms. The war he's referring to is one of those long, drawn-out internal conflicts that has everybody checking their watches (assuming they have one with a year display). It started in the mid-1960s, with its root in the Violencia of the 1940s.

In the foreign media, it's the FARC (Revolutionary Armed Forces of Colombia) guerrillas that tend to get all the headlines, but they are just one of many different belligerents, each of which tends to fall into one of three main categories: left-wing groups (known as guerrillas), right-wing groups (known as paramilitaries) and government forces. Together they've been involved in a special three-way citizen-twatting competition, with the first two also showing a predilection for terrorism, kidnapping and drug trafficking.

The guerrillas sprang up in the mid-1960s to deal with the problem of social injustices amongst the rural poor. The paramilitaries appeared shortly afterwards to deal with the problem of the guerrillas. The demobilisation program arose in the 2000s to deal with the problem of the paramilitaries. Indeed, the whole thing has an 'old lady swallows a succession of animals' feeling about it. And whilst in recent times the guerrillas have very much been pushed back to the margins of the country, all the entities are still very much alive and present in the belly of Colombia.

Continuing onwards, our journey is punctuated by traffic lights, where street performers and beggars come to the car window open-palmed, like human toll booths. Without fuss, Felipe hands them money from a little stash of coins he keeps in his car. He gets a polite and deferential "*Que Dios te pague*," in response, which means something like 'May God reward you' or perhaps 'God will pay you back – I'm kind of between jobs at the moment'.

Heading out of town, things take a turn for the suburban, and then even semi-rural. We pick up his wife and children from the most idyllic high school I've ever seen, sited on a hillside amongst little pathways and trees. I tell Felipe's wife that it looks like a wonderful place to study. She agrees.

"But..." she says, and rubs her thumb against her forefingers as an indication of cost.

Felipe and family live in a village-like neighbourhood which scarcely feels like it's part of Cali, their house being further secluded up a dirt track that winds its way into rich vegetative hills. Not wanting to leave anyone out, or perhaps recognising the potential for sit com-like hilarity, they've built a place next door for the in-laws, too.

"I said to my wife 'Who's going to look out for them? The government?'"

Felipe takes me on a tour of the fertile slopes behind his house. We crouch about on the springy earth as he points out branches weighed down by plummy mangoes and nests of long curving leaves that each bear a tiny pineapple at their centre.

Then I just sit and relax a while, in the company of the well-behaved dogs, and look out over the trees, where other white-washed houses poke out from within. Felipe's daughter brings me a foamy glass of freshly-squeezed juice while her brother feeds the chickens. It's so peaceful here. Even the Cali heat is mostly gone, tamed by the elevation.

It's at an idyll of a slightly different sort that I meet Isabela again. Well, eventually. Realising I'm going to be 15 minutes late, I send her a text. I can't stand being late but somehow I've got really good at it – I guess I just persevered. Fortunately, she's running a little behind, too, and arrives at the mall about the same time as me. Give or take one and a half hours.

At this point you may well be thinking "I would never have stuck around for that long". But then neither would I – nobody does. I waited for maybe half an hour, then texted her, then got a reply saying she'd be there soon, then pondered leaving but thought "What if she's nearly here?" and stuck around another half an hour, then got absorbed in a game on my mobile phone to the point that when she did arrive some part of me wished she'd been even later.

"*¿Cómo estás?*" How are you?

Isabela has a way of delivering even a simple question in a way that makes it feel delicate; intimate even. It's disarming. I know she feels bad, though, because she insists on buying me a hamburger so big it could double as a comfy chair. And the fact she picks up the ticket is significant – the man generally pays in Colombia.

She apologises. I say it's fine. Which it is: she might be late, but I'll be buggering off entirely on some self-centred dance mission very soon, and that's probably bad manners anywhere.

Finding ourselves alone and unobserved, we naturally move closer, sharing each other's personal space. Then, with my exit from the city nearly in sight, our lips meet and we finally share a kiss.

And now I'm the one who feels bad.

Ever so slowly, bit by bit, my dance fatigue has melted away. The scars of the *clausura* remain, but with a few days having passed I've mellowed over the whole situation. I watch the video and it's not half as bad as it felt. Most of the errors are barely noticeable, although the conversation halfway through is still one to watch through fingers.

I go to class again. Marta teaches me some new *vueltas* and I'm back to where I should be: dancing, and happy about it.

By the time my second *clausura* comes round, it's practically an anti-climax. I don't even click that this is what it is at first – Marta just told me she wanted to record me dancing and to get some quotes of me gushing about Cali, for use as promotional material.

After the trauma and nerves of the previous occasion, it's practically a non-event. There are no balloons and no fanfares; there isn't even any choreography – we just get up in front of an audience of staff members and dance a bit for the camera, working our way through the repertoire with Marta doing all the leading. It's solid; unspectacular; fine.

Almost before I know it, it's over, and we're receiving outsized whoops and cheers, the handclaps spanking the walls. I waffle on to the camera about how great Cali is, and how much I enjoy eating the exact same meal for lunch every single day, and then we're done.

It's not only the dance classes I've made peace with – my return to the little salsa club has also passed with far fewer of my customary histrionics. Though at the start of the evening, as ever, there's a bit of a diving board moment. This is often my biggest problem - I try to think my way through it, and you can't.

"In Colombia we don't think too much – we just act," someone at the dance school told me. "You see the car; the bikes? They shouldn't park there but they just do it. And the police don't care."

I take her point. I also sense some underlying frustration with minor parking violations.

Once up, things are much better, though there's still a progression. I find in general that my dance ability improves as the night goes on. At first it's all very mechanical and awkward, like a spider monkey trying to put up a clothes maiden, and there are moves I won't even try. But after several dances it becomes smoother and more aesthetically pleasing. The problem is just getting to that point without losing heart.

"It's a shame you don't drink," a fellow foreigner tells me, "because it would make dancing easier for you."

Actually, it's probably just as well I don't drink: crossing the crowded dance floor is a nightmare even when sober. The whole area is a shifting maze of torsos, with spaces that suddenly appear then disappear again just as quickly. It's like being in a special mashing machine made of people.

And when it's your turn be one of the mashers, I mean dancers, you have to live on your wits. You want to go forwards and backwards? Hard luck – the only space is to your left (oh, it's gone now). You also have far less room to play with – I soon learn to dance with my elbows folded to take up less space. This makes it even more important to maintain tension in my arms – that way, with the tiniest of taut little tugs I can signal a turn to my partner. A compact turn in a compact space.

Not only that, but each woman has her own style. Some are relaxed and carefree whilst others and upright and rigid; some have an attitude of light-hearted fun whilst others maintain a stiffly serious gaze throughout; some seem ill-matched at first but after few dances you tune into each other's style, whilst others straight away feel juuuust right, like eating porridge that you stole from a small bear.

A German salsa expert with years of experience tells me that it's only when you get on the dance floor that you really start to learn, and I can see his point.

There are other things to learn, too, such as the whole thing of who you can actually dance with in the first place. From what I've figured out so far this means anyone in the group, regardless of whether they're single or not. Relationship status is just not an issue. But as Isabela has told me, there are still certain boundaries:

"If she's part of the group it's okay. But if she's sat on another table, it isn't. It will end in *dsh dsh dsh*!" She indicates blows to the face. "It's very dangerous!"

But, aside from all this learning, I've just occasionally started to experience something immensely satisfying. Like when I'm doing a basic turn – one of the few things I can do without really thinking.

You step back, putting your two bodies in tension, your fingers on a precipice of adhesion. Then you pull hard, impelling your bodies back together. Rotating, you break the bond of arms, your fingers instinctively reconnecting as you pass out the other side. Once again, fingers grip and once again you reverse the momentum, guiding your partner back and through a turn of her own. It's such a simple sequence, yet the physical execution of it feels exquisite.

When I finally leave for the evening, I find myself careening down the street, wanting to dance with lampposts... cars... anything. I'm buzzing: I've faced my fears and triumphed, yet again! But it's a short-lived victory, because I know that the very next time I go out the cycle will restart. Once more I'll be stuck firm in my seat, gripped by fear.

My time in Cali is nearly up, but there's still time for one final act.

"*¿A dónde vamos?*" I ask as we leave the restaurant. Where are we going?

"*¡A bailar!*" replies Isabela. To dance!

I don't even know why I asked.

There's something very peculiar about this particular night out, though.

The drill is no different – people chip in for a bottle of *aguardiente*, and shots are poured out and knocked back. Then everyone grabs a partner and skips off to where the real action is, leaving the little plastic cups circling about on a sticky table. A few dances later, they skip back for another shot, swap partners and head out again.

What's different is the music: it's not all salsa. It's not even mostly salsa. The venue is playing *crossover*, which translates to a little bit of everything. Whilst this might seem like a small issue, it really isn't. It's a huge issue. Changing the direction of gravity would be a superficial novelty in comparison. I've suddenly been thrust back into the big, bad world of Latin music that I can't identify; confronted with the realisation of just how sheltered I've been.

I cling to the safety of the cushioned seats, watching the silhouettes shift about in the blue-tinged haze, feeling the vibrations in my body. There's so much to love about these nights out, especially the way that people dance together just for the sheer joy of it rather than romantic intent, and the fact that drinking is a mere adjunct. I just wish I could be up there dancing with them, dammit.

No-one in the group even tries to press-gang me – I guess they realise it's unrealistic here. Bodies sway, stride and circle, legs intertwine and hips are unleashed from side to side. Some movements look familiar, and others utterly alien, but most of them are the same in that they're all out of reach.

The occasional salsa track does play out, but by the time I've heard enough to recognise it, it's far too late: any free dance partners have already been taken. The only time I get to become part of the hot, writhing mass is when either Isabela or one of her friends comes and rescues me, although even then, in the case of the former, it's just that muddling-about thing. I still don't know how to deal with that, and it's clearly my failing rather than hers.

It's at times like this that alcohol probably does make a difference. If I drank then a point probably would come – somewhere between 'I don't care' and 'I can't walk' – where I'd just give it a go. I'd be a human wrecking ball, leaving a trail of devastation in my wake, but hey – I'd be up there.

When my mum and dad used to go ballroom dancing, someone used to announce the dances ahead of time – "The next number will be a foxtrot. A foxtrot."

But since I can't see that happening here, and this situation is likely to occur again, what can I do to improve my lot? Well, being able to identify for myself what's actually playing would be a start. In fact that would be great – there are only so many genres, and it would seem that each one has its own specific dance.

I focus in on what's playing, flapping at the notes as they fly past my head in the hope of analysing them. This track has a complex rhythm section, with a *chikka-chum chikka-chum chikka-chum* sound coming from some kind of scraper, or maybe it's a rice-shaker, and a zany saxophone goofing about over the top. It sounds a touch bonkers – overly fast; cartoon-like even. It also sounds quite familiar, though I'm not sure how or why.

Then it clicks: I heard something similar years ago in an Andean village in Ecuador, on my previous trip to South America. Two dogs were chasing each other round the marketplace as it blared out of the tannoys, making it seem like a Benny Hill chase scene, albeit with fewer bikinis.

"What type of music is this?" I ask someone sat near me.

"Merengue."

Daft-dog music? Merengue. There's a start.

After a few daft-dog tracks, the style changes to something else. Whatever this is, it's less popular – the dance floor clears almost completely except for some close-dancing couples. The music is quite slow and the dominant instrument is a mushy, wandering accordion. What is this – some kind of sea shanty?

"*Vallenato.*"

The next style doesn't really have anything I can get hold of – it just sounds fiddly and fussy, and plicky and plucky, like it's being played on a miniature guitar and drum kit.

"*Bachata,*" two different people lean in to tell me – I no longer even need to ask.

Then things take a turn for the dark and dirty. The rhythm becomes a sparse and moody *THUMP de-THUMP derrr*, with a sentiment like a Latin version of hip hop, all tinted car windows and overdone jewellery. It's the kind of music best suited to being played from the bass bin of a passing vehicle. I've heard this before, for sure – it's bludgeoned its way into my consciousness.

"Reggaeton," says Isabela, sitting one out for a change. "I don't like it." Gauging from the number of people on the dance floor, she's in the minority.

She explains that her dislike stems from the rapper-esque, women-as-objects lyrics. It's a sentiment I might agree with if I had the first idea what was actually being said. The dancing also bothers her, as she finds it too "*sensual*". But whatever could she mean? After all, it's just some innocent woman-bends-over-and-rubs-her-backside-against-the-man-behind-her type action.

There are other ways to dance to it, though. In fact, this is one of the few occasions when I'm implored to join in. Ah well, why not. Our group forms a tight circle of people, all improvising slow, intense and moody-looking moves. It's a bit like the hokey-cokey, but not quite (there's no rushing in and out), which is a shame given that that's the one dance other than salsa I could adequately perform. Still, it's pretty much the exception that proves the rule – even when they don't dance in a pair, they have to find a way of dancing inclusively.

We all have to take a turn in the 'spotlight' in the centre of the circle. Predictably (and thankfully, with hindsight) I get shoved in there very early on. There are no fixed *pasos* in this set up, so in theory you can't really get it wrong, but I still give it a good go, showing off the library of strange and awkward postures that have long been my trademark.

So there are quite a few different genres here, but at least that gives me something to aim at. Imagine coming to a nightclub like this and being able to dance to everything; to never be sat down; to be able to lead a girl onto the dance floor before you even knew what the genre was, confident that you'd be able to dance to it regardless. It seems like an impossible dream. But it's clear that something has changed in me since the *clausura*. I don't just feel like I should do this – I actively want to.

With the club having run out of genres with which to confuse and scare me, the end of the night has come. The lights come on and the bouncer walks round politely trying to convince everyone that it's over. He's right. It's time to say farewell to Isabela; to Marta; to everyone. For now, at least, my time in Cali is done.

Now the real journey begins.

CHAPTER SIX

Ready to Rumba

It's always strange arriving in a new city. It's even more strange when you get to the hotel, open your bag and find that all your most important stuff is gone.

Out of precaution, I'd taken all the things I could least do with losing and put them together in a single, handy steal-it-in-one security pouch. So chock-full with important things was it that it no longer could fit comfortably under my clothing. Instead, the bloated bundle had to hitch a ride in my shoulder bag.

But now that I've opened my bag, I can see that the bundle has vanished and, with the hotelier in Barranquilla not willing to accept a surprised expression as payment, I'm going to have to retrace my steps.

The journey out of Cali had been a great big leafy romp through the mountainous area known as the *zona cafetera* (coffee zone), passing coffee plantations that combed the hillsides with patterns like the surface of the brain.

Arriving in the city of Medellín in darkness, I immediately forged a path northwards. Which makes it sound like I was hacking a route through with a machete, rather than just getting on a night bus and sleeping.

By the time I awoke, the mountains had scarpered, replaced by variations on a theme of 'flat'. With the land barely undulating at all, swampy areas were all that was left to punctuate the territory. I watched, layered-up against the icy blast of air-con, as we passed baking tin-roofed shacks and dogs lolling about in the sun-scorched dirt. A trail of roadside rubbish waxed and waned along both sides of the road without ever quite disappearing.

Finally, the historic port of Cartagena rolled into view. A taxi from the coach station took me deeper in, the tough outer leaves being peeled back layer by layer until the city's majestic colonial centre was finally revealed.

It was here that I stayed for a few days – a pit stop amidst the cobbled streets and the high-rise modernity – before heading along the coast to Barranquilla. But at some point between the two coastal neighbours, my stuff went walkies. So it's back to Cartagena I go to see what I can salvage from this situation.

The computer in the sparse, beach-side police office is switched off, but the mechanical typewriter is switched on. An official thuds away at the old brute, punching onto a pair of carbon paper-separated forms the details of my loss: one driver's license, one bank card, one festival ticket and a small wedge of money in various denominations. Oh, and my passport.

Outside is the gentle swish of the tide on the beach calling out to me to forget it – just let it go. But I can't. I won't be satisfied until I've checked everywhere possible and still not found it. Which makes it sound like the plan. Which it probably is.

I spent the whole bus journey back chasing around the places in my mind. When did it go missing? Was it pilfered from me on the minibus? Did I absent-mindedly toss it out of the hotel window? Did a seabird swoop for it whilst I was on the phone, outside the cafe? I simply don't know. But by the time I've run through my whole day for the seventeenth time, I'm convinced I've not lost it – it's definitely been stolen. Or has it? Arrgh!

The fact that I can't be exactly sure when, where or how it happened is the worst part. Nobody I ask knows anything about it. It's a curiously suspenseful feeling... like you were drinking a cup of tea and put it down somewhere and you're looking round for it. Some part of my brain can't accept that finality: that the tea is gone, and it's not coming back.

Surely it's round here somewhere?

In some ways I wish it had been grabbed from me, because then I'd know. I find myself hankering for the over-zealous filming of everything, like we have in the UK. If could see a video of it being taken then I could know for sure and then let it go. It's a closure thing. Why can't thieves leave compliment slips, dammit?

I don't even know if I could have done anything to prevent it. Did I, as Colombians say, *dar papaya* (give papaya)? In other words, was I open and blatant about my possessions? If you walk about with a plate of papaya, then everyone will take some. Not me – I don't even like papaya – but there are plenty of sneaky types that can't keep their papaya-grabbing mitts to themselves.

Leaving the police office clutching the *denuncia* (crime report) concludes my business with them. There is no talk of recovering items or catching criminals – it's just an exercise in paperwork. Not that they could catch anybody from my own vague recollection.

"My God it could be anyone! I'll order the city to be sealed immediately. We'll catch this scoundrel if I have to check every last person myself!"

It still doesn't quite seem real. How can my stuff not be around anymore? I can still see it in my mind. How is it possible that I don't have it? As tough a proposition as it is, I resolve to just try and forget about it for the time being. I've done all I can, and I've got an appointment with what promises to be the best distraction possible.

Carnaval (Carnival) season is here, and there's only one place you should be for that: Rio de Janeiro! I mean Barranquilla! Though little-known globally, this port city on Colombia's Caribbean coast lays claim to having the second biggest carnival in South America – hence my cross-country dash.

But what is Carnival? The image embedded in my mind is one of scantily-clad people of ambiguous sexual orientation dancing down the street blowing whistles. In fact, some part of me was resistant to coming just out of pure fear: would I have to dance too? Would it be like the Conga? But a friend reassured me that this wasn't the case; that Carnival was basically a bunch of people dancing for you, and all you had to do was look pleased.

For much of the journey back to Barranquilla I've had the azure of the Caribbean Sea off to my left, the crests catching the sun like a line of winking mermaids. But as we near our destination, we take a turn inland and all that inviting water is suddenly forgotten – we're in a clean and modern grid city of low-rise condominiums and business premises in white, yellow and terracotta. Was it on the minibus itself my things were stolen?

I switch to a little yellow taxi cab and head for my

accommodation near the city centre. The streets become gradually more haggard and unloved; an organic concrete disarray seemingly only held in place by the grid-form layout. I walked much of this way on my arrival. Perhaps it was here that my stuff was taken – lifted surreptitiously by someone with sleek feet and sneaky hands.

I doubt I'd be staying in this area at all but for the fact that it's carnival and hence accommodation is scarce. Family-run cafés operate from behind filthy canopies and worn-out paint, whilst beggars in ragged clothing lie slumped in doorways or sometimes just sprawl out on the pavement like basking dogs.

Finally I arrive in the pristine haven of my hotel room, with its air-con blessing and its three-times-the-normal-rate room. And this time I can actually pay.

A backpacker in Cartagena described Barranquilla to me as 'a city without a face' and, whilst I like the feel of the place, I can kind of see his point. It's kind of like you're 'in it', without much of a sense of what that 'it' is. There are no obvious vantage points to give a feel of the city from above, no centrepiece frontage presiding over a body of water and, crucially, no eyes, ears or nose.

What's particularly strange is that we're so near the sea, yet we could be anywhere – you can't even smell the salt. The Magdalena River also passes right by here, but that's kept mostly at arm's length, too. All of which is perfectly fine with me – I've not come here to go kayaking or build sandcastles. Though it sounds like fun now I've said it.

Carnaval proper doesn't start until tomorrow, but there's apparently some kind of folk music-based pre-event entertainment in the city centre tonight – something I heard about via a social networking website.

Social networking is very popular in Colombia, and in at least one instance has had a direct impact on society. In 2008, a 33-year-old electrician called Oscar Morales started a group on Facebook called 'One million voices against FARC'. He was sick of the activities of the left-wing group, particularly when they tried to use as leverage a hostage that they didn't even have.

The unprecedented result was huge marches across Barranquilla and many other places in Colombia, with estimates of total numbers involved ranging from hundreds of thousands to millions.

There aren't quite that many people in the Plaza de la Paz this warm evening, but they're probably still in their thousands. A modern cathedral with an organ-like frontage presides over a huge multi-level plaza filled with revellers. The smell of *arepas* and chorizo sausages drifts about over the crowd and into the warm night air.

People spread out across the multi-levelled plaza in hats and t-shirts and fancy dresses, but mostly hats. Everywhere I look there are wide-brimmed *sombreros* in a distinctive style: straw-coloured woven items, with concentric chocolate bands that radiate outwards on the brim and crown, plus vertical ones on the upright.

All the while, music from a live band insinuates its way through the spaces, drawing bodies this way and that. It's all shakers and rasps and the elastic pinging of hand-played drum skins, like someone chucked a load of rudimentary instruments in a big crate and started shaking the whole thing about to a *pum-pata pum-pata pum-pata* rhythm. Or is it actually *pata-pum*? It's hard to tell after a while. Occasionally, and especially on the faster tracks, a squeaky instrument like a naughty oboe plays over the top.

What have we got here, then?

"Cumbia."

Somewhat atypically, the stage is right in the middle of the plaza, and all round it is a kind of fenced-off moat. The reason for which becomes clear when, during one slow number, costumed couples enter and start parading around inside it.

The women sashay their way by, carrying bundles of candles and wearing beautiful long frilly dresses. Sometimes they gather up the very edges with their hands either side of them, turning it into a big smile of fabric. The men come by in loose white tunics and trousers, red neckerchiefs and the ubiquitous banded hat.

The hat is clearly an iconic must-have item, and the cumbia dresses aren't far behind. I suppose it's a bit like footy fans wearing replica shirts. I wonder if they discuss it at work the next day.

"See the cumbia last night?"

Amongst the crowd I notice a small focal locus of foreigners with locals acting as their guides – it's the people from the social networking site. I go over and get talking to them, but I soon regret it – the next thing I know I'm being dragged off by the hand by one of the guides. Where are we headed? Oh no – not the moat! Wait! I don't even have a cumbia dress!

Too late. We coalesce with the group, and I become one of many people now circulating clockwise. Together we parade round in the gaze of the locals who seem delighted with the smattering of foreigners. All the while, the naughty oboe bleats away frantically on stage, leading us off on a merry jaunt, a scene which hopefully won't conclude with us drowning in the local river.

I have no idea how I'm meant to be moving to this cumbia stuff, only that my salsa *pasos* are useless. In theory I shouldn't be able to get it wrong, because what everyone is doing is so vague. But you can't kid a local: on numerous occasions, someone else in the throng glances at my feet and says "*¡No– así!*" (No – like this!)

Like what? Arrghh! You're all just shuffling your feet! And in a way that looks simple yet defies any attempts to copy! The mumbling I saw in Cali looked pin-sharp by comparison.

It's not the only thing I can't get a grasp on. During one number, the whole crowd spontaneously starts clapping along. All fine and good, except they're all clapping on the off-beat. And they all somehow know to do that. I clearly need some help, so I start chatting to a random local woman who's here with her sister. She's friendly and encourages me to dance round with them.

The excitement ebbs and flows like a replacement for the city's absent tide, and the music is the controller of this. Mostly slow yet gently insistent, now and then it makes a sudden break for it, that rascal of an oboe – which turns out to be a tiny flute – coming into its own. The crowd responds immediately, erupting into a sudden frenzy of excitement and *alegría* (joy), and as dancers, we have to get with the programme and speed up.

"What kind of music is this?"

"*¡Puya!*"

"*¡Así!*" she adds. Like this!

She does that thing with the shoulders. The one where you either shimmy them appealingly or just go into violent, awkward spasms, depending on whether or not you're the author of this book.

"*¡Relajado!*" she says. Relaxed!

She wants me to do it with my arms open, but I can only do it with my arms closed. Closer inspection in a mirror will later reveal that I can't actually do it then, either, and that I have a tendency to bend to one side as I'm doing it. I look like a man in handcuffs trying to escape from a banana suit.

As we continue to circle, I take every opportunity possible to avoid doing it, chiefly by taken long slow guzzles from my bottle of water so she can't tell me off for not dancing, something she otherwise does frequently. I learnt a lot in Cali, I tell you. Finally, one of the guides takes pity on me, and I get pulled out of the moat like a boy being fished from a pond that's too deep for him.

It's been a good show so far. I just hope that the next event won't have quite as much audience participation.

Cesar is a big guy with a big heart. He's probably got a big liver, big pancreas and big stomach, too. Like I said, he's a big guy. He's also of mixed Cuban and European heritage, is probably in his forties (though I could easily be a decade out either side – it's hard to tell) and is staying in the same hotel as me.

An accountant on a year off to explore the world, he travels with a suitcase and an array of smart shirts which, when compared to my backpack and t-shirts, suggests we're probably in different life stages and with different budgets. We're also on different programmes – he's bought tickets to go to see some live concerts whereas I'm on the freebie trail, especially since my things were stolen.

Damn it. I still can't believe it.

Out on the streets, locals with caramel-toned skin breeze past walls of cracked render, women clack along on the broken tiles and the occasional car navigates slowly round street detritus. This *barrio* feels a little unloved.

It's the first day proper of Carnaval and Cesar and I are grazing for breakfast together near the hotel.

"They call this the cholesterol palace," he says, as we pass by a number of heated display cabinets containing deep-fried *empanadas* – golden, breaded pasties which glisten with saturated intent.

Nearby, a string of stalls compete to sell freshly prepared sugarcane juice, the stall holders driving the canes through a mechanised press to harvest the juice within. Cesar buys a cup of the yellowy-green stuff for each of us. It's very rich, and I've had enough after half.

In this part of town, a lot of things are sold on the street, especially paraphernalia for Carnival. Battered kiosks sell t-shirts, daft plastic sunglasses and the iconic banded hat, which I've since learnt is the called a *sombrero vueltiao*.

Despite all the clear signs of how dodgy this part of town is, it's not without a certain charm: the women on the stalls casually call me "*mi amor*" (my love), and I hear men addressing them as "*reina*" (queen), reminding me a lot of Liverpool, where my family in part comes from.

I pull out some money to buy some credit for my mobile phone – you can do this on practically every street corner – and the lady on the stall warns me about *ladrones* (thieves), advising me that you should keep your money "*en las medias*" (in your socks).

It sounds like good advice considering what happened to me, although I must admit to being slightly cynical. Surely, the *ladrones* must know about this ploy, and after saying "Give me everything you've got," they just add, "in your socks."

Cesar and I have different plans so we split up for the time being. With the time of the first big parade drawing near, I take a taxi up to the north of the city, accompanied by a salsa track about 'plastic' (i.e. fake) men and women. It's got a wonderful funky slap bass intro and turns out to be a Ruben Blades number from the 1970s.

I don't know much about Carnival, yet I can already tell it's going to be something other than what I was expecting. Perhaps that's because I thought I'd be watching it from one of the *palcos.* A *palco* is a large, temporary metal stand surrounded by metal fences with an entrance where a man makes you wait to one side for an hour and a half before telling you that no, you can't come in without your ticket, even if you were robbed, and even if you do have a photocopy of the original along with a crime report.

Damn it. I still can't believe I've been robbed.

By far the worst part is the passport. I've got a spare bank card, I can replace the driver's license, and I could even buy a new *palco* ticket if I didn't resent the idea so much. But that little burgundy book was different. It's not the functional aspect – I'm sure they'll have a replacement for me within a couple of days – it's the sentimental value. I loved that passport: we went everywhere together. We still had so many plans. Why did it have to leave me?

It was more than just a government-issued traveller's tick book. I used to love sitting there in quiet moments leafing through the spent visas and expired stamps, enjoying their exoticness. I don't tend to buy souvenirs – the various ink markings and embossed stickers are my souvenirs.

"It's not important," I keep telling myself, "it's just a material possession." Like I've suddenly turned Buddhist or something.

Meanwhile, back at Carnival, the sky is a flag-waving, patriotic shade of blue, making it a wonderful day for a parade. Well, so long as you're watching, rather than taking part, and you've got adequate shade. The air throbs with the constant beat of drums from bands and the hot scent of chicken kebabs follows me down the street. I scuff along, still annoyed by my rejection from the *palco*, and unsure as what to do next.

Further down from the *palcos* are some free areas where people jostle for position to get a good view. It's several people deep at the barrier and the parade hasn't even started, so I decide to take up a position whilst I still can. There's not even the slightest hint of shade, but thankfully I've picked up a cheap *sombrero vueltiao* from a street seller. Hopefully the sun won't turn me too crispy round the edges.

As I stand waiting, some pushing and shoving starts going on. There seems to be a lot of movement with no real reason for it. Something makes me look down, and there I see a hand attempting to unbutton the pocket on someone's shorts. Wait – those are my shorts.

When we imagine ourselves in such a situation, we may like to think we'd react with bravado: shout "*¡LADRON!*" repeatedly whilst pointing at the offender; grab their wrist and thrust it up in the air like trophy; tear their head off and drink from the fountain of blood whilst parading about with their intestines draped about our necks.

"Look who fucked with the writer!"

Of course the whole problem with the archetypal 'give 'em a good shoeing' idea presupposes you're bigger and stronger than they are and/or that they're just an inanimate punchball. It also assumes that the kind of person who would steal from you hasn't been involved in many scrapes before and wouldn't be armed.

It's all irrelevant, as my instinctive reaction is simply to knock his hand away from my pocket. I'm slightly surprised at how little anger I feel, but then all my money, bar a low-value decoy note, is in my socks anyway.

The would-be thief's response is to start moving his hand about to the rhythm of the music, as though he was just dancing all along. I know this is rubbish, so I turn round and look straight at him to let him know that I've got him sussed.

He looks back at me, impassively. It's my first proper view of him. He's just some bloke in his late thirties in dull, non-descript clothing. Which makes me wonder what I was expecting – Snake off The Simpsons perhaps? As it is, with so many of the other revellers wearing fluorescent t-shirts and bonkers neon wigs, he's practically invisible. I look away and he looks away. I look back to him and he looks back at me. Is that it? It's slightly surreal, but then what did I expect? Did I think he'd laugh, say "You got me!" and hold his wrists up?

I turn away. The next time I look back he's gone; disappeared into the crowd.

At first I think nobody else has noticed, but then a guy nearby turns round and tells me "*Hay ladrones*," (there are thieves about) and explains that they try to confuse people by pushing them.

A short time later, after chewing over what happened, I find myself feeling furious, wishing the guy would come back so I can endanger my life with some ridiculous, unsupportable posturing. This gradually relaxes into more of a smartarse stance – in future, I decide, I'll carry a piece of paper in each of my pockets bearing one of those promotional scratch card-type messages: "You haven't won anything this time, but keep trying." Finally I calm down altogether and decide that what I did in the first place was just fine.

Then I find myself thinking about my passport and the other stolen items. They didn't just vanish – a real person physically took them. It's so frustrating to know that somebody somewhere actually knows where they are, right this moment.

By the time the hour mark comes up for how long I've been waiting, I'm rapidly tiring of the whole event: Carnival is apparently just a load of people staring at an empty road whilst others try and rob them. But after an age of impatiently transferring my weight from leg to leg, things suddenly burst into life.

Way down the road, the roadside people are erupting into a flurry of noise and activity – the parade is finally in sight! So... welcome, people with massive comedy papier-mâché heads! Welcome, people on stilts! Welcome, people who think it's a good idea to wear gorilla suits in the scorching Caribbean sun! Thumping music comes from the stacked-up PA systems carried by support vehicles, whilst others carry their own music with them in the shape of drums and shakers and naughty oboes.

Even the city's municipal workers get a chance: construction workers with comically big tools (yeah, I know); street sweepers dancing with their brooms; police officers on motorbikes. I certainly can't blame the law enforcers for wanting to be in the safe bit in the middle – these viewing areas are dodgy as hell.

Really driving the buzz and fervour are the floats. I would say they resembled something of a dream sequence, but that's not quite true, because they don't consist of people falling from heights, missing exams and walking about in their underwear in public places. They do, however, feature things like a huge fantasy bird, a King Kong-sized ape with a beautiful woman in his clutches and a gigantic *marimonda* – the monkey-inspired motif of carnival.

Today's parade – the Batalla de las Flores (Battle of the Flowers) – has been going since 1903, and the event as a whole even longer, so it's had plenty of time to develop a strong tradition.

There's so much to take in that my lasting impression is just a blur of colour and action, yet the party going on down the centre is tame compared to what's happening down the sides. All around me, it's quickly turned into a warzone, with the main weapons being cornflour and foam. Children are hoisted up high on parents' shoulders getting a great view, but also getting caught in great drifts of the stuff. People wander about with monstrous foam beards from recent attacks, and/or powder-white hair, like dusty headmasters.

Being a foreigner certainly gets me plenty of attention. One middle-aged woman tries to foist her 21-year-old daughter on me within moments of us meeting. The daughter and I are both slightly embarrassed by the situation, though when her mother isn't looking she asks for my number anyway.

But before you can say 'age gaps in relationships don't matter if two people really love each other, even if they only met seconds ago', she's run off with her friends, shrieking with excitement: some *telenovela* (soap) stars and famous reggaeton acts have started passing by on open-topped floats. She turns, imploring me to follow, and I tail behind, trying not to look too bemused.

"*¡Baile!*" she says when we get the railings. Dance!

Neither she nor any of her friends are, but that doesn't seem to matter.

I humour her and do something appallingly poultry-like for a bit to the reggaeton from the passing vehicle. But then the self-consciousness becomes too much so I make the excuse that I need some food and promptly run away. I hide out at the food stalls and end up being given a phone number by another girl at a *salchipapa* (sausage and potato) grill. It's that kind of a day.

Finally, some hours after it began, the parade is all over. With nothing left to hold people's attention, the area slowly drains, like a sink half-blocked with fluorescent wig-hair. However, finding public transport back turns out to be a bit tricky – apparently everyone else wants to use it too. With some apprehension, I decide to walk it back to the hotel, no mean feat given it's something like 40 blocks south and another 30 west.

Away from the parade, I can suddenly see how different this northern part of the city is compared to my own neighbourhood: it's all clean, broad avenues with nice cars. Here the cafes are shiny US-style fast food joints rather than down-at-heel family-run cafés. It's middle-class Colombian suburbia. Not that this means they don't know how to *rumba* (party): private parties are erupting everywhere, mostly in confines of concrete front yards made safe by security railings.

Things gradually get ropier as I head back towards the centre. The ashes of the parade are still blowing round: a group of ghoulishly-dressed people sit on a curb smoking cigarettes, whilst scores of cumbia dancers hang around on a five-a-side pitch like they're taking part in a fancy-dress football tournament. Then, as the sun sets, I pass the floats that had paraded by so vibrantly just a couple of hours earlier – parked-up and vacant with only an amputee beggar for company.

Carnaval is taking its first breather.

That night, I head to a nightclub with some of the people I met on the night of the cumbia dancing. It's a swish, minimalistic place with swirling lights that paint bare flesh plum and purple.

I've arrived feeling pretty ready for it – Barranquilla isn't a salsa city, so they might even be quite impressed by my skills – but my confidence dissolves when I hear what's playing. Rather than cowbells, claves and pianos, it's mostly drums, accordions and flutes that pepper the darkness. In fact, they only play a single track of salsa the whole time I'm there – barely enough to even warm up to.

So instead of showing off my moves, I find myself on another mission of discovery asking "What kind of music is this?" every four minutes. It turns out I know the answers already, I'm just short on familiarity: "*Puya,*" (the fast one with the naughty oboe), "Cumbia," (the slow, folky one) and "*Vallenato,*" (the sea-shanty one I heard in Cali). Still, it's ridiculous – how many genres can there be? Nightclub entry in Colombia should come with an instruction manual.

Presumably in order to accommodate the foreigners, much of the dancing is just people winging it in a big circle. This isn't helping me any – as we've established, I already know how to dance the hokey-cokey (aka hokey-pokey in some countries). I try a different tack, and convince one of the girls into showing me some cumbia.

"*Así,*" she says, and gives me a demonstration of the man's footwork. Like this.

"YOU'RE JUST SHUFFLING YOUR FEET!!!" I want to shout out. But this clearly can't be all she's doing, as I can't even get close to replicating it. She shows me again, and I get it wrong again. I'm getting a handle on the nature of it – it is actually meant to be a shuffle – but something about its subtle and indistinct nature means it defies accurate copying.

Maybe that's the point: maybe it's a special secret magic thing, like the Balducci Levitation, where you aren't supposed to understand what's going on because it would spoil the illusion. Like the salsa in Cali, it's yet more of that real, local-style dancing – the passed-down, learnt-it-as-a-kid type stuff – and I'm hardly going to pick it up in a single evening.

Cesar has already given me his own insights into dance culture in this part of the world.

"I think there are only four places in Latin America where the people dance well. Excuse me – it's not very modest – but I would say Cuba, Puerto Rico, Santo Domingo [in the Dominican Republic] and..."

...please say Colombia please say Colombia please say Colombia...

"Colombia."

Hooray! At least I'm in the right place.

"Venezuela also, maybe."

He qualified his appraisal by explaining that these are the places where pretty much everybody has some dance ability – Brazil certainly has plenty of good dancers. But from what he was saying, this shouldn't be confused with the idea that everyone dances like a pro.

"In Europe you have classes – beginner; intermediate; advanced. Everyone wants to be advanced. Some people in Europe dance better than people here. The people here cannot afford to have lessons."

But simply learning all the fancy stuff would seem to be missing the point in his eyes.

"Dance is not just a set of moves to learn. It's a communication between two persons."

My passport is gone and it isn't coming back. None of that stuff is. I'm getting used to it now.

I grimace with embarrassment as I hand over a sweaty note, fresh from my sock, although the ticket tout accepts it without a second thought. This new 'wallet' of mine is uncomfortable to walk on, and I have to pretend to be doing up my shoelaces whenever I want to access it, but wet, salty notes are still better than absent ones. They're tastier, too.

With only two days left of the main parade, the price of the three-day tickets has slumped like a worn out street dancer, so I now feel less resentful about purchasing one. Beside, by being in a ticketed area, I should be able to get some good photos without quite as much risk of my camera being stolen. I decide to fork out.

My *palco* selection strategy is quite simple – I'm after the one which looks the most fun. Moments earlier, from the other side of the street, I saw a 50-something gringo dancing what looked like a passable cumbia right at the front of the *palco* with a girl in a bright yellow t-shirt helping him and everyone else cheering. They seem a good bunch.

A few minutes later I'm sat near him, telling him how much I admire him for giving it a go. He tells me he's from Ohio, but he's been married to a Colombian for 30 years.

"Carnival is a party they throw for themselves."

All about us people are ready for that party, wearing the comedy sunglasses and *sombreros* that are on sale all over.

Particularly common are Day-Glo t-shirts emblazoned with the word Costeño (meaning 'people from the coast') – suggesting a strong sense of regional identity and pride.

Each *palco* has its own band, and ours is no exception. It's mostly percussive but with added naughty oboe – a lot like what I experienced on the first night. Constantly on the simmer, it forges rhythms like a team of expert blacksmith churning out weapons.

With the parade yet to get going, the band is the only source of music, and the crowd chant "*¡Mú-si-ca! ¡Mú-si-ca! ¡Mú-si-ca!*" whenever the musicians have the temerity to take a break for more than a couple of minutes. As I sit there, enjoying my new, lofty position, a bright yellow t-shirt with a young woman inside approaches me, and pulls me to my feet. Okay, so what's all this about?

It clicks.

No! No! No! Wait! You don't understand! I'm not here to dance – I'm just a spectator! Look, I had specific assurances! Dammit why didn't I go for the most boring looking stand?

I'm still working out the least impolite way of making it clear that no dancing is about to occur, when I'm spotted by everyone in a fifty metre radius. Whoops go up all round the *palco*, and I know that, in dance terms at least, I've passed the point of no return. Mind you, I probably passed that point the moment I boarded a plane for Colombia.

The band is tonking out some simple, repetitive and very catchy rhythm with drums and shakers, and suddenly the woman and I are dancing cumbia together. Or rather, she's dancing cumbia and I'm just randomly advancing and retreating whilst sweeping my *sombrero vueltiao* in front of me, in a manner that's largely copied off what I saw the other guy do. It's my bad impression of someone else's marginal effort: the cumbia equivalent of salsa hell.

To great whoops and cheers from the crowd, I shuffle forwards and backwards on the metal gangway, my hat lightly scrunched in my hand. The commotion attracts the attention of people on the other side of the road. Soon hundreds of people are exhorting us from all sides. I can't help but laugh, it being the appropriate reaction to both great fun and to hideous embarrassment. Damn it – I thought the *palco* was meant to be safe.

Cesar reckons that learning Latin American dances out here instead of back in the UK offers a great advantage: you can see the context in which the dance actually occurs. Which would be fine if I could observe it at a distance, and perhaps from behind mirrored glass.

It's with some relief when I'm finally able to give a bow – ridiculously well-received – and take my seat again. As I was told in Cali, Colombians are quite happy for you to massacre their dances, just so long as you look like you're enjoying it.

I ask the girl her name

"*Aisha.*"

Aisha? But that's...

"*Árabe, sí.*" Arabic, yes.

A lot of people from Barranquilla are at least partially of Middle Eastern heritage with the most famous example probably being one Shakira Isabel Mebarak Ripoll. I love Shakira, and I have done ever since my first visit to Latin America some eight years ago, when the Spanish-language versions of her stuff was everywhere. I love her for being the archetypal intelligent, passionate, no-bullshit Latin American woman. Although, at risk of sounding like a muso, I definitely prefer her earlier stuff.

There's actually a statue of her down by the Stadium, though the locals I mention her to barely raise a shrug in response when I mention her name, apparently not feeling a particularly strong connection with her. This is perhaps because she's chosen the international life, and is hence less of a national figure, although it could also be because I'm going off a sample group of about three people.

Aisha gets me up to dance again. Apparently, I'm the fall-back option for whenever the entertainment runs thin. Dammit, this kind of thing would have been so much easier back in the days when I could drink.

"*¡Cerveza!*" says Aisha, making a general request to the people around her. Beer!

She's quickly presented with an unopened can.

Oh crap, now they expect me to drink beer. I can see the dilemma coming a mile off – if I do drink it I'll be betraying my own values (it wouldn't kill me, but drinking should be my choice, not the result of external pressure) but if I don't I'll look like a bad sport. I'm still turning it over in my head when I discover I've got it all wrong. Because she doesn't want me to pour it down my throat, she wants me to balance it on my head.

It's funny how the subtleties of your own skull can go entirely unnoticed until the time comes when you have to balance stuff on it. It turns out that heads aren't flat on top after all: the can wants to lean to either one side or the other and only the cushioning effect of my hair allows it to sit centrally.

I start shuffling forward, gingerly. I can feel the weight shifting on top of my head and know the can is on the brink of toppling. Aisha begins to reach up in expectation... but instead it's me that rescues it, catching it with my balance. It stays where it is.

My movements become more confident – I've got it under control, and the crowd are cheering away – but in the end Aisha decides we ought to quit whilst I'm ahead, and takes the can away before it can topple.

"I don't think anyone could quite believe you kept it up there for so long!" says the man from Ohio.

Just because I don't drink doesn't mean I can't handle my beer.

But there are other reasons why people came here today besides my impromptu pantomime act. Hundreds of dance troupes are scheduled to pass in front of us. In fact, hold up, because here they come: a Jamboree of colour and sound that draws the already wound-up revellers to their feet.

You probably think you own some quite bright clothes. Perhaps you have a garish shirt or blouse, or maybe a pair of trousers you think are pretty outlandish. But if you wore them down the centre of the carnival you'd as good as disappear.

To even just be seen here – to avoid people's eyes filtering you out as irrelevant – you need to be wearing a spangly electric-green bra and briefs combo with tiger face mask. Or perhaps a transparent sequined bodysuit with a massive parachute of fluorescent orange feathers, like an exotic fishing lure. At the very least, you should be parading about in gaudy, light-catching head-to-toe satin, whilst on stilts. Basically, if you're not ten feet tall and glowing then forget it.

Way-over-the-top make-up is also the norm: paint dramatically blooms outwards from eyes and adorns cheeks, sometimes taking the form of visceral splashes of colour, other times consisting of intricate designs of beach scenes and the like.

As if all that wasn't attention-grabbing enough, the participants are also dancing. I have no idea of the genre most of the time, but every now and then there is one I get. Like when some women pass by in their big, beautiful dresses accompanied by men in loose white clothing with bright-red neckerchiefs and *sombrero vueltiaos*.

I now get to see cumbia the way it's meant to be danced, first-hand and unobstructed. It's beautiful and coquettish, yet also elegant. The man shuffles about, enticing the woman with his hat, whilst she in return teases back with her dress, whilst also contending with an eager-to-escape bottle of rum atop her head.

So, carrying the alcohol is actually the woman's role, then. I stare intently, trying to work out if the bottle is attached in any way. Then one drops to the floor, failing to smash, but succeeding in answering my question. Another woman passes by with a can of beer in place of one, presumably having been less fortunate.

There's a whole host of other obscure folkloric dances. The *garabato*, for instance, features the Grim Reaper plus an epic supporting cast of dancers that dance along whilst constantly advancing, like a jaunty invading army. In one sequence he comically swipes high with his scythe at a group of three people, to which they all duck. He then goes low, and they all jump. If I was Death I'd just aim straight down the middle. And I wouldn't play chess with people because it's clearly just a stalling tactic.

Occasionally, individual dancers break from their troupes to come over and rev up the audience, delighting in the spotlight and being adored by the cameras.

"*¡Jueeeeep-aaaa!*" people yell out to express their excitement, it meaning something like 'Hey! Yeah! Come on!'

What would the English equivalent of this folk stuff be? I suppose Morris dancing – something which is an object of derision for many back home. But here people really buzz off their cultural heritage, and I'm buzzing off their buzzing, like an empathic bee.

Aisha would have been in the parade herself but for an injury. It's no mean feat taking part: just walking the distance would be trial enough in the searing coastal heat, but if you're dancing then you're going two steps forward and one step back. Possibly several to the side as well. So, for this year at least, she has to make do with being one of the many in the *palco* looking out for friends and relatives in the parade to cheer on.

Certain characters are motifs of Carnival and are repeated again and again. For instance, there's La Madre Monte, a messy-haired earth-mother type, and there's also the royally-robed figure of Joselito Carnaval, who represents Carnival and its revelry. But by far the most common is the cartoon-bright monkey-like *marimonda*. With its comically simplistic facial features – eyes, mouth and elongated nose – it's a walking ode to the idea of dropping all pretence and just having a great laugh.

The sun is streaming in through the open side of the *palco*, and I find myself feeling quite giddy from the whole experience, carried by the general sense of *alegría* (joy). I'm happy. Everyone's happy. By the time it all comes to an end I'm exhausted from the all the smiling, cheering and waving.

I head back once more through the wildfire parties to my own scruffy *barrio*, where the quietness is almost a relief. Here there are no spontaneous festivities – just shuttered shop fronts. You have that feeling that if you held a party here, someone would grab it from you and run off.

Cesar and I catch up in a little café near the hotel, sat on those white plastic stack-chairs that seem to be everywhere in Colombia. By pure coincidence, some Colombian twenty-somethings from the warm-up night are also there. Cesar has brought his laptop with him, and this becomes the main topic of conversation. The Colombians think he's crazy: getting your laptop out in this part of town is a clear case of *dar papaya*. What will he do if someone tries to take it off him?

"I won't give it to them," says Cesar.

The Colombians don't think it's that simple. What if someone pointed a gun at his head? One of the men in the group illustrates his point with his fingers.

"I will say 'shoot'."

I like Cesar, and I'm pretty sure he means what he says, but I also know from experience that there's often a big gap between our imagined behaviour and reality. Hopefully, it will remain a purely theoretical question.

The parade on day three is very different to that on day two. Whilst the former featured large groups of costumed people parading down the street, the latter features large groups of cost… oh, wait.

I also meet Aisha again, and I'm also expected to dance again, although this time we're high up in the *palco* and no-one notices.

Or at least I think no-one notices.

"I saw you when the girl was showing you how to dance," Cesar will later tell me, "Everyone was looking at you."

So I'm a novelty, then.

"It's funny for them. Here dancing well is normal. Here the people have 40 years of experience dancing. You are just a baby. They don't expect you to be able to dance well. I am Cuban, so when I dance I have to dance very well."

Maybe I shouldn't try and improve at all: being the crap novelty dancer actually has a lot going for it.

With many Colombians having already left town, the final day's parade is on a smaller scale. This time it's mainly themed around the character of Joselito Carnaval – the one who represents the revelry surrounding Carnival. The idea is that Joselito has been partying too much and is now being buried – an act that signifies the end of Carnival for another year.

There's not just one Joselito but many of them, each coming past in their own coffin although occasionally I see one that looks a little too active for a dead person. Mind you, imagine taking centre stage in Carnival and spending the whole time lying down with your eyes closed.

With Carnival all but over, there's an unfamiliar sense of normality about the city. Previously shuttered shops are now showing their faces, and people are just going about their daily business, not one of them covered in foam. The switch has definitely been flicked from 'party very hard' to 'party marginally less hard'.

It's time to leave, and to say farewell to Cesar. But before we part, he has some news for me. He tells me he was walking about in a dodgy part of town – even dodgier than our own – when some guy standing the shadows, made a polite and considered request of him.

"He say, 'Give me everything you've got'."

The guy was holding what appeared to be a gun, although he was stood in the shadows, so it was apparently hard to know for sure.

"So I say 'Okay, okay' and I reach into my pocket, like this."

It was a movement that rattled the guy.

"He says 'No, stop!' And I choose this moment to grab him like this."

Cesar play-acts putting one hand on the guy's throat and his other on the gun. It was at this point he discovered that it was actually just a shaped piece of wood.

"He say to me afterwards that he was just joking."

"And was he?"

"No! He hopes that I give him everything!"

Thankfully, my own interactions with the locals are a touch more pleasant.

"*Qué lindo...*" sighs the cleaner in my hotel room when I tell her why I've come to Colombia. How lovely...

And as I check out, the receptionist insists one seeing some of my salsa footwork. I happily oblige, going through some of the basic *pasos*.

"*No eres extranjero*," he says, "*¡Eres Colombiano!*" You're not a foreigner - you're Colombian!

Well I certainly don't own any paperwork to the contrary.

When I first lost my passport, I missed it terribly. I wanted to give it a big hug, to say sorry for all the times I'd neglected it, and to let it know how much I loved it. Maybe even take it out for a meal, go for a few drinks (well, coffees), then take it home so we could and do what comes naturally between a man and a passport.

But Carnival has put a lot of distance between me and my passport. We've both moved on. All that remains is the divvying up of friends and subtly trying to let on to each other how amazing our new lives are. Of course, that still leaves the small problem of my being undocumented in a foreign land. Let's just hope that's as easy to resolve as I've assumed.

CHAPTER SEVEN

Coasting

I always thought that if I ever visited a consulate, it'd be wearing a white linen suit and Panama hat. Me, that is, not the consulate. In the event, pale-grey jeans and a long-sleeved shirt will have to do. This breach of imaginary protocol doesn't seem to bother Brian, which is just as well since I'm going to need his help – he's the Honorary Consul of the British Consulate in Cartagena.

"In Colombia," he says, "you pay your taxes on the street."

Brian is not some stiff upper-lipped colonial throwback, but an avuncular chap with glasses on a chain round his neck and a welcoming manner. Despite having been out here for decades, there's still something about him that's ineffably English. If he was back in the UK he'd work for Ordnance Survey, and at the weekend he'd race lawnmowers that he'd designed and built in his own shed.

According to Brian, the decoy cash I was carrying in Barranquilla is a good idea, although I should up the value a bit.

"Fifty-thousand pesos will make anyone go away."

That's about 25 US dollars, or 17 pounds sterling.

The consulate itself is tiny – a partitioned office with room enough for Brian and a thirty-something Colombian called Carmen, who works there as a consular officer. The office looks out from above onto the ruins of Castillo San Felipe de Barajas: a multi-levelled pyramidal beast that's baking hard in the Caribbean sun. It makes the air-conditioned office feel all the more serene and unflustered.

Once I'm over the whole "Look at me, I'm in a consulate!" thing, it's time to order my new passport – I can't hang around here undocumented forever.

I'm about to get a nasty shock. Due to a recent change, the British Embassy in Colombia no longer issues passports. Not only that, but nor does anywhere in the whole of South, or even Central, America. I have to send my application all the way to the USA, to the embassy in Washington DC, where they will process my application and then courier it back.

"How long will it take to process it?"

"About six weeks."

Okay, well that's not too bad.

SIX WEEKS?! Is it hand-bloody-woven or something?

I mean, I don't want to be all 'first-world problems' – I accept that prancing about in foreign countries is something of a privilege – but this turn of events gives me a genuine problem. The time immigration allotted to me on arrival is due to expire soon. If I go ahead and apply for the passport, I'll have to hang around in the country illegally for weeks. And then when the new passport does arrive, I'll have to convince DAS – the security and immigration people – to stamp an extension in my new passport. Which they might not be so happy doing if I've been hanging about in the country illegally for weeks.

"Go and speak to DAS," says Brian.

The history of Cartagena de Indias, to give the city its full name, is a lustrous one – it's the port through which the Spanish sent home all the lovely gold they eventually acquired. However, it's also a tainted one, as the port also served as the prime conduit for inbound African slaves.

On the lustrous side of things, the legend of El Dorado had grown by word of mouth into a city of gold, for which many would engage in fruitless searches for over the years. This didn't really matter in the grander scheme, though, as the Spanish went straight to source, mining it from veins and obtaining it from stream beds. Not with their own fair hands, obviously – they set slaves to the task, both indigenous and African.

History lives on in the architecture of Cartagena's old town: wooden balconies lean inwards, sharing ancient secrets with their neighbours opposite; arcading leaps triumphantly along the edges of plazas; and horse-drawn carriages clop down cambered streets, past distempered walls in yellow, peach or ochre.

The whole thing is girded in place by a big, fat, 'you ain't coming in' kind of a wall – beyond which glistens the delicious Caribbean – keeping ancient foes, circulating traffic and any kind of breeze firmly on the outside.

There's a bit more room to breathe once you're out of the centre. Almost too much, in fact – with the shade of the buildings cruelly whipped away, things can get very hot very quickly. Your clothes begin sticking to your skin such that they quickly descending into an undiplomatic mush of damp fabric, propelling even a short journey, such as the one to the consulate or DAS, into taxi territory.

The fortress flashes by as I sit in the little yellow bug, cheesy accordion-based music coming from the stereo. Let me think... *vallenato*, right?

DAS, the Colombian State Security Department, is in a grand old building in leafy grounds with security gates. Any sense of welcome I felt at the consulate is absent in this place of in-trays, processes and stern desks, although the air con brings a rational coolness.

They're curt, in a way that I'm not used to in Colombia. But then as Carmen would later tell me, "If you knew some of the stuff they have to deal with, you'd understand why."

I'm probably the least of their concerns, but they deal with me quickly and I'm happy with the outcome. Yes, they tell me, I can get an extension. I just need to give them an official original document to stamp. A photocopy won't do, but emergency papers will be fine.

Bingo.

With the measured gait of a foreign diplomat, I walk out into the sunlight and call Brian on my mobile. Turned out nice again. Could I have some emergency papers please, old sport?

Brian tells me he can get me the papers, no problem. Oh, but there's a catch: they're only valid for a few days, and once they've been issued I'll be obliged to leave the country. They're not for hanging around with – they're for going home with.

So, in summary, I can't extend my stay without a full passport, but I can't get a full passport without extending my stay.

Damn it. They should give that catch a number.

On top of all this, barring a little bit of salsa, I still can't dance to save my life. This particular point is not an official DAS or Consular line, but probably only because I didn't press them on it.

I can't believe how quickly this has all fallen apart. The sheer timescale of the process has me baffled, too – other people I know who've lost their passports abroad haven't had to wait more than a few days. The foreign office website lists a number of reasons why they've centralised passport issuance in the USA, with saving money right up there, an understandable priority given the global economic recession.

There's a lesson in here: never lose your passport during a fiscal crisis as replacing it in a timely manner probably isn't at the top of your government's priority list. Which is fair enough of course – if they've got any sense, all the money should be going on escape helicopters, travel sweets and plausible moustaches. And yes, that does include the women.

Time is running out, and my only option, as it stands, is to fly home. This is bad enough in its own right – as writer Iain Sinclair puts it, "An involuntary return to the point of departure is, without doubt, the most disturbing of all journeys." – but given the costs involved, it's highly likely that my dance mission would be over.

I can't believe it – I've only just begun.

Despite the Gordian knot being pulled tight, I still have around three weeks before I have to leave, so whilst I think it over and consider my options, I'm going to press on with my dance mission. I just have to carry on and assume it will all work out.

I've found a dance school – a light, airy venue some way outside the centre, with white-washed walls, ceiling rafters and cool floor tiles – so now I just need to choose a dance. In a way, it doesn't seem so important specifically which one I learn: surely whatever I do will increase my overall ability to move with the music. I just need to learn… something.

One option is a modern dance called *champeta*. I keep hearing about it, and every time I mention it to anyone they give a giggle and say it's "*muy sensual*". This cheeky naughtiness gives it an appeal, as does the mystery of not actually knowing what it looks or sounds like. I do feel bashful about the idea, but I also know I'm something of a prudish Englishman and I like the idea of challenging that. Besides, it's only a dance – how bad can it be?

There's another option too: one I witnessed on my first visit to Cartagena in those heady days when I still had a passport. It was evening and I was in a busy square in the old town, the amber lighting reflecting off the polished pavers. Scores of tourists sat eating pizza at outdoor restaurants, the waiting staff buzzing about petitioning passers-by with leatherette menus. My attention, however, was fixed elsewhere: a troupe of wiry, black dancers was preparing for action on the periphery, the men standing bare-chested in neon-green pantaloons; the women in tie-together neon crop-tops and pink-hued grass skirts.

As diners directed the pointy ends of their food mouthwards, the drummers tore into a bare, rapid-fire beat, sending the night air into palpitations, and catching the attention of everybody. Suddenly the dancers were in action, their taut sinews flicking this way and that and their bare feet popping about on the pavers. Pantaloons shimmered and skirts flicked about, barely able to keep pace. It was frenzied yet somehow effortless, their bodies rhythmically tossed and shaken as though by some exterior force.

This was clearly a folkloric dance and an Afro-Colombian one at that. It summoned all my awe and ignorance of African culture in one go: the tribal poundings; the frenetic movements; the rice shaker like insects in the night grass.

Despite there being no contact between male and female dancers, there was also a mildly erotic subtext, with the men breaking into bouts of rapid chest and groin thrusting, pulsating as though in an electrical-induced spasm.

At one point, one of the men started doing a bird impression, with arms high and fingers splayed. But this was no chicken dance –his movements were more a vibration rather than a set of consciously repeated actions. It was like watching a humming bird.

Then came the defining moment, at least in my eyes. The men dropped to the floor, adopted a push-up position on toes and palms, and began bounding – no, ricocheting – through the legs of the women. It was the single most African thing I'd ever seen.

What on earth was this?

"*Mapalé.*"

Excellent. It's always good to know the name of something you specifically want to avoid ever taking lessons in. I mean I'd love to be able to dance like that, but hey – let's be realistic about this.

Back in the dance school it's decision time.

"*Champeta*," I say to the woman behind the desk.

"And *mapalé*," I blurt out, like someone trying to draw attention from their purchase of a massive dildo by also buying a toaster. Although in this case it's a toaster with erotic pictures on the side, and probably just makes things worse.

My teacher is a woman in her early twenties, with a skin tone that a Caleño described to me as *café con leche* (coffee with milk). It's common to Cartagena as a result of mixing between Colombia's three main ethnic groups. She has a slight figure, a glowing complexion, and a loose-fitting t-shirt that she rearranges frequently.

And her name?

"*Yudi*."

Nice to meet you – let's dance!

Or let's not. Let's warm up for at least twenty minutes instead. What is it with all this warming up? It's not like you see anyone doing it in a night club.

We stand opposite a mirror working on individual shoulder movements for what seems like an eternity. Only it can't have been an eternity because we also spend an eternity working on other body parts, too. Following her lead, I thrust my chest right out, then withdraw it to the point that my upper back is curved.

"Like the Hunchback of Notre Dame."

It's surprisingly hard to move the individual elements of the body in this way: other bits tend to want to join them. At one point I get ahead of myself, pre-empting what we'll be moving next, to which Yudi instantly stops. She turns and gives me a raised eyebrow. There'll be no insubordination in this class.

Finally we're done warming up and we're ready to go.

The first dance is the one I'm partly doing out of embarrassment – the *mapalé* (pronounced ma-pa-LAY). We start with the main movement, which is the one that everyone apparently thinks of when they think of *mapalé*. Well, when they're not thinking "What's *mapalé*?"

The move consists of high-speed thrusting of the palms in and out from the chest, elbows stuck out at the side, accompanied by similar thrusting of the pelvis. The top half reminds me of the scene in Carry on Camping where British national treasure Barbara Windsor is exercising her chest so vigorously that she launches her bikini top.

I'm not wearing my bikini today so Kenneth Williams and Hattie Jacques will have to find something else to be scandalised by. Like the sight of me staring intently at a woman's chest and pelvis as she thrusts them rhythmically. I'm obliged to watch in order to copy, but that doesn't stop it feeling kind of intrusive.

The track starts off with a slow introductory section, during which Yudi encourages me to flutter my hands and loll my head about in a generally head-spun and intoxicated kind of way, before bursting into life. This is the manic bit, during which I'm expected to do all the thrusting.

But there's a basic problem here – I can't do it fast enough. We try doing it slowly at first then building up in speed but I still can't hit that top gear, or even get near it. Determined to at least keep in time, I do it half-speed instead. It looks pathetic, like someone jogging the 100 metres. Why the hell did I say *mapalé*?

"*¡Sonríe!*" Smile!

Yudi reminds me a little of Servalan, the baddie from the late 70s BBC Sci-Fi series Blake's 7, only she's not Welsh and she doesn't command a space empire. She's probably working on it, though. The space empire, I mean.

She tries to explain the meaning of the dance to me, but something's lost in translation. From what I can gather, it's something to do with trying to catch a fish. Given the semi-erotic overtones, I'd rather not know what they're going to do to it when they've caught it. But whatever the significance, it's both technically demanding and physically exhausting.

"Smile!"

Yes, okay. I know I should be enjoying it. But I'm not, so smiling just becomes another bodily movement I have to remember, and one which I keep getting wrong.

After half an hour of failed thrusting, Yudi brings the nightmare to a close. She changes the music in the CD player, and I get my first taste of a new genre. Whilst *mapalé* is an established piece of folk heritage, *champeta*, which has its roots in African and Caribbean styles, sounds more like modern pop music. The beat is a bit like reggaeton, only lighter, and without all that brooding intent.

A bunch of sampled effects, like that *viiippp* sound of a DJ scratching on vinyl sets a frivolous tone, a calypso-like guitar steals in over the top, and my God, we're on the beach. And not a serious beach with posturing models, but one where everyone is mucking about and having a laugh.

I can tell before we even get going that this is neither going to be a dance with formal steps, nor one that's likely to have a serious fraternity of purists to offend if you get it wrong. It's wonderfully home-made and lo-fi and I love it already.

"*¡Suelta! ¡Suelta! ¡Suelta!*" calls out the singer, which just seems to mean 'Let go!'

We start out with three simple *pasos*, each of which confirm those expectations, whilst notably denying another – none of the moves are even slightly saucy. This is a profound relief: whilst I like the theoretical idea of tackling a dance that is a touch *sensual*, the prospect of actually doing so makes me want to make up some rubbish excuse and vanish at high speed.

The first of the moves involves tapping the floor with each foot alternately, with the toe turned inwards, making me feel kind of ditsy. The second involves advancing and doing a 'swing your pants' gesture with one leg before retreating again. But it's third one that's the stand-out move: you wag your knees fluidly whilst slowly descending to the floor, before rising back up again, knees still wagging.

It's brilliant; hilarious. And as if that weren't enough, the jelly legs are accompanied by a one-handed lasso action. The whole thing makes me want to jump about and spank my own backside. Which is probably a whole other *champeta* move.

So far, so nuts. And as for the sensual elements... well, what sensual elements?

I'm not really sure I like Cartagena at first – it's just not my kind of place. I don't feel like I'm in Colombia so much as in a film set. For a movie about the effects of tourism.

The streets echo to the clatter of hooves as visitors are paraded through the colonial splendour, which nowadays includes a Benetton store and a Hard Rock Café. Afro-Colombian women in acid-bright clothing carry artfully-carved fruit about on platters on their head, charging dSLR-toting tourists for the authentic photo opportunity. Hawkers sell *sombrero vueltiaos*, hippyish artisans preside over tarpaulins of handicrafts and all manner of other people stop you on the street with their own propositions, some less wholesome than others.

Maybe I needed to be here earlier – say the 17th or 18th century. Though, given the history of slavery in this place, I doubt I'd be saying that if I was black. It's this African connection which is responsible for much of the musical culture in this part of the country: *mapalé* is apparently just a very fast variant of cumbia, which itself is thought to have its roots in African music such as Guinean *cumbé*.

The sea-accessibility that made the city popular in times gone by is the same thing that's responsible for the levels of tourism: Cartagena has long been a stopping-off point for cruise liners on a circuit of the Caribbean, with a pumped-up police presence helping to keep it viable even when things were dodgy in the rest of the country. Nowadays, it's also one end of a major backpacker conduit between Central and South America.

Overland travel has long been tricky between the two continents because of the Darién Gap – the jungle-swathed isthmus at the border with Panama. Darién is a wonderful place, especially if you like seclusion, rare orchids and kidnap by armed forces. It's certainly a great place to visit if you want to write one of those 'My year as a hostage'-type books, although an obituary in the newspaper is perhaps the more likely literary outcome.

Panama actually used to form part of Colombia, despite the physical barrier. But in 1903, amidst politicking over the then-unconstructed Panama Canal, the US helped to strong-arm Panama's independence, and it seceded.

When I was last in Latin America, most travellers heading south from Central America would avoid Colombia altogether by flying over the top. But now that it's back on the map, the sea route has come into its own. The journey from Panama, once only being taken by the brave or foolhardy, is now a chilled-out five-day yacht trip for the party-hostel crowd, complete with en-route island-hopping.

Seeing empty carriages lined up in a field outside the centre cements the idea in my mind that the centre of Cartagena is a façade; a daily play acted out for a transient audience. Of course, the actors in this show are just regular, everyday people trying to make a living, including the highly-skilled *mapalé* dancers, but the sum effect means it's just not my kind of place.

Somewhere I do feel a bit more at home is Getsemaní: a working class *barrio* adjoining the historical centre. It's still within the city walls, and the buildings are still attractive, it's just that some of them could do with a bit more make up. In other words, it's not a preserved reminder of the past: it's right in the here and now. Not that it's untouched by tourism – this is the landing spot for the backpackers, attracted by the mixture of low cost and authenticity.

Locals sit out on steps and chat away in the gentle heat of the evening; phone-call vendors sit at their desks, literally on the street; dogs just kind of skulk about and chew the fat with other dogs. The scent of fried fish drifts out from small, family-run cafes, snuggling up next to dapper new backpacker places that offer muesli breakfasts and free Wi-Fi.

It's in a guest house in this part of town that I meet Carl, a 30-year-old surfer dude from Australia. Like many backpackers, he arrived in Colombia by boat. Unlike many backpackers, he eschewed the expensive yacht in favour of cheap passage on an unseaworthy container vessel with ill-prepared crew, which had to weather a storm.

Carl paints a picture of the water in the sleeping quarters perpetually ankle-height, of things flying off the side of the boat, and of him and fellow passengers lashing things down on deck to try and stop the weight shifting about.

"I thought I was I going to die."

With his tanned torso, salt-curled hair and languid demeanour, he looks every bit the beach bum. This seems to make him a prime target for the scam artists, drug dealers and prostitutes – a disproportionate number of them pregnant – that hawk for business. Whilst I attract a mere trickle of attention, Carl can't walk more than ten or fifteen metres without being approached.

This seems to suit him just fine. He happily stops and engages with anyone who shows the slightest interest, meaning that getting anywhere suddenly takes an age. There are no annoyances in Carl's world – only conversation opportunities.

The drug issue is an interesting one. Before I knew better, I thought the white stuff would be blowing down the streets here. In fact I've yet to meet a Colombian with an interest in it – they seem to be more interested in alcohol. The people who are talking about it, consuming it and generally creating a demand for it seem to be us foreigners. You could perhaps argue that some of the ugliest aspects of tourism are the ones we bring with us.

"Dooo ittt!"

After another inordinately long warm-up, we're dancing again. None of my footwear seems appropriate to this style, so I've resorted to skipping about on the hard tiles in my stocking feet.

Mapalé is danced at a speed which looks highly improbable and yet still manages to be faster than it looks. I complain to Yudi that I physically cannot do what she's asking – my body won't move quickly enough. Her response is to pucker up her bottom lip like a baby.

The truth is that there is something I could do to improve – I could practise. I was going to say 'I could practise more', but that would imply that I practise at all.

When it comes to not practising, I've long been an expert. Whilst at school, I spent a full four years not practising the piano, before joining the school band and adding not practising the bassoon. I later traded them both in for the much cooler hobby of not practising the drums.

It's not just the new dances that are affected by this deficiency – I can barely remember anything beyond the basics of my salsa, either. I guess if you don't use this stuff, you lose it.

Even when my willpower is high and I'm in the mood for it, my attempts are being stymied by some simple obstacles. First off, my room is too small to practise in. Secondly, I don't have any music to dance to. Finally, I don't have anyone to partner up with. The result is that my classes and my practice are effectively one and the same.

It's not going well and I'm definitely not enjoying it. Both my mind and my body are struggling in the Cartagena heat. My ankle socks are leaving damp marks on the tiles and the overhead fan is barely noticeable. Halfway through the class I decide I've had enough and I need a drink break. Yudi is insistent I continue, but I'm equally insistent I stop. And I hold the trump card.

"It's my class, isn't it?"

I take time out for a cold *gaseosa* (flavoured fizzy drink) from a reusable glass bottle. The purple liquid (or pink, or green, or orange) ejects the straw at first as if to say 'this product does not belong inside a human being'. But I assure it that it does, and I'm soon succumbing to a series of less-than-gentlemanly flavoured gasps.

The break from dancing is all too brief, however, and soon I'm back at it again, only now with sugar-coated teeth. Later my t-shirt will be bleaching dry on the balcony, or perhaps in a bag being weighed by the hand-scales at the tiny local laundrette – keeping enough clothes clean when learning to dance is a mission in itself – but for now it swings heavily with sweat.

As well as the Barbara Windsor, which I still can't do, we've been working on another *paso*, where I lunge forward onto one heel, whilst swinging my straightened arms round in a big circle from top to bottom. It's a movement that can clearly only be performed in rooms that have the BSI Kitemark for cat-swinging, thus immediately dooming it to the land of no-practice.

Yudi and I argue over whether or not my knee is bent, which it shouldn't be. I do it again to prove it isn't. But I'm wrong – it is – so I correct it. However, now my elbow is wrong, so I correct that too. At which point my knee is bent again.

It's not the only problem.

"Stronger!"

Yes, very good, but how do you actually dance stronger? Besides, I'm just not muscular enough. Yudi counters by pointing out her own skinny arms, which is a fair point. The *mapalé* dancers I saw weren't beefcakes, either, they were just toned.

"Smile!"

Now there's *paso* I don't expect to master any time soon.

My relationship with the dance might be fraught, but the music is something else. I love *mapalé*. It has a charging feel to it, like the opening credits of Hawaii Five-O, or an angry buffalo belting down a hill or a foreigner attempting a frenetic local folk dance. Well, okay, less so the last one.

The lyrics are something of an insight into the way people use language. In the track we've been practising to, the male singer implores a woman to come and dance, calling her *negrita*. This is an affectionate diminutive of *negra* (black), although if you were to translate it, it would be a bit like calling someone 'blackie'.

Referring to a person by their colour is something I've heard on the street, too. Just the other day in Getsemaní a woman near me called out "*¡Negra!*" (black woman) to her friend over the road, to which the two women came together and embraced warmly.

Plenty of the Colombians I've spoken to have been convinced that there is no racism in their country, due to the intermixing of people and the whole call-it-as-it-is mentality. Whilst this is a nice idea, it ignores the fact that indigenous and African people still tend to occupy the lower strata of society, that they have historically been negatively characterised and that you don't tend to hear people calling out "*blanco*" or "*blanquito*" (white or whitey).

The straight-talk doesn't just stop at race: people that are overweight get called *gordo/gordito* (fatty) and thin people (like me) are *flaco/flaquito* (skinny). If you're fat, then you're fat – why pretend otherwise? I wonder what the Spanish is for thick-skinned.

The *champeta* should come as a respite from the difficulties of *mapalé*, but this is developing problems of its own. Previously I thought hips only had two settings – move and don't move – but it appears there's a lot more to it than that. For instance, as Yudi shows me, you can describe a forward circle with your left hip, then your right, creating a kind of figure of eight.

This, she explains, is the reason for the long warm-ups. The idea is to learn to isolate these body parts so you can move them freely and individually. She gets me gyrating my hips rapidly in a circle, like I'm trying to keep up a hula-hoop. It would be tricky enough on its own, but she also wants me to tonk imaginary high and low *tambores* (drums) with my right hand at the same time.

It takes all the concentration I have to get the hips going quickly enough, and the moment I try and add the hand actions, it all just falls apart. I stop and stand there, frustrated.

"Dooo ittt!"

I do as she says. I try again and again, but I get no closer. But whilst I'm struggling to grasp the move, Yudi is struggling to grasp my struggle to grasp it. To better communicate my problem, I turn to her and start patting my head whilst rubbing my belly. Yes, we can all do that, but we can also all remember a time when we couldn't.

Yudi goes to copy me… but she can't. She tries again and she fails again. She can't do it! Ha – got you there, kid. Perhaps now we understand each other a bit better.

My visa expiry date is slowly nearing, but thus far I've been devoid of ideas of what to do about it. But in a major and unexpected boon, some Colombian guy who works in hospitality tells me he thinks he can help. He likes my mission (pretty much everybody does, especially those that haven't asked for a demonstration) and reckons it's a good thing for his country that I'm able to stay and carry on.

He knows an official, he tells me, and he's sure this guy would stamp my photocopy of a passport. This is perfect as it would cut the Gordian knot in single slice – I'd be able to stay long enough to get a replacement, and everything would be dandy. It's all a bit random but he seems genuine, he's not asking for any money and, hey, it's not as if he can steal my passport.

It's not the only thing that's looking up. Despite my initial reservations about the place, Cartagena is growing on me. I suppose there's a point at which you realise that it is what it is, and you stop resenting it and start enjoying it.

It's not all tourism, anyway – a university sits on the fringes of the centre, with a tidal flow of students with daypacks. And beyond that, the tourist centre proper diffuses into an attractive residential area, where greenery scales the buildings with amorous intent and bougainvilleas shower down kisses from upon high.

Then there's the wall. Thick and salt-weathered, it jags about the outside of the old town punctuated by turrets and cannons. Down below, beyond the peripheral road, a man stands on the rocks fishing with a simple length of nylon. Away to our left, over a stretch of water, is the dog-leg of Bocagrande, a gleaming world of condos, hotels and private clinics, where beach vendors try to hustle a living in front of gleaming altars to wealth.

The whole coastline round Cartagena is kind of messy. In bygone times this translated to vulnerable, and meant Spain had to spend a fortune on fortifications to protect it from folk like Sir Francis Drake. Hero or pirate, depending on your viewpoint, Drake held the entire city to ransom in 1582, and was just one of many people or groups who wanted to destroy, ransack or take ownership of the place.

Times seem a lot less fraught now. There's a faint smell of sea up top, and a breeze takes the edge off the afternoon heat. I stroll along passing a Colombian couple on a wedding photo-shoot, the salty air curling my locks and forming a film on my skin and my sunglasses.

As the day departs, the sky turns a delicious pink, and beyond the gnarled walls, lights start appearing in the high-rise cityscape.

Yes, I like this place. I just hope they'll let me stay.

The café's rigid chairs are pretty much forcing me to sit upright. Carl isn't one to be constrained, though, and drapes himself over them like a beach towel. His neck hangs in such a way that suggests there's not been an ounce of stress in it in a long, long time. We're in a local joint in Getsemaní and strains of accordion are easing their way across the place. This *vallenato* stuff is everywhere.

Carl and I sit there, stapling food to our hard palates. By now, I've acclimatised to Colombian lunch, and I even actually enjoy it at times, something that seems to come and go in waves. Things are a little different here on the coast. They still serve rice, beans and plantain, but there's also more fish, for some reason, and they also serve up coconut rice and *patacones* – plantains which have been smashed with a stone and formed into biscuits.

The relative eating styles of Carl and I are pretty much reflective of our personalities as a whole. I'll still be picking out the bones like it's a game of Operation, whilst he's long finished, and is relaxing with an empty plate and a satisfied smile.

Despite his unwound manner, all Carl needs to spring into action is the right motivation. This comes when a couple of women in tight jeans and skimpy tops arrive, pulling seats out from a nearby table with a squeaky judder.

Carl turns round and commences chatting them up in one single, natural manoeuvre.

"Give me a hand, man."

I do, but he doesn't really need one, and he pretty-much single-handedly sets us up on something approaching a double-date.

"I mean, they're probably prostitutes," he says once they've left. "They looked like prostitutes."

They did a bit. But hey, I might get an evening of dance

practice out of this, so let's just roll with it. Carl's attitude seems to be rubbing off on me.

Prostitution is rife in Cartagena. Indeed it's actually legal in Colombia within designated tolerance zones, and I've heard that a lot of the women in the nightclubs here are engaged in that particular business. But not every woman accepting money is considered a prostitute – some are *prepagos* (prepaids), which is more like an escort, or a mistress for hire.

Hey maybe I could solve my dance-partner problems for good by hiring a *prepago*!

"Oh God – another one of those blokes who just wants to dance."

That evening we head out past the book stalls and the sizzling food stands, and enter the historic centre via the famous clock-tower archway. And there we wait for them, in the triangular square (if such a thing is possible).

It's that twilight hour when the show finally stops, or at least changes: horse-drawn carriages are still hanging about, hoping to give one last tour of the city, whilst women who are definitely prostitutes have begun touting for business.

"I don't think they're going to turn up," says Carl.

This is never going to be a problem for someone like Carl – he just starts talking to some random guy on a nearby bench. Within seconds it's as though the girls never existed.

From my perspective, however, it looks like I won't be getting any dance practice tonight after all, something which simultaneously pleases and frustrates me. I mean, we could just go to a club, but with the momentum lost, the chance to bottle it and go home, avoiding dancing in public altogether, has become the path of least resistance.

It's not just fear that drives me away: I've been struck by a certain lethargy ever since I arrived on the coast, and it's especially been the case in Cartagena. You can feel the languor in the air here. Or you can just come to my hotel room any given morning and see it first-hand. Slow just feels like the right speed.

It's probably one of the reasons for the easy-going nature of the Costeños (coastal people) and the loose-limbed manner with which they walk the streets. Costeños seem to be seen as either laid back or just plain lazy, depending pretty much on whether or not you're a Costeño. Similarly, *cachacos* (people from Bogotá and the interior) are either the epitome of refinement or a bunch of complete stiffs.

However you look at it, even the way the locals here talk is relaxed, with all the words coalescing into a single, long one, and some syllables getting lost in the process, making their Spanish tricky to understand at the best of times.

At least communication between Yudi and I is starting to take a turn for the better. I'm not quite sure what has happened to prompt it, but I'm not questioning it, either.

As a break from all the stuff I can't do, Yudi decides we should do some cumbia. She gives me some simple pointers on shuffling technique and also gets me rolling my hips. The same hips which I now have a growing awareness of. I perform with them for her like some amateur private dancer she hired down a back alley. I like to think.

Even though I just shuffle about unimaginatively for the whole song, she smiles and tells me it's "*muy bien*". I give a bow and she laughs. The ironic bow is quickly becoming a key weapon in my dance armoury. I'm going to start doing after everything from now on, and that includes belching.

"*El baile es una conversación con la música,*" she says. Dance is a conversation with the music.

I love these pithy little dance-related aphorisms – they must get taught them at school.

The *mapalé* hasn't suddenly stopped existing, however, and, with my Barbara Windsor still not at a bikini-flinging stage, we're having a go at what Yudi calls *adoraciones* (adorations). These are where you leap to one side or the other, and throw your arms up in the air and back down again, like you're praising a deity, albeit in a bit of a rush.

Yudi tells me off for not following her instructions correctly. I return fire by appropriating her baby bottom lip – one of the few things she's taught me that I can do properly. She laughs out loud.

Our new-found rapport isn't enough to solve the problem though: I physically can't do the adorations quickly enough. I feel like blaming gravity – my body just doesn't seem to come down out the air quickly enough – but, knowing I'd be on to a loser with that one, I blame my age instead.

"How old are you?" she says in a tone that suggests the idea is preposterous.

I tell her I'm thirty-five. This elicits a surprised look that I'm well used to – people tend to think I'm younger due to my childish immaturity. I mean looks.

Next up it's the *champeta* again, which means it's hula-hoop-and-drum-tonk time. I haven't practised, of course, and guess what? I haven't improved, either. It's like there's some kind of weird connection between the two. Yudi is unimpressed by this, but I've got the antidote for that: I turn to her and pat my head whilst rubbing my belly.

Bite me!

She doesn't bite me, but instead does something far more cutting: she performs the move straight back to me, flawlessly. She's been practising, the little cheat.

"If you don't practice dance, you never can dance."

Practice isn't the only issue, however – she thinks that part of my delivery is fundamentally wrong to begin with.

"You have to believe you're black and strong."

Do you mind – I am black! I mean I am strong! I mean... okay.

"When you dance, you need to have... *actitud* [attitude]."

But surely you need to get to the point where you're really comfortable doing something before you can do it with attitude. I don't tell her this, though, because that's just further proof that I need to practice.

With my time dripping away like sweat from a dancer, I get back to my contact. He's still adamant that he can get my paperwork stamped, and very soon. I decide it's best to phone Brian and let him know where I'm up to, and that I've got everything covered.

It's not the conversation I'm expecting. Brian strongly warns me away from this route: regardless of people's good intentions I could end up with false papers. This would not be good. At the very least, I'm going to need to extend my stay again, so if I go about this the wrong way I could be jeopardising my stay in general.

Another one of Cartagena's heavy wooden doors thuds shut.

I might have little or no control over my passport situation, but my dance situation is different. It would be bad enough having to go home, but imagine doing so without even having given it a real go. It's finally time I did something about this, and I'm going to start by removing those obstacles.

No music to dance to? Fine – I'll just go out and buy some music. No stereo to play it through? Not a problem – I'll play it through my mobile phone. Hotel room too small? Well hey, I'll just dance on the first-floor landing. Should I hear anyone coming I'll just adopt some kind of pensive hand-on-jaw posture.

And so it happens that I finally do it – I finally practise *mapalé* and *champeta* – sticking at it despite the odd interruption from cleaning staff, who I leave to draw their own conclusions.

"Look, a man stroking his chin to world music – must be a Guardian reader."

The jigsaw still lacks one final piece, however – a dance partner. Hanging out with Carl could well be the key to this, as every time I catch up with him he's been out clubbing. I make a note to head out with him the next time the opportunity arises. No excuses.

There's one thing about all that practice though – it wears you out. I lie in my hotel-room bed exhausted yet fulfilled, the fan blades above me chopping into the heavy coastal air. I can't sleep without the fan rotating because it's just too warm, but I do find it unnerving, not least because it has a bit of a wobble.

I reassure myself that, despite the millions of them that must exist in the world, I've never heard of anyone being attacked by one. I close my eyes and drift off into a long and satisfied sleep.

"Dooo ittt!" says Yudi.

She can no longer say it without smiling.

It's the final class in the block that I booked, and we're working on the Barbara Windsor again. Yudi explains that this is the most important *paso*, and shows me a whole raft of derivative *pasos*. If I'm going to crack *mapalé* I've got to crack this. But despite repeated attempts in practice I wasn't able to do it, so what are the chances now?

"I really can't do this," I say to myself out-loud, instantly bringing to mind Henry Ford.

"Whether you believe you can do a thing or not, you're right," he said. "Unless it's *mapalé*, in which case you genuinely can't."

I try again anyway, though. I try again, and fail again. I do reps in trying and failing, like we're in a gym.

Then, suddenly, out of nowhere – BAM – I do it. Not only that, I nail it full speed for all of about 20 seconds. I'm like a kid sailing off down the road for the first time without stabilisers. Whoopee! The practice paid off!

TWANG.

I've ridden straight into a wall. By which I mean I've pulled a muscle in my abdomen. My body won't let me continue. Actually, let's just rewind a moment... since when did you ever hear of anyone pulling a muscle in their abdomen? This dance is crazy.

As a kind of informal *clausura* for the *mapalé*, Yudi gets me to run through the whole track using what steps I've learnt. Practise has definitely improved me, but I started too late for it to have a real impact. I simply can't keep up with the music, and whilst my execution is improved, it's still laboured and slovenly. It's certainly nothing like the exhilarating popping-about that I saw on the cobblestones. My pulled muscle, meanwhile, means I can no longer show off the one piece of progress I have made.

The *champeta* is a bit better. To bring that one to a close, Yudi and I dance together, holding hands opposite each other with me performing various *pasos* and her following my lead. I still can't do the hula-hoop and drum-tonk movement, though, and nor have I ever worked out why everyone thinks *champeta* is so naughty.

Boy do I love the music, though – it's like multi-coloured ice-cream soup. And I know I must be doing something right, because when I look in the mirror I find, somewhat to my surprise, that I've got a big grin on my face.

The next morning when Carl emerges from his room he looks surprisingly rough. Perhaps it's the hangover he's wearing on his face. Or maybe it's the blood-stained white bandage he's wearing on his wrist. There was me thinking that pulling a muscle in my abs was bad – what the hell kind of dance was this guy doing?

The answer is the fan dance, and not the Arabic kind. He tells me that he met a girl in a club, and he took her back to a hotel room. They were just about to "get busy" as he puts it, when suddenly there was blood everywhere. Standing on the bed, he had put his hand in the air and the rotating blades above him had chopped into his wrist, severing a tendon.

Carl, perhaps due in some small part to alcohol, was keen for their night of passion to continue, but the prissy local woman insisted he dealt with his partially-severed limb first. Cue a sequence of early morning cab rides as he went from hospital to hospital trying to find one that could treat him on a limited budget.

"They said they weren't going to fix the tendon – they were just going to sew the wrist up and I should deal with it later. Does that sound right to you?"

Well, I'm not a healthcare professional, but... no, Carl, not really.

He's determined to stay in Latin America, but from an outside perspective it's hard to see how he'll manage that. And he's not the only one clinging onto a dream. I haven't even looked into tickets home yet. I'm convinced that there must be some way of making this work: it's just a case of finding it.

I feel like I'm just beginning to see the first glimmers of developing a body awareness that I didn't even know was lacking – I can't give up now. But unless something radically changes I won't have much of a choice. My mission to dance like a Colombian seems certain to end very soon, and in failure.

CHAPTER EIGHT

Bumper to Bumper

The bus is a rampaging old boar of a vehicle with an imposing snout and grille. It looks like it should be foraging wildly through the undergrowth rather than roaming the streets. I sit on the shaded side, unsticking my bare legs in turn from the vinyl seats. The vehicle snarls into life, then reverses out of its berth, and our journey begins.

With the days running out, and me no closer to securing my stay in the country, I've decided to do the obvious: head off on a jolly to a nearby village and forget all about it. But this is not some thoughtless act of denial – rather, denial has become a conscious strategy. Part of my problem, surely, has been my uptight, English approach to the situation; this inherent need to do things the 'right' way. If only I could be a bit more loose-shouldered and Colombian, perhaps there wouldn't be so much of an issue.

"You must think in Russian!" as some bloke tells Clint Eastwood in Firefox when he's trying to steal a Soviet plane, a situation exactly analogous to my own.

So how about I just travel around undocumented for the rest of the trip? I mean, they're hardly going to hunt someone down for overstaying – people must do it all the time. When I leave, I'll get a fine and a rap on the knuckles or whatever. But so what? I mean, it's just paperwork, isn't it?

Even though it's only a short-range rural machine, the bus still has a DVD player on board. The television buzzes into life, and the title sequence reveals we're about to see the highlights of a previous year's *corraleja* (bullfighting) season. I brace myself for what I imagine will be a wonderful mixture of human skill and animal cruelty.

As it happens, I'm only half-right, and not because the bull spends the whole time being pampered by masseurs. Though in the Colombian version of the sport they do even the punishment out a little by allowing in anybody mad enough (or perhaps drunk enough) to get involved. Perhaps this is why most of the men in the dirt-patch arena are adorned in the less-than-traditional bullfighting outfit of jeans, t-shirt and baseball cap.

The outcome is not unpredictable. To the upbeat gaiety of the Mexican Hat Dance, we are treated to a montage of human carnage. Most men are fleet-footed enough to escape the bull, but not all of them. Bulls fling the unfortunates up into the air, digging them out once they've landed and exacting further punishment.

One participant tries to escape the animal's charge by sliding under the wooden fence at the perimeter of the viewing stand. Just as he looks safe it plucks him out again and tosses him skywards. He lands in anguish and holds his hands up, pleading for mercy. But it's a bull – he might as well try and discuss agrarian policy with it. It flings him so high that he collides with the roof of the stand before crashing back down to the ground.

The extent of each person's injuries isn't clear, but some of the men are left lying lifeless on the floor, as good as dead.

Popcorn anyone?

There's little to see out the window as an alternative – this coastal region is predominantly flat and the fields race by in a blur of yellow with dabs of green. Until, that is, we slow down. Then stop.

We've reached a checkpoint of some kind. A security official boards the bus and everyone starts rummaging around for their *cédulas* – their mandatory Colombian ID cards. Every time anyone asks me if I've got one, I think they mean *celular* and smile and wave my mobile phone at them. It's certainly a good way of getting a confused look out of someone.

Everyone's documents are in order. Well, almost everyone's: some idiot is carrying only a sweaty, torn photocopy of his long-since-vanished documentation, and hasn't even had the good sense to bring the *denuncia* (crime report) that might back up his account.

The official orders me off the bus. Feeling both idiotic and concerned in roughly equal measures, I stand by the dusty roadside while a yet-more-senior official quizzes me. What am I doing here in Colombia?

"I'm here to learn to dance," I say, and tell him about my efforts to appropriate some of the folkloric heritage of his country.

"*¿El mapalé?*"

The very same.

He starts repeating the word in rhythmic tribute, which is pretty much how a large portion of the song goes.

Oh wait – does he expect me to dance? Is this some kind of test of veracity of my story? If so, is my dignity allowed any say in this, or am I meant to just succumb to the moment, like when English footballer Peter Crouch did the 'robot' for Prince William?

Unless, of course, it's a display of authority – for all I know, the people on the bus are all gripping their heads in horror at the unfolding scene.

"For Christ's sake, man, dance! Dance if you value your life!"

Holding my nerve, I simply smile and say "*¡Sí!*", even though some part of me desperately wants to add "No, wait!" and attempt a set of Barbara Windsor lunges.

Given my level of competence in this dance, it's probably just as well I don't.

"Gentlemen, his *mapalé* story is clearly a lie. Take him away."

I stand waiting on the hot road whilst he considers the situation. There is a long authoritative pause. Finally, he relents and allows me on my way, telling me to be careful and to watch my bags. I want to say "I know" but clearly I don't or I'd still have my passport.

"*Tengo confianza en él*," says the bus driver, pointing out a kid on a motorbike. I trust him.

The village of San Basilio de Palenque, known simply as Palenque, isn't on the main road, so a number of *moto* (motorbike-taxi) drivers hang about at the junction with their vehicles waiting to ferry people the mile or two from the bus stop to the village.

A *palenque* in this context was an enclave village formed by escaped slaves, known as *cimarrones* (maroons), to provide solidarity against recapture.

"We shall remain forever within this closed community," they said, "where we shall be free!"

Okay, so I'm stretching the irony a little, here.

Whilst slavery was abolished in 1851, this particular community remains, and is considered a hugely important part of the country's cultural heritage, even gaining UNESCO recognition.

We bump along a dirt track that darts up and down and winds between fields before straightening out, some small houses joining us for company. Stick fences mark out the boundaries of the attached land, with washing dorning the points, like a line of sock puppets.

I'm feeling apprehensive. It's quite unnerving to be told you can trust a specific person – it suggests that trust is somehow an issue. Added to this, a woman I briefly met in Cartagena told me I shouldn't come alone. And now I think back to that official telling me to be careful – I think he meant in general but could he have meant in Palenque? I'm nearly there now, so I'll get a feel for the real situation soon enough.

During a conversation of muffled shouting of the kind you can only really achieve at speed on the back of a motorbike, I tell the kid about my dance mission. To my surprise, he tells me he knows someone at the college who might be able to help, and that he can take me directly there.

The school is a very rudimentary set of buildings with an open area at the centre. It's here the kid introduces me to a teacher. I tell her of my mission and her response is immediate – would I like to see a dance demonstration?

Really? Right now? Just for me? Great!

I'm led into the school courtyard. The primitive buildings; the heat; the scores of little kids all congregating together... it's just like being in Africa. And the fact that everyone is black, of course. I've never actually been to Africa but I did see The Constant Gardener once, so I'm kind of an expert.

The classroom is just a basic shell with a corrugated metal roof and inside, the students – young adults – are stood in two lines, by gender, wearing clothes as bright as a washing powder advert. The young men are dressed in acid-yellow shirts, loose white trousers and straw hats; the young women in white dresses with a black flower print. Discarded items of clothing are draped across chairs and desks, looking a lot like things they've just changed out of.

Okay hold on, this isn't just for me – it did seem a bit too good to be true – they're putting some kind of a show on here.

I'm led into a hall with rows of chairs forming a U-shape around a central space. The sudden, jarring thing – even more than the sight of bright clothes against bare concrete – is the audience. They're all white, or at the very least whiter than the villagers, and they're dressed in an urban style.

By pure coincidence I've arrived in time for a start of a performance laid on for a group of cultural observers who've come here on a day visit from the country's interior. This is nothing like as far as I've come so they should all fuck off. Not that I'm suffering from a bout of fellow-outsiders-ruining-my-authentic-experience annoyance or anything.

The room is filling up. A cluster of local children watch from the doorway, dwarfed by the tall drum next to them. Other inquisitive little faces peep in through the glassless windows, clutching at the metal bars.

When I was at college the lead guitar was the chief instrument of aspiration and/or torture, but here it's all about the percussion. Indeed, the band today consists in its entirety of a couple of male students with hand drums, and someone on maracas.

With everyone finally in place, the show begins. Cadences rise up from the taut drum skins like animalistic spirits leaving their carcasses, or some other African-like thing which possibly exists only in my head.

The young people in the washing-powder clothes take the floor and lead us through a variety of folk dances. There's a real mixture of styles on display here. Some are cheerful, partner-based dances, with do-si-dos and the like. Other are more frantic and closer to the *mapalé*, such as one in which a lone male buzzes about the floor, pattering his bare feet at such high speed they're just a blur of movement, like the Looney Tunes' Tasmanian Devil. I find myself wishing I could do it, despite not quite knowing why.

The thing all the dances have in common is this open, sunny exuberance. In fact, I've never seen people smile so much as they're dancing. Yudi would definitely approve.

A woman with an orange turban takes the floor. After a bout of singing, she looks to the audience for someone to join her in dancing. Now I understand the warnings – the danger in Palenque comes out of nowhere. I avoid all eye contact and try to appear busy, despite the unlikeliness of someone genuinely being busy whilst sat in an audience watching a dance show.

Just for once, however, I'm not the only novelty outsider, and she finds a willing victim amongst the cultural observers. The danger is unlikely to have passed for long, however, so when I'm beckoned out to meet someone, I gladly oblige. His name is Oscar, and he's a stocky local man in his early thirties wearing jeans and a casual shirt.

Within ten minutes, everything has changed. We're sat out on brightly-coloured moulded plastic chairs with a couple of his friends in the backyard of someone's house, enjoying the easy tranquillity. The mottled shade of a tree protects us from the harsh sun of early afternoon, and radio plays out in the background.

There's not much to do, so I amuse myself by watching a duck opening and closing its beak seemingly in time with a radio station jingle about "*!Éxitos!*" (Hits!)

Is it because it's a Saturday, or is life here always this relaxed? I don't know, but I'm not complaining.

Oscar hands me a plate of food from a stock pot indoors: pork in a rich, slow-cooked sauce served with sticky, fibrous hunks of yucca. It's magnificent – the best food I've had since I came to Colombia. I clank it down gratefully, whilst black-skinned piglets snort and roll about in little patches of mud on the otherwise hard-baked ground.

The food isn't the only stewy thing here: Oscar and his friends are chatting away in such a casserole of an accent that I don't understand a thing they're saying. This is probably Palenquero – the only Spanish Creole language in Latin America – and something Palenque is known for. Then again, given the thickness of accents in this part of the country, they could be speaking English for all I know – I still wouldn't understand a damn thing.

After an unhurried repose, Oscar takes me out on a walkabout of the village and its unpaved streets. The buildings vary between ones of bare breeze blocks and others that are rendered and painted in muted yet colourful shades, with stamp-print patterns around the windows. They have a humble, welcoming feel. The church fits this pattern, being an angular construction in pastel shades of pink, blue and yellow, with a bell tower so small I could practically reach in and ring the thing myself.

Palenque is home to 3,500 people, and it seems like Oscar knows all of them.

"*¡Buenas!*" or "*¡Entonces!*" he says to passers-by as a greeting, the former being short for 'Good afternoon!', and the latter just kind of meaning 'So… !'

We pass the main square and the statue of Benkos Bioho, the escaped slave who founded the village in the 16th Century, his face contorted in a rage as he tries to break from his chains. Nearby, some men relax at tables next to a wooden drinks hut, playing what looks like dominos.

There doesn't seem to be much going on in Palenque. Pigs and piglets roam about and kids play football on the up-and-down road surface. We stop to greet a friend who is shelling beans, discarding the green and yellow pods in a big pile on the table. This seems to be a common thing – carry out your business on the porch and watch the world go by. Indeed, Palenque would be approaching a paradise of sorts if it weren't for one thing.

Litter.

It's everywhere, congregating in vegetable plots, skulking lazily about the streets and even coalescing with the dirt to become part of the road. And the source is no mystery – people just seem to drop it where they stand.

"I don't like it," says Oscar. "It's just manners."

Well it's been a nice day, and I feel like I've seen something very different, but I'm going to have to get going soon.

"There's a party tonight," says Oscar.

Ah, yeah, but I can't stay overnight: I've brought no lens solution and precious little money. Besides, there don't seem to be any guest houses.

Oscar doesn't see these as obstacles – I can stop at his place, he tells me. He's modest about what he has to offer, but he's got a spare room, and it's mine if I want it.

"Do you want to come to the party?" he says. "*¿Si o no?*"

This 'Yes or no?' question tag is a favourite of his. It seems abrupt and hurrying at first, but I soon realise it's just a turn of phrase.

The party seems like too good an opportunity to miss, but there are a couple of unsaid things that are bothering me. Firstly, does he expect money? It would be a perfectly reasonable exchange, but I have very little with me and broaching the subject feels awkward. Secondly, is the question of my safety. No-one knows I'm here and, despite my positive experience so far, the warnings have still made me wary. I'm very aware of how vulnerable I am.

I'm still pondering all this when we arrive at a place with a woman outside who Oscar seems to know particularly well. This is because it's his mum. She invites us in to her living room, where pictures hang directly off the breeze-block walls. The ceiling is a corrugated tin roof and the floor is just compacted dirt, yet there is a DVD and television. Oscar puts them into immediate use, putting on some music and imploring us to dance.

You can run but you can't hide.

I've no idea what the music is, and even less of an idea what to do to it, but my dance partner has no such problems. She wheels about in little circles with her backside stuck out, showing off implied tail feathers. The only dance I know that's even remotely like this is cumbia, so that's what I attempt to do, shuffling about in the dirt nearby.

We're not a good match and I feel surplus to requirements. It's a feeling that's compounded when Oscar takes over from me, using his hat as a prop and drawing a big sunny smile out of her. It's also the closest I've seen to him smiling himself – he seems a somewhat melancholic individual, or at the very least is today.

As we leave, he presses me again on my plans.

"Are you leaving today? *¿Si o no?*'

It's time to talk cash. He's as awkward about it as I am, but finally tells me that whatever I'm able to give him; that will be enough.

So that's settled then.

"I want to stay."

Imagine you were in a quaint English village with birds tweeting and not much else going on. Now imagine someone started blasted out music, sending nearby windows into vibrations. Finally, imagine everyone in the village was okay with that.

That's pretty much the shape of it here in Palenque. We're sat out on chairs on the dirt track, music booming from a triangular stack of amplifiers nearby which Oscar refers to as the *picó*, set up on a plot of land which will be the venue for the party. Palm leaves decorate the fences surrounding the plot, the entrance being an archway of yet more palms, creating a sense of occasion.

"Are you going to dance tonight?" says Oscar.

"Yes."

And I mean it. Kind of. I mean, who knows what music they'll be playing.

It's late afternoon, and there's little to do other than wait for the *fiesta* to start. These people seem to fill vacant time very well, whereas I'm just restless. I put my head back and close my eyes to let the time pass, under a reassuring blanket of late-afternoon sun and *vallenato* accordion.

"*Mira,*" says Oscar, bringing me back to the world of the open-eyed. Look.

Over the road, two people are dancing together. They're stood facing each other, feet opposing feet, but from their knees upwards they're a single indivisible unit, hips gently gyrating in unison.

Okay, so we're watching a couple of lovers dancing together intimately. What are you expecting from me, Oscar? A dig in the ribs and some "Phwoar – eh!" type comments? I mean, it feels like a minor invasion of their privacy just looking at them.

"He's not her boyfriend."

Seriously? You mean they're just friends? That's madness!

Party time is getting closer, and a few people are now milling round the venue, so we head over to grab some seats. Music of three different types reverberates from the big stack of speakers: the bonkers (*champeta*), the hip-hoppy (reggaeton) and the accordion-based (*vallenato*). Okay, so at least I can dance to a third of that, assuming the way they dance *champeta* here in any way resembles what I've learnt. It's notable that none of the stuff they played at the show gets an airing – it would seem there's a clear division between their cultural heritage and what they actually dance to for fun.

While we're waiting for time to pass – which has been today's main activity – a gang of children arrives. They walk past us to the concrete porch of one of the buildings and start dancing to the music. Well, when I say dancing, the girls have their backs to the wall with the boys are up against them, and they're pushing their pelvises together, albeit with the boys legs on the outside of the girls', this being the one detail that makes it not dry humping. I guess they're in some way copying off what they see the adults do.

I'd say it was like a behind-the-bike-sheds type scene, but

they're too young even for that. Oscar reckons the youngest is four and the oldest ten. I'm not a prude, but… well, okay, maybe I am.

"What do you think of this?" I say to Oscar.

"It's good," he says, and gives the thumbs up, adding that it wasn't like this when he was young, but that it's good they learn to dance at such a young age.

I think we're seeing the scene through different lenses.

As the night ambles in, the kids disperse and the older party-goers arrive. Unlike at the show earlier on, people are dressed in a casual, urban style, with most women opting for spray-on jeans or hot pants.

The party hasn't started yet, although I'm not sure how I'll know it's begun – maybe someone will blow a whistle or something. Or maybe it won't happen at all, and I'll somehow get away without having to dance. Not like I'm hoping that's what will happen or anything.

I'm part of a group of about a dozen people, sat on a circle of chairs. The dancing will be soon. Is it just me, or is the tension unbearable?

It's just me.

I get chatting to the guy next to me, out of nervousness rather than friendliness. He's sat with what appears to be his girlfriend, although I feel like I can no longer safely make that judgement any more – my social compass is completely scrambled.

Whatever their relationship, she says something to him, and he passes the message on to me. I'm struggle to understand it exactly, but since it contains the words *cerveza* (beer) and *regalar* (to give as a present), I get the gist.

"Very kind," I say, "but I don't drink alcohol."

He looks confused for a moment.

"No – she's wants you to buy her a drink."

Ah, okay. Well, I am the rich foreigner so I really don't mind in principal. The problem is that any money I spend on them is less money to give to Oscar, but at the same time, it seems poor form to refuse. I wander down with her to the bar, sorry, man-with-a-cooler-box. At the point of sale, a single beer for her becomes one for each of them. I buy nothing for myself to save money.

Just when I'm starting to think that this could be a night where my wallet is everyone's new best friend – and I end up having to pay Oscar with my shoes – someone buys me a soft drink without me even asking. Then a few minutes later, someone else walks up with a cup and asks me for some of it. They show a similar mentality towards seating – when there's a shortage of chairs, people just casually plonk themselves on each other's knees.

I like this sharing culture. Accepting drinks from strangers is a big no-no in Colombia according to Brian – there's a risk of them being spiked – but at least if it happens here we'll all end up drugged-out together, in a big pile. As a side note, you shouldn't take sweets from strangers, either. This is especially true if they didn't offer you any.

The villagers even share with the floor – everyone takes a shot from the familiar little plastic cups before spitting it out again. Yeah, that's cheap whisky for you.

"*Para los ánimos,*" someone says to me. For the spirits.

That's what I meant to say.

All this chin-rubbing social anthropology has been a nice diversion, but on the dance floor – well, dirt floor – a few people have actually started dancing *champeta*. And it doesn't look good. Whilst some of the moves are vaguely similar to what I learnt in Cartagena, there's an added twist. They're banging their groins together.

Arrgh! Yudi never told me about this. It's not for the whole song, and it's the men's legs that are on the outside, but still, it's not what I had in mind. I'm English, dammit. We don't do this kind of thing. Still, this crystallises things. I'd better start making my escape plan – the time is soon.

Wrong! The time is now. The dreaded hand is proffered in my direction – the girl I bought the drinks for has decided to reward me with the least reward-like thing imaginable.

I get to my feet with a half-smile and a sense of 'oh crap, here we go', wondering why I didn't leave a long, long time ago. The wheel of fortune has skipped *vallenato* and reggaeton and gone straight to *champeta* again, but then none of them are safe bets anymore.

Palenque, along with Cartagena, is one of the homes of the *champeta*. Its origins are not just Afro-Colombian, also lying in genres such as soukous from Zaire, highlife from Nigeria and various others from Haiti. At least one source claims *champeta* is named after a kind of knife – a reference to the needle cutting the record. In a similar vein, *picó*, which can refer to the whole DJ setup, and not just the speakers, comes from the electronic 'pick-up' on the arm of a record player. Outdoor discos such as this, complete with mobile DJ, are apparently a regular feature of coastal Colombia.

There's a history of couples dance being viewed as scandalous and vulgar before being accepted into the mainstream, with tango and waltz being notable international examples, and with cumbia and many others fitting the same pattern in Colombia. Along related lines, music and dance in Colombia has repeatedly made the journey from black and working-class communities of the coast to the middle classes.

I find the very modernity of some of the popular forms fascinating: salsa hails back to the 1960s, *champeta* only appeared in the 80s and then reggaeton in the 90s. Before that everyone in clubs must have just stood about shrugging their shoulders. A bit like I do.

Sorry, I'm just trying to put it off. The dancing, yes.

We stand facing each other, holding hands. To the home-made sampling and the singer's calls of "*¡Suelta!*" I start cycling through some of the simple *pasos*, stubbing the toe of my trainers on the compacted dirt.

A few whoops come from those round me – I don't think they expected me to be able to do a thing. I make the switch into the jelly legs and lasso, drawing yet more excited noises – this foreign bloke actually knows a thing or two. Not three or four, but not zero. And I'm actually leading – can you believe it? Perhaps we won't have to do any of that other stuff after all.

Ha – right! About a third of the way into the song, she takes over. Suddenly, from nowhere, we're banging pelvises, like a pair of bumper cars. And now the real shrieks and whoops go up. I guess that whilst it might be normal for them, seeing a foreigner doing it is quite something else.

Once I've got over the initial shock, I realise that contrary to how it looks, it doesn't actually feel sexual. It's just an action we're performing, and something to do with the orientation means we're actually just kind of banging hips.

Then she spins round and starts rubbing her backside against my, well, frontside, in a move I recognise from reggaeton. This by contrast seems a lot more saucy. Yet once again, from all that's gone before, I know very well that in this context it's nothing more than dancing.

But it's still dancing, and therefore it's a skill. It's funny how you can see something done plenty of times, but when you go to do it yourself, you realise that you don't know the technicalities. Am I meant to move my hips in unison with hers, or do we go in opposite directions? And if I get it wrong, will be the locals be offended?

"My God – it's like he's trying to have sex with her or something!"

I go for opposites when later inspection reveals it should be same-same. No worries, though – I'm not expected to get it right. Finally, it's over, and we're both sitting down in a post-dance recline, holding metaphorical cigarettes.

"More or less?" I say to my neighbour.

"It was good!"

"Good," says Oscar. "It was your first time."

There's something about the delivery that suggests he's actually saying "It's a process." I'm still buzzing, though – I've just done something that terrified me. Actually, I rather feel like I've just come through some kind of hazing ceremony. They'll probably give me a wedgie before the night's out.

You might think that after this first experience the night just flowed; that I was constantly up there, dancing with all and sundry. But somehow it doesn't turn out like that. Whilst everyone else is getting up repeatedly – the plastic chairs being constantly jettisoned and reclaimed – I find myself stuck in my seat, trapped by several problems.

The first is finding a partner. It's my job to make the approach – that first dance was a one-off – but how do I actually go about it? Can I approach just anyone, or are there hidden rules? I mean, is there a polite way to ask someone to bang pelvises with you?

It's complicated by other factors. I only know how to dance one style – *champeta* – and, as with the crossover club in Cali, once I've worked out the song is suitable, there are no free girls. Plus in the absence of alcohol, I can't even just get leathered and say "Ah, what the hell."

But the real problem is the one in my head. I think far too much instead of just getting up and doing it; waiting for some perfect moment that will never arrive. In the close night, the scent of whisky hangs in the air, and bodies are writhing, colliding and grinding to the deep beat from the stack. But not mine – I'm just sat down.

Not that I don't learn something from the sidelines. Whilst the specific execution differs between the three genres – *champeta*, reggaeton and *vallenato* – the dancing always follows the same pattern. The couples start a 'normal' distance apart. Then, about a third of the way through, they come together. From then on it's all the sensual stuff, which is hip-gyrating, pelvis-banging, or backside-to-loins depending on the genre. Come the end of the song, there's no final flourish or 'dip', as with salsa. Instead, everyone simultaneously de-couples.

"Are you watching?" asks Oscar.

Yes I am, even it still feels a bit like I'm perving. At times I have the occasional double-take: am I really looking at a mass group of people in some form of clothed coitus? I feel like Edward Woodward's puritan policeman in The Wicker Man. And that doesn't end well, either.

Ironically, at least from what I can see, the bona fide couples are the ones who are dancing slowly to the point of it being tender: there's nearly no grinding or bumping.

So yes, I'm learning, but my position has now become entrenched to the point where I'd need a ladder to escape. I don't get it. I've come out here on my own despite the warnings of others, and accepted an invitation to stay with a stranger from an unfamiliar culture on a whim. I've not let inadequate documentation, money or anything else stop me. In other words, I'm way outside my comfort zone. Yet the moment it comes to simply moving my limbs to some music, I can't. It's the lowest hurdle of them all, and yet it's the one I keep refusing.

"Are you tired?" asks Oscar.

The hidden question here is obvious. It's like that pre-*clausura* night in Cali all over again, and if I behave exactly the same, why should I expect it to pan out any differently?

I get up and go for a wander. Perhaps the very act of moving will break the mental impasse. On the periphery of the party, I bump into one of the men from our chair-circle, a short guy in a blue shirt who has a near-visible aura of friendliness. Like Oscar, he also wants to know why I'm not dancing, only he asks me straight out.

I've evaded the issue too long, so I try to be honest.

"I don't know how you..."

"...start?" he says. "Like this."

He holds his hand out.

Oh. Okay. It's really that simple.

He accompanies me back to the dance floor, enthusiastic for me to succeed, and points out a lone woman. Freed by the moment, I make my move, but just as I'm about to reach her, someone else beats me to it. We both look around and he points out another free girl – I'm onto it already, my hand straight out.

In my eagerness, I've completely overlooked what kind of music it will be. Just by some strange musical quirk, it turns out to be the first salsa track they've played all night, and I can dance it better than her. We dance the next one too – *champeta* – and she gives me instructions of when it's correct to start bumping together.

Buoyed by my experience, I go off hunting for more partners. At one point I find myself dancing with a tall, slender girl. Then suddenly, I'm not: another girl has jumped in between us, grinding her backside against me. Refusing to be ousted, the original girl goes round the back of me, so now I'm the meat in a manwich.

To think that, when I started, I thought that putting a hand on a woman's back was a touch forward. I don't really understand the relationship between dance and sexuality here in Colombia, and especially in Palenque, but what I do know is that in this short space of time, my sense of personal space has been completely reprogrammed.

I even end up dancing *vallenato*, by which I mean just kind of standing there pressed together with a woman who mouths out the lyrics over my shoulder, whilst our feet repeatedly clash because I don't actually know how to dance *vallenato*.

Then the numbers start to thin out, and I approach Oscar to ask him what's happening now.

"Everyone has gone home to make love."

It almost seems like an anti-climax.

The next morning, Oscar gives me a lift back out to the junction on his motorbike. I give him all the money I have left, keeping just enough for my bus fare and a snack. It only comes to about 20,000 pesos (US$10; £6.67). I feel embarrassed as it doesn't seem like a fair exchange.

The woman on the bus next to me has a platter of sticky goods on her lap. It was originally atop her head, cushioned on a ring of fabric, but she took the whole thing off to get on the bus – I guess it's rude to wear hats indoors here, too.

I buy a sugary oat-ball from her and sit gnawing at it as the bus growls its departure. I can barely see a thing as I only managed to re-insert one of my contact lenses, and the sensation is the alcohol-free equivalent of a hangover. My body and clothes are coated in dust, my fingernails are full of dirt and I face another security inquisition about my rubbish copy of an absent document. But I don't care, because that crazy experience was worth all of it.

I feel like I'm learning so much about people, about culture, about dance. Unfortunately, one of the things I've learnt is that travelling about on a crappy sweat-addled photocopy of a stolen passport isn't viable in the long term, and it will be even worse once I've gone past my exit date. That budget-destroying emergency flight home is looking more and more like the only realistic option.

CHAPTER NINE

Hats Off

"*¡Miércoles!*"

The photocopier repairman is frustrated with something, but doesn't want to say "shit" (*mierda*) so he's saying "Wednesday" instead, like someone saying "barstool" in lieu of "bastard".

He's not the only one with problems: I'm out of ideas, out of time, and soon to be out of the country. So here I am in the consulate for one last, frantic dice-throwing session. I don't really have much to go on, but I simply won't let it go. It was such a big deal for me to come out here, and I'm not giving up until I've exhausted all the possibilities.

I feel like a distinguished dignitary when I'm in the consulate; like if the country suddenly went to hell we'd all escape together from the roof-top by helicopter. Realistically, if the budgetary situation is as bad as it would seem, we'd probably all just be stood there flapping our arms like *mapalé* dancers, but that's not the point.

Brian is out, but Carmen is in. I like Carmen. She's attractive, intelligent and governmentally-connected enough for a Bond-fling if he ever were to pop into the office for a quick martini, but dignified and self-respecting enough that she'd probably smile and politely tell him no.

Fortunately for me, suffering fools is also amongst her qualities – if she's getting sick of the various wacky suggestions I'm putting her way this morning, then she doesn't show it. Could I apply via the UK where there's a fast-track system? Could I fly to a nearby British Overseas Territory and get a new passport there? Could I make my own passport using craft paper and crayons?

No, no and only if it were really colourful.

Well that really is that then. I really am done here. Oh, hold on, I do have one last idea. Can't we just create a new document which says that I've applied for a passport and I'm waiting for it to arrive? After all, DAS just want something official they can stamp – so why don't we just innovate something official? I mean, who decides what's official and what isn't? Surely it's the consulate.

Carmen thinks a while, then picks up the phone. Wow – this might actually be a goer.

It's the first of a series of calls that she makes to the various stakeholders, both British and Colombian. It's hard to tell how well the other side of the conversation is going, but Carmen is the model of charm and discretion throughout. Her approach certainly puts my own fire-hose approach to diplomacy to shame.

It's clearly an important skill. What is very apparent in each of the calls is that no-one actually needs to say yes. What do they have to gain? Saying no is definitely the path of least resistance. The merest hint of an obstacle and the deal will be off.

Carmen puts the phone down one last time.

It's a yes.

I'd quite like to hang about for a while, enjoying my general sense of disbelief, but this positive result means I've got a lot of work on my hands. What follows is a blur of taxi journeys and paperwork; trips to DHL to post stuff and to the bank to pay the various processing fees. It chews up a lot of cash and takes the best part of two days continuous effort, but it means I can stay in the country and therefore it's worth it.

The next time I go to the consulate, Brian is there. And, what's more, he has something for me.

"This is the first time we've been able to issue this piece of paper."

Brian hands me the stamped and signed document. It feels like a momentous occasion; like there should be handshakes, dignitaries and the flashing of cameras. One quick visit to DAS later and the document has the Colombian stamp of approval, too.

I'm legally able to stay in the country.

With my status assured, I'm finally able to turn my full attention back to why I'm here in the first place – hanging around claiming to be learning how to dance, whilst in reality avoiding every opportunity.

The Caribbean coast has no shortage of dances, many of them with an African influence. There's *bullerengue*, *porro*, *pilanderas*, *jorikamba*, fandango, *pilón* and a whole load of others, all of which are nothing more than names to me.

But rather than learning a new one to add to the list of dances I'm half-arsed at, wouldn't it be better to really nail something I already kind of know? Let me answer that for you – yes it would, and cumbia is the obvious choice. So back I go to the place I saw the most frilly dresses, two-tone hats and head-balancing of alcohol: Barranquilla.

There's something about the latest dance school that reminds me of swimming baths. The walls resound with squeaking trainers and echoing voices and the air is heavy with poolside levels of humidity. Every time I take a breath, I do so genuinely expecting to smell chlorine.

All it's missing is a load of damp-haired children squabbling at the vending machine. And a very young me getting my 10-metre badge for the umpteenth time as a side-effect of my attempts to avoid graduating to the bigger pool – I used to be as apprehensive of deep water as I am of dance floors.

"Cumbia's easy, isn't it?" I say to Juliana, my teacher.

Juliana speaks good English. This in itself is great news as it means that for once I won't have to combine dance lessons with Spanish lessons.

"After *mapalé*," she says, "everything is easy!"

Excellent – that's exactly the answer I was fishing for.

The dance studio is a long low room with fans and mirrors, the veneer on the floor tiles showing wear from years of diligent learning. There's not much time to take it all in, though, as we get straight to work with the basic cumbia footwork. Juliana quickly has me advancing in the basic shuffling *paso*, which actually means kind of sideways-orientated, like a swordsman.

Cumbia music originated in Colombia, with its roots supposedly in Guinean *cumbé*, but spread to various other parts of Latin America, including Mexico, Peru and Argentina, mutating along the way and developing into subgenres such as *technocumbia* and *cumbia villera* (shanty-town cumbia).

The music is recognisable across the board, but the way it is danced in other countries bears little relation to this Colombian style. I've heard from a couple of different locals that the shuffling of the home-grown style is a reference to when slaves used to wear leg-irons, whilst there is also some suggestion that the dance represents courtship between African men and indigenous women.

Before long I'm shuffling – well, squeaking – up and down the well-worn dance floor like a pro; my hips shifting naturally with the rhythm, and my feet kept close like a shackled slave. Which I am, of course – a slave to dance, baby!

Presumably impressed by my lower-limb movements, Juliana soon has me adding some upper-body relatives. Cumbia is an old-school flirtation and involves minimal contact between the partners, so many of these movements are wooing in their nature, and involve using my *sombrero vueltiao* as a prop. And a pretty well-designed prop at that, as I can store it on my head when I don't need it.

First there's the 'sweep', as I'm going to call it, where you advance sideways with arms up and open, like the Y in YMCA, then sweep the hat downwards and in front. This is the one I was aping in the *palco* in Barranquilla.

Then there's the 'distress call' where you wave your hands about your head to catch her eye. Or to urge people to rescue you from the dance floor, one of the two.

Finally, there's the 'waft', where you wave your hat at her hip-region as you both advance. It's meant to draw attention to her seductive hip movements, though when I do it, it just looks like she's farted and I'm wafting it away. Although I suppose this would at least make me a gentleman.

Juliana is toned and athletic, her dark hair slicked back into a pony tail giving the look of a Spanish flamenco dancer. She has an unpretentious way about her and the natural resting position of her face tends towards a smile.

The music has the *pum-pata pum-pata pum-pata* rhythm I just about recognise from Carnival; all shakers and pinging drum skins. It seems to have a really strong 2/4 time, making you want to dance in a very simple left-right marching rhythm. It's music to climb stairs to.

The track we're focussing on today has lyrics referring to the 'King of Cumbia'. This is clearly a reference to, well, me: we're only an hour in and I can already do plenty enough to perform a single dance. I mean, how much more can there be to learn?

Hey – imagine I was at Carnival, and one of the cumbia dancers collapsed, leaving them a man short.

"Is there anyone out there who can help us?" the troupe leader shouts into the *palco*.

"Yes!" I say, vaulting the barrier. "Let me dance instead! I'm an expert at cumbia!"

"I meant help save the dying man."

"Oh yeah, sorry."

"I mean, hey, why not go through his wallet, while you're at it?"

"I said I was sorry."

But he won't let it drop and we end up wrestling on the tarmac in front of shocked onlookers. I have some strange daydreams sometimes.

Given the sheer variety of musical genres, it's helpful when, as with this track, the name of the genre pops up in the lyrics. This kind of name-checking seems to be particularly common with the more obscure genres: the best known *mapalé* tracks in full flow are largely a repetition of the genre name, whilst *garabato* and *puya* are similarly self-referential.

It's this last genre which Juliana suggests we end the lesson with – the crazy snake-charmer music from Carnival. I remember mentally labelling this a dance to be avoided, though I can't quite recall why. I guess I must just have some long-repressed Indiana Jones-esque fear of snakes.

She gets me flicking my heels inwards one after the other – *ba-DAM, ba-DAM, ba-DAM.* I'm meant to do about twice as quickly as seems reasonable.

After my *mapalé* experience I'm wary that I might pull a muscle somewhere weird, like my footwear. But it's only when attention shifts to up-top that I remember why the *puya* is truly out of the question: it's the one with the shoulder shimmy that makes me look like I'm having a grand mal.

I tell Juliana I'd rather stick to what I'm good at, and what I'm good at is clearly cumbia, which I've nailed already. Like I said, I'm the king.

Staying in guest houses can be quite an isolating experience, so this time I've opted for a homestay with a couple that a friend put me in touch with.

With the living quarters elevated onto the upper floor, their house feels more like a flat. As I enter, I'm greeted by a ridiculously low fan with thin metal blades that would do a good line in cheap haircuts if it was ever switched on.

I wonder how Carl's doing.

The place is located in the pleasant and rich northern part of the city's grid-system streets. Here, on the back streets, the streets are quiet and have a hot dustiness to them. It's all condominiums, detached modern houses, and the occasional apartment block, rendered in sun-faded colours, like a 70s postcard.

Barranquilla was once standard-bearer of modernity. It had a whole bunch of 'firsts' on Colombian soil – first radio station, first airline, first planned elite neighbourhood – as well as top notch municipal services. But during the latter half of the twentieth century it fell into economic decline. Although, from what I've seen, it still single-handedly props up the country's neon wig, spray foam and corn flour industries.

Everywhere in this part is gated and grilled, to stop the haves becoming have-somewhat-lesses. If it weren't for the odd horse-drawn rag-and-bone cart clattering past, street-sellers yelling "*¡Aguacate!*" (Avocado!), and dirty, throttling *busetas*, you could almost be in North America.

Ryan is from New Zealand, and is a year older than me. Angélica, his wife, is in her early twenties. Her English is excellent, which is just as well since he speaks practically no Spanish. They've been together for two years, but they only got married a month or two ago and it shows: they give each other little hugs and touches every time they pass each other by.

They're both welcoming and generous hosts, but with quite distinct personalities.

Ryan is a logical and direct guy, and likes to ask "What are you talking about?" if he doesn't understand your point, which invariably makes me think "Yes, what am I talking about?"

Angélica, meanwhile, is all Colombian woman: voluptuous with a round face and a big sunny smile. She's also remarkably open: within about an hour of meeting, she's explaining to me in quite some detail about the intimate health problems she's currently suffering.

"They're very comfortable with their bodies out here," says Ryan.

They're not the only ones – it's not for no reason that I've awarded myself the title of King of Cumbia. I wander in for my next lesson just like dance royalty, except without a robe or sceptre. Which is a bit of a shame given how much cumbia loves its props.

But something's changed – and for the worse. Instead of being fawned over by doting subjects, this monarch is about to be rudely dethroned. No sooner have we started than Juliana is pointing out I'm doing something fundamentally wrong. Instead of gliding along like a glider, I'm bouncing along like a bouncer.

And the problem? My hips.

All this time, I've been throwing them forward in time with each forward shuffle; complementing the movement. But this means that instead of negating the natural up-and-down, I'm exaggerating it. The backwards swing is the one that should align with my advances, not the forward one.

This is no two-second correction: body parts are connected, else we'd all just be piles of limbs, heads and torsos. Changing the hip-movement changes everything: it's like starting all over again.

"Imagine you have a glass of water on your head," says Juliana.

Only if you'll imagine you've got a mop handy. I try it again and again, but I just can't crack it at all. It's like trying to fold your arms the other way: it just feels… wrong.

"Like you are flying."

But the metaphor's not the problem – my body is. My plane remains beset by never-ending turbulence.

I don't get it: it looks so easy and natural when she does it. But then, in the world of dance, few things are as easy as they look. Apart from *mapalé* which, as discussed, is almost exactly as easy as it looks.

There's more. Not only am I moving in the wrong manner, I'm moving on the wrong beat. There are three drums, as Juliana explains: the *tambor alegre* (happy drum) the *tambora* (low drum) and the *llamador* (caller drum).

"You hear that little drum?" she asks.

As mentioned, I used to play the drums, so I do have an ear for these things. I delve around in the music, like a security official searching for a camouflaged drugs laboratory in the jungle.

......*tak* ......*tak* ......*tak* ......*tak*

Yeah, I've got it. It's high in the register, on the off-beat.

"That's the *llamador.*"

Suddenly the syncopated hand-clapping at Carnival makes sense: they were clapping along with the *llamador.* And that's the beat I'm meant to go on.

But even this new knowledge can't detract from my sudden fall. I simply can't catch the timing, and even if I could my movements are all wonky. We forget all the other stuff and practise simply shuffling up and down the hall. But I've lost all intuitive sense of what's right and wrong.

I sit despondently in the back of the taxi on my way home. Earlier the same day I was up there buzzing about in the clouds, but now I can't even get the damn engine started. What's it going to take for me to make a success of this? Maybe I'm just not cut out for this kind of thing. And what's the point of it all, anyway? I mean, unless I discover a hitherto unknown network of cumbia clubs, what use will any of this be back home?

Things are always lively in the flat due to the full occupancy. Ryan works at a desk near the entrance, giving him the semblance of a receptionist, whilst Angélica's health problems means she's also at home, mostly on the games console slaying pixels. Then there's Marina, a friend of Angélica's who's staying with the couple for a while. And finally, there's the itinerant dancer from the UK, here on the questionable notion that learning obscure Colombian folk dances will somehow enhance his life.

When Angélica is allowing the console to cool down slightly, the stereo is on, delivering an unbroken stream of merengue, salsa, reggaeton, (Brazilian) samba and *champeta.*

"My friend says you can dance anything to *champeta,*" says Marina. "You can even make a burger."

She demonstrates, gyrating her hips sensually whilst processing the imaginary foodstuff with her hands – bread… meat… salad… ketchup… more bread – before handing it over. What can I say? I'm impressed. Although I wouldn't normally have so much onion.

Dance is clearly a major fixture in this house, an idea reinforced in my mind when we sit down together to watch Ryan and Angélica's wedding DVD.

The film starts with the ceremony, which consists of a whole lot of Angélica looking beautiful and of Ryan looking for help with the language. From here, the action moves on to the wedding reception, where the newlyweds' first dance is merengue. As is their second dance. In fact all of Ryan and Angélica's dances are merengue, even when the music is salsa.

But whilst he only knows one dance, I'm genuinely struck by how the learning of this has added immeasurably to their special day – it's genuinely touching. It also reassures me that what I'm doing out here has some genuine value.

There is something faintly comical about merengue, however. It largely involves the hips swinging emphatically from side to side, uniting the partners in a rocking motion that looks more daft than flirty. Nonetheless, it's clearly a useful dance and looks like a lot of fun, and I do find myself feeling rather envious.

It soon becomes clear that the Wedding DVD is actually largely just extended coverage of people dancing. For Angélica and Marina, this is bliss: they watch it devotedly for its entire length, passing comment on the various dancers.

Judging from the video, Ryan's dad turns out to be an accomplished *salsero,* executing a constant sequence of *vueltas,* sending her every which way. Marina explains that she found this difficult, as they simply don't do so many turns out here.

"I didn't know where he wanted me to go."

Regardless, he's definitely got something I haven't. When I dance salsa, I spend much of my time trapped in one of the basic *pasos,* plotting my escape to the next. But this guy is right in the zone, switching at will – he's immersed in the music and the physical movements are just following. I'd love to be at that kind of level.

Out of nowhere the reception is interrupted by a great cacophony of noise and action as a troupe of female samba dancers enter in a flurry of whistles – shock therapy intended to lift proceedings. Angélica and Marina reveal that they weren't particularly impressed with them: they themselves can both samba, and had hoped these hired dancers would be better.

It must be tough being a professional dancer in a country where everyone's pretty much an expert.

I'm enjoying my time in Ryan and Angélica's flat, but it's a small place and I sense they could do with a bit of time to themselves. I deduce this from the way Ryan keeps suggesting I go out and see more of the city.

It's probably a good thing for me, too. The dance isn't going well, and I feel like I need a break from all this exposure to it, so I swap the cool air con of the flat for the baking sidewalks.

Up at the nearby mall, palm trees wave from the desertified strips of grass that separate the hot concrete lanes. You'd never know that much of the surrounding coastal area was swampy delta. But there's an unexpected contrast, as pointed out to me by a girl I met at Carnival and briefly catch up with again, now.

"*¡Acá es como un río!*" she says as we cross a completely dry road in the south of the city. Here it's like a river!

She's referring to a phenomenon that commonly afflicts Barranquilla – street rivers. Known as *arroyos*, they can spring up after even moderate levels of rainfall, coursing down the city's inclined thoroughfares. In wet season things can get particularly dangerous, with cars being washed clean down the street. Road signs warn of danger spots, whilst deflective concrete walls and barriers sit at strategic points on the sidewalk, reflecting a sense of inevitability about the occurrences.

There's a more permanent flow of water than the arroyos, however. After a thousand-mile travail from the Andes, the mighty Magdalena River finally prostrates itself to a higher power here at Barranquilla. Rather than expiring naturally, a man-made breakwater extends into the sea adjacent to a spit of land at a point called Bocas de Ceniza (Mouths of Ash). It's only this piece of mid-twentieth century engineering that makes Barranquilla a sea-port, and this is the next place I head, this time on my own.

I peel myself off the taxi's seat and scuffle up the unpaved road; dragging my feet a little feels natural in this climate. Two hard metal lines in the dirt mark the start of an old railway track that runs from the mainland out onto the breakwater. Here, a rickety little *trencito* – an open, metal-framed vehicle with tiny wheels – waits for action, with a few bare-chested local men hanging off its frame. It turns out, however that they won't depart with only one passenger, so instead I accept the offer of a motorbike ride from another young man nearby.

Soon the driver and I are charging along a path next to the railway, hemmed in between a barrier of trees to the left and the brimming river to our right. At first it's all very pleasant – the warm breeze whipping at my clothes and ruffling my hair – but then the land starts to thin out and we have to mount the railway track. Here the sleepers protrude like the ribs of a street dog, and we end up juddering along in a manner not unlike my recent attempts at cumbia.

My innards aren't up to this kind of battering and I have to resort to using my arms and legs as shock absorbers, lifting my backside clean off the seat. The driver tells me he's been doing this job for six years. He must have mush for organs.

As we head out along the spit, a curious anomaly becomes apparent: the water on the right (the river) is a dull shade of grey from the silt it's carrying. But on the left (the sea) it's a wicked blue.

Bounding onwards, we pass through a ramshackle and largely-deserted settlement of small wooden buildings. There's even a tiny railway station with gaily-painted signs and murals that have long since faded. It's like an old seaside town past its heyday, except that it's also a riverside town.

The spit thins out, as do the huts, and we come to a halt – this is as far as the *moto* driver will take me. He pootles off behind me in a trail of dust and I continue on foot, past jeans left to dry on rocks and innumerable discarded flip-flops.

The track eventually gives up the fight, whilst the huts get progressively more basic: wooden poles and plastic sheeting. One has a politician's face from a plastic campaign banner as the wall. I suppose he can at least say he's done something to help the poor.

On the grey side, big container ships pass silently to and from port, whilst on the blue side, sea-worn fishermen sit on rocks, working the waters with lengths of nylon. Spray bursts up around and about them, the sun illuminating the individual beads about their heads. One of them tells me he comes out here for a few days at a time to make his living, sleeping in one of the rough huts, then heads back to his wife on the mainland.

Ultimately I reach the end of the causeway, where the alluvium blooms into the open sea; presumably what gives the place its

Mouths of Ash moniker. Here, a guy is fishing from the end boulders, a skate lying flat on a discarded sleeper nearby.

"*¿Cómo está la vida?*" I call to him. How's life?

"*¡Gozándola!*" Enjoying it!

I really like this country, and this attitude to life. Everything suddenly seems so simple when you only have frivolous stuff like providing for your family to worry about.

Arriving back at the dance school for my next lesson, I'm mentally prepared for my inevitable rubbishness. The gods of dance must be bored, however. Because this time I hit the dance floor and... I can do it! I can shuffle correctly! It's almost as if my brain just needed a bit of time to absorb the new relationship between feet and hips. Or I've been sleep-dancing again – one of the two. It's not like I got much practice in.

My new-found shuffle is not completely instinctive yet – I still have to concentrate – but it's as though the existing wires in my brain have been ripped out and new ones installed. We do some laps of the dance floor to consolidate, and the very same action that felt wrong yesterday now feels right.

There's so much freedom in cumbia that the more moves I know, the better. So Juliana helps further increase my vocabulary, teaching me flirtatious gestures with which to punctuate the dance. In one of them I come to a dead stop and affect surprise at her beauty, whilst in another I offer her my heart. She doesn't accept, though – I believe that's more of an Aztec thing.

"He has to do different things to make her happy," says Juliana. "He has to do many things, like in real life."

I'm meant to do stuff in real life? That explains a lot.

A further gesture involves me dropping to one knee and expressing my adoration for her while she dances around me.

"You look like Shakespeare!"

The turns, meanwhile, are less orchestrated but are my favourite part. You orientate yourself back to back with your partner, albeit somewhat offset. You then gyrate together, eyes meeting across conjoined shoulders, before switching and repeating in the opposite direction. It gives you this wonderful sense of perpetual falling, and in the context of such a slow dance it feels giddily dynamic.

Seemingly from nowhere, I'm well on the way to being able to dance a decent cumbia. Not an amazing one, but a decent one.

Success! Failure! These early extremes are clearly not to be trusted. I feel like I'm learning as much about learning to dance as I am about the dances themselves.

Angélica is busy in her room readying herself when Marina and Angélica's sister come round, so they tease her by loudly affecting sex noises outside the closed door. She pokes her head through the gap, protesting her innocence. She can't do any such thing at the moment – she's ill! But this just means they both wonder aloud to each other how she copes.

"I've got hands! I've got a mouth!" she says. "I've got an imagination!"

Crikey, girl – no-one else needs one.

But whilst everyone else is comfortable with their bodies, I'm still some way short: my new-found cumbia skills don't seem to be translating to extra dance-floor confidence. Once the clanking of dinner-time cutlery has come to an end, Ryan and I sit round a table with the sister's boyfriend, watching the three girls dance, displaying total mastery of their hips.

This hip-based stuff is remarkably sexy. Even a very average woman can take on the semblance of a goddess just by knowing how to work her coastal regions, and these women are already far from average. There are some people, however, who think I've done enough watching other people's movements for one day.

"You're here to learn how to dance," says Ryan. "You should be up dancing!"

"You expect me to get up and humiliate myself?!"

I'm trying to make a joke of it, but yes – why wouldn't I?

Well, today's excuse is that my dance fears are amplified by the girls' very presence. After all, if someone was up on stage playing the trumpet really well, would you really want to get up there and force out a string of bizarre parping sounds? Or even play the trumpet badly, for that matter.

It's actually a bit of a strange social mixture, as everyone is in their early twenties except for Ryan and me.

"We're like the grandpas of the group," I say to him.

"Are you suggesting I'm a cradle-snatcher?"

Oh, well I didn't mean… I wasn't saying… what I meant

was... I'll shut up.

I don't judge Ryan in the slightest, but the age gap thing does highlight a minor frustration for me. Some part of me had kind of hoped I might meet someone out here, maybe even fall in love. But people marry younger here, so the single, available Colombian women I meet tend to be in their early twenties. Whereas ideally I'd like to meet someone that has long since lost all their youthful optimism and is just a worn-out husk of a person with nothing to share but resentment. You know – someone in the same life stage.

I did recently get a phone number off a cute thirty-something Bogotana, and I also went on a date in Cartagena – kept that quiet, didn't I? But given the time it takes to build a relationship (especially with the *poco a poco* approach), and the fact that I'm zipping about everywhere, it's pretty unlikely anything is going to happen.

Angélica, Ryan's Colombian wife, is next to try and convince me to dance, which makes me feel even more ridiculous given her own situation.

"She's just had an operation," says Ryan. "She shouldn't be dancing."

But then I guess it's hard to stop doing something when you're having fun. Just ask Álvaro Uribe, Colombia's president – he was only meant to get a single term of four years, but had the constitution democratically amended so he could run for another four. The electorate, wooed by improvements in the security situation, duly voted him back in. His request for a third term, however, has been denied – it's someone else's turn to take the floor.

Me.

I don't mean I'm going to be president, I mean... oh you know. In a burst of courage, I launch myself out of my chair, leaving my comfort zone behind – such things have to be done quickly so my brain has no time to register complaint.

I take Marina's hand and we begin dancing together to the salsa from the stereo. Now I'm up there I realise I'm actually fairly competent. Okay so my repertoire of turns is extremely limited but I remember what she said about the wedding video, and that calms me down. We even dance a quick bit of cumbia together. It's not long enough to really show what I've learnt, but the fact I can do it at all seems to rather impress her.

Once again, I'm left wondering why it always takes me so damn long to get started.

It's my final day in Barranquilla, and my final dance lesson. I've got all the pieces I need to dance cumbia – I just need to glue them together.

This isn't as easy as it sounds. Although the man leads in cumbia, he has little control over what she's going to do in response because he's not physically guiding his partner. This means he needs to be reactive to her movements, too. Or just use a sheepdog to harry her into position, though I suspect that might breach certain rules of etiquette (not to mention gender equality).

So although the dance seems fairly sedate, my mind courses like an *arroyo* in wet season when I'm doing it, and this means I make mistakes. Sometimes I mess up the footwork and have to pull myself back in line, whilst other times I simply hesitate for far too long as I seek out the appropriate weapon from my cumbia armoury. But after several dances, the progress I've made is clear: we're extemporising entire dances to the music. I've reached a whole new level.

For our final dance together, Juliana changes into a voluminous, red gingham skirt with multiple layers, each trimmed with white lace. It's not the full-length shoulder-down item – sometimes called a *pollera*, and referenced in the famous cumbia track La Pollera Colorá (The Red Pollera) by Wilson Choperena – but it's more than enough for what we're doing. She looks poised and elegant, like a jewellery box ballerina. She doesn't make that sproinging sound, though.

We're lacking the extra props like the clutch of lit candles that the man traditionally offers the woman, as referenced in the *mapalé*-influenced cumbia classic Prende La Vela (Light The Candle). But maybe it's not such a bad thing: Juliana tells me of an accident on stage some years ago, where a dancer caught fire.

"He was in hospital for 3 weeks, then he died. So now we aren't allowed to use candles on the *¿escenario?* … stage!"

The flute and drums start up, and I shuffle towards her, lightly gripping my *sombrero vueltiao*. From here, I gradually weave in my whole repertoire – rushing in and retreating, getting her attention with my arms and making sweeping gestures with my hat.

Juliana responds with a rocking hip gesture that's like the combination of a sideways glance, a beckoning finger and a raise of the eyebrow all rolled into one, the backs of her hands gently resting on those hips, creating a look of flirty mock-impatience.

We dive into elegant turns together, she ruffles her dress at me tantalisingly and, ultimately, I offer her my heart.

We're done.

It's time to pack up and go, and the former won't take long given it only involves putting my hat in my bag. As a parting note, Juliana tells me she's really impressed with my progress: few people pick up cumbia in such a short space of time. I head off into the heat of Barranquilla feeling satisfaction rather than smugness: I can genuinely perform a Colombian folkloric dance.

Well, okay, maybe a little bit of smugness.

I've still got another farewell remaining, however: to my hosts.

It's only been raining for a few hours when we leave the house that evening to head out to a bar, but it's long enough: water has formed into torrents at the edges of the cambered street, and we have to leap over one to reach the car and keep our feet dry. Once en route, the driver has to use something approaching 'the knowledge' in order to avoid the roads that may have become impromptu rivers.

"This is nothing," says Ryan.

Apparently, it frequently reaches a height at which regular footwear becomes pointless.

At least my own journey is starting to look like something other than a washout. What awaits me next, who knows, but in the space of a week I've not only secured my stay in the country, but I've genuinely added cumbia to my dance repertoire. Even the imaginary Carnival bloke would be impressed.

"Forget the old dude – get your arse over these railings and let's dance some cumbia!"

"Oh and drag the body to one side if it's in your way."

You betcha!

CHAPTER TEN

Holy Moly

I've never been sold on the idea of modern-day 'adventure tourism'. For me, adventures should involve chewing your way through undergrowth with your bare teeth, punching gibbons and patching up wounds with wet Sellotape. Going on a well-established tour that sets off daily, led by guides who cater for all your needs is only as 'out there' as going to a job interview wearing a loud tie.

And that's how it's been so far with the Ciudad Perdida (Lost City) tour, a trek to the ruins of a Tairona city hidden on a jungle-clad mountain-side, on which the guides did pretty much everything for us bar the hiking itself.

However, the sight that greets me now, on the third day of the five-day trek, is worth all the mock-exploring and photo opportunities with tourist-weary *indígenas*.

Circumstance (well, okay, a toilet stop) has left me well behind the rest of the group, so there's just me and a guide. We criss-cross a rocky stream repeatedly before arriving at a point on the river bank where a muddy path cuts up and disappears into the steep undergrowth. The guide tells me he won't be accompanying me any further, play-acting that he has sore testicles from mule riding.

"*¡Arriba!*" Go up!

I take the first few uncertain steps on the greasy track, slithering about in my wet sandals. A few steps more and I finally see what the last two days of trekking have been all about.

They're just rough, moss-bearing stone blocks, but after nearly three days trekking, deeper and deeper into the jungle, their appearance is jarring and potent. Each one is like the dull clang of an ancient bell, and together they form a set of stairs that climb upwards into the unknown.

This is it: the entrance to the Lost City.

No wonder the colonial Spanish never found this site. Indeed it went undiscovered up until the 1970s, though local indigenous people never actually lost it – they just kept quiet about it and turned up now and then to trim the borders and pull out any weeds and such.

"*¡Arriba!*" says the guide once more, as though I'm perhaps unfamiliar with the concept. Something about me must scream 'bungalow owner from the Netherlands'.

With Semana Santa (Holy Week) fast approaching and Colombia being a religious country, everything was coming to a halt. This left me with a natural break in my dance schedule, and hence an opportunity to do a spot of more-conventional tourism.

After an arse-wrenching journey up a dirt track in a 4x4, myself and some other foreigners set off on foot into the wilds, complementing the sounds of bird chatter with those of ripping Velcro and swearing in international English.

What followed was two days of uphill trekking on paths that wound in and out of jungle, with only the waxy foliage and the cool river to tame the sun's menace, plus two nights of sleeping on plastic-sealed mattresses, else in hammocks suspended from wooden frames.

Columns of leafcutter ants, on their global deforestation programme, crossed the trail, carrying dismembered plants from one side to the other, despite there being plenty of plants on the side they were already on.

"Why go to so much effort to do something you don't actually need to?" I found myself wondering, during the strenuous trek to discover something that other people had discovered decades earlier, itself part of a bigger journey to learn dances which would mostly be of no use to me once I left the country.

The route traced a path into the jungle-clad foothills of the Sierra Nevada de Santa Marta, which is the highest coastal mountain range in the world. At clear of 5,000 metres above sea level, it's also home to the tallest peak in Colombia, a fact which is even more remarkable given that the range is entirely separate from the Andes. It's a rounded cluster that hangs about on its own; a line-dancer looking for a line.

The mountains are highly venerated by the local indigenous people, such as the Kogi and Arhuaco, descendants of the Tairona people who used to inhabit the coast. There are thought to be 87 distinct groups of indigenous people in Colombia, making up 3.4% of the population, with the ones that have best managed to maintain their cultural identity often being those in remote locations such as this.

Both the Kogi and the Arhuaco peoples have sleek black hair and a rich reddish-brown skin tone, and wear their own subtly different combinations of cream-coloured tunics, trousers and woven hats and bags, making it quite difficult to tell them apart.

We had frequent near-contact with them en route, especially with the Kogi people. They see this cluster of mountains as 'the heart of the world' and the earth as a living being, and believe that many of man's modern activities are hurting the planet. I guess they're just too primitive to understand the full benefits of things like pollution and global warming.

At one point we passed a tribal leader with his arm in a sling – he'd broken it and had been to the nearby city of Santa Marta to get fixed up. Another rode by with a battery-powered radio pressed to his ear for entertainment. But even when they were near us they were distant, and only seemed comfortable talking to our guides. Not that I'd have known what to say had I had the opportunity.

"Hey there! We're the people screwing the planet!"

Their settlements consist of little villages of circular wooden huts with conical, thatched roofs. On one occasion a guide coaxed a family out by the cunning use of bait – lollipops for the children – and they posed quietly for photographs. The tribes are apparently recompensed for allowing tour groups through their reservation, but I still felt uncomfortable.

It's not an easy time for Colombia's indigenous peoples. Some of the groups that survived the colonial era intact, such as the Nukak people from the fringes of the Amazon, are more vulnerable than ever, with displacement due to the civil war and the narcotics trade a particular threat. Of a total population of 46 million, around 4 million of Colombia's inhabitants, indigenous or otherwise, have been forcibly displaced as a result of the conflict.

Back in the here and now, my hamstrings feel as leaden as the stones themselves as I continue ascending, pushing ever upwards through jungle dripping with creepers, to the crunch of dead leaves. Some cumbia would really help me out here. Finally, after traversing well over a thousand steps, I reach the outskirts of the ruins.

I saw the picture postcard photo of The Lost City before I even arrived in the country, so my expectations are low. In fact, I distinctly remember thinking "Is that it?" – it was just a bunch of green platforms encircled by stone. They looked like cake platters without the cakes or statue-less plinths; like theatrical curtains had been opened to great fanfare to reveal an empty stage.

But now, as I reach the shaded outlying part of the ruins, I feel only excitement. Much as I imagine did the looters that rediscovered the site back in 1972.

"What an amazing opportunity to expand our understanding of our proud nation's history and culture," they must have thought as they charged down the hillside with arms full of precious artefacts.

Further sets of stairs carry me higher and higher still, until finally, momentously, I burst out from the upper foliage and into the open. And suddenly there I am, atop the main platter, lifting me up out of the foliage like the open palm of a deity. On one side, rainforest canopy stretches out, rolling out and rearing up into jungle-clad hills and mountains, whilst on the other, tall palms rise up like hosannas.

It's safe to say the photos didn't do it justice.

Behind the site, rounded terraces clamber higher still up the vertiginous hillside, and I can see soldiers milling about up there in their camouflage gear (not enough mossy-stone patterning, evidently).

This area has historically hosted all three sides of the civil conflict: left-wing guerrillas (the ELN, a group which dates back to the 1960s, kidnapped a group of tourists in 2003); right-wing paramilitaries (there to deal with the former); and the army (to protect tourists from the first two).

The guerrillas are the ones who get all the press globally, more usually the FARC than the ELN, but according to the UN, they're only responsible for 12% of killings. 80% of killings are attributable to paramilitary groups, who historically have also done a nice line in human rights abuses and brutal massacres.

The role of paramilitaries has been as the hired militia of landowners, politicians and drug cartels, protecting them from the activities of left-wing guerrillas. Some claim they've also been used by the military as a way of outsourcing some of their less-palatable counterinsurgent activities. In recent times they've been encouraged to demobilise, but this has met with mixed results and some have simply gone on to form criminal gangs.

Whatever the bigger picture is, the military feel like a reassuring presence here in the wilds, and the ones who we've passed on the trail have all been friendly and approachable.

A few of us clamber up the stone steps to where they're based. From here you can see clearly how each of the various circular plazas is outlined by a succession of terraces below, making them look like the contour lines on a relief map.

Eight soldiers sit on a low wall with their weaponry slung about them. This is the military hangout and evidently the best tactical position. It's also, from the look of things, the place where they all get their hair cut. The view is great, but there are some things a photo can't capture: the serenity; the freshness; the military hair clippings.

The soldiers are young and friendly, but seem a little bored. I wonder if any of them were about when British politician Michael Fabricant, on a trekking holiday, had to eat mouthfuls of coffee whitener at gunpoint to prove it wasn't anything stronger.

It doesn't look like there's much for the soldiers to do except listen to their little portable radio and receive haircuts, so I ask them if they ever dance up here. This is partly because of my interest in the subject, but also because I like asking people stupid questions.

"You can't," is the answer, the main obstacle also being the most obvious one – a distinct lack of women.

"They're the only ones," says one, gesturing to the girls in our group.

At this point I make a sudden, unforced confession. Despite there being no bright lamp pointed in my face (other than the big yellow one in the sky), I start blabbing all about my secret dance mission. Some part of me is urging me to shut up, as the outcome is predictable to anyone who has ever watched a Western – some men with guns expect me to dance for them.

With a sigh of resignation, I commence some rudimentary taps with the point of my feet to either side. A big cheer goes up, completely out of proportion with the amount of skill involved – they recognise it as something vaguely *champeta*-like, and that's good enough. Buoyed by this, I switch to the super-daft jelly legs and lasso, to further cheers.

I can see this is becoming a trend on my journey: I successfully entertain a group of people with my novelty-dancing-foreigner routine then come away feeling like I've lost something I can never get back. At least they offer me a haircut, something I accept as I'm in dire need of one.

I perch on a stone and the barber quickly gets started, bringing some discipline to the unruly mess. He spends a good twenty minutes to half an hour snipping away, the scent of rainforest mulch mixing with that of freshly cut hair as the unruly locks are sent skipping down my back.

I look in the mirror and I'm delighted – he's done a very professional job.

"He's an expert," says a fellow soldier.

He then whips out the clippers and shaves damn near the whole lot off, leaving just a regulation tuft at the front. Oh well.

I smile and thank them then leave, treading gingerly as I negotiate the steps back down – some of the stones rock as I tread on them.

"You can't dance *champeta*!" one of the soldiers calls down.

I think he means on the stairs, though it probably applies in general, too.

Two days later, we're back at the small group of huts that marks the start point, awaiting a lift back to civilisation, my hair now tuft-less since I snipped it away with nail scissors. To kill time, our guides propose we play *tejo* – a typical Colombian game that dates back hundreds of years and was played by indigenous people in the Andean region to the north of Bogotá.

Tejo is played on a pitch consisting of two angled beds of clay situated some distance apart. The idea is to stand in front of one of the beds and throw circular metal weights, or *tejos*, into the clay of the other. Adding some spice to the game are the little packets of gunpowder arranged in a circle, which can go off if struck by the *tejo*. This is an infrequent event, though – one Colombian friend told me she'd never managed one even when she'd pitched from 20 centimetres away.

A stocky, shaven-headed guide sets the victory prize – the losers will pay for a round of drinks. Right on cue, five open beers, complete with palate-teasing condensation, arrive from the nearby café. They sit there on the wooden sideboard like a line of golden trophies, waiting to be claimed.

The game turns out to be harder than it looks. The weights require significant force to launch the distance, and a good trajectory is vital: low slung shots tend to fall short and end up half bouncing, half rolling to the clay.

Both the two guides – one on each side – are competent players, with the stocky one particularly good. One of my fellow trekkers, an Aussie, is also proficient, assimilating the technique expertly. Between the three of them, pretty much every shot thuds satisfyingly into the distant clay.

A Swiss bloke and I, however, are in some whole other league, and it's definitely a lower one. One of my many errant shots sends a nearby mule bolting, whilst the Swiss guy has to pursue one of his own down the hill, like it's Gloucestershire cheese-rolling we're taking part in. We also both try our hands at demolishing a nearby building.

Just as I'm considering preceding all of my shots with "Fore!" to reduce the chances of maiming passers-by, something unexpected happens. My shot sails through the air… it wobbles towards the clay bed…

BANG!

Holy crap!

"COME ON!" I wheel about with clenched fists. "WOO-HOO! WHO'S THE DADDY?"

Our team loses in the end, by 30 *manos* (hands) to 29, but I made a bang happen, so I'm the real winner. But before anyone can enjoy their cold beer, a mule, possibly on a revenge mission, clangs into the sideboard and totals all five of them, leaving them foaming their guts out on the wooden shelf.

Holy week is no longer approaching, it's already here, and vast numbers of Colombian families are descending on the coast. I've landed in nearby Santa Marta – a port city with a narrow strip of beach that disappears when the tide comes in to meet the promenade. Not that you can see much of the sand even when the tide's out – it's elbow-jostlingly popular. People splash around in the water, leap off the sea-wall and generally muck about, unconcerned by the fact they're sharing the bay with a terminal for container ships.

The city's colonial centre is elegant at its heart then decays into fading grandeur as it crosses town, the crumbling old buildings housing billiard halls and brothels. Back in the early part of the 20th Century, it was exactly such places that helped spread new music, their jukeboxes playing records from Europe, North America and other parts of Latin America.

Young women in doorways call out to me as I pass, trying to engage me in conversation, but ultimately just resorting to yelling "*¡SEXO!*" down the street after me. I've not had a chance to look it up yet, so I don't know what it means.

Santa Marta was, in fact, the first place settled by the Spanish conquistadors in what we now call Colombia. Arriving here at all was arguably a bit of a gamble given how technology can progress at different speeds in isolation: they'd have looked well marching up the beach in full colonial pomp only to be cut down by laser cannons or molecule disassemblers.

The indigenous Tairona people who inhabited the region at the time possessed no such technology, but they were still determined to resist enslavement by the Spanish. So they left the coastal lowlands behind and sought refuge in the aforementioned Sierra Nevada de Santa Marta. The Spanish ultimately won them over, though – if you can call killing most of them 'winning them over' – and much of their former territory became engulfed in jungle.

It was a common story in other parts of Colombia, with the Spanish attempting to subjugate the indigenous peoples they encountered, or at least those that were non-violent and conveniently-situated. What opposition there was often dwindled pretty quickly as the Indigenous people died out for one reason or another. In fact, whether by direct force, the side-effects subjugation or just the classic gift of old-world diseases, the Spanish seemed quite incapable of not killing the pre-existing local populace.

Slowly the Spanish took a grip over the new territory and forced the non-dead indigenous people into the *encomienda* tribute system whereby they had to provide the Spanish with food and labour, and sometimes even gold, in exchange for the privilege of having colonial overlords.

It's a wonder the Spanish continued to press inland at all given the immediate proximity to the legendary kickback zones of Tayrona (with a 'y' this time) National Natural Park and Taganga. The former is travel-brochure porn – a melange of boulder-strewn beaches, crashing waves and swinging hammocks – and the latter a sleepy fishing village which has been slapped awake by its recent arrival as a prime backpacker destination.

In Taganga I find it easy enough to forget I'm in Colombia at all, let alone here on a dance mission. It made the mistake of being an idyllic village only ten minutes bus ride from Santa Marta, and hiding behind a big hill was never going to be enough. Restaurant signs are in English and Hebrew, and the gentle fluttering of palms intermingles with semi-inebriated voices in a variety of languages.

But the indications are always there if you know what to look for. As I leave, I spot some little kid by the side of the road doing the jelly legs and lasso. Despite carrying stupidly-heavy luggage, I just can't help myself – I stop where I am in the middle of the road and do my own version, my knees straining under the weight. The kid squeals with delight and her and her friends call after me as I stagger off.

"Again! Again!"

I realise that I'm now trundling around a little aimlessly. In Colombia, Holy Week is not just time off, it has a really strong cultural significance, so I should really try and get somewhere that can do it justice.

The not-too-distant town of Mompós is renowned for its Semana Santa parades, as is the much-too-distant town of Popayán. But these things all sound a bit serious, and I've left it far too late to find accommodation anyway. Fortunately, there's another option – there's apparently a place back down the coast that not only celebrates Easter but also offer a little light relief in the process. I think I'll go there.

The land quickly becomes flat again as we head back along the coast, the sudden shockwave of the Santa Marta range receding in our mirrors. Past the town of Ciénaga (meaning 'swamp') we go, famous for the cumbia track La Cumbia Cienaguera and infamous for the 1928 banana plantation massacre, in which striking workers were killed by the army when they refused to disperse.

But the country's history of violence doesn't make more mundane threats any less of a problem. Whilst the Colombian road safety statistics look pretty reasonable by Latin American standards, road safety is still a serious issue, hence the 'No more stars on the road' campaign, which references the black stars painted at the site of someone's death.

Still, religion can help keep you safe. The Virgen del Carmen (one of the Virgin Mary's titles) is the patron saint of drivers in Colombia, and her likeness can often be seen adorning the outside of buses else swinging about inside vehicles in trinket form, watching over the occupants. For some, it's practically part of the driving test.

"Do you have the Virgen del Carmen hanging from your mirror?"

"Yes"

"Then no harm may come to you or those around you. You've passed."

Being more road traffic accident-fearing than God-fearing, I tend to find the sight of functioning seatbelts more reassuring. But trying to find the seatbelt in the back of a Colombian vehicle is like playing treasure hunt in a garden of sponge and fabric. And when they do exist, they're generally tucked out the way in the seat crevices. On the rare occasion that I successfully buckle up, I'm generally the only one that has bothered. And such is the case today.

We've passed through the swampy Magdalena delta region, where breeze-block shanty towns cosy up to rubbish-fringed lagoons, and are well on our way to Cartagena, when everyone makes a sudden surge for the windows on one side of the bus. Something's happened outside. I feel the centre of gravity of the bus shift – were we on a boat, it would be in danger of capsizing.

From bits and pieces I overhear, including much laughter and repetition of the word *pollo* (chicken), there seems to have been an accident involving a livestock vehicle. As we trundle through the bottleneck the doors hiss open and a young member of the bus crew nips off clutching an empty black bag. This is accompanied by more laughter and jokes from passengers – he appears to be off to scavenge for spoils.

We continue rolling along whilst he's gone, gradually creeping up on the epicentre of the accident. Partially obscured by a downed motorbike, a person is being attended to by paramedics. Further beyond, a truck cab lies on its side amidst the trees, battered into submission. The noise on board dies down. By the time the young man re-boards, with a now-bulging black bag, it's to complete silence.

No-one puts their seatbelts on, though.

Things aren't much more reassuring after I change bus in Cartagena – the road is more tortured, and opportunities to overtake fewer.

Colombian overtaking is a sight to behold, albeit in the gaps between your fingers. At first, when your bus scorches past something, you find yourself thinking "I'm glad we're no longer stuck behind that slow-moving truck / car / rocket-propelled dragster". But soon it becomes evident that overtaking is what journeys consist of in their entirety. Having single-carriageway roads bearing traffic of hugely varying speeds demands it.

Night-time, which is now encroaching, brings its own hazards, as drivers rely on the absence of oncoming lights as an indicator that it's safe to hurtle round a blind corner on the wrong side. Which forgets that most animals – even modern ones – don't have headlights.

But the most unsettling thing on this particular journey is the lurchiness. At first the minibus is weighed down to its haunches with luggage and passengers and hence has a certain stability. But by the final stretch it's near empty and the vehicle has taken on the handling characteristics of a vaguely-guided missile. Even my huge frame, and hence relative jammed-in-ness, is not enough to stop me being thrown about within the hurtling metal container.

Finally, we arrive. They pick up the bus and rattle it round until I fall out onto the tarmac, which I grip for all I'm worth.

Tolú is not my intended destination, but it's a pretty good place to stop en route. A holiday town on the Caribbean coast, its main focal point is its *malecón*: a seafront promenade with restaurants, bars and guest houses on one side, and the sea on the other.

Children scream along the surface of the water on giant speedboat-drawn inflatables whilst the rest of the family splash about in the shallows else lie out on small spits of sand, presumably in knowing reference to the sun-worshipping Muisca people of the interior.

Sticky-treat sellers walk the promenade, balancing the platter atop their heads like a cumbia dancer's bottle of rum. They don't advance to the left, shuffling and swinging their hips, though. Which is good, because you wouldn't want to have to flirt extensively with one every time you fancied a snack.

Then night time arrives and the place becomes an adult playground. People sit drinking next to the splashing black void, dance at open-fronted bars or simply stroll the promenade, the smell of the sea salt mixing with that of pizza and hot dogs from food stalls.

But the big thing is definitely the hireable giant pedal cars. These metal-framed beasts prowl up and down the *malecón*, pumping out music, the passengers whipping the streets into a flurry of liquor, rhythms and laughter.

It looks great fun, but I think I'd look a little sad hiring one on my own. Fortunately I get chatting to a group of teachers who are looking at hiring one together, and they invite me to join them.

They elect reggaeton as the music of choice, and decide that, rather than cruising the *malecón*, they'd quite like a tour of the town. The vehicle owner – and hence steering-wheel master – obediently veers off the main vein and onto the back streets.

Only a block or two away from the main strip the mood changes entirely. People sit out on steps in front of their houses and chat with neighbours, whilst others rock gently in chairs. It's another tranquil evening in Tolú. Until, that is, we arrive in our angry, fire-breathing monster, the music blasting the render off the buildings and the lights scorching the fur off domestic pets. Have you ever tried cringing and pedalling at the same time? It's not easy. When we finally return to the main drag, and the ride comes to an end, it's a moment of great personal relief.

As it nears midnight, everyone suddenly remembers why there's a holiday in the first place. The *malecón* and the food areas empty out, and the streets around the church become jammed.

When the Spanish came, they didn't just subjugate and exploit the indigenous, they also indoctrinated them with Catholicism.

"God loves you," they said. "Which is just as well because we couldn't give a shit."

Okay, so that's perhaps a trifle unfair. A lot of missionaries and clergy and so on were vehemently opposed to the Spanish treatment of the indigenous people in Latin America. One group of Dominican friars on the Caribbean island of Hispaniola were particularly fearless in their questioning of the legitimacy of what was going on, taking their concerns to the King himself.

A committee was formed but, in a darkly comic turn of events, they focussed on fixing the legitimacy rather than reducing the maltreatment. The outcome was a piece of legalese called the *requerimiento* – a document to be read by Spanish forces to indigenous people asserting sovereignty over their lands via some convoluted religious reasoning, and demanding acquiescence – or else.

"Oh, and if you try and stop us, any harm that comes to you is your own fault. It says so here."

They read it out on the boat on the way in, proclaimed it to empty huts, or shouted it after the indigenous people as they ran off in terror.

You guys have got a translator – right?

That was all a long time ago, but religion remains an important factor in Colombian culture, with 90% of Colombians self-identifying as Catholics. I've even been the subjected of attempted proselytization myself on a couple of occasions. I guess I must look indigenous.

Processions are happening all over the country, Tolú included. The one here consists of various wooden floats, each bearing life-size models in a biblical scene. Actually, to call them 'floats' is to do an injustice to those that have to carry them. One even has some fellow frolicking about on top, hopefully for some reason other than just to make it harder to lift.

Sorry about that – I'll get down now.

But the biggest test comes on reaching the church, when the bearers have to try to manoeuvre the floats in through the doors. It's a bit like trying to get a new sofa into the house except everyone doesn't then jump on it once it's inside. And there's more praying. Well, maybe about the same amount of praying.

Having watched for a long time in reverential silence, a collective sense of "Right – that's that done!" passes across the crowd and everyone gets back to the serious business of pedalling about in oversized toy cars and getting trashed. For me, however, it's an early night, as I'm moving on in the morning – I've got a festival to get to.

Viiippp! Viiippp! Viiippp! Viiippp!

Champeta plays from the stereo of the suffocating heat-trap of a bus as we wait to depart. Today's fellow passengers include a man carrying dual spearguns, like some kind of outlaw fisherman, and another sticky-treat seller.

The heat is flushed out by the breeze as we pull away and charge along a country road. Shortly, we arrive in a small town where I change to another bus. This one smells of fish, possibly due to it being full of fish – we're definitely getting more rural. We're also getting more there. In fact we are there.

San Antero is a sleepy little town with few more than a handful of dusty streets. *Motos* with vinyl seat-covers bake in the midday heat, their drivers waiting in the shade for business. A fisherman walks by with crab-filled nets that hang from a pole over his shoulders, which he bears like some kind of maritime crucifix. A couple of seated men slide draughts about on a worn-out board.

There doesn't seem to be much going on here, but I'm pretty sure this is the place, so I go hunting accommodation on the back of a curvaceous, scantily-clad woman. Customised motorbike seat covers are normal in Colombia, and 'oiled-up woman in skimpy bikini as seen from behind' is a favourite.

From guest house to guest house we go, but every single room is taken. What is this place – Bethlehem? I'll probably wake up in a manger tomorrow, spitting out straw, which if nothing else will at least remind me what the morning after a heavy session used to feel like.

In the end I settle for something pretty basic – a bare concrete shell with a bucket-flush toilet and a hand-scoop shower. It's rough, but that's okay, because I've not come here for a weekend of foot spas and Balinese massages. I've come for the twenty-third annual Festival del Burro (Donkey Festival). Now that's what I'm talking about!

I sit out in a café by the crossroads, which form the focal point of the village, and wait for donkey-related things to happen. A bus cruises by, embellished with decals of Jesus, Rambo and a surfing Bugs Bunny – the holy trinity. The sticky glass bottle keeping my company slowly empties, but nothing else changes.

I'm not sure what's happening here, and no-one seems able to help. San Antero is the kind of place where everyone knows everyone else's business, yet nobody apparently knows where any of the events are taking place.

A woman in the cafe thinks I'm missing something important, but she isn't sure what or where. Some other bloke assures me that the parade will come past here, but doesn't know when. In fact, if it wasn't for a guy selling little models of donkeys from a table by the roadside, I'd be starting to question whether this was the right place after all.

It's almost predictable that it falls to someone from out of town to point me in the right direction. I leap onto the back of a scantily-clad woman and melt it across to a defunct bus terminal on the edge of town where the action is. And by action, I mean fancy-dress contest. For donkeys.

Jesus rode a donkey into town, at least according to a well-known book. But what Jesus probably didn't do – unless the apostles glossed over it – was adorn his donkey with a wig, lipstick and gold body paint with the intention that it looked like Shakira. The donkey in question seems fine with this, not to mention uncommonly good looking.

It's not just the donkey that's come dressed up, either: its generously-curved female owner is also decked out like said pop star. Indeed they're both attired in very similar gold spandex outfits.

Shakira has some serious competition though. Amongst others, there's a donkey in period military uniform, a library-donkey ('Biblioburro') with a shelf of books on its back and an enviro-donkey sporting models of the earth and sun.

I've arrived just as the judges are deliberating, having missed the bit where each owner explains the intellectual concept behind each donkey's getup. So I don't have to wait long for a winner to be announced. And the honour goes to Biblioburro, with its message 'Neither distance nor low social class are reasons not to receive education.' Which is a rather sensible message given it comes from an animal, and one wearing massive comedy glasses and a *sombrero vueltiao* at that.

I'll later discover that Biblioburro is a genuine concept – a travelling library in the Magdalena valley region with a fleet of two donkeys – although photographic evidence suggests that the one here may be an homage rather than one of the originals.

With a dull scuffle of hooves and the occasional squeaky grunt-honk, the donkeys depart the terminal and trot back through the village in a convoy, led by an effigy of Judas who, with his long hair, beard and mal-fitting suit, looks like a rocker in his first office job.

I have to jog to keep up as we pass locals stood out on vantage points and sat on doorsteps of their painted houses, coastal beats coming from a *picó* casually set up in someone's front yard.

As we continue, the procession grows. Any local boy who has access to a donkey has brought it out for the day and joined the procession, like it's a classic scooter rally. They lean back astride them on saddles of straw, sacking and wood. A few horse-mounted police in green fatigues also join the throng, showing up the donkeys for just how small they are in comparison – a grown man would be as well riding around on a tricycle.

By the time we reach the city centre, the streets are packed with donkeys and beeping vehicles (I'm trying not to swear). A band of musical mercenaries has also joined the procession, adding brassy squeals and the popping and snicking of freeform snare-drum rhythms to the clopping of four-legged beasts.

They certainly love their donkeys out here. But there's more to this than just plain affection. The T-shirts on sale hint at this, with slogans such as 'You never forget your first love'. It turns out that there's more than one way to ride a donkey, and doing so in a less-then-biblical manner is apparently a rite of passage for local boys on some parts of the coast. Now there's something you don't see on Blackpool beach.

According to a documentary by Vice, the young men don't want to be seen to be virgins, because you're not considered a man until you've had sex. However, these are traditional, rural communities, so sex before marriage is out of the question. Enter the donkeys. Or rather 'enter the donkeys'.

A billboard in town warns about the dangers of unprotected sex, yet keeps curiously quiet about the risks of rear mounting an animal that is fabled for its kicking.

In the end I can't keep up with the procession any longer – two feet are two too few – and I have to let it go on without me.

Come the evening I head to the site of the evening's festivities. People are referring to it as the 'stadium', but it's actually just a huge fenced-off patch of ground on the edge of town with a temporary stage, a plethora of beer tents and a massive inflatable advert for *aguardiente*.

Whilst the main venue is still quite sparsely populated, the wooden marquee adjacent is already full. A makeshift affair of wood, plastic sheeting and swinging light bulbs, it's buzzing with activity.

I can't really see exactly what's going on from outside, so I bustle my way in through a crowd which consists mostly of men of the polo-shirt-and-cap fraternity. At the heart is a dense circle of people surrounding an open ring of dirt, demarked by wooden fencing. A timer clock hangs down on a cord. Off to one side, some cockerels perch on wooden beams, and opposite me a pair of roosters are held up in front of the audience: one white, one brown.

Ah, okay. Not the place to take an animal rights protester on a date, then. Or maybe exactly the place.

Money changes hands like I've only previously witnessed in cheesy fight-scene parodies, never in actual fights, and the cocks are let loose. Immediately, they launch into each other, pecking and clawing at each other in a flurry of feathers. This drives some of the beer bottle-clutching onlookers into a frenzy, shouting out what I presume is complex tactical advice.

The only sign of progress is the white bird's plumage, which is developing a blood-pink tinge. I've read that in some cock-fighting, the birds have spurs or blades attached to them, though I can't tell if that's the case here. As the fight builds, people push in front of me – everyone wants a better view. I peck at a few of them in annoyance, but I just get funny looks.

Suddenly, the white bird starts to falter. It ends up on the floor, the brown one stamping all over its head. It's hard to tell how much this is a bona-fide fight technique and how much it's just a dumb bird wandering about, thinking "Where did the other guy go?" But whatever it is, I've seen enough, and leave.

As night encroaches, the party cranks up in the main venue. A good deal of the town folk have made it here, as well as a pretty high proportion of its donkeys. Some people have ridden here on their steeds in a manner reminiscent of the *salones burreros* (donkey taverns) they used to have in Barranquilla, where folk would tie them up outside, like a slightly comedic Wild West.

Judas is here, too. He's parted company with his mount, though, and is now hanging from an impromptu gallows. After some time they cover him in petrol and set fire to him, because hanging's too good for him. Or maybe it's not good enough. Or maybe they just want to make sure, lest he spring back to life and start betraying people.

Then fireworks burst in the sky and a night of revelry begins. Musicians take to the stage at the far end of the field, and the party hits full flow. Spray-foam fizzes through the air, rum – the liquor of choice on the coast – is splashed about and everyone close-dances, circling tenderly with their partners to the strains of live accordion.

I meanwhile stand on my own drinking plasticky water from a sealed bag, fished from the melt water and floating ice of a vendor's cooler box. Finding someone to dance with is surprisingly difficult – everyone is either a teenager or in a romantic clinch. This is typical rural Latin America: "Quick - let's get married and have kids before we're all old and twenty and everything!"

For all the difference it makes to me, they may as well be playing Christian music, a genre which does exist in Colombia, and which I have yet to see anybody move to. It's a curious niche with eighties-style synth-pop at its heart, and musically, it's not converting anybody. Or at least anybody who thinks music is sacred, and not something to be casually defiled by a group of amateur musicians with a cheap keyboard, no matter how repentant they are.

I find myself hypnotised by the slow padding of opposing feet circles on the dirt-patch field. With no-one to dance with, I'm in danger of having to ask one of the donkeys, and we all know where that might lead.

It's time to turn in.

As far as breakfasts go, the fried egg *arepas* and *gaseosa* (fizzy drink) which I have the next day would probably make a good hangover cure. But since I don't get hangovers anymore, it just makes a good hangover substitute. Fortunately, there is a local opportunity to relax and rejuvenate which doesn't involve sugar, deep-fried snacks or the carnal knowledge of animals.

All along the Caribbean coast are examples of a geological

feature known as the 'mud volcano', and San Antero has its own. So, along with an Aussie filmmaker I've met in town, I take a *moto* to the local one.

It turns out to be a partial misnomer: there is no cone, no lava and, perhaps most disappointingly of all, no volcanologists running about on fire. What there is, however, is a pit full of gloopy mud ten metres in diameter, with a drop of about a metre from the lip to the gooey stuff.

When we arrive there's an attractive woman in a bikini standing on the precipice. By the time we've changed into our shorts, she's been replaced by a human-shaped blob making a fresh trail of brown through the surface algae. She's not alone in her 1950s B-movie predicament, either – seven or eight other humans have also come to an untimely (and rather brown) end.

The Aussie and I decide against the genteel wooden stairs, plumping for a more direct entrance. We climb down to a lower lip, and stand in the Caribbean heat ready to leap (diving head-first would seem imprudent). I hold my nose, as I always do when jumping, even when it's onto a hard surface. There's that customary pause to think "Oh crap" – a sentiment which I'm more than familiar with from my various brushes with dance – and then I just go.

SPLUCK.

I'm stood waist-deep in mud, still holding my nose. Laughter rips through the air, largely from the brown monsters on the other side. I want to cross the goo pit to mock-berate them, but there's no chance of that: although my limbs can move freely, actual forward displacement is near-impossible.

It's a peculiar predicament. I can't feel the bottom with my feet – it's all just squidgy – so there's nothing below to push against. At the same time it's seemingly impossible to sink: the mud just refuses to accept me any deeper than I already am. So I'm just kind of held there in a gooey stasis. Not that it's unpleasant: below the sizzling surface, the mud is cool, and has a smooth, slimy consistency with a slight graininess and the occasional submerged twig.

I'm still only partially covered – my painfully-white upper torso is still unblemished – but then peer pressure intervenes, the mud-beasts expecting me to complete my baptism.

"The people demand it!"

It's actually a wise move given that I'm stuck fast and exposed to the midday Caribbean sun. I smear it all over my chest, face and neck, plastering it right through my hair – well, what the heck – then lie back on the surface and make a mud angel. In time it dries out and I have to reapply it to stop it caking hard. I guess I'm getting my spa treatment after all.

It's a fine way to spend an Easter Sunday, which is just as well as leaving any time soon could prove to be a problem. The Aussie and I each have a return *moto* booked but, given the difficulty moving, we'll be lucky to make it out before sundown. We start heading for the steps and inevitably, given we're both adult males, it turns into a competition. A really weird, slow competition.

The best technique turns out to be to drag oneself along the surface. But despite all our effort and grim determination we're still like a pair of racing snails, trails and all. The discovery of a helper rope under the surface speeds things up dramatically – now it's like we're being dragged along a slithery jungle trail by a Land Rover.

Finally we make it out, and get baptised – well, hosed down – by the local washer women just in time for the *moto* home. There's a whole load of giggling from the two that are washing me, possibly because they don't see many foreigners here, but maybe also because of my difficulty in retaining my shorts about my waist.

The festival is now nearly over for the best part, but there are still a few events scheduled at the stadium. Like the unmatchable exhilaration of the *chipi-chipi* (shellfish) shelling contest.

The shelling is done by putting large quantities of the *chipi-chipi* in big metal bowls and flipping them rhythmically. Several women line up against each other in front of the stage, and commence, with a *shick-shick-shick* sound. From what I can work out, they have until a man has climbed a pole behind us.

The duality of this event creates a strange tension, the crowd switching their focus between the shellers in front, and the pole-climber behind. No-one can possibly tell how well the shellers are doing, but what else can you do as a spectator other than turn your head back and forth?

The pole climber reaches the top and holds his hand up in triumph, bringing the contest to a halt. He's invited onto the stage where he's presented with an electric fan, which he thrusts aloft like a sporting trophy. I swap bemused glances with a middle-aged Colombian with an accordion over his shoulder, an exchange which I find strangely reassuring.

I leave the revellers behind as they gear up for another night of *vallenato*-based merriment, and possibly a few awkward can't-remember-the-name-of-the-donkey-you've-woken-up-with type moments.

Easter is nearly at an end. With relative normality about to resume, it's time to kick on and learn some more dancing, though which dance I learn, and indeed where, is still open to debate.

Religion clearly has a major influence on Colombia, even if its key dates aren't always celebrated in a way the church might approve of. But, from what I've observed so far, if there's a single unifying belief system in Colombia it's dance.

CHAPTER ELEVEN

Flat Out

It's raining outside.

A couple of middle-aged guys in checked shirts and jeans chew the fat at a nearby table, whilst an old one-armed bandit hacks up and spits out the theme from man-with-no-name. I chew on a pastry, like it's a cheroot, and ponder on the wall poster for a recent cowgirl competition.

I'd spent far more time on the coast than I'd ever intended, in part due to those troubles with my passport, so I decided it was time to make a break for the interior, flying back to the capital and then heading out of town over land.

It's not all mountains and valleys in Colombia's interior. East of the Andes is a huge, flat region of grasslands that sweeps out towards the Amazon jungle and upwards into Venezuela. This region – the Llanos (Plains) – is so unrelentingly level that the inhabitants probably get vertigo just from standing on their tip-toes. And it was there that I was headed. To the Llanos, that is – I've stood on my tiptoes before.

Clouds haunted the asphalt as the minibus forged its way through the creases and folds of the outer edge of the Andes. As we reached the last high point of the range, I got my first view of the Llanos. In the gaps between various epic billboards advertising jeans, the plains, sticking to their promise, stretched out endlessly without a single perceptible undulation. Somewhere down below, right on the hem, was Villavicencio – known to Colombians as Villavo (pronounced vee-YOW).

And that's where I am now, guzzling on a plastic cup of *café con leche* like the grizzled drifter that I am, the coffee's skin adhering moustache-like to my top lip.

Once the rain abates, I take a walk. My trainers make a slick sound on the pavement and the white-washed concrete buildings gleam in the sudden sunshine. It's not coastally hot, but it's still t-shirt weather, and everything smells of rain. Some guy dressed in jeans, checked shirt and cowboy hat works a fruit stall, chopping pineapples with a machete in the way that Rooster Cogburn never did. The *sombrero vueltiao*, meanwhile, is nowhere to be seen.

I'm in cowboy country. And by that I don't mean there's an abundance of incompetent tradespeople. These wide expanses are prime cattle-farming territory, and working the grasslands since colonial times are the Colombian equivalent of gauchos known as Llaneros (people of the plains), a term that also seems to apply to people from the region in general.

But what kind of a dance culture would such an environment inspire?

It's time to find out.

"It's harder than the *mapalé*."

The name *joropo* is thought to come from the Arabic word '*xarop*', meaning syrup. It's the main dance in the Llanos, and has therefore become my next target. Of the two dance schools I've located, one looks larger and more professional, but the smaller one has the edge in having someone in attendance when I visit – a bloke in his early thirties called Carlos.

Carlos has a crop of dark hair, and that sunny *mestizo* skin I've seen so much of in Colombia. He's quite short with a solidity of body, without actually being fat. I'd say he looks typically Colombian, but the very idea of anything being uniformly typical here seems more and more ridiculous.

Where were we?

Oh yes.

"No it isn't," I reply having suddenly become an expert on all dances, even ones I've never tried. "Perhaps it's more complicated, but I've heard that *mapalé* is the most difficult there is, especially because of the energy you need to dance it."

I know what I'm talking about here – I half-learnt a bit of *mapalé* and I've watched a good thirty seconds of *joropo* on the internet. The fact that Carlos teaches both of the dances in question is irrelevant. As is the fact that my failure at *mapalé* means some part of me needs to classify it as the most demanding dance in the history of the universe.

Once it dawns on me what I'm actually trying to do – negotiate in advance how difficult a dance will be to learn – I let it drop.

Later that same day I'm back for my first lesson. The outside of the school could be someone's house with its white-washed exterior wall. Inside, however, is the now familiar trinity of tiled floor, mirrored walls and the spoils from competition wins.

There is one item a little out of place, though: the car at one end of the dance floor. Maybe this place doubles as a parking school. As I'm standing there waiting, some bloke climbs in and drives it out through a pair of double doors, which is a bit of a shame as I've always wanted to know what it would be like to dance with a hatchback.

At first, I'm not sure how I feel about Carlos being my teacher. Specifically the fact that he's not a woman. He might be an expert in the male role, but who do I partner up with to actually dance? But then learning from a woman provides the opposite problem – you can dance with them but will they understand the nuances of the male role given it's not the one they usually perform? Ideally I'd have two teachers: one male and one female. And a specialist physio. And a sports psychologist. And someone fanning me whilst I'm fed grapes.

In the end I cut through this by just talking to him. He tells me it'll be fine – he can teach me the steps, and he'll get me a dance partner when we need one.

The dance floor is intimidatingly large, especially given that, short of hiring a car, I don't have anything to fill it with yet. But then every dance journey starts with a single *paso*, and Carlos is soon demonstrating the *paso básico* (basic step) of *joropo*.

He slaps the floor once with each foot. Then he slides the first foot backwards. Then he does the same thing again, but with the order of the feet reversed. Two strikes and a slide. Two *golpes* and a *resbalón*. So what we're dealing with here is a three-beat bar, like a waltz. We practise side by side, looking down at our feet in the mirror like we're in a shoe shop.

I stutter at first – I can see what I'm meant to be doing, but the messages I'm sending to my feet seem to be getting corrupted in transit, like the telegraph line is down. But I soon reach the point where I can do a run of them joined together, a sequence which lasts as long as it takes for me to notice I'm doing well, at which point I immediately trip up.

"*Dan-DAN-tsss... dan-DAN-tsss... dan-DAN-tsss...*" says Carlos.

He's not being a weirdo – these are the sounds I should be making with my feet, and he thinks it helps to vocalise them. The two *golpes* make up the '*dan-DAN*' part, and the sliding bit is the '*tsss*'. I copy him both in terms of footwork and vocals.

Thankfully, the music is a lot more impressive than our beatboxing. In fact, when Carlos puts it on for the first time on the portable stereo, I'm somewhat taken aback by its beauty. It's highly string-orientated, with fluttering guitar-rhythms and harps that are lulling at times yet commanding at others. It sounds refined yet folky; halfway between the ballroom and the barn, like Rodrigo's Concierto de Hoedown.

All of which would be fine except for one thing. You would think that picking out the beat in a waltz would be like picking out the trees on a plain – I mean how hard can it be? But it's easy to get lost amidst all those complex string patterns, so it can quickly become like trying to pick out the Sagittarians in a herd of cows.

Despite this, I am making ground, but I'm missing an important piece of kit. My suede-soled shoes just aren't 'spanky' enough - I should be sending sparks flying when my feet strike the floor – but as it is I'm just buffing it. What I need is a pair of *cotizas.* These are the typical flat-soled leather sandals that *joropo* is danced in, featuring a large stretch of material at the front and a single strap behind the heel to secure them. I go for a wander around town after my lesson to see if I can find some.

Villavo seems safe, but it wasn't always like this. In fact, this whole city had been out of bounds until fairly recently, a victim of the armed conflict and of crime in general, despite its proximity to Bogotá. Mind you, safety is still relative, and the moment I pluck my camera from my bag, a local tells me "*cuidado*" (careful).

Shops in Colombia are often grouped like-with-like, and it's as much the case in Villavo as anywhere. For instance, there's the street of flower shops, where women emerge in clouds of pollen and perfume to try and entice me inside. Then there's car-repair street, where big hands turn wrenches and the oil is ingrained on the concrete forecourts.

To these national staples, Villavo adds its own specialism. Right in the centre is a street of workaday cowhand shops. I follow the scent of virgin leather and head inside one. Saddles are stacked-up, topped by immaculate coils of white rope. Bridle parts hang from the ceiling, and riding crops and spurs adorn the walls. Everything you could need for life on the ranch is here, cowboy hats included. But for all the essential Llanero items the cowhand shops stock, they don't seem to have any *cotizas*.

The best bet would seem to be shoe street (nay district) with row upon row of cheap footwear. It's here I spot my first pair of *cotizas*: hideously decadent with white and brown animal-hide for that straight-off-the-dead-calf look. But they're overkill for the task at hand – I just want something simple to practice in. I end up finding a suitable pair in a little corner shop for 6,000 pesos (US$3; £2) – a couple of basic, flat leather soles with some cheap fabric attached. Yeeha.

Whilst I'm waiting to put them into action, I decide to act on a suggestion of Carlos's – that I go along to that evening's group class to watch some more advanced *joropo* dancers in action.

It's a great idea, although I can see the danger a mile off – that of getting dragged up to join in. I'm not even close to being ready, so that's not happening. Pre-empting the problem, I decide to turn up deliberately late so the class will be underway when I arrive. Unfortunately, I do the job too well: I'm so late that I'm on time for the next class.

"Are you here to dance?" asks one student at the door, fascinated by the rare sighting of a foreigner at the school.

No chance! You folks will all be doing all sorts of crazy shit, and I'll be walking round with a map and a compass trying to locate the beat. And even supposing I find it, I'll then celebrate by doing the same *paso* on the spot for the next hour.

I sit on the chair and watch everyone warm up. They do this by playing follow-the-leader – trooping round the room in a snake-line, copying the steps of the teacher at the front. I can see straight away that they're actually all different ability levels. In fact, some of them are barely more advanced than me.

"Bollocks to it!" I say and stand up.

No, I don't. Somehow, my ingrained dance-floor avoidance

gets the better of me, and I just stay sat down. I keep telling myself I should just get up; just do it. But my backside remains firmly stuck to the seat. What is this ridiculous fear, damn it? I mean, so what if I get it badly wrong? Do I think it'll really make headlines?

Novice dances badly

"It's as though he had limited experience," says eye-witness.

I try to gee myself up, to reason my way off the chair, but to get up and dance now would look weak, and make it obvious that fear was the thing stopping me. If I stay sat down, at least I'm being decisive.

Halfway through the lesson, I decide I've had enough. I've overthought it and nothing's going to change. I do stand up, but it's so I can leave. I slope away feeling far more ridiculous than I could possibly have done had I just given it a go. To paraphrase a fellow Englishman (one Guillermo Shakespeare), a dance-coward dies but a thousand times, a dance-brave dies but once.

I must be making serious inroads into that thousand.

If there's one good thing that comes out of my failure to join in the class, it's a determination to work harder at my dancing. Which is just as well, as it's beginning to hit me how complicated *joropo* is. And if I don't get stuck in, it'll just end up as a half-arsed bag of odds and ends, as with the *mapalé*.

So, not only do I commit to daily practice, I also decide to adopt a more high-intensity approach; signing up for two lessons a day instead of one. Whilst this misses the point in some ways – there'll always be dances I'm rubbish at, and I should just get comfortable at being rubbish – it's still progress.

Back in my hotel room I take the opportunity to break in my *cotizas*, like a pair of wild colts. It also means the guests in the adjacent rooms get to play the game of 'What the hell's that noise?'

When I come in for my second lesson – or rather pair of lessons – it's clear the practice has paid off: I've got the basic *paso* down pat. *Bravo*! But learning to dance on the spot is about as useful as learning how to drive on the spot, so now I need to learn to move about – doing what Carlos calls *desplazamientos* – whilst maintaining that *dan-DAN-tsss* rhythm all the while.

"In a square," says Carlos, and has me going forward, left, back, and then sideways again.

The problem with this is that once I'm travelling about my brain struggles with the idea of creating a distinction between the slaps and the slides. My tendency is to inadvertently drop the sliding and just end up walking, and I can do that already. Moving backwards creates a slightly different failure, in which I end up sliding backwards at speed on alternate feet. But whilst I might not yet have mastered the basics of *joropo*, at least I can now moonwalk.

Upping the ante still further are the changes in tempo. The songs tend to start quite unhurried, in a variant known as *pasaje*, but they frequently switch partway through to the urgent *recio*. These switches in speed are exciting to listen to, but a bit of a nightmare in dance terms: There you are, happily cantering along on your dance-horse when the damn thing has a funny turn. The next thing you know you're belting along with one hand on your hat and the other on the reins, doing your damnedest not to fall off the back.

Not allowing me to rest on the laurels that I haven't yet earned, Carlos pushes me further still up the learning curve: he's brought in his daughter for me to dance with – a lithe girl in her late teens. I'd have preferred someone taller, but then you can't have everything in life or I'd be dancing with that hatchback.

We face each other holding hands, which is apparently the *joropo* way. Carlos explains that the man's posture is meant to be slightly bent over and have forceful intent about it. You also need to hold your arms wide and firm so that when you're driving – sorry, leading – there's no slack, and hence no delay in steering column response.

Sorry, I'm obsessed.

We do the *desplazamientos* together in a square. It's a mess; far more so than on my own. I simply can't do the footwork and drive a woman about at the same time. She'll have to take a cab.

"Listen to the sound," says Carlos.

As I continue to try and slap-slap-slide my way round the square, Carlos's wife, who's just been watching thus far, joins in with the advice giving. She and Carlos alternate, each picking up on a different issue.

"I don't want three teachers!" I say, trying not to sound irritated, but failing.

His poor daughter hasn't even said a word during this, but I'm frustrated and feeling the need to exaggerate. Maybe what I really need is lessons in not being a pain-in-the-arse. I've never lost the habit of bleating out excuses for my every mistake. Plus whenever I drop the beat I feel the need to go back and start again – I can never just muddle on through.

"It's always complicated whilst you assimilate it," says Carlos, not even slightly irked by my manner.

I would say Carlos has the patience of a saint but perhaps that's the wrong way round: perhaps saints should be described as having the patience of Carlos, or even just that of my dance teachers in general.

That evening I do yet more practice, shuffling about the tired floor. I reward myself for my dedication by taking a taxi up to a place called La Piedra del Amor (The Rock of Love), a mountainside restaurant that looks out over the plains.

I sit outside gazing into the infinite and enjoying a cup of *agua de panela con queso* – a hot, sugar cane-based drink with added cheese, the latter glooping slowly down from my plastic fork. Way below, Villavo clings onto to the edge mountains as if for safety; as if it could drift aimlessly for days in the great wide expanses were it not attached to something.

Out there are the mega-ranches. Go far enough, and the plains turn to rainforest and the Amazon Basin, the largest drainage basin in the world. Here Colombia meets two of its neighbours, Peru and Brazil, a peculiar zip tag of land giving Colombia access to the Amazon River at Leticia, the location of a war with Peru in the 1930s.

A river wriggles away from the Andes next to Villavo and into the great space, splitting into loose strands, yet remaining strangely flat, as though the whole scene is compressed into two dimensions. The sun says its farewells before dropping behind the mountains, turning the water a glinting silver, like a clatter of spurs. At this point, a strange insect rattling begins emanating from the hillsides, a kind of folkloric percussion accompanying the reggaeton coming from the restaurant.

Bursts of lightening in the far distance illuminate the distant sky, zapping the ground beyond the horizon. It's as if they're keeping the Llanos in check, lest they get any funny ideas about undulating. Soon, darkness is creeping across the wide expanses and lights erupt across the plains, defining little settlements and networks of roads.

The lights are starting to come on in my dance world, too, and by the time I have my next pair of lessons, my practice is clearly paying off. As a result, Carlos decides it's time to add something new – *zapateos*.

I could tell you that *zapateos* are rhythmic footwork patterns, similar to those in flamenco (indeed, *joropo* has primarily Andalusian influences, along with African and indigenous elements). I could also tell you that *zapateos* are unique amongst the dances I've encountered here so far in that they're meant to generate sound. But it would probably get the message across better if I told you they're a cross between stamping and tap dancing. Stamp dancing, then, and who doesn't like the idea of that? Well, apart from dance partners with open-toed footwear.

Carlos and I do the shoe-shop thing again, with him launching into the first *zapateo*, and me trying my best to copy.

B'dam-BAM... b'dam-BAM... b'dam-BAM... b'dam BAM...

I have to grip onto the bar that runs round the perimeter of the room for support, as the combination of slippery-soled *cotizas* and violent stamping is threatening to put me on my backside. Carlos suggests I wet the underside of them, which I do, running the tap on the undersides in a little bathroom.

They work a lot better after this, albeit with the added toe-curling sound of wet grit being scratched against smooth tiles. Perhaps I should pour black paint on them instead – I could make one of those dance footwork diagrams for future reference. Actually the hardest thing to record is the rhythm itself. After all, short of writing it down on a stave, how do you remember a rhythm?

We work our way through a whole bunch of *zapateos*, including various syncopated rhythms, one of which is intended to sound like a horse galloping (or "Gallop-eeng" as Carlos says, in anglicised Spanish). Perhaps we could just dispense with the *cotizas* and use a pair of coconut halves instead.

Then there's the one that Carlos calls the *metrónomo* (metronome), which he demonstrates by pretending to fire a machine gun with his hands. It's very fast and, appropriately, I'm all over the place from the recoil.

As previously mentioned, thanks to several years as the school drummer my sense of rhythm is pretty good; bordering on the Catholic in fact. And in at least one way *zapateos* are like drumming – when you try and speed up, it's easy to become tense, but this makes the outcome slow and erratic: if you want to do it quickly, you have to stay relaxed.

The hardest one turns out to be one where I have to do two consecutive strikes with the same foot, which means I have to shift my weight about – if I've got any weight on a foot I can't move it with any kind of haste.

I watch myself doing it in the mirror, my body leaning subtly from side to side as I slap the floor, making it look like some kind of Fred Astaire routine. I'd shout "Gotta dance!" if it weren't for the fact it would confuse the hell out of Carlos.

By the end of the lesson we've gone through seven different *zapateos*, and I can successfully do all of them.

"*¡Excelente, Neil!*"

I'm pleased with this, but I'm also suspicious as I've been here before, and it's never that straightforward. When is the horse going to buck me off?

There's not a great deal to do in the centre of Villavo, so in my spare time I just tend to wander around. I often get out to the main square which, rather than celebrating some general on horseback, has a huge ceiba tree with a canopy that extends right out across the square as though in widescreen format. Pigeons flap-walk past ice cream vendors and food stalls, and people sit chatting on the encircling steps.

It could just be my perception, but there seem to be a lot of people carrying injuries that look distinctly motorbike-related: a woman with a big burn on the inside of her calf from touching the exhaust pipe with bare skin, for instance, and numerous others with various bandages applied to their arms and faces. Levels of motorbike ownership seem particularly high here, a reflection, I'm guessing, of the high cost of cars rather than of rebellion. Carlos himself owns one, and arrives at all his classes in the obligatory reflective waistcoat.

Of course I could have got it wrong – perhaps the injuries are from *coleo*: a Llanero sport performed on horseback where cowhands 'tumble' cattle by twisting their tails. It's just as well for the men involved that the bulls aren't manually dextrous as I imagine the concept would also work in reverse. It would certainly make for a fairer fight.

Back at the dance school, I find I was right to be suspicious about my progress. We're not doing anything new, but for some reason everything is now awful. My *zapateos* and my *desplazamientos*, which should be fresh and crisp, are like a bag of old salad. Yet I've been putting the practice in, and I've doubled the lessons, so what's going wrong?

I know this much – I've only been here a matter of days, but I'm already kind of bored. My days consists of dancing, writing about dancing, practising dancing and not much more except perhaps the aforementioned wandering about. It's not helped by the fact I don't know anyone outside of the dance classes – just service personnel like the friendly-but-distant guest house receptionist.

Even the food is grinding me down. There are few places to eat of an evening, and my budget has taken a hit with the passport incident, so I've got into the habit of eating in the roasted chicken joints that are so abundant in Colombia. I sit with a metal platter of roasted chicken, boiled potatoes and a lonely little *arepa*, my fingers slipping with the grease as I pull the chicken apart with the surgical gloves they provide, washing it all down with a sticky *gaseosa*. The staff try to look happy but aren't.

The fact that the dance is coming on so slowly adds to the malaise. Maybe I need a break.

"At times when I'm learning to dance," I say, "my motivation is..."

"...on the floor," says Carlos.

He thinks for a while. "Some people [at group class] have been learning for months and they can't do it as well as you."

He's right. I have actually only been doing this a matter of days.

"Many Llaneros don't know how to dance," adds another member of staff who just happens to be passing.

My mood has lifted a little by the time the second lesson of the day comes round. Which is just as well as we're adding yet another storey to the wobbling tower of *joropo*: elaborate turns known as *figuras*. How many elements does one dance need?

You know that thing where people link arms and go round and round in circles facing opposite directions? No, not marriage – the other one. We do something akin to that, except with added elegance. Once again, I'm practising with Violeta and taking instructions from Carlos. With one form, called *cuellito*, he has Violeta and I clasping hands behind her neck, giving it a semblance of a headlock, and requiring me to be quite gentle lest I wrench his daughter's neck in front of him, which might not go down so well.

At the end of each of the *figuras* I'm required to spin Violeta a couple of times, one-handed.

"*Como un lazo*," as Carlos puts it. Like a lasso.

All this would be fine, or at least passable, if it wasn't for the footwork – you have to do the two-slaps-and-a-slide thing the whole time, whether you're putting your partner in a half-nelson or simply lassoing them. This creates the whole head-patting stomach-rubbing thing again: I can be performing the simplest of *pasos*, and doing so very comfortably, but the moment I go to spin my partner – an act that involves little more than raising my hand above her head – the whole thing collapses.

We practise, practise and practise some more, and I dance until my t-shirt is tugging down with sweat. Violeta is wonderfully light on her feet, but that alone is not enough to rescue me. It feels like we're getting nowhere.

"I'm much worse than yesterday," I hear myself say.

Having two lessons in a day seems to have doubled the pain, but not the progress.

Carlos looks bemused. "Neil, in just a week you've learnt the basic steps, *desplazamientos*, footwork..."

Not only is he physically steady on his feet, but even mentally he seems to have a low centre of gravity. And he's right, of course – I've covered a lot of ground in a very short period of time. I should know better by now, as ups and downs are clearly part of the process, and this is a difficult dance. But then motivation is not a rational argument – it's a feeling.

I'm not likely to improve too quickly, either – I can't practise combining the *figuras* with the basic *paso* back at the hotel, because I don't have a dance partner. Carlos suggests I go back and practise with a broomstick. He's joking, but it's not such a crazy idea – if there's one thing I learnt from Cartagena it's that you can't allow small obstacles prevent you from practising.

I've already changed accommodation once in Villavo for this very reason. Initially, I stayed in a brand new place where the light pinged off the surfaces, but I soon switched down-market to somewhere with sunken beds and a worn-out floor simply because it had more space to practise in.

Back at the ranch, I don't find any broomsticks, though I do find a plastic chair in a utility area with a concrete washboard and the smell of drying linen. I have a go dancing with it, whisking it about the tiled floor, but I can't get it in a sufficiently satisfying headlock. It's tiring holding it up, too, although less so once I convince the cleaning lady to get off it.

I end up ditching the prop and just twirling my empty hand in the air as an accompaniment to the footwork. But even then my success is limited – it feels like my brain's overheating. I'd stamp my feet in frustration if that didn't feel like yet more practice. I finally give up on it for the evening. I just don't seem to be getting anywhere, despite all my application.

I really need that break.

The scent of green stuff blasts through an open window as we charge along the asphalt. It's my first real view of the plains at ground level, as up to now it's always been obscured by buildings. On one side of the road, the Andes make a meaningful start to their ascent into the clouds, whilst on the other it's just flat, flat and more flat – the transition really is that sudden.

We continue eastwards, past the occasional water tower and tin-shack gas station, but mostly acre after acre of grassy farmland demarcated by flurries of white fence-posts. Blue skies filled with perky white clouds race across the surface of the partially-flooded pastures, trapping cows on floating islands of green.

The Llanos has two distinct seasons. The dry season is now coming to an end and the wet season starting, so we're pretty much on the cusp between the two. In the latter, the region floods extensively, turning much of it into wetlands and creating a habitat for water birds.

Every now and then we pass the entrance to a ranch: a driveway stretching away to a homestead hidden from view by trees or by distance, but never by undulations. Many of the ones in this area seem to be for Colombian tourists – it seems unlikely that the gigantic, winding water-slide we pass is for the cowboys. Or the cows, for that matter.

I've cancelled my lessons for the day in favour of time-off, and a trip to the Llanero town of Puerto Lopez, some 90km out of Villavo. After entering town we cross the thing that allows this place, hundreds of miles from the coast, the right to call itself a port – a heavily-engorged river bearing a couple of barges.

Puerto Lopez is famous for being the geographical centre of the country, the location of which is marked by an obelisk atop the only hill in a very large radius. It seems an unlikely coincidence that it's in exactly that spot, though, to be fair, I doubt many people would come to visit if it was in the middle of a flooded field.

Up here, along with the few handicrafts stalls that such a remote site can sustain, is another splendid view over the plains. It's different to that of the Piedra del Amor in that the territory is wilder and less developed, and what flooding has already occurred is really apparent. It's a melange of light-green grass, dark-green woods and silver bands of water that just goes on and on for miles – my eyesight is defeated long before the patience of the plains is.

It's worth noting that, despite this location marking the centre of the country, you could draw a line through this point on a map such that pretty much all the towns and cities are on one side – the side with the mountains and valleys – and very little is on the other. Despite the Llanos and Amazon regions collectively comprising about half of the country's landmass, they only hold a tiny proportion of the population.

Cowboys aren't the only inhabitants: eleven different indigenous groups live here too. Then there are the guerrillas – French-Colombian Ingrid Betancourt was held hostage in the plains' Guaviare department by FARC guerrillas having been kidnapped whilst running for president in 2002. Military personnel secured her release six years later by tricking her captors: posing as a non-government organisation, they whisked her away by helicopter, purportedly to the then FARC leader Alfonso Cano, but actually to freedom.

Northeast of here the plains continue unabated into Venezuela, spreading across both countries in a broad swathe. And the two countries don't just share the plains, they share Llanero culture –

joropo is Venezuela's national dance. They have a shared history, too: together they formed part of the Viceroyalty of New Granada under Spanish colonialism, and then of Gran Colombia following independence.

Perhaps these ties are part of the reason why they sometimes fight like siblings. There have been particular problems in recent times over political ideology, their differing stances with the US (Colombia is close, Venezuela isn't) and the Colombian allegations that Venezuela provided a safe haven for Colombian guerrilla forces.

Some Colombians have told me they love Venezuelans, how they're essentially the same people, but not everyone shares this viewpoint. One woman from Villavo tells me there used to be graffiti saying "*Mate un Venezolano, gane un yoyo,*" (Kill a Venezuelan, win a yo-yo), which sounds a lot less apposite in English as it doesn't rhyme. It's a rubbish prize, too.

I head back to Villavo not sure if I've benefited from the break, but grateful for the chance to experience a little more of this region.

Come my final pair of lessons, something about my dance has changed, and for the better. As with the cumbia in Barranquilla, it's like some time to assimilate all the new material was all I needed.

Under Carlos's tutelage, Violeta and I work on the *figuras* again, like the headlock and the lasso, and now I'm mostly able to maintain my footwork at the same time. Even my attitude to mistakes is different – when I do something rubbish, I stop and laugh, with Carlos laughing along, meaning that any frustration is completely defused. I can see where Yudi was coming from now, though perhaps I had to arrive at this understanding myself to really get it.

Carlos encourages my grid-like *desplazamientos* to become something more free-form, and also throws in a little gentle clockwise rotation. After all, the end goal is fluidity rather than adherence to rigid structure. Essentially, we've progressed to a waltz – or "*vals*" as Carlos puts it, making him sound like The Count off Sesame Street.

I'm waiting for the next new element to be added, but there

isn't one. I've been here barely a week, and I now have all the basic ingredients I need to dance *joropo.* It makes the despair of just a couple of days earlier seem all the more bizarre now I have a little distance.

"Okay Neil," says Carlos, as we prepare for one last dance, "with *berraquera*!"

"What's '*berraquera*'?"

"With grotesque words!" says Violeta.

Ah, okay. I've learnt all the moves: it's time to show some real Llanero attitude.

Violeta and I formally present ourselves to the audience – i.e. Carlos – then it's time to head off into the wild plains of dance.

To lulling strains of harp, I lead her off at a canter on a journey round the sweeping expanses of dance floor, waltzing her about and performing some simple *figuras.* I like these *pasaje* intros - they give me time to warm up.

And I need it, because now the music is accelerating into the fast *recio* section. I throw in some quick rat-a-tat bursts of *zapateos,* meting out punishment to the slippy tiles, then lead her away again, this time apace, mixing in all the *figuras* I can remember.

I do my darndest to do all this with *berraquera.* When we're waltzing, I whip her about assertively, my arms firm. When we go into spins together, I pull our arms tight like harp strings, so we turn that fast we can feel the forces pulling us outwards. Also so bystanders can come up and twang us for a laugh.

Some six minutes after we began, the music draws to a finish, and we roll up by the porch of the ranch once more. It wasn't flawless – the whole performance was riddled with niggly errors – but, my God, I can actually dance a passable *joropo.*

"I told you it was harder than *mapalé,*" says Carlos.

This is more like it.

I'm relaxing in the garden of an up-market restaurant eating the most succulent and tender meat I've encountered since I arrived in Colombia – a Llanero speciality called *mamona* (marinated calf meat). The inside is pink, the outside has the colour of a well-worn saddle – though thankfully not its flavour or texture – and once in the mouth it melts like the sun over the plains. Suddenly all those wearisome nights of practice and fast food are gone and forgotten.

Mamona isn't the only memorable meal I've had recently. During my brief stopover in a rainy Bogotá, I tried a local dish called *ajiaco* in a little café, waves from passing cars lapping up against the pavement outside as I tucked in.

Ajiaco, Bogotá-style, is a creamy chicken stew with potatoes, hunks of corn and the vinegar bite of capers (as one frustrated foodie said to me "They've got capers, so why do they only use them in this?"). Yellow-green in colour with a swirl of cream on top, *ajiaco* has a heartiness that sets it aside from thinner Colombian stews, like the soup-like *sancocho*. I loved it instantly and spooned it into my mouth until I felt bloated.

There is clearly some really good food to be found in this country, you just need to know where to find it. And perhaps be willing to pay more than a couple of dollars.

Back in Villavo, I'm with Heidi, a smart, professional, dark-haired *mestiza* woman in her early 30s that I've been put in contact with by a friend. She's friendly and approachable, and has kindly agreed to help me find some real *joropo*.

She suggests we go to Acacías, a pleasant little town about 15 miles from Villavo, and a spot she knows well. So we take a minibus there together, go for a bit of late afternoon wander by the river and have a *raspado* – ice shavings mixed with syrup – in the park.

But these things are just the support acts, because next she leads me to a place with a shiny floor, mirrors and massed ranks of cheaply-made-but-expensively-won trophies. Whatever could this place be? I have an idea, though I can't say for sure as there's no parked-up motor vehicle to verify it.

She has a chat with her friend and dance teacher, Sebastián, who agrees to round up a posse of his dance students to put on a show just for us. Sebastián is in his late twenties and is articulate and passionate about dance. Something about him reminds me of a mechanic I once knew from Wigan, and this familiarity makes me like him even more.

As we wait for them to arrive, Heidi enlightens me on the subject of *joropo*, and specifically how the *pasos* often relate to the rich wildlife in the Llanos. The plains are host to a whole range of creatures beyond cattle, such as armadillos, crocodiles and spectacled bears, plenty of which depend on its seasonal transition into wetlands, so there is a lot of material. The man's steps, she explains, mimic that of a bird called a *garza* (heron), and she play-acts this by kicking her feet back. It does indeed look a lot like the *paso básico* (basic step).

Sebastián also knows plenty about this, and tells me that another *paso* is based on a wading bird called the *gabán* (wood stork), which has to take a long run up to take off, like a plane. Well, a plane with big striding legs. Add to this the galloping and lassoing, and this dance is not just the culture of the plains, it IS the plains. All that's missing is a giant otter *paso*.

Whilst we're chatting, six students – all children – arrive, and within minutes they're in costume and ready to go. The boys are dressed in black jackets and trousers with black felt fedoras, making them look a little like the gangsters in Bugsy Malone. Their partners, meanwhile, are wearing purple satin tops paired with iridescent frilly skirts.

The speed of their arrival and preparation might be impressive, but it's nothing compared to their dancing. The first pair head straight for the centre of the dance floor without a hint of fear and, as the strumming commences, away they go.

The boy is hunched over, his arms firm, and he is in total control both of the dance and of his partner as they slap-slide their way through the opening. Soon he's flying through the *zapateos* – *tackata tackata tackata* – leaping into the air and spanking the floor; splitting the air in two with firecracker snaps – *rat-a-TAT... rat-a-TAT.* All this time his partner provides a simple, blank canvas of a *paso* for him to show off against, something called the *escobillo* (brush) – *joropo* is clearly a very male-orientated dance.

A crowd is beginning to gather in the broad entrance to the dance school, reminding me of that night in Cali. In the heat of the enclosed space, the boy throws his partner into a spectacular and seemingly endless sequence of turns and pirouettes that turn her skirt into an iridescent strip, creating a breeze greater than any of the fans could.

The dancers finish to a warm and well-deserved applause. I feel honoured to have had the chance to see what the dance is supposed to look like – these kids are *calles* ahead of me.

"And now," says Heidi, "you!"

I've seen enough dance schools now that I could probably build one myself. And I've also been in enough situations where

I've been required to dance that I've finally started to see them coming. So the response is already poised on my lips, ready to go.

"No!"

I'm quietly pleased with this – if you're going to be a coward, at least be a decisive one. There's no way I'm getting up there in front of that crowd, especially after such a brilliant display. All I'll be doing is making the kids look even better, and I'm just not that generous a person.

"*¡Sí!*" says Heidi. "*¡Tú!*"

Good comeback.

"*¡No!*"

"*¡Sí!*"

Oblivious to our squabble on the sidelines, Sebastián introduces the two other pairs of dancers. Once more, the strumming begins and once more the dancers are spanking, sliding and spinning, spinning, spinning. Whilst the style holds no surprises, what does catch me off guard is how much they're enjoying it – they're taking genuine pleasure from the simple (ha!) act of dance. I'm not enjoying their performance quite as much as they are, however, because I'm consumed with something that would probably never occur to them: how to avoid dancing all together.

The show ends with all three pairs dancing together in a synchronised routine. Various locals have told me that Acacías holds – or perhaps held – a record for having the most couples dancing *joropo* synchronously (performing the same actions at the same time) although no-one I speak to can quite agree on the number of couples, and I'm quoted variously 400, 1200 and 1500.

Today there are only three, and when they're done and step off the dance floor, there are no longer any children for me to bravely hide behind.

"Now!" says Sebastián, "Neil's presentation!"

Checkmate.

I walk out and take the hands of the girl, under the lights, The wait is mercifully short – just enough time to glance back to the set of expectant faces and give my now customary 'here we go again'-type sigh.

The strumming begins, and I lead her straight into the *paso básico*. Hearing the tune from the beginning is an early win: it means I know where the *golpes* lie and don't have to go riding all over the plains looking for them.

I switch to *desplazamientos*, waltzing her about the unfamiliar floor. My footwork is a little erratic – it's always the first thing to go – so I focus on trying to make it sound right. I'm determined to produce that *dan-DAN-tsss* rhythm. I'll do it with my mouth if I have to, damn it.

My partner launches into a spin of her own accord. I take this as a sign that I'm not engaging her enough. I take the hint and start putting her through a few *figuras*. The amorphous, multi-headed creature that is the crowd is pleased with this, though I do sense it's holding back somewhat.

Wait, I know what we're missing – *zapateos*.

My well-worn trainers may have all the snap of a soft biscuit, but if there's no spanking then it's not *joropo*. I commence attacking the floor, keeping it simple so I can drive what sound I can out of it by sheer force of will. At this the crowd monster erupts, bellowing and clapping. Boy, do they like the floor to be stamped on in these parts.

The music fades out, and our dancing follows likewise. The crowd adorns us with a metaphorical laurel wreath of appreciation, and I give a bow. It's the first proper public performance I've given since my salsa *clausura*, and I'm floating several feet above the plains. Now I'm out the other side all my nerves have gone and I actually feel disappointed that it's over – they cut the music just as I was getting into my stride.

Sebastián and I thank and counter-thank each other to a faintly ridiculously extent, and everyone seems to be impressed disproportionately to the skill I showed. I guess it's not every day an outsider rides into town and shows you a bit of your own culture.

Later I'll have mixed feelings about it as I mentally play back my performance: pride at having done it, yet melancholy because I know I could have done it better. But for now I'm exhilarated – this dancing lark is addictive.

"*Hola. Hola. Hola... Hola. Hola. Hola...*"

We've arrived at El Pentagrama club back in Villavicencio. Despite sounding more like a witch's coven, this is one of the city's most renowned *joropo* venues.

En route from Acacías, I found myself picturing some kind of packed local hoedown, an idea which made me feel strangely anxious. I don't know why that bothered me – surely the more people that were there, the less conspicuous I'd be – but it did.

Inside the venue the band are sound-checking, hence the repeated welcome. As we squeeze through the thickets of wooden furniture, I find I couldn't have been more wrong in my prediction: we're the only customers in the entire joint. I don't know whether to be relieved or disappointed.

We take seats in the middle, at the front, separated from the band by the square dance-floor. Suddenly having a reason to exist, the band burst into action, filling the venue with the beautiful and expansive music of the plains. The harpist, the lead guitarist of the genre, strums and plucks at his big brute of an instrument, backed by an electric bass, maracas and a tiny little guitar.

The singer personally serenades us, coming down off the free-standing stage with his mike, offering it to us to have a go ourselves. He sings songs like Ya No Le Camino Más (meaning something like 'I Don't Chase Her Any More') which, according to Heidi, is a well-known number with lyrics that compare a woman with a bull.

"It's *joropo*, Neil – dance!" says Heidi and gestures towards her cousin, who has come with us.

"Do you dance *joropo*?" I ask.

"*Sí.*"

Oh well, there was always the hope. I sit there a bit longer, trying to work out where the *golpes* fall, but I've not been listening from the beginning, so I'm struggling.

"Dance!" says Heidi, with a look of near-derision at the fact I'm still sat down.

She's right – I should just get up and give it a go. If I put the *golpes* in the wrong place, so what? But I'm also feeling conspicuous, what with there being no-one but us and the band. There are too many people! There are too few people! One thing I'm never short of is an excuse.

Bollocks to it.

I pull Heidi's cousin to her feet and lead her off to the empty space, trapped between the watching eyes of both Heidi and the band members.

We smile at each other and, as I start warming the dance floor

– *dan-DAN-tsss... dan-DAN-tsss...* – the other people present just melt away.

She's not as light on her feet as either Violeta or the dance student in Acacías, so I can't quite whisk her about in the same whirlwind manner. It's like driving a regular hatchback rather than one with power steering, if you'll excuse the comparison (although there's probably a *joropo* song about that). But hey – she's not a professional, she's just a regular Llanera. This is the real deal.

We try a few *figuras*, which are great fun, albeit for the wrong reasons – I mislead her and/or she misreads my intentions, leading to a few moments of us laughing more than dancing. But I don't care: I'm revelling in this shared medium of self-expression and mutual-humiliation, and buzzing once again at having overcome my dance fear.

"You dance well!" she says to me as we sit back down at the table.

Despite my glee, the truth is that my relationship with that seal-breaking first dance remains unchanged. The only time I'm able to overcome my fear of it is when I've so been completely backed into a corner that the humiliation for not dancing is greater than for doing so. It's been the same the whole way along.

Still, one thing's for sure – once the first dance is out the way, it's one heck of a lot easier to get up each subsequent time. Soon I'm pulling both my companions up at will, like some kind of cheap in-house dance whore. At first I have to plan every *figura* a couple of bars in advance, but after a few dances I hit a rich seam where I somehow need a lot less planning – I pretty much just do it. It's not free-flowing self-expression, but it's not far off.

By the time the group of ten-or-so young people from Bogota arrive, I'm in my element. Not knowing any *joropo*, they sit there, drink *aguardiente* and watch whilst the foreigner dances *joropo* with the locals.

"This is just how we roll in England," I want to tell them.

It isn't, of course – we actually just sit about getting wrecked like they're doing – but they don't know that.

It's raining outside.

I sit with my knees hunched up in the tiny space, watching as the rivulets of rain stream along the minibus's side windows. We're bounding from town to town along the rippling green fringes of the Andes, with the sodden mountainsides on my left and the inundated fields on my right. Water alternately pools on the windscreen and is swiped away again with a judder.

The wet season is closing in.

I didn't have high expectations of the plains, but they gave me so much more than I could have imagined. The time has now come to head back for the coast to hopefully pick up my replacement passport, and maybe see a little something along the way.

My visit to the Colombian Llanos is over, but my dance mission is truly springing to life.

CHAPTER TWELVE

In the Valley of the Blind Drunk

Okay, let's get this out the way early – I don't like *vallenato.*

I now find it very easy to recognise this genre of music. There's an accordion part that consists of so many notes in succession that any semblance of a tune, let alone hook, is lost entirely; vocals that sound like the singer is heavily constipated; and lyrics that ramble on artlessly and interminably, like someone reading passages from a photocopier repair manual.

But I think the thing that bothers me most is how similar it all sounds. In fact, I'm not convinced that every last *vallenato* song hasn't, in fact, been generated by an algorithm developed as part of a government programme to pacify the coastal masses.

Obviously, there's the occasional catchy number – every genre has its gems – but to reach the stage where I can even recognise the odd song has taken tens, maybe hundreds, of hours of forced listening in taxis, supermarkets and cafes.

And in all this time, the only instance of *vallenato* inducing positive emotions in me was when Diomedes Díaz's song Listo Pa' La Foto was playing on a little *buseta,* and an old guy sang his own version, changing the words so that it was no longer about a man declaring that his lover had replaced him, but instead about him declaring that she was late for her period. Something which everyone on the bus found amusing. Well, except for me as I had no idea what his replacement word '*retraso*' meant. But I looked it up in my dictionary when I got back to my guest house, and laughed really loudly to compensate.

So, in summary, I'm probably not what you'd call a fan of *vallenato.* Which is a shame, really, especially when you consider that it's effectively the national music of Colombia, that I hear it every single day of my existence and that I'm about to spend a whole weekend and more at a festival dedicated to it.

"It's a nice city; a green city," Carmen tells me over the phone. "They don't just have *vallenato* music here; they have *vallenato sentimientos* [feelings]. It's very traditional."

She's talking about Valledupar, a city which, despite being some distance from the sea, still falls under the loose banner of 'coastal'. But Carmen's not calling to give me convenient quotes for my book – nice as that would be – she just wants to let me know that my passport is ready for collection in Cartagena. As if I needed another excuse to make my stay in this city a short one.

It had been something of a novelty to experience undulations again as we began winding up into the mountains in failing light. The novelty soon passed – the road was heavily pitted in places, unsurfaced in others and swung between left and right as frequently and violently as Colombian politics.

Just in case anyone had somehow nodded off (despite this only being possible via a blow to the head with a heavy implement) we made a late night stop at a military checkpoint, at which all the men had to troop off and have their papers checked. Interestingly, some of them gave the soldiers warm handshakes, presumably because out of respect or because they felt they were doing a good job, rather than an ironic thanks for waking them up.

It probably goes without saying that I also had that night-bus staple, the daft neighbour. On this occasion, it was a kind yet slightly nutty woman from Antioquia department who was conducting an experiment into how many toddlers she could fit on her lap before they started cascading down onto me.

She babbled on to me incessantly and was determined to relieve me of my earplugs which she declared "*loco*" (crazy). In the end I gave them to her knowing that this was one occasion on which I would probably get more sleep without them. Then I remembered that I was on my way to a *vallenato* festival and I cursed my loss.

Things are very different in Valledupar to Villavicencio, and it's not just the heat. As I walk about the centre the very streets themselves feel like they are in a state of repose. It feels strangely village-like, with low, white-washed houses that dazzle in the sunlight, and fruit trees everywhere – Carmen was right. Looming away in the background, meanwhile is our old friend of the Sierra Nevada de Santa Marta, now separating us from the Caribbean Sea.

Our proximity to the mountains means there are a few indigenous Arhuaco people here from the mountain's foothills: they walk about quietly in pairs in their simple white garments, black hair spilling out from beneath flat-topped knitted beanies.

But the people mostly seem that bit more open and expressive here, and I pick up a mixture of excitement and mild suspicion at my outsider status that simply wasn't there on the plains. Young women giggle as I pass, and men stare at me in cafes, which is the way round I prefer it.

"Hey! *¡Acá!*" Here!

Walking down a side street, some kids in their early-to-mid teens are trying to get my attention. My instinct is to walk on – I'm used to people trying to stop me on the street, and it's never good news. But this place seems different, so I turn on my squidgy heel and wander back. Their faces lift at my return, and they engage me in conversation which consists mostly just of them telling me the names of English football teams.

So excited are they by meeting a foreigner that they insist on taking me on a tour of the local streets. One of them is carrying a small wooden *guacharaca* (rasp) – one of the key *vallenato* instruments – and starts scraping away rhythmically – *screeeeek-scrik-scrik screeeeek-scrik-scrik* – as we walk down the street. To which a policeman, stood next to his parked motorbike, instinctively starts drumming on his seat – *poom-poom-pa-pa poom-poom-pa-pa.*

We end up sat out on plastic chairs on the pavement in front of one of the kid's houses. A proper *caja* (vallenato drum) appears from somewhere – policemen's seats aren't traditionally part of the percussion – and suddenly we're all sitting there playing *vallenato.* Well, two-thirds of *vallenato,* anyway, because we're missing the accordion. And five-sixths, or whatever, of our group, as I'm not doing anything but listening.

It's a beautiful day, and they're all just lounging on the street making music and singing along. They invite me to join in with the rasp and then the drum. I don't know any of the appropriate rhythms, but I just rattle out what I can on each instrument, drawing the attention of passing locals, who can't help but stop for a look at the foreigner.

"You're a tourist attraction!" says one of the kids.

No-one is impressed by my rhythms, however, and I'm quickly relieved of my duties so they can show me how it's really done.

"Clueless foreigner – he can't even make it sound like it's been generated by an algorithm."

I might not like *vallenato* but I love the accessibility – everyone can have a go. All you really need is a drum, a scraper, an accordion and a singer who sounds like they're lifting a heavy object. You don't even need electricity. In fact, there was once a tradition of bands playing music on the streets in Colombia – it was one of the ways the working class had access to it.

Vallenato means 'born of the valley', the valley in question being the Upar, which also gives its name to the city itself (Valledupar is just a contraction of Valle de Upar). Apparently, farmers travelling the region to sell their cattle would make music to entertain themselves, using the rasp, drum and flute. It wasn't until later that the European accordion replaced the flute as the main instrument of torture. With the drum likely being of African origin and the rasp indigenous, it's arguably another example of Colombia's tri-ethnic heritage.

Due to the poor communications network of the days, the farmer-musicians were also news bearers and would sing their tidings, in line with the tradition of both Spain and West Africa, spawning the culture of the *juglar* (minstrel). I'd probably be more interested in global affairs if the news was disseminated like that.

One boy charmingly tries to set me up with his 17-year-old sister. Not being entirely deterred by my response that she's too young, he insists that she can teach me to dance *vallenato*.

Just as an aside, why does no-one ever try to whore their 30-year-old sister to me? Or even their 30-year-old mother for that matter? At least then I'd have some decent motivation for learning to dance to this music. Although in reality we'd probably just end up sitting there gazing into each other's eyes whilst I slagged it off.

I decline the boy's offer, but it does set me thinking – whilst I've met Colombians who go to formal classes, I've met far more who seemed to just have picked it up from all their friends and family in natural social situations. Dance is an organic thing, so why learn it in a regimented way? And *vallenato* would undoubtedly be a good dance to learn. After all – it's everywhere. The downside is that it's *vallenato*, and I'm just not sure that I have the reserves of sanity to cope with that.

It might be a weekday night, but the main square is buzzing – tonight the festival begins in earnest. There's more than one venue during the festival, but the events in the main square are free and as a result are very popular. Not that this logic ever followed with chlamydia.

Revellers have packed the place out; their *sombreros* all facing the same way like sunflowers that seek out the accordion. The only space is around the outside, where vendors sell drinks from battered polystyrene cooler boxes, cans of beer bobbing about in the meltwater like flotsam from a wrecked Spanish galleon.

I walk about in my t-shirt, the residual heat of day lingering like a chord and the mountains nothing but a craggy silhouette. Apparently, I'm going to learn some *vallenato*, so I'd better see what I can do about that.

I stand on the edge of the throng, watching the now-familiar sight of Colombians having fun. Hands wave frenetically in the air and foam spurts skyward amidst a mixture of cheers and screams, which might make sense if it wasn't accompanied by strains of accordion.

There's an ebb and flow of energy, but things are never allowed to die down too much. "*¡Arriba! ¡Arriba! ¡Arriba!*" yells the singer, meaning 'Hands up!' in a non-Butch Cassidy and the Sundance Kid kind of way. This immediately reignites things; the crowd obediently going mental once again.

Vallenato singers are like Hollywood trailer announcers, in that they all sound like the same treacle-voiced guy. In my mind I have the image of a 50-something Brylcreem lothario, chest wig poking out of unbuttoned shirt, so it's a surprise to me that pretty much every one is some clean-cut type in their twenties or thirties. None of them ever take it one step further and surprise me by being a woman, though.

All of which is very interesting, but I still have the problem of trying to locate a dance partner.

Now, how to get involved in some dancing? In the centre is a bit of a crush, so that's no good to me. I wander a bit further out trying to become part of what's going on, but that's easier said than done. There are lots of big, impenetrable groups with no obvious entry point, whilst other people are in couples and probably don't want to be joined.

I try the "Hey, how's it going?" approach with one random group, but they seem disinclined and it doesn't really go anywhere. I'm picking up intrigue but also reticence.

I head out to the periphery. Low colonial buildings mark the perimeter of the square including one with an elegant first-floor balcony that must have looked out upon many a musical mush-fest.

Middle-aged locals relax on plastic chairs they've carried from their houses, with one such woman telling me that life here is about "*divertirse*" (enjoying yourself), whereas when she lived in Italy, it was "*trabajo y casa*" (work and home), that was important.

There's a brief interlude as a man in a *sombrero vueltiao* yells at a guy on the floor. The latter is soaked through having apparently been kicked through a big puddle. I try to get a closer look, but somebody gently pulls me back and I don't resist – Colombians have a well-honed sense of when to stay the heck out of things.

As the evening progresses, the *vallenato* concert becomes just some annoying noise 'over there'. It's hard to see how I'll ever learn this dance given that I can't even motivate myself to listen to it.

Some college kids that have heard about my dance mission come up and quiz me about it. It's a conversation which heads off in a predictable direction, although the more this happens, the more I'm finding I enjoy it.

"This is *joropo*," I say, and lay down some *zapateos* on the street in front of them, thudding the tarmac in lieu of spanking it.

Others take note and come over. Enjoying the attention, I go through a few *pasos* of each of the different dances I've tried. By the time I reach the end, I've drawn a small crowd of entranced locals.

"You dance well!" says one.

It's true: as long as there's no partner to complicate my partner-dancing then I'm great. My repertoire is growing, too. Salsa, *champeta*, *mapalé*, cumbia and *joropo* – it's quite a list. Shame I don't seem to be able to add *vallenato* to that list.

Come the early hours, I'm wandering back down a quiet, pedestrianised side street when I happen upon some blokes sat out on chairs. Their accommodation for the night is in clear sight – a line of hammocks slung between urban trees.

They call out to me but I feel wary. This is not like with the kids – these are grown men, it's late at night and I'm well outnumbered. Still, they seem pretty much encamped, and it would be a bold tactic to mug someone knowing you're not going anywhere. I stop to talk to them, although my danger antennae is still twitching.

They tell me they've come from various other parts of the coast to see the festival, but the high costs of accommodation during Carnival means they're going to have to rough it if they want to indulge their love of amorphous musical mush.

I tell them a little about my own adventures, to which one of them asks me if I know about "*la primera mujer Costeña*" (the first woman of the coast). What are you on about? A presidential wife, or something? Oh no, wait – you mean…

"*¡El burro!*" The donkey.

They all laugh out loud.

"*¡La burra!*" one of them corrects me. The female donkey!

Yes of course. How ridiculous of me. Imagine a man having sex with a male donkey. I mean that would just be weird, right?

The subject moves on to that of me: How come I can afford to swan about like this, learning to dance as a lifestyle choice? I've barely begun to pick a way out of that one when someone else starts asking me about my family. In an instant, I feel rather vulnerable: these questions are practically custom-designed to arouse my suspicion.

Ever since kidnapping became trendy in the 1970s, pretty much everyone's been at it. The left-wing guerrillas like FARC and ELN for cash or political capital, the right-wing paramilitaries and drug cartels to intimidate and criminal gangs for all sorts of reasons. Even I've been thinking about doing it: Stockholm syndrome is probably my best chance at finding a dance partner.

"If you get kidnapped, the ransom's coming out of your money first!" my dad said before I left the country. I think he was only half joking.

It's still a better deal than my own government, who refuse to meet ransom demands on the basis that it just fuels the problem.

And considering the only negotiation technique I possess is the 'Oh pleeeeease' method, I'm probably best avoiding such situations altogether.

The result of all this is that I enter 'I'm not worth the trouble' mode, and find myself saying something unexpected.

"My parents are dead."

It would be news to my parents.

"Siblings?" asks one.

Okay, so this could get out of hand really rather quickly. Do I stop now, or bluster on in the same direction and create a horrible litany of death around me.

"Cousins? Aunties? Uncles?"

"None."

"You must have friends?"

"Dead. All of them. Well, except some very poor ones which I have to support despite having no money myself."

That's the other thing: I'm also in the strange situation of trying to infer that I'm on the verge of destitution, despite coming from a wealthy country. Which, on the face of it, just makes me look incompetent.

I've just about managed to change the subject to something less death-related, when a previously-unseen member of their group arrives. Interested in who this foreigner is, he instinctively asks if I'm here to visit family.

It all goes very quiet.

"His parents," says one of the men, "are dead."

The others look down, else shift their gaze awkwardly. This poor foreign guy: he's got the whole world as his playground, but he's got no mum and dad.

It's with some relief that two of the younger men change the subject to Colombian women. Sanity, at last. Until, that is, they start playacting their oral sex techniques, and looking to me, seemingly for approval.

Guys – can we talk about my dead relatives again please? It feels less weird.

Vallenato is already everywhere in Colombia – it holds the place hostage, especially the coast – but in Valledupar it's even more everywhere. It's the Japanese Knotweed of Colombian music.

I'm out on a trip to a local mall when a band begins playing on a little stage between opposing shop fronts. A crowd forms and quickly swells, engulfing the escalators and flower beds.

It's not an isolated occurrence: I'm picking up some essentials in my local supermarket, when an in-house trio, set up between the shelves of beer and fizzy pop, begins subjecting shoppers to live *vallenato* amid the dangling '*¡Oferta!*' price signs.

It blows out the windows of passing taxis and through the open fronts of cafes. It's the soundtrack to vendors trying to sell me *sombreros vueltiaos*, stopping me to demonstrate how foldable and roll-upable their hats are – an indicator of the quality.

Even back at my accommodation there's no respite: the old classic El Pollo Vallenato (The Vallenato Chicken) infiltrates our rear courtyard from a group of musicians next door. I mean, I like the fact that it's live music, but that really is where the appreciation ends.

I'm not the only one who doesn't like the stuff. In another supermarket (I seem to be spending a lot of my time in Colombian supermarkets), I get chatting to a model dressed as a pirate, the prevailing wind of accordions blowing across our sails as we talk. She tells me she's here from out of town for the duration of the festival on a promotional job advertising rum.

"I hate *vallenato*," she says.

The things we do for work. And I don't mean the indignity of spending all day in a supermarket dressed as a pirate – I'd do that for free.

Still, it's not like you can change the channel – a futile act anyway given what will invariably be playing on the others. All you can really do is accept it. Besides, I can't help feeling there must be something in this genre just from the way other people react to it.

When I was in the shopping mall, for instance, a middle-aged couple came round the corner to be confronted by the live music. Their reaction was to put their bags down and start dancing with each other – something I've never seen anyone do in Manchester's Trafford Centre. It was a touching moment, the music inspiring spontaneous tenderness between two people who'd probably just come out to buy some bog roll.

I'm sitting amidst the plants in the back courtyard, listening to the gentle flurry of notes. I suppose hearing live music played well isn't such a bad thing. In fact in some ways it's kind of relaxing, like someone strumming an acoustic guitar. In other ways it's uplifting, the cartoon-like notes leaping over the fence and bounding towards me with puppy-dog eyes.

Okay, stop it. *Vallenato* is awful. It's like some kind of state-sponsored musical subjugation technique, and I must resist it with all my strength.

But the pirate and I are pretty much on our own. In fact it seems like everyone has come to Valledupar: I recognise various acts from the Festival del Burro and Carnival, and I even bump into the donkey-festival Shakira – minus donkey – in an ice cream parlour. People don't just want to be here, either, they want to be seen to be here: some of the candidates for the upcoming presidential election are also in town.

I get into a conversation about politics with a university student from Colombia's coffee zone. His name is Steve, and he's wearing a hat, sunglasses plus a fake moustache which keeps falling off at inappropriate times – having already given him a pseudonym, I may as well put him in disguise, too. Actually, I could describe him as anything, really, couldn't I?

Steve is an eight foot-long basque-wearing monitor lizard driving round Colombia in a gigantic hollowed-out onion.

He has some good things to say about soon-to-depart President Uribe. He tells me how, not all that long ago, families had to spend significant proportions of their income on securing themselves and their homes, but that things are better now. A good security situation is good for everyone because it means people aren't spending all their money on simply trying to protect what little they have – they can genuinely invest in the education of their children; in their future.

But then Steve has his own reasons for his interest in security, which date from when he and his family lived in the Llanos.

"My brother was kidnapped."

At its peak in 2000, there were over 3,500 recorded kidnappings in Colombia. Over the next ten years the figure fell to around 200. So it's much better than it was, but that's hardly consolation for those affected, and the current figures would still be an outrage in most countries in the world.

"It was the same in that house; that house; that house," he says, indicating up and down the street he is picturing.

Kidnapping doesn't always take the form of a long-term abduction. There's also the *secuestro express*, which is a quick kidnapping where they request a reasonable sum of money, instead. This often takes the form of the *paseo de milionarios*, where a driver and accomplice take you from cash machine to cash machine, maxing your card out. For this reason, it's the done thing to order taxis by phone instead of hailing them on the street – they're less likely to be rogue.

It's not like there's always physical coercion involved, either. As mentioned earlier, one method is to drug targets with scopolamine – *burundanga* as it's known here – perhaps enlisting the help of an attractive woman. The drug renders the target functionally intact yet suggestive, and hence extremely vulnerable.

Steve doesn't go into the detail of how his brother was captured, but he says that his captors demanded money to secure his release. His family paid up.

"What happened?"

I mean they got the money they were after, so they returned him, right?

"They killed him."

Oh my word.

I try to fill the silence with fumbled questions, to say the right thing, but it's only me that feels awkward, not him.

"It was ten years ago. Today is a different chapter."

They moved to a different part of the country and ultimately did the only thing they could – they got on with their lives.

We're on the vacant edge of town, at a roundabout with a centrepiece statue of a female cumbia dancer. Taxi doors slam all around and the night air sings with chatter and the splashing of alcohol.

Steve and I, plus a few others from the guest house, have headed out to the Parque de la Leyenda – a stadium which was purpose-built for the festival, and where most of the bigger turns will be playing. I've come out of a sense of obligation rather than desire, but I'm feeling a lot more engaged than I was before.

I get a strange tinge of nervousness as we walk between the security fencing and into muffled range of the stadium music. It's the same sensation I experience when I'm going to a dance class, or about to perform inter-cranial surgery on a friend.

Round a corner we go and there, in front of us, is a concrete half-bowl stadium, cradling a halogen glow. As the stadium grows in size the music becomes clearer. And then I get it – that tingle of joy that comes with musical recognition. I know this one! It's the missed-period song! Ha!

I hurry through the final ticket checks and inside, dashing through the concrete underbelly. I can see a broad opening: there's the stage! Stage lights illuminate the moisture in the air, sweating up from the audience and into the night. The music is clear and focussed, no longer defeated by distance and obstacles; the air bursting with rich, throttling accordion, like a musical two-stroke engine.

"COME ON!!!" I yell, raising my fist in the air, surprising myself almost as much as the drinks vendor stood by me.

We charge up into the banked, curving terracing of the amphitheatre looking for gaps in the crowd. Unrestrained joy boils off the audience. People are not only singing along; they're inhabiting the music, not unlike the assembly at a congregational church. Everyone loves *vallenato*.

For the moment, at least, I'm part of that everyone. I'm like a non-football fan getting caught up in the fervour of the world cup, or someone who only takes crack-cocaine every now and then. The urge to dance is irrepressible.

Shame, then, that I don't know how.

Dancing *vallenato* is easy according to Colombians. Mind you, there are probably surgeons who say the same about thoracic surgery, but that doesn't mean I'd like to have a go at it without first understanding the basics. Fortunately, the environment here is perfect for getting a primer: the terraced steps mean a lot of people are dancing apart which means I can observe the *pasos* in petri-dish isolation, like some kind of mad (dance) scientist.

The old guy on the step below me is my first subject. The fact that there's someone of his generation dancing at all is one of the great things about *vallenato*. Unlike, say, reggaeton, it brings together old and young, rich and poor, totally drunk and just very drunk. I watch intently as the man goes forward on one foot, brings the other one forward to join it, then does the same thing backwards. Easy peasy.

A couple nearby, meanwhile, are doing a simple side-to-side motion, and throwing in the occasional turn. Despite the confines of the step, they are also rotating clockwise as a couple, which seems to be a common component of partner-dancing. There's nothing here that I can't do.

Not that this stops me struggling with it when my chance comes. One of the guys in the group introduces me to a university student who's standing couple of steps in front, suggesting we dance. She's hesitant at first – who is this guy? What are his intentions? But I explain my mission and she agrees.

My own forwardness in doing so almost passes me by. Whether it's because my dance confidence is increasing or simply because I'm being carried away on a wave of *vallenato*, there's definitely something new about my attitude. It's not a lack of fear, just a refusal to accept it: you've got to give these things a go, as first-time thoracic surgeons would doubtless agree.

I take her in a salsa-like stance, placing my hand on her upper back.

"We can dance apart, too," she says.

I interpret this as meaning 'don't dance so close to me' and switch to just hand-holding. At first I just copy the old man's *pasos*, but it's not going well: our feet are getting mixed up, and I'm spending a lot of time looking down. I should have known that it couldn't be as easy as it looked. But my partner is patient, and ultimately we get a whole lot of rotating done.

So that's *vallenato*. But that still leaves *vallenato*, *vallenato* and *vallenato*. Because this genre actually comprises of four different sub-types, each with its own variations in music and dancing style.

From what I can tell, *paseo* (what we've just danced to) is the most common, and has a nice, comfortable speed to move to; *son* is slow and lends itself to close, romantic shuffling; merengue (not to be confused the musical genre of the same name) is fast and has a stronger two-beat sense to it; *puya* is even faster and has a frantic, mental rhythm.

I struggle to tell them apart, but then even the locals aren't always 100% sure, as I found out on a previous occasion when I asked someone what we were listening to.

"*Merengue. ¡No – puya! ¡No – merengue!*"

The next track in the stadium is in the *puya* rhythm. I've no idea how we dance to this, but my partner knows exactly what to do.

"Like this," she says and shimmies her shoulders forward.

Arrrghh no! If there's ever a Colombian citizenship test, that'll be on it. And I'll fail outright.

I reluctantly perform my epilepsy imitation for a while, before inventing a toilet excuse and casually fleeing mid-song.

Not all the acts that evening are *vallenato*. One is a young and poppy group that comes on and plays something halfway between ska and Russian folk. At one point the lead singer comes to the front and does some rhythmic pelvic thrusting. In the UK this would just be seen as sleazy, but here he has the women enraptured.

The singer demands all the single women in the stadium make themselves known to him. Many begin emitting high-frequency noises and waving their hands in the air, including a woman stood a couple of steps in front of me. Then she suddenly stops, gives her boyfriend an embarrassed smile and apologises.

Now the singer wants to know if we want to hear some song or other, during which he'll presumably say "*¡Arriba!*" a bunch of times, thrust his pelvis rhythmically and make enquiries into the sexual availability of all women.

"*¿Si o no?*"

"*¡No!*" says the guy next to me.

"*¿SI O NO?*" says the singer, looking for a more emphatic 'yes'.

"*¡NO!*"

I agree. I never thought I'd hear myself saying this but FOR GOD'S SAKE PUT SOME *VALLENATO* ON.

Steve has quickly settled into a cycle of drinking and sleeping. Unfortunately, each cycle is considerably shorter than a day, which means that by the time I'm ready to go out the following night he's already asleep.

This makes things a bit trickier in terms of finding someone to dance with – I find it much easier to get chatting to strangers if I'm already hanging out with someone as there's less pressure, so it's more relaxed. And the stadium brings with it its own set of particular problems – you don't really have time to assess the situation whilst walking up the stairs that separate the viewing terraces, and approaching people from behind isn't a good strategy either. Unless you plan to garrotte them, in which case it's perfect. But if I'm going to learn how to dance, I need to be with people, and ideally not garrotted ones.

One thing I do have in my favour, however, is the intrigue of being a foreigner. I wander round the near-full stadium and find the end row of a terrace with a couple of women.

"Who is it?" I ask them, gesturing towards the warm-up act.

I don't remember their answer, and it wasn't important anyway. I thank them and turn my focus back to the act, feigning indifference. Before I know it they're trying to get my attention, and are aiming the stream of usual questions at me – Where are you from? What are you doing in Colombia? How is it possible to spend so long on the coast and still be so pale? Well, okay, not the third one, reasonable as it would be.

The older of the two is a healthcare professional working in reproductive health. She tells me that when she toasts, instead of saying the traditional "*¡Salud!*" (Health!) she says "*¡Salud sexual!*" (Sexual health!).

I suggest we dance together, but once again encounter reluctance. Perhaps the natural progression from *vallenato* is unsafe sex.

To be fair, I've heard from a few people now that women are wary of getting a *mala fama* (bad reputation), and that even just being seen to get too close to a foreign guy can get people talking. Besides, I am just a random stranger that rocked up next to them, so perhaps my expectations are unrealistic. And just because most Colombians are happy to dance straight off in such circumstances doesn't mean they all are – they're not some homogenous mass.

Whatever the issue, my new friends and I stand there and dance next to each other in a line, together but apart, and I'm grateful for their company.

Dancing might be important to me, but it's not everyone's top priority. In fact, the whole stadium – the whole festival, even – is on a collective mission to get very trashed indeed. Even as we stand there, vendors walk past holding up litre cartons of rum and empty beer cans clatter to the floor. In fact, drinking was the original adjunct to the music. It was only when the festival came along, the first of which was held in 1968, that dancing really became part of the fun, and many still see drinking as its natural partner.

"*Vallenato* is music to sit and drink alcohol to," as a friend from Barranquilla told me.

Clearly not everyone sees it like this – pretty much the entire crowd was dancing at the festival in San Antero. Mind you, *vallenato* is rich with incongruities. For instance there are the CD covers – despite this being folk music, many of them, especially the counterfeits on street stalls, feature oiled-up bikini babes in a way that I don't think Fairport Convention albums ever have done (although I should probably check). And then there is the fact that this is traditional, rural music and yet nowadays it's often played in stadia.

Tonight's headline act – Carlos Vives – is in some ways the epitome of this last point. Whilst his style spans numerous genres, Carlos is the person who's probably done more than anyone else in recent times to broaden the appeal of *vallenato* and spread it beyond Colombian shores. However, since he achieved this by funking-up old classics from *vallenato*, he's done a fair amount of purist-irking. This shift to commercialism has been referred to as 'dressing *vallenato* up in tails'.

But then there's a history of this that pre-dates *vallenato*: In the early 20th Century, the elites on the coast used to have bands playing to them literally dressed in tails as a way of making music with some black roots more 'respectable' (which actually seems to have meant 'whiter').

As *vallenato* has become yet more mainstream and commercialised, the festival has continued to evolve. I've already heard a local saying how elitist the festival has become: at least with Carnival, he said, you can enjoy the events for free on the street. Here much of the festival, including the finale, is only available for those who can afford it, and everything has been shifted to a weekend to accommodate visitors from out-of-town.

Not that any of this is likely foremost in the minds of those watching Carlos prowl the stage, his curly locks bounding along behind him.

"*¡Qué hombre!*" shouts some guy in front of me. What a guy!

Carlos and the other stadium acts will go on until the early hours of the morning, but even when the concert is over here the parties will continue burning long into the night at *parrandas*. These are private events which are much closer to the traditions of *vallenato* than the stadium interpretation, and many of them won't even get going properly until the sun is up and stretching its arms once again.

From what I've heard they're also quite extraordinary booze-fests. So whilst it would be good to go along just to experience it, the thought of a gig where everyone is wasted, with people vomiting onto their rasps and snore-droning on their accordions, somehow doesn't appeal. I decide to save myself for the following evening.

Steve's destructive cycle has a flat tyre, but I still manage to drag him out to the main square the next day. It's the big accordion competition for God's sake: we have to see one of the rounds at the very least!

Have I been body snatched?

The *acordeonistas* are already showing off their talents when we arrive. At times they play in short bursts with the ends quite close together, whilst at others they draw the concertina right open for a longer section. Whatever they do, it's always a controlled musical action, squeezing and caressing, never a rough manhandling. Meanwhile the people in the crowd are performing similarly loving and tender actions with their bottles of beer, rum and whisky.

The accordion players of *vallenato* produce quite a distinctive type of melody, too. This isn't like the Lambada where the player lays down a simple pattern of notes – a good *vallenato acordeonista* can keep a tune bubbling away constantly, producing a discordant river of notes, which is no mean feat.

"You can't just go like this," says Steve, moving his hands together and apart really quickly. "It's actually quite hard."

Whilst he knows more than I do about *vallenato*, Steve is on almost as much a voyage of discovery as I am, and this is his first visit to Valledupar. In fact, with the improved security situation, many young Colombians are just beginning to get out and explore their own country for the first time – my Facebook feed hums with their excited photos.

One of the competitors is playing a seriously intricate solo, taking us on a full-blown journey through accordion, which builds and builds like he's constructing some great edifice in the sky, appropriate given that the festival's inspiration this year is the legendary Rafael Escalona and his song La Casa En El Aire (The House in the Air).

Steve and I turn to each other and exchange a look of awe. The skill and dexterity involved must be immense. Unless I'm missing something and accordions actually come with a 'demo' button. In some of the tracks, the other instruments get a quick chance to shine on their own, too. Which is fine, but if we start getting into 70s-supergroup style 20-minute percussion solos, I'm outta here.

"And on rasp!"

Despite my new-found interest, there's only so long I can hang around in the city centre during the daytime – Valledupar is crushingly hot at the best of times – so we decide to head down to the river Guatapurí to cool off.

The entire population of Valledupar at some time or other has instructed me to head down there, and today it seems like they've all come down to check that I've made it. The grassy bank is heaving and we have to weave round family after family, each of whom is sending out sweet barbecue smoke signals else cooking something up in their stock pot.

Felipe told me about this back in Cali – it's called *paseo de olla* (pot tour) and is a form of picnic where families cook the stewy soup of *sancocho*, or similar, using the river water.

The river practically makes a sizzling sound as I dip my toes in, the coolness riding up my chest as I sit down. The current is quite testy, so I sit facing upstream and allow it to press me against a submerged rock, the water gurgling all about me like an endless *vallenato* number. Even the river is busy during the festival, the shallows being full of people relaxing, clutching beer bottles as though they were floats.

As I sit there, a guy with an accordion wades into the river just upstream of me. My God, this stuff really is everywhere. You could check in to a sensory deprivation tank and some dude with an accordion would casually float up next to you. And, given the recent transformation in my opinion of the music, he'd be very welcome.

The *acordeonista* is joined by a rasp player and a drummer, the latter with a plastic chair. Soon they're serenading a river full of people, the music mixing in and out of the sound of rushing water, the current sloshing up against the underside of the drummer's seat.

I sit in the sun, listening to the music and watching men leaping off boulders and into the drink. It's not quite as hazardous as the high bridge downstream of here, where they make particularly daring leaps, but it still must take something. After a while I notice that some of the boulder-leapers are able to simply crouch slightly and just go. Others, meanwhile, crouch, then stand back up, then crouch again, and then go, like they had to psychologically set themselves.

What I don't see is anyone who stands there and takes a good look, says "Oh fuck," talks themselves out of it, talks themselves back into it, and ultimately only goes through with it when the level of insistence from bystanders means that their levels of personal shame have started to exceed those of their fear.

So I can't entirely relate to it.

It's the last night of the festival. Tonight, the judges will appoint a new King of Vallenato – a title which could propel the winner to a record contract, if they don't have one already, and relative superstardom.

I haul an already-flagging Steve up to a strategic spot next to a group of girls so we can casually ask them to dance when the time is right. This part of the plan works well although the next bit – getting one of them to dance with me – doesn't. One of them, an accountant from Cartagena, does at least keep nudging me to tell me I'm dancing well in my solo style, which I suppose is better than nothing. Marginally.

The music I'm dancing to is that of the five finalists, backed up by drums and rasp as part of the classic three-piece. We might be in the stadium, but this is far from the Carlos Vives sound – we're right back to *vallenato* basics.

Their fingers fly about the fingerboards delivering note sequences with the same verve and emotional expression as guitar licks. I find myself fantasising about ditching the dance quest in favour of staying here and learning the accordion. Some of them even sing whilst they're playing, which must be like trying to do *zapateos* and *figuras* at the same time.

Even the physical instrument holds an appeal for me. The lacquered wooden body comes in many different colours, but a red, marble-effect seems especially common. The classic design means they look like time-weathered items, each carrying its own story of whisky-soaked *vallenato* duels that went on right through the night, the two-tone bellows expanding and contracting like the underbelly of some mythical beast.

Presented to the audience at this point is a guy from Hohner, whose three-row button diatonic accordion is the iconic instrument of the genre. This prompts Steve, in between gulps of beer, to tell me about the legend of *vallenato*. He explains that, due to an accident on the high seas, a crate of Hohner accordions washed up on the Caribbean coast, and the local people recovered them and taught themselves how to play from scratch. The result was a style of amazing complexity. When a recording of someone playing in this style first made it back to the Hohner company in Germany, they simply couldn't believe what they were hearing.

It's a nice story, even if it does have the delicate fragrance of bullshit hanging about it. For a start, after about twenty minutes, they'd be saying, "But it all sounds the fucking same. And for God's sake give that man some laxatives before he explodes." Mind you, tonight the *vallenato* really does all sound the same: all competitors have to play the same pieces for purposes of comparison.

Finally, after all the musicians have demonstrated their ability, the judges announce a winner: a gentleman called Luchito Daza is the new King of Vallenato. I'm not sure if this means he can knight people with his accordion, but it's certainly a fitting end the festival. And, with Steve having drunk himself to a point where I can no longer tell if he's repeating himself, because I don't understand a single word he says, it seems like a good time to leave.

The polished floor of the transport terminal is alive with feet and luggage as every man, woman and accordion tries to make a break from the clutches of alcohol, and escape to sanity.

On my own coach, which I had to book days in advance, a film is cranking up as we prepare to depart. It seems like every time I take a coach they're showing the least (or possibly most) appropriate film ever for this country – a Hollywood kidnap film. Perhaps it's because in this fantasy world, all the baddies get mullered (killed, that is, not drunk – this isn't a *vallenato* concert) and the victim is rescued unharmed.

But I'm not even paying attention this time – before my coach pulls away I'm already engrossed in the music playing through my headphones. *Vallenato.*

My attempts to learn a dance via osmosis have had mixed results. But whilst I can't say I've learned to dance *vallenato,* I do seem to have learned something I could barely have imagined before I came here: I've learned to appreciate it.

With my passport waiting for me at the Consulate in Cartagena, it's time for one last hop to the coast before charging conquistador-like into the interior. I've seen so little of the inside of this country that I don't really know what to expect: both Cali and the Plains would seem atypical, whilst Bogota, being a capital, is surely a law unto itself.

So I have many new places and new challenges ahead of me, I just don't know what they are yet. But wherever I go, I need to get better at finding partners to dance with, or there's precious little point to this journey at all.

CHAPTER THIRTEEN

The Rhythm Inside

"*Los cachacos no pueden bailar nada,*" says the woman, expressing a common local sentiment. *Cachacos* can't dance at all.

Cachaco is a blanket term applied to someone from Bogotá, or the interior of the country in general. The term can sometimes carry a negative connotation, part of the coastal-versus-interior we're-better-than-you cultural fisticuffs, but I'm going to use it here as neutral shorthand.

I'm not a *cachaco*, or whatever the British equivalent is – I was born only about ten miles from the coast. This effectively makes me a Costeño, which goes at least some way to explaining my natural dance ability and chilled-out demeanour. Furthermore, us Brits are all islanders, making us doubly laid-back. We spend most of our time just swinging in hammocks.

I'm at a *verbena* (street party) in a Cartagena backstreet. Music blasts out from between wide-open shutters, filling the sultry night with *vallenato*, salsa and *champeta*. Couples dance in the street against a backdrop of distempered render whilst young men sit around in a group on plastic chairs playing cards and drinking *gaseosas*.

A stocky black Costeño with a hearty smile is dishing out rum to anyone who wants it, after first tipping a little plastic cup of the stuff onto the ground, as happened in Palenque.

"It's for the spirits," he says. "*¿Entiendes?* Like the dead. It's something symbolic"

I love street life on the coast – even when there's nothing going on, there's something going on – but my time here is drawing to a close. A couple of days ago, I strolled into the consulate and picked up my new passport from Carmen, thus cutting the umbilical cord with Cartagena and making me a free man. It's time to head to the interior and see if what they say about *cachacos* is true, and hopefully get some serious dance practice in the process.

The coastal plains are gone, replaced by lush, rolling hills, which I'm seeing from the inside of a slightly less lush (but just as rolling) bus. Rather than charging in to the interior on a long-distance coach, I've decided to slow down so I can see a bit more of the country en route.

Being on the back row of what is a pint-sized vehicle, every time we go over a bump my backside and the seat part company. Sometimes the impact is so hard and sudden that I emit involuntary sounds, and on at least one occasion I have a good go at destroying the overhead light cluster with my head.

So it's something of a relief when we arrive at the riverside town of Magangué although, as per usual, I left it a touch late in the day to depart, and the sun is well gone by the time I get there. Without the breeze of the coast, it's a hot night. It's also a dark night, as the lighting in my part of town is permanently on dim, making the whole place feel very low-key, and only half existent.

What the town lacks in light it makes up for in sound, with the various bars and clubs competing to be the least pleasant environment to relax with a drink. Not that I'll be getting any dance action tonight – despite all the whumping, they're near-empty. Instead, all the activity that evening is focussed on the evening fitness class, where the young women of Magangué are dancercising, and the young men are gawping shamelessly through the windows.

Back in my hotel room, the big fan stirs the moist air whilst a grasshopper pings about the edges of the tiled floor – this town is crawling with insects. I trap it under my shoe, not quite having the heart to kill it. The next morning I wake to find it dead inside my shoe, with lots of little ants scurrying about outside. Did the ants move it and then forget where they put it, or did the grasshopper hide from them, but then croak? I'll never know.

Down at the port, water taxis line up along the rubbish-strewn bank under a flurry of little Colombian flags. The river is fat and bloated here, and seems even more so because of the lack of elevation. My plan is to head along the route of the Magdalena river and into the highlands, like the conquistador Gonzalo Jiménez de Quesada, although hopefully quicker and with fewer attacks by indigenous people.

But I've got my eye on one last, quick stop before I head for the hills – in the town of Mompós - so after a short spray along the river in a water taxi, I take to the land again. This time it's in a *colectivo* (share taxi) with pleated curtains in the windows, the rear tyres kicking up dust as we pull away, heading off past a young man walking a cow.

Trapped in a swampy lowland, where the Cauca and Magdalena rivers converge, the pace of life in Mompós is a step down from the coast, even. Folk sit out in front of their houses on rocking chairs, giving me friendly smiles as I pass, whilst cats roll out and stretch behind window grills. Colonial buildings bake in the midday sun and the corners of concrete sidewalks slowly disintegrate into the road. Green paint gradually peels off a door in a decades-long process, revealing the previous coat, also green. Time doesn't flow here – it oozes.

Once upon a time, Mompós was a trade rival for Cartagena, albeit one that favoured contraband, but the shifting river course rendered it a backwater. Now most of its cargo is a never-ending supply of branches and river-weed, and the occasional banana-laden canoe. We're still definitely more coastal than interior though, the ratio of *vallenato* to other music proving an excellent barometer.

I sit at an open air café on the low-key riverfront eating fish with rice and *patacones* and a squeeze of lime. It's good, tasty stuff – have I mentioned that I like Colombian food? I repose and take in the surroundings. Wrought-iron lampposts line the bank of the river and stairs descend elegantly into the turbid water, giving it the sense of a flooded street in Victorian Britain, and that a hansom cab could pull up at any moment.

Mompós is a place that inspired Colombian writer Gabriel García Márquez, and he's not the only famous name to be linked here. In the main square is a plaque quoting Simón Bolívar: "*Si a Carácas debo la vida, a Mompós debo la Gloria,*" (If to Caracas I owe my life, to Mompós I owe my glory) referring to the local men with whom he fought to victory in Caracas during the struggle to free Venezuela – then a province of the Viceroyalty of New Granada – from the Spanish.

Bolívar was the great liberator, and you can bet the Spanish would have offered more than a yo-yo for killing this Venezuelan. He rode across South America freeing a great swathe of it from Spanish rule, and is now immortalised in the army of statues that marches across this mighty continent, and also in the name of streets, towns, currencies, and even a country (Bolivia). Mompós itself is located in the department of Bolívar.

I'd argue that his greatest triumph was leaving Mompós at all. I could easily stay and laze about here for weeks. But I need to press onwards to the interior and get dancing again. I head out before sunrise the next morning: you have to leave this place before it's woken up or it can hold you in its grip for good. Also because that's when the minibus leaves.

My head judders against the glass as we head by road to El Banco, another riverside town and one with a proud cumbia heritage. En route, a couple of my fellow passengers – a pair of middle-aged local women – press me to stay, telling me they'll find me someone to teach me the local variant of the popular dance. I politely decline – my sights are set firmly upriver, on the interior. These *cachacos* had better be keen dancers.

Here, as at Magangué, the river is wide broad and high, Water is the dominating force in these parts, not land, and the sheer volume of it is intimidating. A pontoon ventures out into the powerful flow, the paint on its sides criss-crossed with scars from boat strikes, whilst the river itself is beset by mysterious eddies and swirling currents that can only hint at the activity underneath.

Once our *chalupa* (water taxi) is full, we fire off upstream, plumes of spray flying past the windows on either side. Ah, life on a riverboat: the throb of the engine; the smell of gasoline; the people at the back complaining that water is coming in. We stop and drift awhile in the middle of the flow, whilst one of the crew bounds along to the back and fixes something, before setting off again in a less drown-worthy state.

The Amazon may be a mighty river, but in the context of Colombia it's a mere lieutenant: the Magdalena is the admiral. Whilst the Amazon merely brushes the country's edge, the Magdalena forages right through the heart of the country before waving a wistful farewell at Bocas de Ceniza.

The Magdalena River became a key trade route during colonial times, but traversing the river was a nightmare, especially upstream. Before the advent of steamboats in the mid-19th century, it took a bare minimum of 25 days to get from the coast to Honda (near Bogotá). Wheat flour being carried downstream to the coast would often spoil due to the heat and moisture, and it wasn't the only thing: the indigenous people that the Spanish brought in to work as boatmen had a ridiculously high death-rate.

But if the indigenes thought they had things bad, at least they didn't have to have to wedge themselves between restrictive fibreglass seats for extended periods of time, as I do now. It feels like a medieval torture device, and each stop – and the opportunity to stretch – comes with great relief.

All the way up the river we stop at floating pontoons serving local communities, both in terms of passengers and also delivery of goods – I see sacks of grain, boxed televisions and even a motorbike being delivered during our journey. Sandalled feet shift about at eye level, whilst locals hang about on the bank sporting 'chicken bags' – shoulder bags bearing a live chicken whose legs are thrust out through holes in the bottom. Sometimes we just stop directly at the grassy river bank to drop items off at an individual homestead – the river is something of a lifeline in these parts.

We're someway upstream now, but the river is still intimidatingly broad in places, and littered with floating river-weed, logs and all sorts of other natural traffic, sometimes with large birds, such as egrets, perched aboard. Despite the complex surface currents, the river has quite a lazy feel. It's only when the boat is lashed in a pontoon that its true velocity and might become apparent, gushing through the mooring at a frightening pace.

There's very little to see beyond the low banks as we continue our journey upstream – no unsightly factories, no big towns, no nothing – just open pastureland with trees and the occasional glimpse of distant Andean foothills. We're now in the Magdalena Valley, and the ranges are growing silently in might beyond the horizon on both sides.

Seven or eight hours after leaving El Banco, we draw in to the terminal at Barrancabermeja, the same place where Quesada left the river and took to the mountains. I, too, leave the river behind here, along with any sense of ambiguity of location – this is most definitely the interior.

Everyone loves San Gil. Set in the eastern cordillera of the Andes, it's the adventure-sport centre of Colombia, and is on the to-do or to-did list of both foreign backpackers and Colombians alike. People come here to paraglide, cave, raft and generally interact with the rugged landscape in every way they can short of rubbing the red soil into their eyes and licking the rocks.

It feels great to be up in the mountains, even if it is the lower boughs rather than the snow-dusted peaks. For me, the Andes is more than just part of South America – it is South America. I love the sense of rarefied air; the musty smell that the Andes practically owns; the fact that if I want to my door to stay closed in my room I have to employ a rock provided for the purpose. But what I really love is the clouds. There's nothing quite like Andean clouds: big raucous loofahs floating in the sky; stupid curly wigs covering chains of green hills; blasts and explosions like a medieval battlefield.

San Gil has its own identity within that, of course. Streets rise up from the centre in a concave sweep with ledge-like crossroads at the top, and I spend much of my time either leaning forwards or backwards, depending on whether I'm going uphill or down.

It's also a place with its own local culinary local delicacy, that of fat-bottomed ants – the Queen song that never was. I can confirm they taste coffee-like, rather nutty and maybe even slightly chocolatey, with a hint of cigarette ash. Although the problem with eating something like ant is that it's very hard to actually enjoy it: even if the flavour was exquisite, you'd still spend your whole time thinking "I'm eating ant."

But enough of all that – what's the dance like here?

A local restaurateur in her thirties tells me she doesn't like the way that they dance to reggaeton in places like Cartagena. The girls get pregnant at a very early age, she says, and she links this to learning intimate styles of dancing whilst too young.

"This kind of dancing should come later."

So the early indications, admittedly from a sample group of one, are that attitudes are more reserved.

I head out in the evening with a couple of female backpackers from the US and a Colombian guy, the inclines testing our ankles.

We sit having dinner in some middle-class rib-house (rib-cage, surely) and I tell them about my mission. The outcome is inevitable: they want me to demonstrate the various forms.

I'm beyond comfortable with this now – I actively relish it. I get up and work my way through my repertoire, giving little kicks and spasmodic thrusts; shuffling my feet, wagging my knees and slapping the floor.

They're impressed, of course. But it's all smoke and mirrors – throw an actual real-life partner in there and I'd be nothing like so polished. I'm becoming some kind of dance impersonator, maybe even a dance raconteur. But that was never the aim. Dance is something that should be done, not just discussed.

Furthermore, I can see disturbing signs that my tools are beginning to seize up through lack of use. *Joropo* is the latest thing to go awry, resembling a set of rusty old stirrups. I haven't practised it with a partner at all since I left the Llanos, but then how could I have? It's like trying to spin plates when you're missing an important piece of equipment. Like the plates. All of which makes me wonder what will happen when the time comes to do the show. You know – that thing I'm pretending I'm going to do.

Meanwhile, it turns out that the girls are novice salsa dancers themselves, and they make it their own mission to find somewhere to dance. This makes me feel strangely uncomfortable: the downside of being a dance raconteur is that it raises expectations to unrealistic levels, as well as making it almost impossible to refuse. I might be getting more confident, but the bar is getting raised too.

"I'm on a mission to dance anywhere and everywhere!"

"Great – shall we go dancing?"

"No."

As it happens, no dance establishments appear to be open on this midweek evening – if *cachacos* really can dance, they're choosing not to tonight. The girls aren't so easily beaten, however, and back in their hostel dormitory one of them puts her laptop on her bedcovers and flips open the lid, releasing tinny-sounding claves, cowbells and timbales into the room, like a flock of strange birds.

But even then there's a problem: the girls both know one of the *en linea* (cross-body) styles of salsa common to the USA. I try dancing Cali-style salsa with one of the girls, but it feels like I've brought Lego to the party, and she's brought Stickle Bricks. Not only that, but my salsa skills have degraded to the point where I'm struggling to lead effectively. I'm also getting seriously short on turns. I've no idea where they're all going – there must be a big pile of them lying about somewhere.

After a few minutes labouring, we go back to where I'm most comfortable – standing on the sidelines and theorising about it. If there's one thing you can say about me, I talk a mean dance. But even then we have compatibility issues.

"There's this shine..."

This what?

"Shine..."

She demonstrates writhing up and down on the spot like a mermaid. It looks quite sexy, but I'm not sure what it has to do with dance, or at least my newly-formed conception of it.

"And while the woman is doing that, the man is doing this."

She strikes a leaning pose with folded arms, like a stubborn sailor.

This leads into an anecdote about how she was once dancing with a partner from her class, when he went into a shine and she didn't know the appropriate 'answer'. The guy threw his arms up in the air and walked off, mid-dance. Now, you see, that's what I'd call dancing like a twat. I mean surely that misses the whole point of partner dancing? As has been pointed out to me, dance is not just a set of moves to learn – it's about a human connection. It's a conversation between two people and the music.

I'm quite surprised by my own strength of feeling on the subject – it would seem like I've genuinely internalised something of the dance culture here. I've started thinking about it in aphorisms, too, and that's got to be a sign of something. If only my dance skills were as advanced as my dance ethics.

Tunja, my next stop, is a town of many clocks, all of which seem to tell the wrong time, on initial impressions at least. It's also a town with a sense of humour: they built the centre on the top of a hill and the bus station near the bottom, which, in a city nearly 3,000m above sea level, is a pretty cruel trick. The place feels yet-more-Andean-still than San Gil and the buildings smell like an old cupboard. That's had sheep in.

Heading onwards through the mountains has brought me here, to the capital of Boyacá department. I'm looking for a place where I'll at least be able to practise, and maybe even learn something new, and I'm hoping this is it.

The joyful self-expression of the coast seems a long way away, muted by the mountain chill. Something tells me I'm unlikely to come across a *verbena* here. The racial mix is very different, too, with the people being mostly *mestizo* (a mixture of European and indigenous ancestry). Dull, heavy clothing is now the norm, including a kind of heavy woollen poncho called a *ruana*. Patternless and neutrally-coloured, it's effectively a big, wearable blanket, and seems to be favoured by the poorer and more indigenous-looking people, like the woman I pass selling fresh fruit and veg off a hand cart.

I watch as business folk in suits and other locals cross the big square that marks the centre of town. These places fascinate me. In villages, towns and cities right across Colombia, the square is a meeting place, a mini-marketplace and a social hub, and it comes in all different sizes.

The one in Mompós, for example, is a small, rectangular effort with gnarled old tree roots and dusty soil beds. Men and boys sit around with brightly-coloured coffee flasks, selling tiny cups of *tinto* coffee for 200 pesos (10 cents; 7 pence), whilst other folk sell lottery tickets, mobile phone calls or fresh orange juice. There's even a guy selling second-hand books, laid out under a scattering of freshly-fallen leaves.

The one here at Plaza Bolívar (named after some bloke or other), meanwhile, has a very different feel. It's modern and paved, and surrounded on three sides by squat, yellow-and-white colonial buildings with a brutal concrete town hall on the final one. Its lack of benches mark it out as more of a thoroughfare than a place to stop and chat or buy stuff.

Today's cross-square traffic is slightly different. A moving hubbub traverses the *plaza*, with the green fatigues of police officers and the snapping cameras of journalists caught up within it – someone important must be about. I get closer and find at the centre of it all some guy pressing the flesh. A few *ruana*-wearing types, who look like they've come in for the day from the country, seem especially keen to shake hands with him, although it's not clear if they're aware of his identity or if, like me, they've just been drawn in out of intrigue.

"I met someone really important today!"

"Who?"

"Dunno, but great, eh?"

Some people are chanting "*¡Santos Presidente!*", so naturally I assume it's Juan Manuel Santos – the favourite for the upcoming elections. But it turns out to be fellow candidate Rafael Pardo – by coincidence, both are campaigning here on the same day.

Santos is a particularly well-known character – he was Minister of Defence for some time under the current president (Álvaro Uribe), and is seen as his natural political successor. The firm hand of Santos seemed to be a factor in bringing the country's violence under control, though not without controversy: it was during his tenure that the '*falsos positivos*' (false positives) scandal occurred. This was where soldiers murdered civilians and dressed them up as guerrillas in order to claim government rewards. I've seen the resulting '*Falsos Santos*' and '*Santos Positivos*' graffiti in a few different places now.

Santos's nearest rival is Green Party candidate Antanas Mockus – a Colombian of Lithuanian descent with the appearance of a cool, avuncular hippy. You just look at him and think "lentils". It's not just his appearance that is outlandish – he is well known for his novel approach to problem-solving. During his time as Mayor of Bogotá, he introduced mime artists to mock traffic-law offenders at a time when road rage was a real problem in Bogotá (humiliation was seen as a bigger punishment than fines), set up a program offering food in exchange for guns, which were then melted down into babies' spoons and took a shower in a television advert to promote water-saving measures.

Under the tenure of Mockus (and another Mayor, Peñalosa) murders in the city fell from 80 to 22 per 100,000 people, presumably because everyone was too enthralled by what crazy shit he'd might get up to next.

"I lived through the whole transformation there," a Mockus supporter in San Gil told me. "I think it's a time of change."

Mockus certainly seems to have the educated-youth vote sewn up. The party's branding of a yellow sunflower on a green background beams out from their t-shirts and wristbands, whilst the enthusiastic social media squawkings of the university and post-university crowd barely mention another name.

Santos, meanwhile, seems to have support in a less-visible but perhaps greater part of the electorate: people who consider themselves realists; who lived through the worst Colombia had to offer and have no intention of doing so again. As far as they're concerned, Santos's approach has made a difference, and he's the natural successor to Uribe. Why change something if it's working?

So a vote for Santos is a vote for continuity, whilst a vote for Mockus is a vote for change (not to mention outstanding beardsmanship). Polls have shown Santos as being ahead for some time, but Mockus is closing. Just to spice things up, Mockus has recently revealed he's been diagnosed with early-stage Parkinson's disease.

I don't know why they need all the security round these guys, though – it's not like any politicians have ever been bumped off in Colombia.

Ahem.

Back to far more important matters, and Tunja seems as good a place as any to find out what *cachacos* know about dance. The tourist information office puts me in touch with a woman who runs dance classes in the town. I'm quite excited by the prospect of learning something else, particularly as I already have a dance in mind – one that's been there ever since I saw the wedding video in Barranquilla. It's time to learn merengue!

It isn't time to learn merengue. Apparently, Tunja isn't famous for this dance – I'm getting confused with the Dominican Republic. The teacher suggests I add a more traditional number from the interior to my repertoire, such as the elegant *bambuco* or its cousin the *torbellino*, and invites me to come and see the class that evening.

In the meantime, I go to visit a piece of local history. Boyacá department is a particularly appropriate place for candidates to be canvassing: the region was one of the main arenas in the struggle for Colombian independence, and hence the country's right to elect its own presidents in the first place. The site that I'm on my way to visit is steeped in significance in this regard.

The asphalt highway carves its way between roaming patchwork hills populated by scratchy little farmhouses. Knackered old cars sit adjacent, clinging grimly onto life, whilst clothes hang from any part of the buildings that are vaguely sticky-outy. From the clutter surrounding these dwellings, it would seem that nothing is ever thrown away.

If it wasn't for all the flags and the visitor centre, it would be easy to miss the site. You certainly wouldn't know it was significant to look at it – it's just a small bridge crossing a humble river. It's the kind of thing you'd only be pleased about if it was in your back garden, or perhaps if it was symbolic in the formation of your nation.

This is Puente de Boyacá (Boyacá Bridge), or at least a reconstruction of it. It was here that Simón Bolívar and his troops defeated the Spanish in battle in what was the definitive point in the liberation from their European rulers. Such was its importance that even now, new presidents of Colombia are traditionally inaugurated on the same date as that battle: 7th August.

Spain was particularly vulnerable at the time, limping as it was through war with Napoleonic France and a couple of bourgeois revolutions. Within a few years it would be expelled from the American mainland entirely. Following the Battle of Boyacá, the ruling Spanish viceroy scarpered, and the liberating forces went on to claim lots of highly populous areas, and ultimately secure the country's liberation.

With the Spanish vanquished, the former Viceroyalty of New Granada, roughly comprising of modern-day Colombia, Panama, Venezuela and Ecuador, formed a new republic of Gran Colombia. However, political wrangling and financial turmoil meant it soon dissolved into its constituent parts (with Colombia and Panama sticking together). Which is just as well for me or my dance mission would be one heck of a lot longer than it already is.

The journey back is in driving rain – a special kind of rain that's well suited to road journeys. The guy next to me is one of a number of *campesinos* (rural farmer-types) on the *buseta*, wearing wellies, jeans and a dirty *ruana*. The smell of wet wool fills the vehicle and the floor is muddy with footprints – many of these people are on their way home after a hard day's work outdoors.

My *campesino* neighbour looks straight-out-the-field, and probably is. Everything he's wearing is functional and the dirt is ingrained in his skin from hard labour. It makes me feel self-conscious about the various artisanal bits and bobs I've accumulated on my wrists, to the point that I pull down my various warm layers to cover them. In an urban environment they look fine, but in this setting they look as comical and frivolous as high heels. Which I also surreptitiously conceal.

This region was originally the territory of the indigenous Muisca people, the starting point of the El Dorado legend, but through various mechanisms the *mestizo* (mixed European/indigenous heritage) population increased and the regular indigenous population declined. Come independence, *mestizo* people were in the majority in many places, even in traditionally indigenous towns like Tunja.

In this new era, moves were made to improve rights for indigenous people and integrate them further into Hispanic society, resulting in further racial mixing still, with the result that very few 'pure' indigenous people remain. A gradual homogenising (well, 'whitening') of the population via miscegenation was something of a goal of the Hispanic elites at the time, as they saw the indigenous people as inferior and holding the country back.

Back in Tunja, it turns out I won't be learning anything for the time being. We must have got our wires crossed, the dance teacher and I, as when I turn up at the venue that evening I can't find any class taking place. I try again the next night, only to find the building locked. I feel like the Spanish looking for the legendary Lost City of Gold – wondering if dancing really exists in these parts, or if it's just pure legend.

The weekend is generally my best chance of getting some dance practice: it's when the clubs open, and when everyone gets out and lets their hair down. I've missed out on far too many opportunities in the past, and unless I can meet some folk here I'm in danger of missing out yet again. Okay, so I could probably go in to a club alone, but that makes me feel like a spare part, and the fact I don't drink just exacerbates it. I could really do with making some local friends and taking it from there. Social networking sites might help in a bigger city, but here they've drawn a blank.

I try hanging out in some of the little café bars on the perimeter of the square so I can get talking to people. When that doesn't reap any rewards, I resort to going out into the main square itself. Asking women straight out to come to a club and dance with me seems a touch forward, so I approach people under the semi-truthful guise of wanting to know good places to eat, although now

I just feel like a cross between a market researcher and a pick-up artist. It feels curiously underhand, despite the fact that my underlying motivation is perfectly honourable.

The group of female psychologists I talk to are kind enough not to strip my hidden agenda bare and parade it about in front of me, but that's about all: after they've helped me to find a pizza place that's about twenty yards away, they make their excuses and leave.

This isn't working. Perhaps going somewhere smaller would mean I'm more likely to meet people. I decide it's worth a shot, so the next day I leave town and head towards Sogamoso, a sacred city in Muisca times but now looking a little tired, and with more concrete than they probably had back then. From here I take a minibus that clambers up the mountainside, leaving the town way below, past houses with their own little patches of farmland and the occasional rudimentary *tejo* pitch.

As we ascend, I ask a pair of women in their twenties if they know of any accommodation. The fact I can't tell them which town I'm going to – because I don't actually know – doesn't help, but one of them takes the challenge on, and embarks on a sequence of phone calls. Hanging up for the final time, she tells me the name of a guest house then politely returns to nattering with her friend once more. I've not found myself any dance partners, but at least I know roughly where I'm going now.

All this time we're pointing up into yet higher reaches, pushing me back into my seat and making my ears pop. Finally we crest a brow, and the nose of the minibus starts pointing down for a change. Spread out below, is the geographical feature I was roughly aiming for.

Laguna de Tota (Lake Tota) is the largest natural lake in Colombia and amongst the highest located. It looks serene from on high: sat within a broad crater-like bowl, its gently-pitted surface reflects the light in teasing glints. Accompanying the view is a scent that's quite sharp, maybe even acidic, and vaguely familiar. It stays with us as we descend, as though it's trapped in the natural depression and can't escape. Dammit, what is that?

We begin circling the lake at a distance, separated from the water's edge by furrowed plots of land bearing sage-coloured shoots in regimented rows.

"These are onions," says one of the women, breaking away

from conversation.

That's it! Onions!

It's not the only local produce, either: signs on the outside of humble buildings announce '*Sí, hay trucha*' (Yes, we have trout), and we pass cage farms submerged at the water's edge. I'm going to hazard a guess that the local speciality is trout and onions. In a freshwater sauce.

The woman turns back to me again and briefly outlines the *leyenda* (legend) of how the small islands in the lake were formed. My Spanish isn't good enough to fully grasp it, and my (no doubt entirely incorrect) version has it that some guy got really drunk, danced a lot, then got dizzy and fell in. Something like that. Unless she's just telling me some local gossip.

After skirting the lake on a road that meanders between houses and plots of land, we draw into the main town, where the bus drops us all off. The two women point out the hotel, then say their farewells and head in a different direction. I guess that approach needs some tweaking.

The friendly young man running the place gives me a room with a view over the lake, although some straining of the eyes is required: the water is a mere sliver of blue, and is separated from us by a good mile or so of patchwork allotments.

Aquitania is a quiet little town, and a weekend refuge for folk from Bogotá. The place has isolated, end-of-the-road feel, even if being on the ring-road that circles the lake makes that a rather improbable proposition. Whereas many Colombian towns have a mall on the outskirts of town, or at the very least a chain supermarket, this is a land of family-run corner shops. Even then, those shops have a bare-shelved, communistic feel about them, with none of the shiny consumerism of the city.

Something tells me I may have got it wrong coming here.

I sit in the square and watch the town's elders wander about pensively, lapping at ice creams, and quietly chatting under the tufted sky. Many of the locals are wearing fedoras and *ruanas*: what was a smattering in Tunja has become a full-on craze. Even little kids wear them, often complete with cute little hoods. Another quirk of the town is that people have suddenly gone from addressing me by the formal *usted* (you), to the medieval-sounding *su merced* (your mercy). Easy chaps – I'm not a conquistador! Although if you know where there's any gold going spare…

Very few buildings feel the need to rise above two storeys, hence the place is dominated by the cathedral with its twin golden domes, which presides over the main square, even if it's the small trout restaurants that I personally find exerting a greater power.

The church/square setup is a common feature of Colombia. In this part of the country, the Spanish wanted to proselytise, civilise and generally control the indigenous people, but this was difficult because they were spread out all over the shop. So they build new towns for them, featuring a square and a 'Who's the Daddy?' religious edifice.

Then there's the thing I'm going to call the shop-pub, for want of a better composite noun. They look like shops, with a counter and shelves and fridges, but they also have plastic chairs and tables. The main (in some cases only) product is beer, lined up on the dusty shelves only one bottle deep, like an identity parade.

"Here's the culprit officer – the one responsible for all that stuff I did last night."

There are so many of these little establishments in this small town, you'd wonder how they could all make a living. There are several on each street, little backstreets included, and presumably many of these places only stay open by virtue of their regulars, who sit about building edifices to the great god of beer with their empties.

It's getting late, so I head into a café for a hot chocolate. A popular salsa track is playing on the radio and I find myself tapping along. A glance to my left and I see that a group of four friends are also doing likewise, and we exchange smiles. The moment the song – Yo No Sé Mañana by Luis Enrique – hits the chorus, we all spontaneously burst into song laugh-singing the words in unison.

The laughter dies down and I end up sat with them, chatting about life, music and onions. For a while I even think we'll end up dancing somewhere, if indeed there is somewhere to dance. But no – they're all turning in early, despite it being a Saturday night. Whilst in Cali I was practically being press-ganged into dancing, here it's like dance doesn't even exist.

The hotel receptionist is sat on the wall outside the hotel when I get back. He greets me with a friendly smile and asks if I'd like to join him in a nearby beer-shop. Well why not? A few moments later, I'm sat at a table with him, his friends and a selection of bottles in varying states of emptied-ness.

The group consists entirely of young men out on the beers, yet they talk with the kind of reserve and mildness you'd expect in a church. We discuss for a while about the upcoming election and other things that seem inconsequential out here in the sticks. Then without warning, things come to an end: someone points out the time and there's suddenly a big rush to get the bottles off the table.

"It's because of *la ley zanahoria*," one of them says.

Ley zanahoria (carrot law) is the popular name for a ruling that it was brought in by Mockus to combat the various problems associated with staying up all night getting wasted, with the 'carrot' bit being a Spanish-language pun for someone healthy.

He also experimented with a more gender-specific curfew in Bogotá, holding a night without men, in which all the men had to stay at home, followed by the exact reverse, to make a point about how violence and crime are male-dominated. It feels like one of those nights tonight given my single-gender company and lack of dance opportunities. But hey, at least it's keeping crimes against dance down.

The bar closing turns out to be a minor inconvenience: they lead me a few doors down into what seems to be Aquitania's only nightclub. Finally! It has a fairly rudimentary set-up, but there are tables and chairs and there's a dance floor. What more do you need?

Well, someone to dance with would be nice.

"Neil!" shouts a voice over the top of the music.

Huh?

Oh look! It's the girls I met on the bus! They're sat with their various partners and other friends, and they're all pretty drunk by the look of it. But that doesn't translate to any equivocation over intent: "*¡A bailar!*" they all insist, and push me in the general direction of their twenty-something friend. At last, I get to dance. Okay, so I get the impression this is more about the novelty of seeing a foreigner dance with their single friend than any Cali-style press-ganging, but I don't really care. Come on, your mercy – let's dance!

I take her warm hands in my cold ones and lead her to the floor. We're halfway through a *vallenato* number, which seems strangely out of place in this chilly little corner of the country. The result is a little uncoordinated, both because she's a little tipsy and because I can only dance *vallenato* as it's never meant to be done –

on my own – but hey, practice is practice.

Despite being inside, it's still pretty chilly, so people are well-wrapped up. There's even a couple dancing in *ruanas*, which I sight to behold in itself. But add the sheer weight of clothing to the breathlessness that comes with altitude, and the dancing feels laboured and ploddy. No wonder most people here would rather drink than dance.

We've only just got warmed up when it's all over AGAIN – the lights come on and we're ejected into the still night. No-one is ready to turn in just yet though, myself included, so we decamp into the main square. Some fumbling for money occurs followed by the materialisation of bottles of *aguardiente*.

It's about now that I notice that everyone is rattling about to the brink of toppling, as though we were in the grip of an Andean earthquake. People in this town seem to be cut from a different cloth: one that's been soaked in alcohol. The *vallenato* festival is the only place to have come close.

There's not just more drink here – there's more peer pressure too.

"One swig," says a pink-eyed bloke, proffering the bottle. "Just one. Just one. Just one."

I politely refuse, to which someone passes comment about me being less than a man. I try to get him to qualify this, but someone else pulls me away telling me it'll just end in a fight. It's like being back home.

I'm only staying up in the hope of another dance, and I eventually manage to persuade someone to put some salsa on the stereo of his parked car. In other parts of the country, this would spur off a frenzy of dancing, but here nobody seems bothered. Even my new-found dance partner requires some persuasion before I can lead – or rather support – her through a sequence of leaden, mutually-uncoordinated moves.

But then there are always idiosyncrasies to be overcome. Some partners are so loose-limbed that I find it hard to lead them, because when I push or pull their arm, their body just stays where it is. Others themselves want to lead, making us like a pair of drivers wrestling with a single steering wheel. Then there are the ones that seem to misread every turn, regardless of how clearly I'm signalling (or at least think I am). Others, as I say, are a tiny bit tipsy.

The evening staggers on, eventually collapsing in someone's flat with a party that is aborted as quickly as it is initiated due to the memory-depriving effects of alcohol.

It really is time to leave.

I don't know if *cachacos* can't dance or won't dance, but from what I've seen so far, a lot of them pretty much don't dance. Indeed, the more time I spend in this country, the more I realise that there's no such thing as a typical Colombian, so arguably the idea of dancing like one is somewhat flawed in itself.

On a personal level, despite my best efforts to practise, I'm still nowhere near where I want to be. If I want this trip to have been worthwhile – to arrest my fading powers and to come out of this as something even approaching a half-decent dancer – I'm going to have to get out there and dance a whole lot more. Otherwise, I'm doomed to be nothing more than an impersonator.

CHAPTER FOURTEEN

Black and White

Phwooaarrrr!

Ay ay ay!

Hubba hubba hubba!

I just wanted to get that out the way.

Colombia has changed a lot in recent times, but probably nowhere quite as dramatically as Medellín. Until fairly recently, this was a place to be avoided: the most murderous city in the most murderous country. It was the epicentre of drugs, assassinations and kidnapping, and the erstwhile home of Pablo Escobar, a major proponent of many of these activities; the home of everything that Colombia is infamous for.

But with Escobar gone, and a modern metro in place, the city – the second most populous in Colombia – has undergone a remarkable renaissance. This is in part due to the the transport network, which branches out to encompass the poor *barrios* on the mountainsides by use of a novel cable-car system known as the Metrocable. This innovation had a big impact, yanking previously isolated areas into a tighter embrace with the rest of the city. Whilst this might sound like a recipe for a self-service poor-rob-the-rich setup, in practice it means the poor are integrated into the city rather than being left marginalised in ghettos.

But exciting as integrated public transport is, it's not the first thing that most people, or at least most men, think about when they think about Medellín.

"*Las mujeres de Medellín...*" as I heard one guy sighing to himself in San Gil. The women of Medellín…

The women here are famous for being the most beautiful in the country. Indeed, the only place where this would appear to be disputed is in Cali, where they insist it's Caleñas who top this league. Indeed, there's a well-known Colombian salsa track by the name of Las Caleñas Son Como Las Flores (Cali Women Are Like Flowers).

But then beauty isn't in short supply in this country, and nor are plastic surgeons, with Medellín and Cali in some kind of cosmetic face-off. Breast augmentation is particularly popular but backside implants are also common, presumably to help counterbalance the augmented frontage.

It's hardly a surprise that plastic surgery is a must for many Colombians given the pressure to conform to the ideal of beauty. Even the shop-window mannequins in Colombia are astonishingly talented. I've been tempted to ask one out on a date before now.

A Colombian barman called Jorge, here to visit friends, tells me that *paisa* women (women from Medellín and the Antioquia region) are reputed to be "*en la calle como damas, en la cama como putas*". They supposedly have really great personalities, too, if you're into that kind of thing.

Paisa women do actually have a reputation for being warm and caring, whilst *paisas* in general are considered very hardworking, and perhaps with good reason – they built the region into the industrial backbone of the country during the first half of the 20th Century.

Jorge isn't a *paisa* – he's from Bogotá. He takes a lot of stick for it in these parts, but says that you just have to take it.

"*¡Al que no quiere caldo se le dan dos tazas!*" He who doesn't want soup gets two bowls!

I'll have to remember that ruse next time I'm hungry.

It seems a long time ago that I was in the capital city, chickening out of going to that nightclub. But I can actually dance a bit now, and my dance confidence is on the up.

With this in mind, I've decided to check into one of the main backpacker haunts – it seems like a good opportunity to see what progress I'm making, and other foreigners should make a good barometer. Added to this, it's a nailed on cert that I'll meet some people who'll want to go out at night, sparing me the problems I've faced in other places. So I join the melee of a dorm room, bagging the top bunk of a metal-framed bed.

The legend of Medellín's women isn't lost on the backpacker

scene, as I found out from a New-Yorker when I was in Cali.

"My hostel was like a frat house," she said. "All they talk about is women, and they try to find women, and it's all just like 'women, women, women'."

Sounds awful – you'd have thought they'd have learnt to veil their intentions by now like the rest of us.

The men in my room aren't trying to find women, but that's because they're buried face-down in sheets, hiding from the daylight, whilst rucksacks spew their contents out like drunkards into what little space there is between the bunks. I'm clearly not going to get any practice done in here, making it all the more important I get myself out at night.

But at least I've got my base sorted – now I just have to decide which direction I want to go with my dancing.

Medellín (pronounced meh-deh-JEAN by locals) is the home abroad for one of the best-known of all Latin American dances, albeit one more commonly associated with Argentina and Uruguay – tango. This is the sultry and seductive one, where the woman flicks her calf upwards inside the man's leg. It's all red dresses and lipstick; slicked back hair and moustaches. It's all, "Oh God I so want to, but we shouldn't... oh let's... oh but we can't..."

The reason for Medellín's link with the dance is an unfortunate one – it was here, in 1935, that legendary singer-songwriter Carlos Gardel died in a plane crash whilst at the peak of his powers, an event that sealed him and the city together in an eternal, tragic clinch. Tango is still held in special regard here, even after all this time, and can be found in special *milongas.*

It's a difficult dance, however, and learning it would be a whole mission of its own. I know enough to know that the end result would likely be just another dance anecdote. No, what I need is a quick win at something practical, and I've got just the dance in mind. It's something I can pick up in a few days; something I can use in clubs all over the country; something that will make me look ridiculous – and that's if I'm doing it right.

It's time to roll out the big guns. It's time to finally learn merengue.

It's a grey day as I stroll through downtown Medellín. A fearful shelf of cloud competes with the architecture for which can be greyer, whilst taxis spray past, yellow against monochrome, like something out of a colour accent photo. Despite this, there's a sense of industry and purpose, from the people that pass by in suits to the folk selling cleaning products from the roof-rack of their car.

Medellín is sited in a narrow valley with gently sloping faces, the buildings flowing into its irregular floor plan and creeping up its wet sides as if by capillary action. Stalking across all this on concrete legs is the metro. I've taken it a couple of times already and I do so again now, the boxy cars whisking me along at eye-level with apartment windows. It's a transcendent experience and I can only imagine the difference it must have made when it opened in 1995, suddenly lifting people above the urban grit and grime, not to mention crime.

My new dance school is located in a pleasant, leafy *barrio* with lawns, birds and window bars, its trees dripping on me as I walk about. I like this part of town, not least because I can wander around without that perpetual sense of danger. Of course, it could be that I am one wrong step from a brutal death, but it doesn't feel like it and that's the important thing.

The school itself is pretty big with numerous dance floors spread over a couple of floors. It's also pretty busy: a group of teenage boys are running through a sequence of boy band-esque moves as I enter, and people are coming and going, stopping to check the group-class timetables on the noticeboard as they pass.

In signing up for classes, I'm also signing up for a challenge: my desire to learn at such short notice and in such a concentrated manner means that I have a different teacher for every class. Quite how that will work out remains to be seen.

Merengue originates from the Dominican Republic and, as with all the styles I've learnt so far, the musical genre and the dancing style go hand-in-hand. Like other Latin dances, it was born of a fusion of European contradanse (line-dancing with partners) with African rhythms. Both the African influence, and the form's possible origins in Haiti, were actively denied by Dominican scholars right up to the 1970s: they wanted it to be purely Dominican and Hispanic. The idea that it might be Haitian was like the Cornish being told that their beloved pasty originated in Devon.

The lyrics and the movements associated with merengue were

originally considered very saucy – immoral even – but then the genre was championed by tyrannical president Rafael Trujillo (in power from 1930 to 1961) who made it the national music of the Dominican Republic, and enabled its change to a more socially acceptable style. Indeed, the style went through many alterations over the years before finally reaching mainstream international acceptance in the 1970s. It's now a really common rhythm in modern Latin pop and blessed with a constant flow of new numbers.

The dance style has a variety of suggested origins, from people honouring a limping war hero, to slaves coping with leg chains (not unlike the cumbia), to the fusing of African dance with the French minuet.

I've watched people dance merengue before, and the main thing that stands out to me is how ridiculous it loo… sorry… is how the hips swing from side to side. This hip movement is true even for the men, creating a sight that would make people shudder back home, and indeed anywhere else where people are still in denial over the existence of the male hip.

The upper part of the body, however, has me in awe: the partners perform all sorts of intricate turns, often without letting go of each other's hands. It's possible this is where the name comes from – the dancing being like a whisk going round beating eggs into a froth. It's brilliant and bewildering, like high-speed Twister for arms. This is one of the reasons I'm so keen on learning merengue – so I can get stuck into all those turns.

But for now, all that magic up top will have to wait. It's the bottom half of the body where the foundations of this dance are laid, and the first teacher insists I need to nail these basics before indulging in anything more extravagant. I say 'I' but actually it's 'we': a young Danish backpacker from the hostel has agreed to join me for the first lesson.

The music sounds too fast and complex to dance to when you first hear it, but it actually breaks down into a very simple one-two marching beat. You still have to get the action correct, though, and the key to this, our teacher maintains, is not to think in terms of moving your hips. Instead, you bend each knee alternately, and this induces the hip movement. The woman then accentuates this movement, whilst the man keeps it understated.

To the now familiar *chikka-chum chikka-chum chikka-chum*

sound (made by a metal scraper called a güira) – the Danish girl and I stand next to each other, bending our knees on alternate legs like a pair of wonky-limbed idiots. She's more of an idiot than me though – or maybe less of one – because she's the one who's really struggling with it. Whenever she bends one knee, the other one bends a little in sympathy, as though she's practising a lob-sided crouch. She just can't seem to separate the two. For me it comes a lot more naturally. It's as though all that body-part separation practice in Cartagena was going in all along.

We both work at improving, standing on the spot and bending our knees with the music, the silence between tracks filled by the gentle spatter of rain filtering through an open window. By the end of the lesson, the Danish girl is good enough that we're able to dance together, or at least bend knees together. The teacher helps us to add the most basic *vuelta* (turn) of all, and the next thing we know we're partaking in some rudimentary merengue.

"You have the rhythm of a Colombian!" the teacher tells me.

I'm in a great mood as we head back out into the rain, marvelling at how quickly I've assimilated merengue into my lexicon of dance. I seem to have a successively higher level of confidence as I go into each new genre – I just know I can do it and I just seem to be picking things up more quickly than ever. This is great – it suggests that I really can improve my general dance ability, even when I'm learning steps that aren't obviously applicable elsewhere. I can't wait for the next lesson, and all the crazy *vueltas* it will bring. I'm on a dance-induced high.

This, of course, is not the kind of high Medellín is most famous for. When it comes to cocaine, Colombia was originally more of a refinement and distribution centre for coca – the primary ingredient – but has also been a major place for the harvesting of the leaves since the 1990s. Peasants are enlisted to do all the labour-intensive stuff, which they presumably do because they like the thought of helping spoilt foreigners to get wrecked, rather than because they're exceedingly poor.

The coca leaves are processed into cocaine and its sub-product, crack-cocaine, in laboratories. If that last word conjures up images of scientists in white coats working in conditions of fluorescent sterility then you should replace that with one of people working on an earthy hillside under a tarp.

From here the product is trafficked out. At one time this was done with speedboats, though stealthier methods have been employed in more recent times, such as semi-submersible craft or even submarines. Other methods include the use of people as mules, or even the adoption of wacky subterfuge such as the replica world cup made from cocaine that was intercepted at Bogotá airport.

The US has historically been the main market. Like some drug-addled loon, it can't get its head straight over whether it loves the stuff or hates it. It accounts for half of global cocaine consumption, yet has been at war with drugs since 1971.

Back in the day, it was all about the big cartels, and the key figure in the Medellín cartel was Pablo Escobar. He was considered a Robin Hood character by some, presumably because he used some of his riches to advance causes of the poor, rather than because he lived in a Nottinghamshire forest and had a penchant for archery. But he was also responsible for the deaths of a great many people, including all 107 on a domestic flight, bombed in an attempt to assassinate a presidential candidate.

Politicians, judges, journalists and so on have long been the kind of people who have been targeted in the name of political influence, along with their friends and families. Escobar had a system known as *plata o plomo*, where targets were given the choice between taking a bribe – *plata* (silver) – and taking a bullet – *plomo* (lead).

Escobar was eventually persuaded to surrender and was put in prison. A big prison which he designed and which looked suspiciously like a drug lord's mansion. From here he was able to carry on pretty much as before, and when the authorities tried to move him elsewhere he escaped. His reign came to an end when he was tracked down, dying during a gunfight in 1993.

In the late 1990s, the US and Colombia developed Plan Colombia: a US-aid program which included activities such as wiping out crops via aerial fumigation, and a military approach to dealing with leftist guerrillas. These close ties with the US, however, have caused friction between Colombia and some of its neighbours.

By knocking off the top guys, the main cartels were largely broken up by the late 1990s. Drug exports still went on to peak in 2000, but the pattern since then has been one of decline.

But even if the efforts have had some success, in the bigger, international picture there is still the problem of the so-called balloon effect. This is where you squeeze it in one place and it grows bigger somewhere else. Or maybe it's where you let go of it and it farts off round the room at high speed. Or it could be where you pop it and it goes bang. I can't remember exactly. Damn these metaphors.

WHUMP

That's the all-too predictable sound of me falling back to earth. I was certain that teacher #2 was going to be impressed by how far I'd come, and that we'd be going straight into learning some turns. But no – my meringue has fallen.

My hip and leg movement are wrong, apparently. They're so wrong, in fact, that the teacher wants us to spend the entire lesson focus on getting them right. This would be fine if it weren't total rubbish: the other teacher told me my footwork was fine, and that I had the rhythm of a Colombian! Why should I trust the second teacher over the first? I tell her I'd like to learn some turns anyway, but she's adamant: the footwork is the foundation, and this must be dealt with first.

I rationalise, telling myself that she's an experienced dance teacher; that I should just trust her and forget what's gone before. I think out loud, saying how it's probably a good thing that I've got a different teacher for every class. After all, in the real world you have to dance with lots of different people, and they all have varying styles.

"I like that philosophy," she tells me.

I'm just not sure that I believe it myself.

With the Danish girl having decided against further lessons, I have my dance teacher's full attention in helping me make the corrections. The problem is that my meringue isn't stiff enough. By which I mean my leg-straightening isn't marked enough. We drill hammering them back into place, so they're absolutely straight, and use this to mark the time, rather than the bending of the knee.

Once she's happy with this, it's time to take it to the next level – moving about. You don't just dance merengue where you stand; that would be about as much fun as driving on the spot. Instead you have to go for a bit of a wander carrying the hips from side to side the whole time.

"Like pushing a *carrito* [shopping trolley] round the supermarket," she tells me.

I'd like to see the supermarket where swinging your hips like that was considered normal. Although for all I know that's every supermarket in the Dominican Republic.

As the lesson comes to an end I'm short of where I'd hoped to be, but hey – at least I've got the foundations right this time. Out on the street, I'm still moving my hips from my own lesson. I've got the hip-swinging motion down to a tee, and this new, better merengue action seems to be stuck fast, integrated into my gait. It doesn't even seem silly any more – mere familiarity has dealt with that. Before you know it I'll be out in the clubs of Medellín demonstrating to the local women my suitability for bearing children.

NO!!!!!!!!!!!!!!!!!!

I've got the legwork wrong? Seriously, you must be having me on.

It's my third lesson, my third teacher, and, now, my third time spending an entire lesson on the basics. This time, it's the hammering back of my legs that the second teacher taught me that are the sticking point. Also, she thinks my movements are too mechanical.

"More fluid," insists the teacher.

This is an outrage! Whoever heard of meringue being too stiff? Actually, do you know what is a common problem with meringue? Weeping. I really need to resolve this. Ideally, I'll get all the teachers together in the same room. Then I'll lock the door from the outside. There is no stage three.

Okay, so it's possible that the second teacher would also have picked up on this in her own time, but whilst I keep changing teachers I'll never know. It could be they have incompatible ideas about merengue, and I'll just be locked in a perpetual cycle of correction and counter-correction. What I do know is that my meringue, as it stands, is not nearly ready to serve. Reluctantly, I renegotiate my position, committing myself to a longer stay in the city so I can have this same teacher every time.

I'm still not ready to take on the turns, though – she won't let me progress until I've got the footwork nailed whilst performing various salsa-like *pasos.* I feel like a learner driver who's being kept away from corners until he's mastered straight lines. Which sounds perfectly reasonably now I've put it that way.

It all comes down to the same thing, not just for me, but for everyone, as betrayed by the line of ballerina pumps that hang from the ceiling by their ribbons. They look elegant from a distance, but up close the heels are fraying and the toes are battered and filthy, telling a tale of countless hours of sweat and repetition.

So I stick with it. And all the hard work with a consistent teacher ultimately pays dividends. Come the next lesson, I finally reach the point where my footwork is solid enough for me to graduate to the upper body.

The turns in merengue are slower than those in salsa, and are less strictly tied to the rhythm. We start with the simplest – where I lead her round in a circle with one hand – but soon progress to the point of using both arms to turn her. This puts my own arms in a twist, meaning I also have to do a turn to 'resolve' it, my arms passing over my head.

This is it! This is the merengue I've seen people dance; what I've been aiming at. After all those false starts, I'm finally able to do turns which leave you one wrong move away from permanent entanglement.

Success.

But it's one thing to push round your shopping trolley in private, and quite another to get it out there and fill it up with groceries. I need that practice.

Saturday night starts in pleasant, low-key fashion. The rain has cleared up, leaving the temperature at the city's agreeable best. Indeed, one of Medellín's titles is 'The City of Eternal Spring'. Myself and some fellow hostel-dwellers sit out on the sloping grassy plaza in the centre of the *zona rosa.* musical genres from the various open-fronted bars combining to create an awkward mix of music, like a truck with a misfiring engine carrying pots and pans down a bumpy road.

We drink and we chat, but mostly we watch the other revellers as they pass us by: women in strappy tops and men doing the casual t-shirt thing, all of them looking fresh and maintained, their fragrances mixing in the air the same way the music is.

Looking at the women, it's easy to see why Jorge describes foreign men in the city as being "*como un ventilador*" (like a fan). I assume he means the type that oscillates left and right rather than one that hangs from the ceiling and spins, although that would still be an appropriate reaction. And whilst the appropriate intellectual thing to do might be to stroke our chins and discuss gender roles in post-feminist society, instead our night degrades into a game of 'natural or plastic?'

Body vanity isn't purely confined to the women – there are quite a few men showing off gym-built bodies and funky tattoos, frequently topped off with a pair of impenetrable sunglasses. But there are still double standards at play. As Felipe pointed out to me in Cali, terms like *perro* (dog), *zorro* (fox), *adventurero* (adventurer) and *sinvergüenza* (scoundrel) all have positive connotations when applied to men, but when applied to women they are all just synonyms for 'bitch'.

Not everyone in Medellín is anatomically perfect: parts of the city are inhabited by grossly oversized people: individuals with trunk-like necks, thunderous buttocks and fingers that start hugely fat and just about manage to taper down enough to look vaguely useable. These are the bronze sculptures of globally-renowned, Medellín-born artist Fernando Botero, who specialises in exaggerating form to the point where conventional proportion is forgotten. Which is starting to sound like a common theme.

My friends and I go to find some action, hitting a nearby venue that is half bar, half disco and pretty-much all dancing – Medellín is partly built on the textile industry, and evidently these *cachacos* are cut from a different cloth. But I can weave some decent patterns myself these days, and I'm actually looking forward to getting out there and putting my new moves into practice.

If the idea was to measure my achievements by comparing myself against other foreigners, then the most telling comparison is perhaps not what I can see, but what I cannot. Despite the heavy influx of tourist and ex-pats in this part of town, there are hardly any in the Latin-music establishments such as the one I'm in now. Most of them have gone out to rock clubs, sidestepping the dance problem altogether.

"*¿Quieres bailar conmigo?*" I ask a girl who is stood alone. Do you want to dance with me?

I've really come of age of late – I've gone from trying to avoid it to actively seeking it out from complete strangers. Shame, then, about the outcome: the girl wags a schoolteacher-like finger and walks off.

Ouch.

Trying my best to remain unperturbed, I move on and get chatting to a group of locals; some friendly guy in the group gesturing that I should dance with one of his female friends. I smile at her. She wags her finger at me. The girl next to her goes further, putting up her hand like a stop sign then joining some friends behind a nearby table, as though needing a physical barrier for protection. A third attempt, this time with a girl stood on her own, meets with a similar fate.

What is this? I thought *paisas* were supposedly to be friendly. If anything, this is even worse than Boyacá – at least there I didn't have people dancing all around me, taking the piss.

"Woo-hoo! How's the dancing going, Englishman?"

Even my friends are happily dancing away with locals despite not having anything like my repertoire. The lone female in our group – the one I shared my first merengue lesson with – just can't stop, even when she's indulged enough in the local liquor that she can barely stand. Dammit – what is it about good-looking, drunken Scandinavian women that enables them to get a dance with the merest gesture of the hand?

At first I think the issue might be age, but whilst I'm not a kid, I'm definitely not an old man, and besides, Nick, a Kiwi in his late forties who has come out with us, doesn't seem to be having much difficulty.

I feel like I just need to abort this mission and start a fresh one elsewhere. Thankfully, Jay, a fresh-faced young Englishman in our group, also fancies a change. He suggests that me and him go and hit another club.

The new venue is loud, close and dark, and Jay and I walk the length of it, through the hustle of chairs, looking for girls to dance with. The problem is similar to the one I've had at festivals – you need a bit of time to suss out the dynamics of the various clusters of people. A woman stood on her own, for instance, is almost certainly with someone else – maybe a female friend, or maybe a boyfriend. Given how cheap life can be here, it seems prudent to wait and find out which.

Jay makes the first approach, asking a girl who's sat at a table with her friend. I can't hear the answer but I can tell she's declined by her body language. Specifically, she's still sat down. He's unperturbed, however: "If you watch the locals, they get turned down, too." Good spot, Jay – that's reassuring.

Next it's my turn to have a go. I spy with my little eye, something beginning with 'W'.

"*No.*"

Technically that begins with an 'N' – I was actually thinking of 'Woman' – but I take your point. This time, however, I'm ready for the rejection, and I've thought up a riposte in advance.

"What an insult!" I say in a tone that's teasing, flirty even. "I'm a guest in your country, and you won't even dance with me?"

And hey – it only goes and works. Her reward is to have me tread all over her toes to *vallenato.* The next track, bizarrely, is a piece of *música llanera* (music of the plains). But just when I think I'm going to get the first opportunity to practise my *joropo* in an age, my new-found partner excuses herself on the basis that whilst I can dance to it, she can't.

This isn't really working.

Jay and I end up standing by the bar, scoping for potential partners. We're not making any progress and as time goes on, we're at risk of looking like 'the two desperate blokes'. Which, of course, we are. Then Jay has a master-stroke: he smashes the unsaid rule we've both been observing, and goes and approaches a guy. Who just happens to be stood with two girls.

They banter for a bit whilst I practise my 'spare part' *paso.* But soon enough Jay beckons me over and together they welcome me to the conversation, all smiles and open body language. That we end up dancing is a natural progression.

For the first couple of dances, I watch from the sidelines as Jay and the Colombian guy take the floor, partnering the two girls. On their return, some appropriate music comes on and I don't need a second invitation – my meringue is finally ready to be served.

Away we go, bending our knees and swinging our hips. I lead my partner through as many of the *pasos* and *vueltas* as I can remember, and suddenly I'm one of the other people, the types that I've stood and watched. Okay, so my repertoire isn't very big, and I have to think before I execute each move, but by the time I return to the group, I've more than made an impression.

"You dance very well!" says the bloke, and the two women

agree, lavishing me with praise.

It does feel like there's an unsaid "...for a foreigner" in there, though – it doesn't flow yet, and I know it – but it's still a great feeling.

"I'm well impressed with your dancing," Jay tells me. "You really know what you're doing."

But I'm more impressed with his. He has no formal dance skills, but it doesn't matter. He somehow manages to approximate, filling in the gaps with all sorts of daft disco moves. He has the courage to get up and give it a go, and whichever of the two girls he's partnering ends up dancing with a big open-mouthed smile.

I guess I can still learn a thing or two from my fellow foreigners after all.

One thing that definitely distinguishes me from most other foreigners is my musical recognition. Salsa, merengue, reggaeton, *vallenato*... almost without noticing I've reached the point where I recognise pretty much every genre on the musical platter. But every now and then one can still come up that isn't part of my lexicon, and leaves me stumped.

One such type keeps cropping up here, tonight. It has a fussy, fiddly sound to it, all plucked strings and finger drumming. I watch a couple of girls dancing to it on their own – the signature element is that they terminate each *paso* by rolling one hip up into the air, their foot leaving the ground in the process.

It looks like it's meant to be elegant, but is a little too close to someone letting out an exaggerated fart, or maybe even like a cock-legged dog urinating on a lamppost. Which are not the images of a woman you'd want etched in your mind.

"What is it?" I ask one of the girls, a sentence I've not had to utter in quite a long time.

"*Bachata.*"

Ah, yes. I'd forgotten all about that genre.

She insists we give it a go, and I'm game. It will only be later that I realise I didn't even register fear at the thought of trying something entirely new. Not that this emerging boldness means I can get the hang of it: despite it being a simple 1-2-3-4, we keep going out of synch with our feet and I don't know why. The fact that it's danced very close – she gets me to interlock legs with her – means I can't even see to find out.

"Good," she says, although it isn't really. Not unless you hold toe-tramping in high regard.

I've been told that Colombians in general don't dance bachata very well, as it only made it here as a mainstream music in recent times. But they still do it better than me.

Back at the hostel, I bump into Jorge again, and take the opportunity to ask him about the whole dancing-with-locals thing. It's a subject he's more than familiar with. In fact, I get the impression Jorge plays 'counselling bartender' to foreign men on a regular basis, especially given that many of them, as he puts it, "*se lo dan a mamar a un cocodrilo en ayunas*" (They'd let a fasting crocodile give them a blow job).

He's impressed by my 'guest in your country' line. "*¡Suave!*" he says (smooth!), although I think he's being kind, as in effect it was a novelty line that got me a single dance rather than a strategy that demonstrates a full understanding of the situation. He does have some advice for me, however.

"*¡El que muestra el hambre no come!*" He who looks hungry doesn't eat!

It's time to leave the smell of unwashed socks behind for that of plastic car interior. The Danish girl and Nick have offered me the chance to join them in a hire car on a quick romp through the *zona cafeteria* (cafeteria zone) as Nick keeps calling the *zona cafetera* (coffee zone).

Nick has recently driven down through most of Central America, making him the closest thing we've got to a matador of the road. As we head out through the congested suburbs, he does his best to drive like a Colombian, pulling out and overtaking in the face of oncoming vehicles. As with me and my dancing, however, he's still got some way to go to match some of the locals – not once does he try and pass in such a way that I instinctively have to cover my eyes.

We soon leave the congestion – and decent radio reception – of the city in favour of the mountains, the asphalt weaving this way and that in its quest to stay atop a narrow ridge. Onwards we go, following the undulating road through the misty heights to the radio soundtrack of accordion and white noise, like some kind of avant-garde musical experiment, before dropping down into a furrow with a sloshing river – the River Cauca, in fact.

Perched on a hillside above us is the historic mining town of Marmato, on a spur off the main road. Way before the white stuff came to prominence, gold was the principal economic force in western Colombia. The Spanish used the indigenous workforce, and later African slaves, to do the dirty work of mining, then shipped the end product out of Cartagena. Slavery was finally abolished in 1851, some 30 years after the Spanish were booted out.

We grunt our way up the winding dirt-track, but our path is blocked part-way up by a stricken vehicle, so we abandon our vehicle for a brief walk. As it happens, we're right by a small-scale gold refinery, if you can call it that. Men in wellies with skin the colour of roasted beans work a primitive production line that follows a stream down the hillside, under cover of a tin and bamboo canopy. We greet the men over the sound of chuntering machinery. From what I can see, the system takes in rubble, churns out gold and turns the adjacent stream black in the process.

We leave Marmato and press further south through the crinkled edge of the central Andean chain. As we do so, the scenery starts to change: hillsides that had been rugged and largely untouched become tidy with contoured greenery, like some fussy mother has slapped them back with a touch of spit and a comb.

The change is due to another product that Colombia has exported a lot of over the years: black gold. I'm not talking about oil, though this does exist in Colombia (there is large-scale extraction in the Llanos, and Barrancabermeja is home to Colombia's largest petroleum refinery). No – these are coffee plantations; rich green bushes tracing out regular lines across the whole complex landscape, creating a manicured beauty.

Colombia got into coffee in the 1850s, and it quickly became its chief export; the USA, with its seemingly insatiable desire for things that make you twitchy and give you a fixed stare, being the biggest consumer. But the Colombian coffee industry has since fallen on hard times. An increase in supply globally has driven down the value of the product, leading many plantations to resort to tourism to supplement their income.

It's late in the day as we thread our way up the access tree-lined road to the hacienda, but there is just enough time left for a look around the place. We park up and a guide welcomes us and leads off round the farm in the twilight.

Our antennas immediately start twitching with the familiar scent as we walk between waves of waxy bushes, plants all about us bursting with little olive-green berries. Between the plots, all sorts of other vegetation grows: heliconia, pink banana and the local variant of bamboo for starters. These are rich pastures indeed.

The higher grade coffee gets exported, presumably in special coffee submarines, else is served up in upmarket domestic cafes. The lower quality beans, meanwhile, end up on the streets of Colombia as *tinto*. Most Colombians drinking the latter have no idea that the quality is so low, but then, given the income levels of the lower strata of Colombian society, Pandora's coffee tin is probably best left shut.

Some distance from the plantation owners' house is that of the employees. Here, gnarled labourers hang about in doorways, watching as the fresh-faced Dane frolics with a kitten. According to the guide, when they want a night out they go and party in the local town, sometimes dancing but also listening to *música popular* which, as she puts it, "is a type of music that you use just for drinking".

We end up sitting out on the veranda of the main house, drinking freshly-ground arabica amongst the insect noises. We could be in the 19th Century. Well, if it wasn't for the plastic chairs. And the electric grinder. And my ridiculous luminous t-shirt. In fact, pretty much everything except the concept of sitting on a veranda, come to think of it.

Coffee is also strongly associated with our next stop. The small town of Filandia is famous for being home to the *telenovela* (soap opera) Café, Con Aroma De Mujer (Coffee, With The Aroma Of Woman), whose creator went on to write the original (Colombian) Ugly Betty – Yo Soy Betty, La Fea.

Telenovelas, also known as *novelas*, are the classic Latin American soap operas, featuring unfeasible amounts of posturing and face-slapping, and more affairs than there are regular relationships. It's one continuous stream of jealousy, infidelity and blackmail.

It's hard to know just how representative this is of the culture here, though as one Colombian told me, "Cheating is the national sport." Which leaves me wondering… if cheating is itself a sport, how do you cheat at it?

Attitudes to infidelity – or male infidelity, at least – are definitely different here. The general undercurrent that I've picked up is that infidelity on its own is not all that bad – at least not if the man is doing it – so long as you're not overly blatant or disrespectful about it. A British friend of mine found this out when she discovered her now-erstwhile husband was being unfaithful, and decided to discuss it with her friends.

"But they're just his lovers," they told her. "You're his special lady."

It's enough to put a counselling bartender like Jorge out of business.

"My wife doesn't understand me. Fortunately, three of my five lovers do."

We even have infidelity to thank for emeralds, of which Colombia is the world's largest producer. According to Colombian mythology, the Muzo god Are created a couple, Fura and Tena, and granted them eternal youth so long as they remained faithful. But the woman (Fura) strayed and hence began to age rapidly. On seeing this, Tena made a direct appeal to the god of melodrama, stabbing himself in the heart and dying. Fura wept at the loss and her tears became a green-coloured variety of $Be_3Al_2(SiO_3)_6$.

But how do people go about having so many flings without being caught? Even if you're "*más mentiroso que un brasier*" (a bigger liar than a brassiere), as a certain barman would put it, you've still got the problem of location. The answer is love hotels – garish establishments where couples can fulfil the physical aspects of their relationships in privacy. They even include hidden car parking to avoid comments like "Isn't that Juan's car parked outside that tawdry sex palace?"

Errant partners aren't the only customers at such establishments: it's typical for Colombians to live with their parents right up until they get married, presumably so the men don't have any awkward gap between their mothers waiting on them, hand and feet, and their wives taking over. Gender roles are pretty strong here. But that still leaves them needing a place to consummate their pre-marital relationships, and once again the love hotel fits.

One source tells me that they smell "reassuringly" of chlorine.

We leave Filandia and head to the city of Pereira to drop the car off, beads of rain running up the windscreen. After parking up one last time. Nick, the Danish girl, the car and I all wave goodbye to each other, and that's that.

My momentum naturally seems to be carrying me south, so I just let it, the hills of the coffee axle giving way to the long flat stretches of the Cauca valley. The roads here are practically die-straight after those of the mountains, and are bounded on both sides by sugar cane plantations – another major Colombian export.

When I arrive for a quick, unannounced pit-stop in Cali it's with the expectation of more dancing. Cali, however, is closed. Not only is there no press-ganging, there are no clubs open in the first place. That's because something important is happening; something more important even than dancing salsa. Well, okay, perhaps that's exaggerating. But either way, it's the first round of the presidential elections.

Not that this stops me learning altogether: a chance meeting with a local dance teacher gives me the chance to dig further into the issue of dance etiquette. He explains that it's common for foreigners to be turned down. "Who is he?" he tells me they're thinking. "Maybe he can't dance well." But even locals can get rejected, for lots of different reasons. "If your clothes are dirty..." he says by way of example, thumbing the hem of his white t-shirt.

Alternatively, he explains, a girl could turn you down purely because her friend did. But afterwards, she might turn to the first and ask "Why didn't you dance with him?" and her friend will shrug and answer "Just because." Which sounds a lot like what happened in Medellín.

Then there's the language you employ. I've always tended to ask "*¿Quieres bailar conmigo?*" (Do you want to dance with me?) because it doesn't sound too pushy. However, I've since been told that this can just sound weak. The best thing to say is apparently a confident "*¡Bailamos!*" (Let's dance!). That's if you say anything at all – you could simply offer a hand.

I had no idea there was so much to this.

Quite a number of cities in Latin America have the moniker 'The White City'. Arguably, the Colombian title should belong to Medellín, given its former associations, but the honour actually goes to the southern city of Popayán, where I arrive next, and whose colonial centre consists of array of whitewashed buildings.

This, allied with the trim greenery of the central square gives the place a feeling of tranquil splendour. You certainly wouldn't know it was ravaged by earthquake in the 1980s.

The backpacker trail has proved itself to have certain advantages, so I decide to stick with it a while, ending up at a hostel where the staff always seem to be studying the bible, and where a fire extinguisher hose points in your face at reception between protective metal bars. I'm guessing this is to deal with *ladrones*, although I suppose it could also be for blasphemers.

It's a Tuesday night, and a group of us wander the streets hoping to find someplace suitable. We're in luck: a whiff of music on the street leads to a small upstairs bar. Nestling within are tables and chairs, and a whole lot of other people who fancied a drink and a dance on a weekday evening.

Like a lot of Colombian venues, the furniture layout seems to have been chosen specifically to prevent dancing. Indeed, some places are so overly-full of chairs and tables that the dance floor is an abstract concept. And it's one thing to jostle about between other moving bodies, but getting into an elbow fight with a seat is just plain ridiculous. Not that such a thing would ever stop Colombians dancing – you could fill the place with razor wire and people would still go for it.

Within our own group there's a more natural barrier: there are only two girls, and their dance skills are limited.

"Go up and dance with some of the locals," says one of them, a curly-haired German.

Good idea! It's ages since I've been rejected.

"It's easy for you," she says. "You're a man – you can just go up to them."

No, it's easy for you. You're a woman – they'll come up to you.

As if to confuse both of us, it's me who is approached, and by a man.

"May I?" asks a big fellow, gesturing towards the German girl.

Presumably he thinks we're a couple and he doesn't want to disrespect me by going straight to her. Flattered as I am by the idea that I have any say in the matter, I accept that I don't, and refer him to the owner of the body in question.

"Ask her."

She takes his hand and he elegantly whisks her away. *Suave, amigo*. Seizing the moment, I immediately head over to the group of people he came from, and approach a man sat with his partner.

"May I?" I say, gesturing towards her.

"*¡Sí!*" he says, although "It depends what you plan to do with her," would also have been a perfectly reasonable answer.

She looks a little unsure at first – who is this guy? – but she comes round to the idea, persuaded by her partner who is perhaps flattered by the display of respect.

She follows me to the nearest space where I lead her through a passable, if rather mechanical, merengue. She's a far better dancer than me. In fact she keeps misreading my leads, and trying to do things which are far cooler than I was ever suggesting, making me very aware of my own limitations. Indeed, there's a high standard going all about me. You clearly can't generalise about people from the interior.

Once we're sat back down again, some other guy comes up and offers a partner swap for me and the German girl – and I mentally assimilate another technique.

"It's like speed dating," says a Belgian backpacker, who has been watching from the sidelines.

It isn't like speed dating. Whilst back home, the offer of a dance can be just the first in a chain of steps that will result in one of the two parties sneaking out of the other's bedroom the next day with their clothes under their arm, here in Colombia it just isn't so. Unless of course I'm the one missing something and we're all going to end up in love hotels come the end of the night. In which case I'd better start practising my macho posturing (or at the very least my slap-receiving).

The whole time I've been in Colombia, the message has been there again and again: dancing together does not, on its own, signify intent. At the same time, what would you do if you saw someone you fancied? You'd ask them to dance, of course. So how can you tell if there's something in it?

As one of my Caleño friends explained to me, if you want to know if someone fancies you, you have to look for other indicators. A woman striking up a conversation with you mid-dance might be one example – useful to know information in a country where she could grind her backside against you and it mean nothing. It's a particularly cruel trick for a beginner like me though – dancing and talking at the same time is advanced stuff, like singing and playing the accordion, or running and putting in a contact lens.

It's been a very useful couple of weeks. I've finally started getting the practice I've craved, and I've had the chance to see just how far I've come since my days of being a clueless outsider. As an unexpected bonus I also seem to have learnt a lot about how to get a dance in the first place.

It's too early to start celebrating, though. For one thing, I'm very aware of how limited my repertoire is. The elaborations which could make it really fun still elude me. In fact, here in Popayán I find myself actively avoid dancing with the same person twice in succession: I've used up all my moves in the first dance – several times over, in fact – and I'm embarrassed by the idea of suggesting "Hey! Let's do exactly the same thing again!"

On top of that, my dancing simply doesn't flow. I never get in 'the zone' because I'm too busy thinking about what my next move is to be able to really let go and enjoy the present.

Put it all together, and I have that overwhelming sense that I'm not really much of a dancer. I can just wing it long enough to convince a partner I can do it, at which point I scarper. I remind myself of all the ground I've covered, of how much I can do that I couldn't do when I arrived, but I can't quite shake the feeling that I'm something of a dance fraud. There's clearly another level above me that I have to get to – the question is how to reach it.

CHAPTER FIFTEEN

Deep Down

The flat expanses of the Cauca Valley are long behind us. As the road presses southwards, the separate strands of the Andes entwine together into a single cord, creating a land of vicious peaks and tumbling gorges. Tracks tether smallholdings to the highway for fear they may otherwise be lost forever in the void, whilst rogue streams blast frostily under the road. This is wild country.

At one time, this was one of Colombia's more troublesome journeys due to the threat of guerrilla activity and banditry. But a lot of places are sensitive at the moment now that we're in the election window – it's a time when various factional groups like to send out reminders of their existence. The start of a regime can be a troublesome time, such as in 2002, when the presidential palace in Bogotá came under attack from FARC mortars during the inauguration of Álvaro Uribe.

The results of the first round are in, and it's the realists who have had their way: Santos has beaten Mockus by a clear margin, whilst the other candidates are nowhere. A second round will still be necessary, but it's widely seen as a formality for Santos. Another outcome, arguably of equal importance, still hangs in the balance however: that of my dance project.

My next stop is Pasto, a town of breezy colonial old-builds and anonymous new-builds, with churches that peek out from every other street corner. Like a lot of places in Colombia, its grid-system streets are home to yellow taxis, ambulant chorizo sellers and a large, paved plaza which has somehow gained the title of 'park'. But there's a subtly different feel to the place, too.

Perhaps it's due to the location: despite being on the Pan-

American highway – the road network which links America from top to bottom, with a break only for the jungle of the Darién Gap – the city is so far south it feels disconnected. We're now closer to the capital of Ecuador than we are to the capital of salsa, the border being a mere 50 miles away.

It could also be because the town casually backs on onto the gentle slopes of an active volcano, Galeras, which watches over the city and its residents whilst quietly brooding and plotting its next move. It would steeple its fingers if it had any.

Or maybe it's subtleties of food: alongside the rice, beans and chicken, there's a golden-fried patty of 'What the fuck's that?' next to the regular staples. Actually I recognise it instantly – it's a *llapingacho*, or potato and cheese croquette – it's just I haven't seen one since I was in Ecuador years ago.

The ethnic makeup is different, too. Whilst in other regions the indigenous people were largely running away and dying from illnesses, the local population in the South was busy surviving the Spanish conquest relatively intact. Pasto, like most places of any size, ultimately capitulated to the irrepressible trend towards *mestizo*, but even today the South still has pockets of indigenous people, like in the villages around the chilly Andean town of Silvia, where the bowler-hatted Gumbiano people live.

On a brief side trip there on market day, I asked one of the heavily-clothed indigenous locals what kind of dances they got up to. Standing there, amidst the thud and clatter of potatoes hitting scales and the steam drifting up from bubbling stockpots, it was hard to imagine them being into bare-chested feasts of eroticism. He explained to me that he didn't believe in dance because he was a Christian. Which is somewhat ironic given you can actually prove that dance exists.

But Pasto is bigger, and so, hopefully a better bet: there must be some crazy local dance which I can invest time and energy in learning, before casually forgetting again in a short space of time. After all, I've learnt dances of the valleys, the coast and the plains, so I might as well collect the set, and it would be a nice addition to the show I keep pretending I'm going to do.

"Why am I doing this?"

If there were such a thing as a corporate de-motivational speech, my inner voice would be a big earner on the circuit. I'm on the way to a dance school group class, and my brain is looking for excuses for me not to do it; reasons why it's not just okay but somehow even preferable for me to skip the class, like I did in Villavicencio.

"Why am I going to this? I really don't need to. I've signed up for some lessons already. I can just skip this, no bother."

I've overcome so many obstacles to get to this point, yet this internal one remains.

"I really don't need to do this. I won't even gain anything from it. It's a waste of time."

Okay, so this is true in some ways. When I went to the dance school to enquire about group classes, I also signed up for some individual ones, so it's hardly all or nothing. On the other hand, I can't come away knowing less, and it'll be good practice. But this whole argument is bogus. Going to a dance class should not be a big deal, and the fact that there's any internal discussion at all says a lot.

There's more to this than just what I might learn. This about dignity, self-respect and not running away terrified in the opposite direction. It's about lying in bed tonight feeling smug rather than stupid (not that they're mutually exclusive, of course). I have to do this – for me.

The thoughts continue, one after another, trying to convince me to turn back. They come disguised as friends, clothed in reason and, hey, only acting in my best interest.

"It'll be fine. I can just go back to the guest house and chill out, then treat myself to some good food and do some reading. None of this stress – it'll just be nice."

Tell you what, brain: you keep talking and I'll keep walking.

My feet make progress along the red tiles of the pavement, past vendors frying fresh crisps in vats of bubbling fat. Locals walk by dressed in conservative work-a-day attire: a bit like Tunja but without the *ruanas.* The air is getting cooler as evening approaches and I'm glad of my jumper.

The building that houses the school comes into view ahead of me. As I get close enough that I can read the sign, my mind gives up on subtlety and starts barking protests.

"It's still not too late – you could turn and leave right this second! No-one would even know you'd been here!"

Into the building I go, my trainers giving little squeaks of protest on the polished surface. I turn the handle of the door and the dance studio opens up in front of me.

It's a gymnasium-like place with a peculiar mixture of things hanging on the wall: animal-skin drums and a rustic wooden xylophone mix it up with a Bruce Lee poster and the national flag of Korea. I guess the place doubles as a martial arts school. Hopefully the two disciplines don't run at the same time – I suspect that merengue would make a less-than-effective defence against Taekwondo.

A group of fellow students, ranging in age from their teens to their fifties, are changing into gym pants and t-shirts on the far wall. I walk over and take my jumper off and stand there clutching a water bottle. I unscrew it, glug some water I don't need and replace the cap. I do it again. Some young guy turns to me: am I here for the class?

Deep breath.

"*Sí.*"

And there is no time to change my mind. A woman strides out – our instructor – and we line up opposite the mirrored wall – opposite our reflections – looking like a drug rehab football team in our collective mismatch of both garb and demographics. It's way too late to stop now, short of bolting headlong out the door.

Some music starts up and the instructor leads us through the warm up. There are some salsa steps in there, and something that seems a bit like hip hop, but they're all simple. Hey, I can do this! Just try and stop me! Well, not too hard, obviously, but a little bit, just to flatter my ego.

As if having heard me, an ache starts to form at the base of my skull, perhaps an effect of the altitude – we're about two-and-a-half kilometres above sea-level. It's not a problem, though, as realistically it's not going to bother me unless we start leaping about like lunatics.

We start leaping about like lunatics. It's like head-banging with a hangover. Still I'm determined to push on through it. Around me, the rest of the group are working through the moves with accustomed familiarity, although I can see already that there's a wide range of ability.

A female instructor takes centre stage to teach us some

vallenato. This is Alba – owner of the school and the person I've already signed up with for individual lessons. Perhaps surprisingly, given our location in the Andes, she looks to be of mixed African and European heritage, rather than *mestiza*. But then this actually makes a lot of sense as we're actually not all that far from the Pacific Coast which, like the Atlantic, has a high concentration of Afro-Colombian people.

With a voice that is low, yet also soft and powdery, she leads us through the basic *pasos*; *pasos* which I'm delighted to see I got almost exactly right during my stint of self-teaching in Valledupar. But dancing in Colombia is not something you do on your own, so I shouldn't be surprised by what happens next.

"In couples!" announces Alba.

I look around for a partner, but everyone else has already pounced, and there is only one woman left – a short lady who looks rather well-to-do. As we come together, it becomes apparent that the top of her head only comes up to the bottom of my neck. We both laugh out loud.

If there's just one thing that all these months of dancing has taught me, then that would be a fairly poor return for my investment. But if there really was just one thing, then it would be this: I need to stand up straight, even when my dance partner is shorter. In fact, this new-found habit has started spilling over from dance and into everyday situations. This is a good thing. Dance seems to be gradually boosting my posture and sense of body awareness as a side-effect. The downside is that bending over feels patronising, and I miss that.

I've got one hand in the air, clasping hers, and have the other on her mid-back. We're pretty close, and I'm getting whiffs of hairspray as we move, but looking at the other pairs, I can see we're meant to be a lot closer. After my time on the coast, I'm more than comfortable with this, but we're in the Andes now, and I'm aware that things are a tad more conservative here, so I don't want to just pounce on her.

Alba, however, has no such qualms.

"*¡Pegado!*" she says, and pushes us together. Stuck together!

Brilliant – our personal barriers are overcome in an instant. It doesn't last long though, as the moment Alba's back is turned, we spring apart again.

How odd. Is she uncomfortable with the closeness? She doesn't seem to be – she looks relaxed; passive; unperturbed. Perhaps she's physically incapable of holding that position. Or maybe I'm part of a psychological study in proxemics. I try to decrease the distance by moving forward as we're dancing, but we're not getting any closer, and I don't want to push it.

Alba, however, with her coastal sensibilities, won't stand for it.

"*¡Pe-ga-do!*" she says, pressing us together once more.

And as soon as she's gone, we spring apart again.

It must be a deliberate choice by my partner. So what else can I do but let things continue as they are, her lower back stuck out in avoidance and my own in sympathy.

"*¡Pegado!*" says Alba, exasperated.

But Miss – it's her, not me!

There's still room for it to get worse as the class moves onto an even tighter clinch. In this, the slowest, closest form of *vallenato* dancing, your feet stay planted to the spot whilst your hips move in unison, describing conjoined figures of eight. This can only happen, however, if you have full bodily contact. As opposed to being in some kind of weird sumo-hold.

I completely respect my partner's right to assert her boundaries – if that indeed is what's happening here – although it does make for a somewhat frustrating situation in the context of a dance class.

"It doesn't mean anything!" some part of me wants to say, conveniently forgetting how putting my hand on a woman's back felt improper just a few short months ago.

It's with no small amount of relief on my part – and hers too, I imagine – when we finally move on to other, less-conjoined dances such as salsa and merengue.

Come the end of the lesson, I step out into the cool night air and realise that my headache is long gone, having silently dissipated without my even noticing. What's more, my fear of dance classes has gone the same way. All that pre-class internal squawking now just seems hilarious. Why was there ever a problem?

In the early 1820s, Bolívar and his supporting armies were gallantly riding around liberating the country, with one Antonio Nariño, previously exiled from South America for his political activities, leading the charge in the South. When the latter and his forces arrived in Pasto, however, they came across something of a problem.

Antonio Nariño: "We've come to liberate you!"

Everyone in Pasto: "Fuck off!"

The clergy in Pasto had done a splendid job of not only proselytising the local populace, but also of convincing them that to defy royalty was to defy God, meaning their allegiance lay firmly with the Spanish royalist forces. This stubbornness to join with the rest of Colombia in its new found freedom is partly responsible for Pastusos being seen as slow and backwards, and hence the butt of many Colombian jokes. They had Bolivar tearing his hair out as Pasto's location made it a direct obstacle to the liberation of Ecuador. Ultimately the Bolivarian forces took affirmative action.

I've got one for you: What do you call someone who doesn't give in, even when all their agriculture and livestock has been destroyed and they're faced with death or exile? That's right – a Pastuso! Even when the liberating forces finally took the place, a good two years after the fall of Popayán, the locals still sporadically rose up and fought back. This despite the fact that the USA had already formally recognised the newly formed Gran Colombia as a country.

Pastusos are not the only ones that can be stubborn. Whilst not necessarily prepared to suffer years of terrible hardship for the cause, I'm still pretty determined to push on with my dance programme for the time being, the latest episode of which will see me learning a dance typical to Nariño department: *guaneña.*

The original musical composition of La Guaneña was apparently a rousing war hymn – something to pound your chest to – although the interpretation that starts playing here today hardly seems to fit that description. Its Andean nature, however, is undeniable – from the first moment it's all guitar and panpipes. I'm reminded of the train journey from Bogotá all those months ago, not to mention many of the times in my life I've been in lifts. Still, as long as I don't end up dancing to a cover version of Hotel California, I'll be happy.

The first *paso* is a bouncy one, with both hands behind the back and elbows out. It's a bit like 'I'm a little teapot', except I'm a quite a big teapot and I appear to have two handles. Let's not mention the spout. From here, we stand facing each other and twist about the waist so our elbows meet, like a pair of similarly dysfunctional teapots greeting each other. This move, Alba tells me, is based on a bird, presumably the teapot-bird.

Alba bounds about, hair bobbing about her face as she does, and I copy her as best I can. Other *pasos* are similarly poised and springy, and I find I'm spending much of my time on the balls of my feet. It's similar in some ways to another dance I saw in a public space in Cali. I point this out to Alba, and do a half-arsed impression. She tells me what I saw was another Andean dance called *sanjuanito*.

As far as first lessons are concerned, it's quite a good one. Of course, I know enough by now not to put too much stock on early success. In fact, it's almost reassuring when, come my second lesson, I find that I grasp the *pasos* I learnt in the first lesson about as firmly as one could grasp mountain mist.

The 'I'm so crap at this' blues then arrive right on cue. Understanding that they're just part of the process helps prevent them becoming full-on blues – they're more like cyan or teal, which actually have a lot of green in them – but even so I find myself moping more than I am bounding.

The distractions don't help, either: a troupe of school children are dancing in another part of the hall, which means that I'm practising my *guaneña* to techno for at least some of the time. Meanwhile, some kid rides a little pink bicycle repeatedly round the lot of us, showing a strong awareness of the concept of taking the piss for someone so young. But then in some ways it almost doesn't matter whether or not my lesson resembles an amateur circus – just getting that bump back down to earth out of the way is progress in itself.

Not that this is enough on its own – if I really want to progress, then I need to spend plenty of time practising back at base. It's not even open for discussion any more – it's just something I do.

My hotel room smells heavily of cleaning fluid and the smoke from my next door neighbours (I set fire to them because their cigarette habit was annoying me). Still, it's big enough for me to spring about pretending to be a teapot, and that's all anyone can really ask of their accommodation.

On the television, President Hugo Chavez of Venezuela is warning that if Santos gets elected, the two nations will end up going to war, whilst on the shuffly streets below, salesmen with microphones jabber on about trousers. I meanwhile spring around on the wooden floor, gradually adding new movements to the lexicon I hold in my muscle memory.

As my lessons continue, I decide that it's best to switch to the tranquillity of Alba's private dance studio before I have to contend with people being fired past me from canons. Sited on the first floor of a shop-house building, the place is small, yet still manages to squeeze in a desk, a lectern and a bookcase stuffed with encyclopaedias. Oh, and a dog that occasionally bounds down the stairs to see how my dancing is coming on. Which is pretty good, thanks, doggy.

The practice is definitely paying off, and we've actually got something approaching a routine, including bits where I take Alba's shawl and parade it around in front of her, like a gloating thief. If only the *ladrones* at festivals operated with such a display of showmanship, they might take fewer beatings. Or possibly more, it's hard to say.

Some of the moves I learn are vaguely reminiscent of other dances I've learnt. We cavort round in circles in a foot-sliding *paso* whilst I hold an imaginary hat aloft (it's cumbia!) before doing some linked-arm turns (it's *joropo*!).

But dancing is not just about mechanically moving an arm here, or a leg there – each one has its own character that you have to attune to, making a dancer something like an actor playing different roles. *La guaneña* is neither commanding like *joropo* nor flirtatious like cumbia. And whilst something about it makes me want to sing Zip-a-Dee-Doo-Dah as I go, that feeling is somewhat tempered by Andean meekness. It's like "I'm quite happy, but some group or other is probably about to march in and subjugate me and my people, so I'm not counting my chickens. Especially as I don't have any anymore."

In the space of a week or so, I've largely got to grips with another new dance. Meanwhile, another weekend is approaching – how many of these flaming things are there? Once again, I'm ill-prepared for it, but Alba has a suggestion for me: why don't I come out and hit the town with her and some friends?

"Yes, of course!"

I don't know quite when it happened, but I seem to have become a yes man. I don't even need to be stood in front of a baying crowd any more – I barely hesitate. Okay, so I barely hesitated previously, either, it's just my answer is now the opposite.

"Do you know anyone else in your hotel?" she asks.

"No, no-one."

"Well, it would be better if you could come with another person."

Okay, I get it. I can't just rely on her to provide me with dance partners – I need to try and bring one of my own.

So that's a problem. But there's a bigger one – one which starts to grow from the moment I give my answer. This isn't just any night out: I've just agreed to go out to dance with my dance teacher. This is not like going dancing with anyone: I'm going to feel under scrutiny for the whole night. She'll notice any mistakes I make. There's nothing I can do that will impress her, because she can do it all already. And more besides. And better.

At the same time, I'm not going to back out – I'm beyond that kind of thing now. Besides, it's Friday night and the alternative is another exciting night in.

In some ways the situation should give me a sense of freedom – whatever I do, I'm going to fail, so there's no pressure – but that somehow doesn't ring true. I've been here too long to play the dumb beginner card. I should be able to dance by now, whatever that means. I just fear we're going to discover that I can't.

I like Pasto. In particular, I like the late afternoon, when the light turns the surrounding crown of green hills to velvet. I like the cafes here, too. In the warmer parts of the country, cafes are open-fronted establishments that flirt brazenly with passers-by, but the ones in Pasto are more enclosed, making them seem cosier.

I sit in one such cafe, peeling the skin from a mug of *café con leche* from my upper lip and thinking about the coming evening. It's an important opportunity, and not one to be missed. Not that it'll give me a chance to dance my *guaneña*: if I want to do that, I'll need to find a *peña*, a traditional Andean bar with live music and dancing. Perhaps the twenty-something lady in the funky glasses who's sat at the table next to me might know.

"Do you know of any good *peñas*?"

Her name is Clara and yes, she does. In fact, within minutes she's leading me out of the café and down the street to show me one. She casually introduces me to a handful of friends we meet en route and, in the biggest coup of all, even suggests she might know someone who could partner me that evening.

So that goes quite well.

That evening in my hotel room I feel excited and nervous. This is a big deal – it's like a show in its own right. In fact it's worse than a show, because I won't be able to hide my mistakes with distance.

Out of my window, the sky is turning lilac. Beyond the roof-tile landscape, visible but out of reach, is the distant freedom of the hilltops.

I flap my hands about *mapalé*-like to dry them – so I can insert my lenses without also inserting towel fluff – then pull my hair into some kind of shape with a little clay. I put on my least-holey jeans and my only trainers, and head out onto the streets, jacket over shoulder. Then I put my jacket on because it's chilly.

The evening starts in a less-than-auspicious manner. When I meet Alba at the agreed street corner I discover her group actually just consists of herself and a female friend. We'd had our wires crossed – I was actually meant to bring along another man. It's just as well my new café friend didn't get back in touch in time – I've seen enough *telenovelas* know that any attempt to juggle three women is never going to end well.

As we walk past the bouncers into the blue of the nightclub, I feel almost as nervous as during those early days in Cali. I sit at the table on the edge of the dance floor, hiding behind a ginger beer, and try to switch it all round in my head. This is not so bad. In fact, if anything, it's a free dance lesson in-situ. Not only that, but I'm about to get loads of much-needed practice. Besides, if anything, Alba is likely to be impressed by how much I know. And why all the negativity? It's going to be a good evening, dammit!

Wrong.

Okay, so I'd expect my bachata to be appalling, so when that comes to pass it's kind of alright. Assuming you're not one of Alba's toes. And the reggaeton... well I can't dance reggaeton, so when I fail on that score, too, it's almost to be expected. But when my salsa doesn't go well, there's clearly an issue.

A big part of the problem is that Alba is leading. This shouldn't come as a surprise given the fact that she's my teacher, but it's not what I'm used to in a night club. What's more is that following is not as easy as I'd imagined – it's clearly a skill in its own right. You have to be alert to the intentions of your partner, light enough on your feet to be able to react quickly, and to have at least some idea of what you're being expected to do. All men who whinge at how much harder it is having to lead, please take note.

It quickly becomes a nightmare. Alba starts doing all this crazy stuff I don't recognise, and I simply can't keep up. I end up inventing an on-the-spot *paso* because I seem to have nowhere appropriate to put my feet. What's worse is that I keep dropping the rhythm, and if there was one set of *pasos* I thought I had engraved in my head it was those of salsa.

It briefly crosses my mind to impose my will and reverse the relationship, but this would mean forcing this hugely-experienced dance teacher to adhere to my limited set of moves. I feel uncomfortable with the idea, especially since Alba, like Marta, is a real *coqueta* and shaking her tail-feathers is part of her personality – what right do I have to cage such a bird?

At the same time, following is a crushing experience. There's probably a whole discussion around the area of gender roles in dancing and their wider reflection on society, but the fact is that I'm meant to lead, and if I don't – or can't – then I'm not doing my job.

Alba leans in and tries to make a few comments, but they just get lost in the Latin throb. In fact, I let them. I can pick up the general gist anyway: your dancing is cack. The breather finally comes when I dance with her friend, with whom the ability gap isn't so big, and who, crucially, lets me lead. But by now my confidence is shot, and the whole thing is mechanical and wooden, if it's possible for something to be both.

We emerge from the saturated rhythms into the cold slap of night, my ears ringing in the silence. A street grill nearby sends out scent-signals of sausages and the like, but I'm not hungry. I'm in a kind of daze.

"You have to improve the *movimiento* of your hips," says Alba.

She thinks a while, then decides to leave it at that. And that's possibly the worst thing – she seems to be holding back. I try to explain to her that I'm not used to following; that I'm unfamiliar with her choice of *vueltas*; that I'm one of those people who says things in threes. But deep down I feel like I'm just making excuses. My salsa – in fact a lot of my stuff – is pretty rubbish. I still dance like a twat.

At this rate, there'll be no show at the end, and hence no redemption for the *clausura*. And if there's something worse than my dance ability being part of a process, it's it not being part of a process. I'll just skip back to the UK, back to boring nights in the pub, back to being the guy leaning on the bar making out like he can dance when he can't.

I smile at my partners and thank them for a good night, then traipse back to my hotel; to the tired bedspread and the crunk of old springs. The worst thing is that it's confirmed what I've thought all along: deep down, I'm crap at this.

If I can't pick up dancing under these circumstances – dedicated to the pursuit, in a country where dance is such an integral part of the culture, and after all these lessons and all this practice – then when can I? I'm just wasting my time.

CHAPTER SIXTEEN

Very Improving

As the sun rises over the terracotta roof tiles of Pasto, some part of me is rebelling. I might not know everything, dammit, but that doesn't mean I know nothing. If Alba had any idea how much I'd learnt during my travels, she'd have a lot more respect for my abilities.

So down at my *guaneña* class that day, I slip into my well-practised dance raconteur bit. I start by telling her about my *mapalé* experience and doing, admittedly, the one and only *paso* I can deliver on demand: the Barbara Windsor. The *mapalé* is quite an exotic dance for these parts – she can't fail to be impressed by that.

Oh yes she can! I've got it all wrong, she tells me. Putting my hands in front of my chest like that is a common mistake, and it means the movement of my chest is *bloqueado* (blocked). Stung by this, I dive into something a quick demo of the cumbia I learnt in Barranquilla – something in which I'm assured of my competence. Try that for size!

She corrects me instantly, telling me I should be moving my hips in a circle. I'm practically beyond help by the time I switch to the *champeta* and the jelly-legs *paso*, her response being that this isn't something you do in *champeta*.

NO!!! You're destroying everything I've learnt; putting all my dances in a big bin and telling me I've wasted months and months of my life.

I resolve not to show her anything again. I remind myself that dances like cumbia can vary greatly across the country, that Pasto is not the world capital of *champeta* and that dance teachers are strident folk who think that their way is the right way or else they'd be no good at their job. I've got a new saying: If it's broken, pretend it isn't and carry on.

Or, alternatively, just make the same mistake again. At the very next opportunity, I tell her that the only thing I know about reggaeton is that you're meant to stay really loose. I demonstrate this by dropping my shoulders – something I saw Jay do in Medellín.

Guess what? It's wrong! If anything, she tells me, it's the opposite. I don't know what dance would suit a slumped body and a sullen face, but I reckon I'd be good at it in my current state. The good news is that this is where the smashing of beloved items stops and the moulding and firing of new ones begins.

The next number will be a reggaeton... a reggaeton.

With its music videos that tell of chicks and cars on tap (which is a bit confusing given both taps are marked with a 'C'), reggaeton is the self-styled bad boy of modern Latin music. It's also the most modern of all the urban genres, having only gone mainstream in 2005-6, when it hit the big time with the US-based Latin audience with hits like Gasolina by Daddy Yankee.

Musically, it's a mixture of reggae, dancehall and hip hop, along with various Latin influences. It started out as *reggae en Español* (Spanish-language reggae and dancehall) in Panama in the 1970s and 80s before maturing in Puerto Rico into the incarnation known today. But the real signature of reggaeton – the prime identifying feature – is the *THUMP de-THUMP derrr* of kick drum and snare. That drum pattern is known as Dem Bow, after the dancehall song by Shabba Ranks that helped bring it to prominence. And once that beat swaggers moodily into the room, the talking is over and it's time for business.

Reggaeton is a genre that divides Colombians, some of whom dislike it due to sometimes misogynistic lyrics, and the overtly erotic nature of the dancing (a style known as *perreo*). But the lyrics don't bother me because I can't usually work out what they're saying, and by now I'm so desensitised to the sight of such moves that if I were to burst in on a couple having sex, I'd be perplexed as to why they were dancing on the bed. Furthermore, there are plenty of women who actively love both the music and the style of dancing, especially on the coast.

Interestingly, reggaeton is the one mainstream Latin dance in which the woman could be said to lead. Although it probably says a great deal that the only way she's able to achieve this is by actively objectifying herself, or at least simulating it.

The first move Alba shows me involves me being poised with my knees bent, thrusting my shoulders backwards in a slow and deliberate manner which makes me feel strong and manly. It's a good start, but we're not going to do all the saucy stuff are we? Of course we are! Why wouldn't we? In fact, Alba tells me, if you try to dance with a girl on the coast and it's not *pegado*, she'll likely just walk away in disgust.

This kind of forwardness is also open to misinterpretation, particularly where foreigners are involved. I heard about one girl from Cartagena who went out to a club with some European bloke, just as friends, and danced reggaeton with him in the typical, saucy manner. On a subsequent night she was out with him again, plus a couple of other foreigners, and danced the same way with all of them. The end result was the Dutch guy getting upset with her, saying "I thought we had something special!"

"There's danger with this kind of dance," the person who related the story to me concluded.

We move onto a number of pelvic movements, which remind me somewhat of the tragic groin-thrusting done by drunkards in suits who've gone straight from office to pub to nightclub. The subtle yet crucial difference is that the thrust is done backwards, not forwards, and this completely changes the dynamic. Soon she's making a table of her back, which I have to rhythmically run my hands down (putting drinks on it would just seem disrespectful).

This impromptu reggaeton class is just the first part of a general dance-improvement programme that encompasses all of the urban styles I've learnt so far. Were we in a film, this part would be a cheesy montage set to music.

Vallenato is next in the clinic, with Alba teaching me something that has almost universal relevance: an elegant move designed to initiate the dance. In this, you gently, almost seductively, drape your partner's hands over your neck. Or, if you're like me, yank them into place like the start of a martial arts manoeuvre.

"*Suave*," she says. Gently.

In the merengue, Alba not only teaches me some new *vueltas*, but a new approach in general. She has us dancing about, clapping our hands together, pushing each other apart and coming back together again, and all sorts of other stuff.

"At times with *elegancia*," she says, "At others – *¡loco!*"

Even my bachata gets some attention. And suddenly I'm able to see why my partners thus far have all ended up with blackened toenails: it's because after rolling your hip upwards – known as a *golpe* – you move the same foot again, which you can't do if you've instinctively transferred all your weight to that foot.

"*Uno, dos, tres, GOLPE. Uno, dos, tres, GOLPE.*" says Alba, leading me about the room with our legs sensually interleaved.

I'm now able to recognise bachata almost immediately due to the Dominican music's trademark fiddly-twiddly guitar plucking. I'm also picking up a recurrent theme in the lyrics.

I've yet to hear a bachata track that was "Hey, we're in love – high five!" Instead, they're about people being dumped, deceived and generally crapped on romantically. They're about the love you wish you could have, or the love you maybe did have before cocking it up royally. In fact, more than anything else, bachata tracks seem to be about pain.

By way of a dance progress test, Alba decides to present me with a prop. What will it be this time? A hat? A shawl? A dog? Try a white plastic chair – she wants me to go and do a merengue routine with it. It's hard doing cat's-cradle turns with something so rigid, lifeless and devoid of emotion, but then people had to dance with me when I first arrived, so I would be hypocritical not to. And, hey – at least she doesn't want me to dance reggaeton with it!

She wants me to dance reggaeton with it. Well, whatever you might think of me, I'm not about to simulate sex with an inanimate object.

"I'm English!" I tell her, "I'm a gentleman!"

And, no, gentlemen don't prefer plastic chairs.

"So the English are gentlemen, and Colombians are crazy, yes?" she says, affecting offence. "*¡Oh bueno!*"

With the customary "What has my life come to?"-type sigh, I advance to the plastic chair with manly intent, *coquetear* (flirt) with it and intertwine my legs with its own. I even turn round, put my leg between its own and start thrusting my butt at it: Alba has explained that swapping gender-roles can be a good way of making reggaeton less intimidating for an unfamiliar partner. Liza Minelli's saucy chair-dance to Mein Herr in Cabaret seems awfully tame all of a sudden.

One final hurdle remains before I can sign off from my lesson – a choreographed performance of *la guaneña*. Alba has me dress up in loose white clothing plus hat and poncho like a local indigenous *campesino*, although I arguably look less peasant-like in this getup than when I'm wearing my travelling garb.

Away we go, bounding about in the work fields of Alba's studio. As is common with folk dances, the movements in the *guaneña* are much more literal than with the urban ones. We work our way through the dance's numerous courtship references which, unlike in cumbia, seem to be less about flirting and more about the realities of a long-term romantic partnership. Like the one where we get wrapped up in the shawl together and go skipping off, and the one where she's cradling a baby. There isn't one where I try to hide several other women under the shawl without her noticing, though.

The dog feels left out and trots round the dance floor trying to join in the performance, though frankly, it doesn't seem to have been practising. And the bit where it pretends to have had my child is just insulting.

The dance comes to an end with me on one knee and my hands in the air exalting my partner. With the dancing all done and dealt with, Alba treats me to a hearty farewell dinner, ultimately sending me on my way with a straw hat as a gift. Another chapter in my dance journey has come to an end.

Ideally, I should now seek out the chance to show it off somewhere, which in this case would mean a *peña*. So that's what I do. Peering in at the one near my guest house that evening, I can see it's packed with Pastusos sat round tables, with a busy dance floor and a live band playing some merengue. Perfect – let's go in.

"It's full," says the woman at the door.

The one Clara suggested has no such issues. In fact, so un-full is it that the band are hanging around outside smoking cigarettes and waiting for someone to play to.

I guess it'll have to wait.

It's not long gone 7am and I'd really rather be asleep. Instead I'm sat in a permanent state of head-loll as the minibus bucks about on its way to… where was it we were going again?

"*¡Vamos a Túquerres! ¡Vamos a Túquerres! ¡Vamos a Túquerres!*" my fellow passengers yell-sing. We're going to Túquerres!

Ah yes.

It came as a welcome surprise when I got a message from Clara inviting me to go hiking with her and her friends. It feels slightly less welcome now, however, as they playfully taunt my attempts to sleep: I feel the heat of a camera flash, and the sound of a group of people loudly awarding me the nickname of '*perrito de taxi*' (nodding dog).

Everyone is in their twenties and thirties, though you wouldn't know it – it feels like we're on a school trip. Together we've requisitioned a vehicle and driver with the intention of hiking to a volcanic crater lake known as Laguna Verde.

The minibus pulls up at a petrol station, and an attendant comes to the driver's window.

"*¡Vamos a Túquerres!*" yells one of the group to the attendant before the driver can get a word in. The chant goes up once more, forcing the driver and attendant to converse through bemused grins.

After stocking up on food in a corner shop at the now-fabled town of Túquerres, we take a jeep out to the trail head. This is accompanied by more singing and laughter, and a whole lot of me getting ribbed in ways I don't quite understand.

Spirits fall a little as we climb out the jeep, our legs finally taking responsibility for our weight. We're at about 4000m altitude in an area of elevated moorland, but a mist has enveloped all of this high ground with the visibility reduced further by a gentle blanket of rain. Ecuador would be visible from here on a clear day, but as it is we barely see the path ahead. We'll certainly be lucky if we see anything of the *laguna*.

I force my wet fingers into a pair of gloves, everyone around me getting similarly layered up, and we start our ascent. As our boots scrunch the silty trail, one of the older guys in the group – Jandro – decides that a bit of music would liven things up, and starts playing US chart music on his Blackberry. Music on a mountainside? You'd get hung for that in England. Well, okay, that's an exaggeration. In fact, had La Violencia happened in England it would just have been a mass outbreak of tutting and counter-tutting.

The treeless scrub is much better adapted to the climate than we are, with much of the vegetation consisting of tufts of coarse grass, ground-hugging growths and peculiarly-adapted plants. One has leaves like vertical tongues, like it's trying to lick the moisture out the air, whilst another has berries that catch the attention of one of the girls in the group.

"Can you eat them?" she asks.

"Try it!" say three different people in unison.

The idea of food is now in our collective mind-set, and people start pulling out their rations.

"Crisps?" says one girl.

I turn, expecting to see an open bag, but I'm mistaken – she's actually offering me a bag of my own. In fact, she's brought enough bags for everyone. Other people follow suit, handing out big handfuls of wrapped sweets and whole blocks of crackers.

I meanwhile cling silently to my single pot of yoghurt and half-eaten bar of chocolate, very aware of how mean and cold-hearted I must look. It's frustrating – whilst I am actually both of those things, I'm usually so much better at hiding it.

The weather still has room to get worse, and soon we're being lashed with rain. Most of us, myself included, are wearing waterproof cagoules, but Clara's energetic boyfriend isn't, and is taking a soaking. Wait a minute – this is my chance. I plough through my bag, and whip out a reflective waterproof sheet – a single-usage item meant for emergency protection from exposure when you're trapped on a mountainside.

He looks like a joint of roasted meat and he rustles like tinsel as he walks, but he's a whole lot better off than he was. I meanwhile feel like I've earned my place in the team. So we both feel more comfortable. A little further down the trail an old man coming the other way asks me if he can borrow my gloves, but he's not shared any food with me so he can fuck off.

Cresting a high ridge, we start our descent into the volcanic crater. With mist still robbing us of any view, we smell the lake long before we see it, catching frequent whiffs of sulphur as we half-walk, half-slither down the treacherous path. It's only as we are nearing the very bottom of the basin that the thing we came to see finally emerges through the vapour. But when it does, it's unmistakable: a glorious milky-emerald body of water, with sand-like white shorelines; a glowing fissure of beauty amidst the craggy landscape; Laguna Verde.

We park up on some rocks in front of this ethereal gemstone of water. Here the sharing continues, not only of bread, cheese and ham but also of jokes and of complaints, with "*hace mucho frío*" (it's very cold) ringing out from all quarters. The temperature is becoming a genuine problem now we've stopped walking, and we're all feeling it.

Not that this stops the goofing round. One guy is wearing a bright yellow rain-poncho with a big bulge at the front where he's sheltering his girlfriend from the weather.

"I'm a chicken!" he says.

"A pregnant chicken!" I say.

This is his cue to strut about, comically.

"*¡Sí!* A pregnant chicken!"

They just never stop. No wonder Bolívar was exasperated.

"*¡Bailamos!*" insists Jandro, getting to his feet. Let's dance!

He's joined by a couple of the girls and soon they're bobbing about on the volcanic rocks, to the tinny strains of Lady Gaga. When this doesn't generate the requisite heat, they resort to just doing star jumps – I guess it must be some folkloric thing. The weather steps up its efforts, whipping us with rain and wind, but it's kidding itself – it would take more than that to break the Pastuso spirit.

"*¡Calor humano!*" says someone. Human warmth!

"*¡Calor humano!*" everyone agrees, and we all huddle together, penguin-like, on a rocky outcrop, sheltering together under the stretched-out yellow poncho which flaps and judders under the onslaught.

Human warmth. How apt.

Pasto has been good to me but I feel like I need a break from my mission – it's all been a bit intense of late – so I decide to take a break in Colombia's equatorially-named neighbour to the South.

Ecuador and Colombia are old friends. In fact, they were both part of the short-lived Gran Colombia, along with Venezuela, at a time when unity was strategically important as a defence against the Spanish royalist forces. The three countries share near-identical flags of gold, blue and red, born of this common heritage, and representing (in Colombia's case) the country's gold, its two coastlines and the blood that was spilled in gaining independence. Modern relations between Ecuador and Colombia are generally good, although things heated up in 2008 when a Colombian task force crossed the border uninvited as part of an attack on FARC rebels.

I spend the first week or so in the relaxing little town of Mindo, up in the Andean cloud forest. It's good to be out amongst nature: the chatter of exotic birds... the patter of rain on leaves... the hurtling of US exchange-students on zip lines... I myself mostly sit out in my shorts by a gurgling stream, writing up notes and occasionally looking up to watch clouds tickle the forested hillsides.

Despite being off-duty, I'm intrigued by what the place might have to offer in dance terms, and head to a little club. It's the mustiest, most Andean-smelling establishment I've ever been in, like they had to herd out a flock of sheep in order to open up for the evening.

I've noticed a distinct change in music since arriving in Ecuador: *vallenato* has been entirely absent and, as if to add strangeness to weirdness, one bus journey I took involved non-stop bachata, like more than one track an hour was normal.

The club continues this trend for the unfamiliar, playing quite a bit of Caribbean-sounding stuff I don't recognise. The other people in the club mostly hang around the edge of the dance floor clutching drinks for safety, as though it's a lake and they can't swim. The only people splashing about are a group of kids doing a reggaeton circle, which is mostly just an excuse to push each other into the middle for a bit of an arse-kicking.

Finally some salsa comes on, and a few couples tip-toe out into the shallows, including a pair in front of me who do the same *paso básico* for an entire song without executing a single turn. The only person I notice show any real ability is a girl in her twenties, here with a group of female friends.

Come the next track, I head over to offer her a dance. It turns out she's from the USA, and not only that, she learnt in Cali. We push out onto the empty dance floor and quickly hit our stride in the basic 'ta-da!' *paso*. I spin through her arm and put her through a few turns – basic stuff.

To my surprise, folk stood round the outside of the dance floor start whooping, cheering and even clapping along. My repertoire might be limited, but it's still apparently impressive for Mindo. Perhaps this is it; I've reached the zenith of my dancing ability, at least in relative terms. I should get it on a t-shirt: 'Impressive for Mindo'.

Eventually, the mosquitoes which are silently tearing my lower legs to shreds get the better of me and I head off to less itchy climes – the market town of Otavalo.

Sited in a nest of volcanoes that wear clouds like they're toupees, it has a more indigenous feel than anywhere I visited in Colombia, with the possible exception of Silvia. The general ambience of Andean docility, however, is very familiar. In fact the *guaneña*-like *sanjuanito* has strong ties with this region.

Big women – or at least very heavily clothed women – amble by, their sleek hair drawn back into a single plait. Some have a blanket-wrapped baby on their back whose eyes peep out over the top. Other folk ascend hillsides in the back of pickup trucks with trailers that serve as public transport.

Here, many of the local shops bear signs telling you you're not welcome if you have a respiratory illness. I swear that in Colombia they'd be just like "Come in – give us a hug!" Or maybe not. Maybe they'd offer you cocaine and/or kidnap you. I've seen the films: I'm not going near that place.

Down in the famous market the colours run rampant while the mountain sun sears the ground between parasols. Stallholders preside over blankets and cardigans with noisy zigzags. People wearing hats sell bags featuring woven images of people wearing hats (and possibly selling bags). Others sell root vegetables and chilli peppers off sheets on the ground.

It's the kind of town you could spend some time, and that's exactly what I do, relaxing in a little *posada*. The young manager of the place, an Ecuadorian who grew up in Europe, mentions that there are a couple of *peñas* in town. I quite fancy visiting one, having missed the chance in Pasto, and she kindly agrees to take me. Which is all well and good, of course, but does she have much dance experience?

"Just the five years learning ballet and modern dance."

I'll take that as a 'Yes, I'm practically a teacher,' then.

We head there together, along with some other foreigners from the *posada*, down streets of tessellating hexagonal pavers. I know I should be feeling confident after the dance-improvement montage, but I'm actually a bit edgy. After all, the last time I went to a club with an expert it was a disaster.

Once inside, we clatter our way through the maze of furniture to a table of our own. The place is pretty big with a stage and a proper dance floor at its heart, although it's only maybe a quarter full of people. A live band is happily knocking out a bit of everything – salsa, merengue, bachata – and people are actually up and dancing. It's not Cali, for sure, but it's certainly not Mindo. Particularly popular is cumbia, to which people dance a kind of two-step, entirely unrelated to the coastal hat-driven flirtation. There's also some Andean folk stuff, albeit without a hint of *guaneña*.

My new friends and I sit talking for a while in a group, but I know I need to act before I think about it too much. On comes some merengue – there's my cue. I offer my hand to the hotel manager, and lead her away, my innards tight like a drum skin.

"Walk with me," she says, taking the lead.

Damn, damn, damn. It's like the Pasto nightclub all over again.

"I can dance merengue," I say, and gently take the wheel back from her.

I'm a little stiff at first – it's the first dance of the evening – but leading stiffly is still better than the alternative. My confidence growing, I lead her through one turn, then another. She's a darned good dancer – light and perky, like a little Andean cloud. But then hey, I'm not bad either these days. By the end of the track, I'm going right through my extended repertoire, even teaching her a turn she hadn't come across before.

"Don't take this the wrong way..." she says as we head back to the table.

I prepare to take it the wrong way.

"...but you dance really well for a white guy."

So do you! So do you! Ha! Sorry I mean... oh look, I'm just a bit giddy.

It's the first of a number of dances we share, and not all of them go as well as that first one. My still-embryonic bachata, for example, is genuinely poor compared to her own elegant swayings. But she won't need to go to hospital afterwards, and that's a big tick in its own right.

I move on to dancing with a Californian backpacker in our group who has some rudimentary skills. By now I'm well warmed up, and I whisk her off, putting her through figure-of-eight turns and dancing at times with *elegancia*, at others *loco*. She turns out to be the perfect practice partner, as I can teach her without having to worry about boring her through repetition, as she needs the practice too.

Suddenly I'm eating the merengue for breakfast. Almost unnoticed it's become near-instinctive. My God, for the first time in my life I'm dancing in a way that just flows. It's not that it doesn't require thought – it does – and I certainly make plenty of little slips, but the moves are just coming to me, and I'm smiling, laughing and expressing myself. It's exhilarating.

Back at the table, my fellow gringos are really impressed. This actually comes as something of a surprise to me, as I hadn't really considered I might have an audience.

"Where did you learn to dance?!" says a fellow Englishman.

"Colombia."

By the time I get back to Pasto, something important has changed.

All over the country, the second round of voting has been held, and the results have been collated: Santos will be the next president of the Republic of Colombia, having won by a landslide. With the social media generation being by and large Mockus voters, my Facebook news feed reads as one continuous lament, youthful idealism having being crushed by hard-headed pragmatism.

The election result is not the change I was referring to, though. Now I'm back in Colombia, it should be time for me to kick on and get the dance going again. But there's a problem, and it's one I couldn't have foreseen: I simply don't think I can be bothered.

It only becomes apparent when I try to go to a dance class. I get halfway there and change my mind and come back. Not out of fear, or paying too much heed to my internal voice, but because I just can't be arsed with it. The thought of it just makes me feel tired.

At first I think I must just be having an off-day, but the longer I hang around in Pasto, the more the feeling grows. I decide it's something best left alone for now, and take time out to visit a nearby lake. It makes little difference – when I come back I still have no dance hunger; just regular hunger. So I go to a restaurant and try out the local speciality of *cuy* (guinea pig), the rodents being cooked mounted on wooden poles, their little paws stuck out helplessly in front of them, until their skin is amber and crispy. But even feasting on small, helpless animals doesn't seem to help.

With my dance appetite showing no sign of returning, I decide to catch up with a couple of my friends, Clara and Jandro, and their *calor humano*.

If there's one thing I've learned about Pastusos it's that they don't consider themselves to be the butt of jokes. Rather they are the jokers – the country's natural comedians – and everything is an opportunity for a gag. During the trek, I asked one of the group if everyone leaves Pasto when the volcano erupts, given the town is less than five miles away.

"The tourists leave," she said, "but we all stay and take photos!"

Actually, I really do hope that was a joke.

Remembering my original request, Clara suggests we all go together to a *peña* where we can dance the night away. It's a good idea in theory – I'll be able to show them some of the skills I've accrued, and maybe even put my *guaneña* out there. But once again I feel strangely ambivalent about it all and I decline.

I swing by to visit Alba. She's delighted to see me again and has a suggestion for me: why don't I go to swampy Tumaco? I could stay with some friends of hers at this coastal town and learn *currulao*, a dance from the Pacific. *Currulao* is a music and dance genre of Afro-Colombian heritage. It's set against the gentle, sandy plink-plonk of marimbas, with handkerchiefs playing a particularly prominent role. I've not touched that coast yet, nor experienced any of its dances, so it would certainly make sense.

Like much of the Pacific coast, Tumaco has some serious safety issues, and Alba tells me I'd spend most of my time in the hotel, on the beach or in the dance class. Which actually doesn't sound too bad, really, especially if you exclude the dance-class bit.

I don't know what's come over me. I feel like it should inspire me, yet it doesn't – it's just more of the same. Still, it would be good for the dance routine in Cali. Ha! The dance routine. Like that's happening. I'm the kind of person who dusts myself down and presses on with stuff, but it feels beyond even that.

I potter about in my hotel room trying to make sense of the messages my mind is giving me. A mini-marathon is being held today in Pasto and the stragglers are continuing to pass through, despite the failing light. My urban dance has improved so much recently that I should be overjoyed. On top of that, I've just had an extended break in Ecuador. I should be champing at the bit, like a Conquistador's horse, so why am I visualising the galleon home?

Maybe it's like when people get ill the moment they take a break from work, or others simply keel over and die right after they've just retired. Or even like that thing when you spin round and round and then stop suddenly and fall over and go "urrrghh". What I'm saying is that perhaps the break was the opportunity my brain was waiting for to just collapse in its armchair – CRUNK – and say "I think I've just broken the armchair."

Travel takes a toll on the mind and body. And with months and months behind me of going from place to place, learning all this stuff and never really having anywhere to call home, I guess I'm just burnt out, and the thought of doing yet more learning has broken me for good.

The runners continue streaming past outside. I feel like I'm running a marathon and I've hit a wall. No, I mean an actual wall. People are cheering and clapping on the runners who pass, shouting "*¡Siga, siga!*" (Go on, go on!). But I don't want to carry on. I'm sick of learning how to dance. I just don't care about it anymore.

I've had enough.

CHAPTER SEVENTEEN

Beauty and the Beats

People warned me that the back road over the central cordillera of the Andes was largely *destapada* (unsurfaced), and also notorious for the threat of guerrilla ambushes, but what nobody bothered to mention was how beautiful it would be.

The vehicle winds through the interlocking eaves of a secluded valley, a glistening river for company, whilst the late-afternoon sun warms up glorious, cow-laden pastures. We bounce along to the tinny strains of a strumming guitar – *corrido,* a fellow passenger tells me – occasionally squeezing past an indigenous local guiding a laden donkey. I recline, at least to the extent that one can in a cramped bus, and inhale. Life is good.

The serenity doesn't last, however. Soon we pop out of the valley and onto open moorland, exposing us to the elements. Dust particles from the road seep inside and hang in the air, giving it a gritty bite, whilst the wind whistles about us, pulling at the vehicle with monstrous hands.

We battle on, gaining altitude and getting progressively more remote, passing a solitary house in the middle of nowhere, heavy rugs being swatted about on a line outside. Still we press on, beyond the point of habitation. The grasslands die away, replaced by a misty, treeless páramo with thousands of stumpy *frailejones* – rare and bizarrely beautiful pineapple-like plants – glowing yellow from the few late rays that have braved it through the gloom.

As we continue to climb, our surroundings mutate into something more hostile still: tightly-hugging vegetation, dripping with moisture, that forms impenetrable barriers on either side of the road. The view ahead, meanwhile, is held hostage by thickening mist and failing light.

Then, out of nowhere, a mighty metal cylinder booms towards us, punching a hole in the ether.

What the hell's that?!

Oh my life – it's a tank! Guerrillas!

No, hold on – since when have guerrillas owned tanks? It's the army. More parked tanks follow, along with an army encampment. And men walking round in military reliefs. And a little café serving trout.

The back of the mountains finally broken, we descend in darkness, quickly and quietly slipping back down through the ecosystems, towards the sanity of the Magdalena Valley below.

Being a valley city, Neiva is hot, and has little breeze to temper it. I sit in a dusty central park, where sand stands in for soil, and eat *plátano maduro con queso* – mature plantain baked and split in half with cheese melting in the gap. A splash of orange from a little stall, coffee from a walking vendor and that's breakfast. I love Latin America – you can just graze.

There's a festival on in Neiva – I knew that before I arrived. But even if I hadn't, I would have guessed it the second I saw the giant inflatable liquor bottles that adorn the centre – a reminder of every citizen's obligation to get wasted and dance the night away.

This time, the flimsy pretext for partying is Reinado Nacional del Bambuco, a festival which combines a beauty pageant with a celebration of *bambuco*, a traditional genre from the interior. Not long ago, I'd have been coming here to learn how to dance it, but I've had enough of all that – I'm just here to kick back and enjoy the show. Watching attractive women dance: I can probably cope with that.

Come the evening I make my way down to the *malecón* (waterfront). The city is sited on the inside of a bend in the Magdalena river. A thousand miles after it began, it will be ejected in sooty plumes at Barranquilla, but here it's young and fresh-faced, with no idea of the adventures that lie ahead of it.

The festival proper won't get going for another couple of days, but there's already a run of temporary open air bars with quite a few people hanging out. Corn blackens on grills in the warm evening, the air thickened further with popular Latin rhythms. Chairs scrape on concrete and dirt as people get up in pairs to rotate to merengue, salsa and *vallenato*.

Good for them.

I continue up the *malecón*, passing some woven-bracelet sellers. This is something an entire street industry is built around, one staffed by young-ish, alternative folk who travel from festival to festival displaying hand-made items on wooden boards.

The ones here seem pretty nice and friendly, but this contrasts quite strongly with a travelling band I happened upon whilst I was in Ecuador who, like me, had recently headed south over the border.

The problem started when one of them stopped me to show me his wares. I wasn't interested and respectfully waved him away. Unfortunately, he didn't want to be waved away. He stepped in my path and started talking at me, rattling off words at a speed that I couldn't keep up with. "*Flaquito*" (skinny) he kept calling me in particular, which I might not normally mind too much given the predilection for straight-talk. But something about his tone suggested he meant to insult, and his parting comment was that I needed to "*engordar*" (fatten up).

I swatted him away and walked on, but my sense of annoyance grew with the distance. How dare he say all that stuff to me that I barely understood but was probably insulting! I was half-hoping he was still there when I headed back the same way later, and half-hoping he wasn't, knowing what I can be like.

But he was there, stood chatting with another vendor. I got a good look at him this time. How could he tell me to fatten up – the guy was practically the same build as me! But, knowing I could have got it wrong, I decided to use his own language back at him as a test – if he took it graciously, then he meant no offence by it.

"*¡Hey flaquito!*" I said. Hey skinny!

"*No,*" he said, "*tú eres flaquito.*" No, you're skinny.

Life must be tough on the streets, what with the lack of mirrors and all.

"You're skinny, too!" I said, measuring his bicep using my thumb and forefinger as callipers.

He countered this with more high-speed vitriol. I hate arguing in a foreign language – it's like going into a swordfight armed with a cucumber. This time he was flashing the word '*marica*' a lot. This can mean 'gay', but is more often used as slang for 'friend'. Which was it this time?

I played it back to him to find out. He erupted in stream of unintelligible invective. But it was a stream which ran dry the instant he spotted a potential client passing: he made the seamless switch into sales mode and approached them.

"Is there a problem?" his friend asked me, stepping in like a tag-team partner.

I figured this could go either way. Actually that was nonsense – there were two of them and one of me, and on the evidence of how I choose my battles I was clearly an idiot. I decided the best thing I could do at this point was to be assertive and just tell it how it was.

"Your friend insulted me."

His face softened.

"Ah, he's just rude."

This turned out to be the end of it. The other guy finished haranguing passers-by and soon we were shaking hands and agreeing to drop it.

"We're hippies!" said the placatory one.

With the word '*marica*' having been bandied around so much, he took the opportunity to make it clear that he and his friend weren't.

"We hate gays," he said.

I see.

At this point I felt obliged to attempt some gentle re-education. I explained that gay people in the UK are treated very differently to over here, and that most people don't have a problem with homosexuality. At which point it all went quiet. We walked together in silence.

Look, whatever you're thinking, just say it.

"Are you gay?"

My talking about gay people made him continue to wonder, he said. Which makes perfect sense of course. In fact, you could probably catch it just by looking at one.

I could easily have dealt with this by telling him the truth – that I'm not – but it really shouldn't have mattered, and nor should it have been an insult. I tried explaining the latter part of that without revealing the former, but talking around the issue was getting nowhere. I ultimately conceded that I couldn't just casually expect to change deeply-ingrained beliefs just-like-that. After all, Rome wasn't built in a day. They were probably all too busy having gay sex.

"I'm heterosexual," I said.

"Ah! You're a man!"

Dear Lord. But with that, we could suddenly all relax again.

Such attitudes are common amongst Colombians. The suggestion that a person is gay is generally a negative one, and if you're a celebrity it can even be potentially career-damaging. Indeed, when *vallenato* legend Silvestre Dangond was faced with similar rumours, he went off on a two-minute on-stage diatribe about how gay he wasn't, before launching into a song called El Gran Varón (The Great Man). Even women dancing together is seen as distasteful by some – if there are too many girls, they should either wait their turn or find a guy willing dance with the both of them at once.

We made a detour so the guys could have a smoke with some other hippies – propped up against a wall down a little side street. It's a chance for them to kiss some local women, the feisty hippy explaining to me that they have "*vaginas como vino*" (vaginas like wine) – the cue for another free oral sex demonstration.

I also got to see why wrist-thingies are an ideal source of income if you're a hippy: you can make them whilst you're idly hanging about talking about peace, love and how much you hate gays. On the down side however, it clearly doesn't provide much income – the ones I met were living from hand to mouth. And that's without considering this curious, nagging anomaly: if you choose to invest so heavily in traditional roles of gender and sexuality, doesn't having a career in needlecraft put you on slightly rocky ground?

Together, the two hippies and I headed off to see something else of the city. En route, crossing a road, I paused to let a car through. The feisty hippy, however, carried on, forcing the traffic to stop.

"*Los calles nos pertenecen,*" he said. The streets belong to us.

Everything belonged to them, yet somehow nothing.

We ended up in a square surrounded by bars where we bumped into another hippy with his own board of wrist-thingies. We sat together in a plaza, the three of them drinking and exchanging stories. All was free and easy. Until, that is, they leapt to their feet in sudden confrontation.

The feisty hippy, who was pretty drunk by this stage, threw some swings at the new guy. The new guy, however, was too quick and alternated between fending off the blows and trying to reason with him. The feisty hippy broke off as though to think about it, but it turned out to be just a ruse that allowed him to grab an empty bottle.

At this point, the placatory hippy waded in – thank goodness. I was glad to see someone had the sense to break up this nonsense.

"Just hands," he said, and confiscated the bottle.

Ah. I see.

Without warning, the situation changed again. Something the new hippy said inflamed the placatory hippy, who instantly became the bloody-angry hippy. Sensing this was a much more realistic threat, the new hippy ran off at pace with the bloody-angry hippy in pursuit. I would have joined in, encouraging everyone else to do the same, but there was no merengue playing.

Colombians are all too familiar with conflict. Following the collapse of Gran Colombia and the death of Simón Bolívar, the political powers said "I suppose we'd better split up into liberals and conservatives then." Both sides were basically the same – liberal – but, due in some part to the narcissism of small differences, the distance between them grew, as did the enmity. It was a divide that would be responsible for numerous bitter conflicts over the years, and was at the heart of the Thousand Days' War at the end of the 19th Century, which cost in the region of 100,000 lives.

Back in Ecuador, the hippies ended up on the perimeter of the square, the new hippy trying to use parked cars as obstacles to his being attacked. At a nearby bar, some muscular blokes in their thirties and forties were sat outside, drinking beers. As the two hippies chased each other about, occasionally exchanging blows, the men rose to their feet, holding their beers and roaring with laughter; laughing right at them, right at the fighting hippies.

I decided to leave before things degraded further. I mean with the hippies rather than the politics. The latter goes without saying.

Back in Neiva, there is no such hostility, but there is also no party as yet, so I head out of town for a couple of days to visit some local badlands – the Desierto de la Tatacoa. It's great having all this freedom from dance: I can do whatever I want.

A battered old Renault 12 takes me out from the nearest town and into the emptiness. The windscreen wipers have no blades attached, which probably says something about the climate in these parts. Big candelabra and prickly pear cacti roam the cracked landscape amidst thinned-out patches of grass and dried-up watercourses. In one particular area the lands get really bad: crinkled terracotta ridges that form a maze of gullies and channels, like a rusty, dried-up brain.

We swing off the road and arrive at my accommodation for the night – an isolated little farm-come-guest house with barn-style split doors. Clothing hangs on a barbed wire fence demarking the site from the vast area of fractured, putty-grey plains beyond it. Chickens scratch about the yard, goats tear at solitary green tufts and a dog slinks about, patrolling its territory.

I tap away on my computer in the evening warmth, with a family with three kids also sat out nearby. One of the little ones comes over to investigate, petitioning me to play some music on my device. Ultimately I relent and put on some *mapalé*, mostly just to appease him so I can get on with my work.

His little face lights up. He commences singing out of time with the music, and pops about, thrusting his hands out. They learn it at school, apparently. My concession is a mistake – every two minutes or so he demands another burst of *mapalé*. Thankfully, he's soon distracted by the arrival of his siblings.

"*¡Mira! ¡Un ratón!*" says one. Look! A mouse!

What, where? I scour the dusty ground around my chair.

"*¡Que baila reguetón!*" That's dancing reggaeton!

"*¡Mira! ¡Un gato!*" squeaks another. "*¡Que baila vallenato!*" Look! A cat! That's dancing *vallenato*!

There's no hope for them. They're only kids, and their brains are already addled with dance. But if they were hoping to see an *extranjero* that's dancing Bolero – or indeed anything for that matter – their luck is definitely out.

I feel decidedly scruffy sauntering about the cocktail party in jeans and trainers, though I'm grateful that I at least had time to swap my crumpled t-shirt for a crumpled shirt (I scrub up well, you know). My new acquaintance, however, is much better prepared than I, being attired in smart shoes, trousers and pressed shirt. His name is

Pablo, he's a straight-laced thirty-something and he's my host – I've managed to arrange a homestay with him and his extended family.

The party is a pre-festival mixer featuring the previous overall winners from the *bambuco* pageant's 50 year history, as well as the regional winners that are vying for this year's crown – nearly all of the country's 33 departments represented. It's easy to tell the regional winners apart from the rest of us because most people don't walk around in a beautiful *pollera*-like dress with a sash over the top that says '*Señorita*' plus a department name. Though not for a lack of wanting.

In between my face-stuffing with party food – *los canapés nos pertenecen* – Pablo introduces me to his friend. Esteban is a slim *mestizo* bloke with a friendly and self-assured smile, and has a vested interest in the festival – he's the dance partner for one of the departmental queens. We sit there discussing the relative merits of said participants though, if I'm honest, their dancing ability is barely mentioned.

"My wife said to me, 'You weren't looking at her face – you were looking at her tits!'" says Esteban, translating their Spanish-language conversation into English. "Can you say that? 'Tits'?"

You certainly can, Esteban. In fact, if you're going to stare at some in front of your wife, you may as well.

The dance in which the departmental queens must demonstrate prowess is a specific flavour of *bambuco* called *sanjuanero*. This is not to be confused with *sanjuanito*, something I do the moment it's first mentioned to me. Just to confuse matters further, when I demonstrate what I think is *sanjuanero*, but is actually *sanjuanito*, Esteban corrects me and tells me it's *la guaneña*.

"If you'd come earlier you could have learnt *sanjuanero*!" Pablo tells me.

Yeah, shame. Are there are any more canapés?

Back in Esteban's pad, we all sit down and watch a TV recording of one of the regional qualifying rounds for the competition.

"It's me!" says Esteban.

It is, too. He cuts a dashing sight in his black trousers, frilly white shirt and blazing-red neckerchief. But the competition isn't really about him – the men are the blank canvases against which the women will be judged. Given each man can partner up to three women, they must perform both consistently and flawlessly.

The women are clad in sumptuous dresses: a tight, white bodice and bursting open into a broad ruffled collar and cuffs up above, and blooming into a voluminous, layered skirt section down below, decorated with embroidery and appliqué. According to Pablo, *sanjuanero* dresses cost almost US$1000 new, or US$250 to hire. Yet below all this finery the women are bare-footed – a nod to the genre's peasant roots.

The song El Sanjuanero was created in 1936 and the accompanying dance choreography in 1960, so it has the weight of tradition behind it. The dance is balletic yet carefree, and even gently flirtatious; reminiscent of lovers skipping through the meadows of a royal retreat. Yet despite the untroubled nature of the genre, this is a serious performance – there is no room for errors on the night.

"They spend maybe two months learning the routine," says Esteban, "then they do this [the festival tournament] and make a mistake."

This is the gauntlet of the one-off performance – quite a thing, as I well recall.

"This part is very difficult," says Esteban.

The woman playfully relieves the man of his hat and places it on the floor. Three times he goes to retrieve it and three times she drags it teasingly out of reach with her toe.

"Because of her balance, she has to stand exactly like this," says Esteban, leaning forward slightly with a leading forearm.

"She can't be like this, or like this," he says, and demonstrates some very minor adjustments.

So technical expertise and practice are both crucial, but when something does go wrong it's important you react the right way, too.

"There was a hole on the stage and she put her foot in it," he says. "She was going to stop. I had to shout '*¡Sigue! ¡Sigue!*'" Carry on! Carry on!

That's great, but there is a simpler solution. One that means you have no demands and no stress, and which makes life so much easier. You could just not do a performance at all.

The weekend is nearly here and the festival is now in full swing.

The city swelling with new arrivals and things are going on all over the city.

In the morning, the departmental queens don bikinis and take part in a river-parade on individual wooden launches. One by one they float down the frisky young Magdalena, waving at the crowd, whilst locals drink beer and cheer them from the river banks, many using slanted tree boughs as vantage points.

Come the afternoon, it's the turn of local *chivas* (rural buses) to get dressed up for a parade, the sides and roofs festooned with bicycles, furniture and even a live donkey, like a reversal of Buckaroo. Sounds from the various *palcos* and amplifiers bleed into one, creating a beat-laden cacophony in which no individual tune can be discerned.

Man, I love Colombian festivals.

I knew those two events would be fun, but it's the event that I'm least bothered about that ends up being the one that captures my attention the most.

When we arrive at the venue that evening there's only standing room remaining, and even that is quickly running out. Tonight is the folkloric revue: each department will put on a music and dance show representative of their region, with their own queen as the star.

The tension is building: competing bands hammer out rhythms into the close night air, snake charmers squeak away and hands wave giant posters and cardboard cut outs of the queens. These are the *barras* – groups of noisy fans that form part of the entourage for each department. According to Pablo, the *barras* actually get scored, and this goes towards each contestant's final total.

The build-up is a hot mash of shrill whistles, squeaking oboes and bleating brass. People are clapping and yelling and other people are trying to talk to each other over the clapping and yelling. But the moment the first department takes the stage, the crowd falls hush.

The acts are up in alphabetical order of department – no doubt a perennial thorn in the foot of those from Vichada – but in my own mind I split the country into the physical regions.

When the coastal departments are up, the air resounds with hot tribal thuddings; the knock-knocking of the *llamador* and the *shicka-shick* of cylindrical metal shakers. It's accompanied by a medley of dances I've become very familiar with: the flirty shuffling of cumbia, the shoulder-shimmying of *puya* and the hard-bodied popping of *mapalé*. They're crowd pleasers, all of them. Well, I'm part of the crowd, and I'm pleased.

"We like the music from the coast, but they don't like ours," says Pablo over the din. "They think it's boring. Maybe they're right."

I'm brought right back to those early days in Cartagena, sweating it out and being told to "dooo ittt", and to Barranquilla, balancing a can on my head in front of a very forgiving crowd. Heck, it's easy to forget it, but I even lost my passport. How am I even still in the country?

Harps are the main order of the day for the Llanera departments. They go through a repertoire of string-based stuff, gentle at times but building up to thrilling bouts of *joropo*, sparks flying as the men's feet strike the floor, the girls being spun ruthlessly about with *berraquera*. Suddenly, I'm back on the infinite plains, along with my near-infinite list of things to learn just to perform a local dance.

The memory cues just keep on coming as we continue our tour of the country. We're treated to *la guaneña*, which confirms my suspicions that a dog isn't meant to be involved; to various ruana-clad numbers from those eastern mountains; to *vallenato*, which sounds just as good whether played at a festival, at a supermarket or in a river.

The coffee-zone departments do a dance which Pablo tells me is *recolectar café* (collecting coffee), and seems to involve quite a bit of the man trying to rest on a chair whilst the woman gets annoyed with him, not unlike me and Isabela in that Cali nightclub.

The capital, meanwhile, provides us with some prim and proper upper-class colonial numbers straight out of a period drama – all umbrellas, powdered wigs and sticks up the backside.

"*Pasillo*," the man next to me says.

I don't recognise it but I still feel the connection. Dear old Bogotá, where my journey began; where I sat in the taxi on the way from the airport with no idea what the hell I was listening to, let alone how my journey and mission would pan out.

And all that's without going into the places I've never been to – jungly Chocó, desertified La Guajira and the vast, vast Amazon, not to mention the many islands that lie off the country's shores.

There's such an astonishing diversity of culture that it's hard to believe it all belongs to the same country. Yet at the same time, there's still a sense of a combined national identity, a major part of which is a love of music and dance. They might be African, European and indigenous; Costeños, *cachacos* and Llaneros; yet they're all Colombian. They're simultaneously divided by their culture and united by it.

Between acts, the *barras* continue to cheer and hammer out their own support, the air pulsating with more rhythms than I could hope to identify.

God, this is great!

Dance is not the only thing Colombia has increased my appreciation of – the costumes are amazing in their own right. It must be crazy backstage, clothes getting thrown up into the air in some cramped space with little make-up boxes propped up between crossed legs and running lists stapled to the walls. My own show in Cali might not have gone well, but now I find myself relishing my memories of that nervous energy and the sense of being part of something bigger.

Yes it's scary, but you feel so alive... how often in our lives do we get the chance to experience something like this? Yes, there's that risk of failure and humiliation, but without that it would barely be worth doing.

Many of the performers make a Buck's Fizz-like use of layers, whipping off the top clothes to reveal another set underneath, thus negating the need for a costume change between genres. If I were doing a show, that's what I'd do.

For the first time I get to see cumbia done as intended, in which the woman, in a massive, heavy dress, and presumably with another costume underneath, decides, "I'm not hot enough – I'd better balance a stack of lit candles on my head". I never thought I'd find myself lamenting never having danced with candles.

Props are in heavy use in general. Neiva's own department of Huila has two people pretending to weave a massive hat as they perform a *guavina.* A couple representing the former British island colony of San Andreas do a routine consisting of both calypso and polka, during which they symbolically cut off a ball and chain and discard an umbrella. The Amazonian region of Caquetá does one where the woman is armed with a spear and the man, rather less threateningly, with a shrub. Another department, meanwhile, has the jolliest machete-based dance imaginable.

Props are great! I'm going to have props in mine! Well, I mean, you know, theoretically, if I were doing one, then that's something I would probably consider.

Everyone is itching to leave as it's getting late, but no-one wants to because they're all waiting for Valle. Meaning Valle de Cauca, the home of Cali. Ah, salsa. The first dance I tried, the first one I messed up in public – reason enough never to try such a thing again. I remember it all so well; the nerves, the build-up, the sucking so badly.

"It's a process."

It still bothers me.

The familiar *tokk-tokk-tok... tok-tok...* of the clave starts up accompanied by a sassy brass section. How did I ever not know that this was salsa? Then in bursts a manic hammering of cow bells, like the end of the round in a boxing match, or a mail train charging through a level crossing, or a cow with a bell round its neck getting very, very excited. A bit like I am now.

The two dancers on the stage kick the air, wheel through turns and lifts and even do that thing with the shoulders. My skin stiffens and the little hairs rise up like a dandelion clock – if there was even the faintest breeze in this city, they would be carried away.

It doesn't get any better than this.

SURPRISE!!!

I'm pretty sure my own birthday shouldn't be a surprise, but I've been so caught up in other things that it kind of is. Especially as it was actually a few days ago. I mentioned it in passing to Pablo at the time, but here in Colombia people happily celebrate a birthday all week, which goes some way towards explaining why there's a group of people stood at my bedroom door with a cake.

"*¡Cumpleaños Feliz!*" they sing in chorus. Happy Birthday!

But just because it's your birthday doesn't mean you get the day off, something I always resented as a school child. And a university student. And a company employee.

Today's key task is to pick up tickets for the finale from the hotel on the main square – one of the city's fancier joints, and the place where all the departmental queens are booked in. Their faces are plastered all over the shop fronts adjacent to the entrance in an attempt to fly-post them into the minds of the judges.

Inside, queens from previous years are floating about the lobby.

"Look," says Pablo, "– there's Miss Colombia."

Ahead of us stands a slender woman with tousled hair and skin like a golden beach. I have no idea if it really is Miss Colombia, but Pablo's knowledge on such matters seems solid enough and she certainly has the looks. I suppose I could always ask her opinion on world peace and see how rehearsed her response is.

After repeated nudging from Pablo I reluctantly go up and ask to have a photo taken with her. She's wearing a long macramé cardigan with wooden beads that cascade right down to her knees. It's a combination that makes her look dressed down yet effortlessly refined. I'm wearing my favourite t-shirt. It has a picture of a dinosaur on.

Pablo tells me that some people think her nose is flawed. I look at her again – it's an astonishing idea. Put it this way: the only justification you could have for Photoshopping her would be if you wanted to see if you could make her look average. But then, as with the hired dancers at Angélica's wedding, it's always going to be hard being declared the most beautiful woman in a country with so many contenders.

Before the *bambuco* queen can run a similar gauntlet of public perception, there's still the main parade to go. Experience has taught me that such events have their own specific anatomy, so by now I'm well prepared for how it will unfold.

Knowing that everyone is going to be trying to go to the same place at the same time it's really important that you put down an early marker for the day by getting up late. Throw your host's delicious and carefully prepared festival food (pork in an *adobo* of herbs and beer) down at ungratefully fast speed and run out to the street where no taxis or buses are stopping because they've all been chock full for hours.

Once at the site of the parade, walk up the street trying to find a viewing point. Not having acquired tickets in advance, you should blag your way into a *palco*. You are now in perfect position to experience the heckling of legitimate entrants into the already-full *palco* (and if you think being in an overcrowded temporary metal structure on stilts is dangerous, you want to try standing in the way of Colombians trying to party).

And that's just about where we're up to.

"*¡Fue-ra ¡fue-ra! ¡fue-ra!*" comes the chant from the crowd. Out! Out! Out!

Quite the reverse is happening: the man on the gate is continuing to let people in, on the flimsy pretext that they actually have tickets.

"*¿Por qué no ma-dru-gó? ¿Por qué no ma-dru-gó? ¿Por qué no ma-dru-gó?*" the chant continues. Why didn't you get up early?

Yeah, you slackers!

Most people are in too much of good mood to care. A guy stood outside the *palco* blows an air horn in time with the angry chants, just because he likes the rhythm, whilst a young bloke taunts his friend in the queue below, calling down to him "*¿Por qué no madrugó?*"

What anger does remain dissipates as soon as the parade starts and the queens start coming past on their own individual floats, separated by Carnival-esque groups of *marimondas* and stilt-walkers, and troupe after troupe of dancers.

All around me, people are wearing the local apparel of cream-coloured panama hats and lightweight ponchos. A lot of the men wear their ponchos folded and placed over one shoulder. In fact the crowd would probably look quite distinguished if there weren't factional foam-based wars going on at the same time.

The event ends with a horse parade, which in theory is an opportunity to see the skill of graceful horsemanship, but in practice is a chance to see people drink enthusiastically and make mobile phone calls whilst mounted on horseback, which is arguably just as impressive. But soon even that is done, and everyone drifts away over the discarded beer cans, plastic cups and cardboard party hats.

Another parade has come to an end.

It's not just the *bambuco* festival that's entertaining people this weekend: there's a bit of a football tournament going on too – the World Cup is taking place in South Africa. Most games are on at breakfast time due to the time difference with the host country, thus taking the edge off any party-in-the-street vibe, but *El Mundial* is still a big deal here, and the fact that the official anthem is a Shakira number adds to the sense of connection.

They love their football here in Colombia. Amongst the best known Colombians in living memory are Rene Higuita, a goalkeeper best-known back in England for his casual execution of a 'scorpion' flying back-heel kick mid-game, and midfielder Carlos Valderrama, of whom there is a twenty-foot high statue in Santa Marta, complete with curly wig.

But in Colombia football has also been inextricably tied in with the country's other problems, and when Colombian footballer Andrés Escobar scored an own goal in the 1994 World Cup, he was murdered upon his return.

In the absence of their own team (Colombia haven't qualified this time round), people are cheering on all the other South American countries in the cafes, bars and lounges of Colombia. Well, not quite all of the other countries. In fact when one team in particular is playing, everyone seems to rally against them.

"I hope that Argentina get knocked out!" says Pablo's mother as they square up to Germany.

Why's that then?

"Because they're vain."

It's a common perception. Another person I speak to, a taxi driver who couldn't care less about the football, still wants Argentina to lose because he thinks they're arrogant.

But the object of all these football games isn't to chide Argentina – or at least not solely to – it's to end up with some kind of footballing climax. You've got to have a decisive moment of some kind, haven't you? You can't just go on a big long journey then stop. There needs to be a finale; closure; completion. There needs to have been a point to it all.

It feels a lot like an international football match in the indoor arena that evening. Vuvuzelas are blowing, bands are playing and everyone is generally getting pretty worked up. This is the crowning glory of the festival: the event at which a *bambuco* queen will be elected. But this can only happen after the final event, and the one that's arguably the most relevant: the *sanjuanero* dance contest.

Esteban is here to perform, and sits right by me, along with his wife, in his white shirt and red neckerchief combo. He only has one dance partner this evening, but it's enough, isn't it? He sits there looking as calm as he does refined, unperturbed by the noise that roars out from the stalls all around us and rains down from the balconies above.

Esteban doesn't really get nervous anymore, he tells me – he's been at it since he was 13, and he's now in his late twenties. The same doesn't apply to me, however. The tension of the wait is almost unbearable – I'm feeling nervous by proxy.

The music, which I'd barely noticed before, is really growing on me, which is just as well given the exact same track – El Sanjuanero – gets played over thirty times in succession. It's light and airy yet also stately and proper, like one of those understated national anthems you hear at the Olympics.

One by one, each of the queens takes to the stage with their partners, absorbing the heat of the lights and the stare of the camera lenses. The dance commences, and together they play tug-of-war with the neckerchief, wending this way and that – an axle connecting the two dancers in their saltation.

The judges' scoring is silent, but the crowd's isn't, and the audience members let out almighty collective whoops and groans at key moments. She missed the hat with her toe! Cue people crossing themselves and others fainting.

It's that one-off performance thing again. It doesn't matter how many times you got it right in practice – when it comes to the stage you've got one chance. You stake your entire reputation on a few brief moments of neckerchief playfulness and hat footsie.

It seems like a stressful world to inhabit, but I can think of a worse one – one where we never push ourselves; never put ourselves under pressure; never put it on the line, mostly just out of fear that it might not go to plan.

Not that you would think this was a pressure situation from watching Esteban – when his turn comes round he makes the whole thing look effortless. Not only does he provide the flawless canvas, but he beams the whole time, his very demeanour relaxing his partner and urging her to enjoy the experience.

It takes hours to get through every departmental queen. If I was organising it I'd just get them all in a big wrestling ring – last queen standing. Maybe that's why I'm not organising it.

The heat and humidity have built in tandem with the tension over the course of the evening, so by the time the judges come together to deliberate over the finalists, the crowd is a sweaty-palmed mess. But eventually there's nothing left to discuss and it's just left for the PA to stand up and break the silence – and the hearts of all of the hopefuls. Well, all but one. Because we have a winner.

Step forward… Señorita Cundinamarca!

The process of choosing the queen can apparently be intensely political. Pablo says that several years ago a lot of people thought that Señorita Putumayo should have won, and when she didn't, the crowd began shouting "*¡Putumayo! ¡Putumayo!*" to which Señorita Putumayo promptly fainted. Not that these competitions encourage melodrama, you understand.

Such tournaments can harbour bigger controversies still: one former Colombian 'Coffee Queen' was disqualified for being married – which surely throws the reign of monarchs all over the world into doubt – and was more recently in trouble for her alleged part in a drugs ring. None of which is as damaging as missing a hat with your toe, but it's pretty serious all the same.

The former queen is ceremoniously de-crowned and the new monarch takes her place, receiving a tiara-like silver headpiece and the title of Reina del Bambuco (Bambuco Queen). I hear some grumblings about the exact choice of the finalists, but the general consensus is that the new queen is a worthy winner.

She must be glad she made the journey out to this oft-ignored little nook of Colombia, but even for the tear-mopping losers it was surely better to have been involved and lost than not to have been involved at all. Life might be easier without these tests – without the stress and the nerves; the pressure and the expectation – but it's certainly a whole lot more interesting with them.

As for me, I think I may have regained something I'd lost. More than that, I think I may even be ready to perhaps start thinking about possibly putting on a show.

CHAPTER EIGHTEEN

Showdown

A man pushes an ice cream cart around the back streets to an irritatingly repetitive tune. Out on the main drag, cars whump along the fuming highway's concrete sections. At a traffic intersection, a man balances a bicycle on his head, then puts it down and starts juggling machetes.

Hey there Cali – have you missed me?

I'd like to say my final test awaits me here, but I can't because it doesn't. In fact I'm going to have to organise the final test myself before inviting people to come along, like a condemned man building his own gallows and then billposting the event about town.

At least I'll have some help in the matter.

"Welcome to heaven's outpost!" says Marta, purring, this being another of Cali's various nicknames.

We sit on chairs in her lounge, the acid zing of *lulo* singing in my throat, and discuss what lies ahead. My dances fit neatly into two categories: urban and folk, and doing four of each seems like a reasonable number. It will give me a chance to show off the breadth of my repertoire, or at least demonstrate just how crushingly mediocre you can be when you spread yourself too thinly.

There's a problem with this programme, though: eight full dances, averaging four minutes each, would run to about half an hour of solid dancing. This is completely unworkable – every single minute of dance will require many hours of preparation and practice – so we decide to cut it down to a third of that. At ten minutes long, the planned routine is doable, but it's still a whopping five times the length of my original *clausura*. On top of that, I've got the added complexity of having to master eight different genres.

For the urban dances, Marta tells me I have the use of Laura, which makes her sound like a pool car. The folk dances, however, are more problematic. After all, where on earth am I going to find someone with a working knowledge of folk dances from all over the country?

"Neil," she says with a wry smile, "I think I know someone who would be perfect for this."

I've daydreamed a lot in my life – daydreamed about football; daydreamed about motor racing; daydreamed my way through entire jobs and even relationships. But having made the concrete decision to go ahead with the show, something odd has happened – I've started daydreaming about my project. Gone are the regular, unrealistic fantasies about becoming Formula One world champion, replaced by unrealistic fantasies about putting on a great performance.

Such daydreams frequently come to me when I'm sat in the dark on coach journeys, as there's little else to do. And on the journey back to Cali I found myself engrossed in exactly such a daydream. But it was not this that the journey was memorable for.

We were on the final stretch of flat, straight road, the bordering fields of sugar cane hidden by the night, when there was an almighty thud, a sound like spraying granite and then the continuous rasp of night air. From what I could make out, one of the windows opposite was now heavily frosted with a black hole in it.

The vehicle carried on regardless. Nobody moved, not even those next to the window. This was crazy: why weren't we stopping? Wait – maybe this was a known ploy used by bandits to bring coaches to a halt, and these travel-hardened and violence-weary Colombians knew better. We'd presumably stop once we were clear of any danger. But twenty minutes down the line nothing had changed save that the bus had started getting chilly. People were putting on extra layers as though that was job done. So I went through the cabin door and told the driver.

It was news to him – he pulled over and switched the lights on. A fist-sized rock lay baldly in the aisle. Directly next to the window were a mother and son, sat politely amidst jewels of safety glass. Apparently, they would rather have sat there the remaining two hours than bother anyone. They were actually naturalised Spanish rather than native Colombians, but none of the locals seemed to think it their business either.

It was actually the third time during my stay in Colombia that there's been some kind of problem on board a coach, and the third time it's fallen to me to say something.

Johana, a Caleña friend of mine who runs a café, tells me she would have spoken up, and that she also makes a fuss when people queue-jump. Manners in Cali are in decline according to Johana, and she describes to me a bygone era when dogs wore top hats, cars curtsied and *arepas* helped old ladies across the road.

I certainly relate to the queue-jumping annoyance. Queuing is the done thing in Colombia, as it is back home, but queue-jumping is rife here, and something which most Colombians only tolerate with quiet annoyance. It makes me wonder who these people are that queue jump. Do they acknowledge each other, like Apple Mac owners, and Mini drivers?

The restraint which greets acts of disrespect seems peculiar given the country's history of violence. Mind you, I've heard it said on more than one occasion that these things are related: people are scared to complain for fear of retribution.

Acts of vengeance are an unfortunate part of Colombian history. In 1948, during an era dominated by fierce Liberal-Conservative rivalry, Liberal Jose Eliécer Gaitán was widely tipped to win the presidential election. The likelihood of this, however, diminished significantly when he was shot dead. The presumed murderer was himself hunted down and killed by an angry mob. The fury spread and Bogotá and other cities across Colombia became engulfed in an orgy of violence, looting and arson, known as the Bogotazo. People were killed and the streets burned incandescent with rage.

It was still nothing compared to what was to come as the trouble moved to the countryside. Even before the murder of Gaitán, things had been hotting up, but now they got really bad. Brutal, politically-aggravated vengeance became the order of the day during this period – known as La Violencia (The Violence) –

with the death toll over the next ten to fifteen years reaching an estimated 200,000 to 300,000. Colombia was a country drowning in its own blood.

La Violencia finally came to an end around 1958 with an accord between the two political parties, but the shadow of this era still looms, not least in the form of the armed groups that emerged in the period that followed.

At a museum in Bogotá, with the bicentennial of Colombian Declaration of Independence approaching, I saw the following visitor comment:

"After 200 years we're still uncivilised. We haven't learnt to value our freedom and all that we've been given."

Backstage in the narrow, street-side academy I'm engulfed both by the hugs of familiar staff members and the memories of bygone performances. Swivelling fans disperse the scent of sweat, dance pumps kick at the fourth and eighth beats and muscles in mismatched Lycra expand and contract. Everybody is working hard and nobody is chatting about dance over a skinny latte.

This is it: the place I made a mess of my salsa *clausura*; the place where Marta qualified that performance of mine by saying it was "a process"; the place I'll be dancing again in several weeks' time.

What am I getting myself into? I really don't need to do this. I've done the important stuff – why don't I just skip the show?

Brain noise – don't you just love it?

Laura is here, too. She still has a warm smile, still only comes to about half my height and is still an excellent dancer. She's my very own blank canvas.

I've got four dances to prepare with her, and it would be nice if we could bind them all together in some kind of narrative. I've given it some thought already, and I've come up with the entirely fictional story of a foreigner who comes to Colombia not knowing how to dance, and meets a local or two who show him how.

But I see that as gloss – first we have to pick the dances. Salsa and merengue are obvious choices, given I can actually do them, and bachata has been growing on me too. It would be nice to add something typically Colombian to those three, but the obvious candidate – *vallenato* – is a bit short on razzmatazz. How about *champeta*? It would certainly give these Caleños a taste of something new.

There's a problem with this, though: Laura has never danced *champeta* in her life, making me the expert, but since I barely remember any of what I learned, that makes me the teacher of something I don't actually know how to do. Still, I'll deal with that when I come to it, by which I mean I'll completely ignore its existence and pretend this constitutes some kind of plan.

With the basics attended to, it's time to make a start on the first dance – bachata. So out come the fiddly-twiddly miniature guitar and drum kit, and on goes the track Por Un Segundo by Aventura, current darlings of the bachata scene.

I have done a little preparation for this, at least mentally. During one of my coach-based daydreams, I cultivated the idea of my partner and me doing extravagant flying 180-degree kick-turns across the width of the dance floor – a move I'd invented in my head – arriving back together to do that decisive *golpe*.

It's a fantasy that lasts as long as it takes for me to try and do it. Apparently, I can't just magically move my body in any way I choose just because I'm able to picture it. Furthermore, the chances of Laura being able to match my stride length are fairly slim.

We go for a toned-down version of it, one that has shorter steps and not quite as much supernatural leaping. To this Laura adds some heel-and-toe cha-cha-cha footwork that looks great but leaves me in danger of falling over and taking her with me. There's a long way to go, but every dance journey starts with a single step, even if it's a poorly-timed and badly-executed one.

In a way I don't have just one dance journey, but two – I'll be preparing for the folkloric dances in parallel. And when I meet my other teacher, Fernanda ('Nanda'), I can see why the mental juxtaposition tickled Marta – it's like we were separated at birth. Assuming I was born a short, black woman that's somewhat on the larger side. I tell Nanda about my dance journey round Colombia and she lets out a raucous laugh that clatters off the walls and rings about the whole studio. Something tells me we're going to get along.

Nanda asks me to show her what *mapalé* I know. It doesn't take long – I do my now-discredited Barbara Windsor, make a failed attempt at the cat-swinging move, and we're done. Fortunately Nanda knows more than that and we get to work straight away. The Barbara Windsor can stay, albeit with some minor remodelling, but pretty much everything else will be new, including some frantic *puya*-esque inward flicks of the heels. I'm learning this dance again from scratch.

Nothing is private on the shared dance-floor and the merest mention of *mapalé* has piqued everyone's interest. My lesson becomes the focus of attention, with students and dance instructors alike wanting a piece of the action. At one point four of us are stood in a row all trying the same *mapalé* move, like some kind of demented chorus line. I'm comfortably the worst.

A discussion starts up regarding what other *pasos* that could be integrated into my routine.

"The caiman," says one of the instructors.

"What's the caiman?"

He drops to the floor and demonstrates – and suddenly I'm right back in Cartagena. It's the one where the men ricochet along doing something resembling press ups. It's still the most African thing I've ever seen. We're doing that. I've decided. We can't not.

Have I changed? I think I might have changed.

For the second *mapalé* lesson, we switch to a different venue in a nearby *barrio*. This studio is even narrower and has a small kitchen annexed on to it, which would have been perfect back in the time when I used to make excuses not to dance.

"Poached eggs, anyone?"

Also we've been joined by a friend of Nanda's – a man with owl-like features in his thirties called Miguel. He just looks like a regular guy off the street, but his credentials are revealed as soon as he dances – he demonstrates a balance, suppleness and ease of movement that cannot be faked.

Miguel is here to help with the men's actions, and his first input is to have me starting the dance with a commando-style roll from the side. This is followed by animalistic sweepings of the floor with my hands whilst in a crouched position. After this comes a bunch of *pasos* that I can't do properly, and at the end is the caiman.

Putting the *caimán* at the end is my idea. Nanda and Miguel both think I should start the dance with it, but then they're not the ones who would have to do a shitload of push ups then spring to their feet and start dancing vigorously.

I try it out first on its own, labouring down to ground level.

The floor is one of those hard surfaces that looks and feels dusty even when it's just been cleaned. It feels strange to be down there, with your nose where people's feet go.

It takes a lot out of me to do the bounding-along bit, and the palms of my hands smart and swell a little. I'm no human ping-pong ball, but I can do it. I do it again, going through Nanda's legs this time, which is how it's meant to be performed. Miguel explains to me that *mapalé* is heavily sexualised – it's a statement of intent – although anyone who thinks doing press-ups underneath a standing woman is sexual needs to get out into the field a bit more. Or perhaps join the fetish scene.

On my third attempt, a jolt of pain shoots through my hands and I spring to my feet, clutching my searing fingers. I pace about in silent torment, fingertips throbbing and burning, and mouth open for a silent yell. It takes a full couple of minutes for the pain to subside. Given this will be the last act of the last dance, we could have a problem here. Me yelling "AAARRGGGHHHH!!!" at the audience is probably not how I want my show – indeed my whole adventure – to end.

It's a special day today.

Colombian flags hang proudly from many residential buildings, whilst down in Parque de las Banderas (the Park of flags), a big stage has been erected and thousands of people are bobbing about, enjoying the live music in their corporate-sponsored, cardboard *sombrero vueltiaos*. Such hats are a bit of a novelty in these parts, and few people have the real thing.

It's not a huge celebration because the event being commemorated is the first attempt at independence in July 1810, which was about as successful as my first *clausura*. Known as the Patria Boba (Foolish Fatherland), it was triggered by Napolean-shaped troubles back in the Spanish motherland. But the freedom from the Spanish was short-lived as they re-conquered Nueva Granada just a handful of years later. It would be another decade or so before the job was done properly, and independence truly achieved.

I bump into a few friends down at the event and stop for a bit of a dance – Johana will later tell me she saw me on local television

– but I don't stay long as I've got other stuff to be getting on with. Such as sorting out my accommodation.

After a grand tour of the spare rooms of Cali, I finally settle on one in a house in historic San Antonio. It's a modern, open-plan residence with courtyard out back and a lingering smell of vacuuming, and I'll be sharing it with some fellow renters who mostly hide themselves away.

My room has a tiled floor and is dominated by the world's firmest bed. There's also a desk – actually an old sewing machine table with cast-iron treadle – and a small balcony which might be nice were it not completely enveloped in a security cage. But it's a base, it's clean and it has plenty of space to practice in. And it's that last one which, come the weekend, is my prime focus.

Practice is both tedious and difficult, but then, as people say of such things, you don't have to like it, you just have to do it. The *mapalé* is particularly taxing, knocking the breath out of me with its sheer ferocity, and there are only so many times I can run through it. By day three, my muscles ache from the exertion, and the knockable bits of my limbs are all bruised from repeated commando floor-rolls on unforgiving surfaces.

I feel beaten. I feel tired. But more than anything I just feel old. Maybe my age finally caught up with me. Maybe these African dances are a young man's game. Why am I even doing this? What am I trying to prove? Am I actually physically capable of doing eight dances in a row? And come the *mapalé* – the final dance of the evening – will I even have anything left in the tank?

Self-doubt isn't the only problem – there are also the interruptions.

dddrrrriiiinnnngggg.

Can someone get that? I'm upstairs.

dddrrrriiiinnnngggg.

Come on folks, it can't be for me – no-one knows I live here.

I mentally brace for further rings, but there are none. Several minutes later I hear a loud metallic rattle come from my balcony. I open the door to be greeted by the security cage vibrating violently, before coming to a rest. I press my head to the metal bars and look down. Dusting himself off below is some guy in ragtag clothing. He must have been on the cage. But why? And how the hell did he get there? I conclude he came down from above. And no, I don't mean heaven.

"Why were you on the roof!?" I shout.

"I wasn't on the roof!"

This is one of those technically-correct-but-deliberately-missing-the-point kind of answers, isn't it? He holds up an empty plastic bottle, and tells me, practically hissing, that he needed water but I wouldn't answer the bell. I shout down to him a couple more times, frustrated with how much my Spanish degrades when I'm angry. He waves me away and walks out of sight, shaking his head.

What the….? You were attached to the side of my house! How is that possibly my fault?!

I charge downstairs and out the door, re-locking it behind me in case this is a ruse. But he's well gone – he must have run off the moment he was out of sight.

It's only once I've calmed down that I figure it out. He knocked on the door to see if anyone was home, and the empty bottle was his alibi in case someone was. Like the guy at Carnival, he stood his ground when caught, because running away is admittance of guilt – not a good idea in a country with a history of violent retribution.

Johana tells me that the wrong thing to do was try and reason or engage. I should just have yelled "*¡VÁYASE!*" (GO AWAY!), making it damn clear what the score was.

Others take an even harder line. Some time in the 1970s, social cleansing became a grisly feature of some cities in Colombia, with the extermination of undesirables including prostitutes, beggars and petty criminals – so-called *desechables* (disposables). Their bodies would often just get dumped in the river.

It can't be much fun for these people, living on the fringes of society, but that doesn't mean you can afford to be naïve to the threat that some of them pose. Johana tells me how she was walking down the street one day when she saw a dishevelled man walking in the opposite direction. Rather than giving him a wide berth, she respectfully treated him as another member of society and maintained her line.

As they passed each other he lunged at her and punched her in the stomach – leaving her doubled over – and carried on walking. It was only later that she noticed her jacket had jagged puncture marks in it – he'd actually attacked her with a broken bottle and only the thickness of her clothing had protected her.

With the weekend gone, it's time to get back to the classroom; to the light sprinkling of sweat on skin; to glugging at water every twenty minutes; to feeling fatigued but pushing on – always pushing on.

Something's changed since I last took classes here. I'm not looking for excuses any more, nor for breaks when I don't need one. When we need to drill something, I just get up and do it, again and again. I don't need to be coaxed any more – I'm doing this because I want to. It's only when my concentration has truly gone, and mistakes start creeping in, that I let myself take a breather.

Over the next couple of lessons, the *mapalé* routine starts coming together. Not only that but my fitness is also coming up to scratch, perhaps due in part to the motivation of practising with Nanda – she's a lot bigger than me, so if she can do it then I've got no excuses.

I really like Nanda – she seems like she's constantly on the verge of erupting into a big, hearty laugh, yet she's serious and professional at the same time. We flap about opposite each other, like a pair of exotic birds. Some things are fitting into place whilst others, like the caiman, aren't getting done at all. I suggest we swap roles: she should do the push-ups through my open legs. She lets out a big throaty laugh and play-acts her boobs banging against the ground.

A major bane of mine are those pesky 'adorations', where you're meant to bound forwards and backwards whilst throwing your hands up to the heavens. I'm used to the upper body part, because that's how I dry my hands prior to inserting contact lenses, but, as in Cartagena, I physically don't feel like my body returns to earth quickly enough. For some reason gravity doesn't apply the same restrictions to Miguel, whose movements I'm trying to emulate.

The *mapalé* is nowhere near ready. But time has only one *paso* – forward – so come the next lesson we need to get another plate spinning. For this class Nanda is running late and, with time a valuable commodity, we're forced to start working on the *guaneña* without her.

As the studio resounds with panpipes, Miguel sets about trying to teach me more *pasos*, but I stop him. My brain already resembles a precariously-filled cupboard of the throw-it-all-in-then-slam-the-door variety. Besides, the idea is meant to be demonstrating what I've learnt all round the country, not what new stuff I've been able to cram in at the last minute. Contrary to the approach I've taken to every exam I've ever had in my life.

Working with what I already have, we construct a theoretical routine, suggesting different *pasos* to each other by acting them out and then scribbling them down in order. But we reach a point where we really can't progress without actually dancing it, and Nanda still hasn't arrived. So what now?

No matter how broad-minded and liberal I consider myself, I can still feel strong mental resistance to the idea of dancing with another man. It doesn't make much sense. Dancing with a woman isn't by itself a sexually-motivated act – no man would let you dance with his wife if it was – so why should there be a problem? Miguel doesn't care: he's a professional. It's all on my side.

I let out another of those big sighs and take him by the hand, my comfort zone rolling its eyes in the background.

Crikey, aren't men's hands big? I know I should have worked this out before now – I've shaken plenty in my time, and I even own a pair myself – but I'm just used to partner's hands being those delicate little things.

With Miguel in a fetching shawl, and me ensconced in my role as protective husband, I feel like we're in the Colombian equivalent of I Now Pronounce You Chuck & Larry. But for Miguel this is serious business and all his focus is on the mechanics. He implores me to be more hunched and *tímido* (shy), explaining that whereas coastal dances, are very much "*¡Mírame!*" (Look at me!), the Andean ones have a quieter aspect and are more humble.

When Nanda finally does arrive – with a big smile and a "Sorry!" – her talent and experience means she picks up our choreography very quickly. The only problem is the final manoeuvre. The idea is that she stands in front of me with her back to me. We both do teapot turns such that we end up looking each other in the eye each time. But Nanda keeps turning the wrong way at the start, with the result that she appears to be looking for me, whilst I'm desperately trying to hide. It's comical, but it's also frustrating.

Back on the urban front, our attentions have switched to salsa.

This is a dance which comes with added pressure given its associations with Cali. On the positive side, this is definite Laura territory, and she comes to the first session with the core of a routine scribbled down on a wire-bound notepad.

The music we've decided on is La Rebelión (The Rebellion) by Joe Arroyo – a much-loved classic whose lyrics reference slavery in Cartagena. I've done a quick bit of editing of the track to shorten what is quite a stop-start intro, but this has meant removing some of the key lyrical content in the process. I just hope the audience won't think me some kind of historical revisionist.

Amidst the dramatic piano punctuation and wailing trumpet refrains we work through the moves, the fans blowing like the breeze atop Cartagena's walls. Laura's routine is a *sancocho* of cool ideas featuring high-speed footwork, a smattering of turns and even a fancy lift. It's perfect for a couple of accomplished salsa dancers, like her and her dance-teacher boyfriend, who've had their own fair share of success in international dance tournaments.

With me involved, however, it's less of a good match: the footwork in particular features *pasos* of such speed and complexity that each one is a challenge in its own right. The *patinetas*, for instance, break down into a foot slide, then an about-turn and finally a cha-cha-cha of footfalls. No matter how slowly I do them, I can't seem to get them right.

Yet whilst some of the *pasos* are technically problematic, the real difficulty, as Laura points out will be "*la memoria*". Memory was one of the main failings with my first *clausura*, all those months ago, and that time we were only doing one routine. This time I've got eight.

"It's a lot," says her boyfriend, himself a dance teacher.

If a pair of salsa professionals think I'm pushing it, then I'm definitely in trouble.

At this point it still feels like a theoretical concern, but that very evening, when I go to practise, the problem leaps in the air in front of me and demands to be caught.

I'm there in my bedroom, my notepad flattened open on the sewing machine table. I perform a step – or at least try to. Then I stop and look at the notepad. I try another step. Then I'm back to the notepad. Again and again this happens – I simply can't get anywhere without checking my notes to see what's coming next, something that I'm guessing is probably frowned upon in dance shows.

Not only that, but the stop-start nature means that the sequence doesn't seem to be going into memory at all. It means I can't focus on the moves themselves, and it's profoundly affecting my ability to practice. If only there was some way of memorising the running order first.

I once heard a memory expert talking about how you can remember long sequences of playing cards by assigning a meaning to each card, then creating some kind of story that fits the order in which they appear. If it can be done with playing cards, then why not dance moves? It's worth a shot. I sit down, my stocking feet working the treadle, and set about trying to find a meaning for the moves. What is each one most reminiscent of?

The resulting story is a little odd. It starts with me changing light bulbs before heading across town on a quest to fix some faulty shoes, before high-fiving a cobbler who broke his leg whilst sweeping the floor. It would make a shit film, but then the point isn't to create a compelling narrative arc – it's to remember a sequence of moves. Besides, I've seen a lot of independent cinema and there's definitely worse stuff out there.

Things are still a touch fitful at first as I have to keep pausing to recall the story, but soon even that disappears: the *pasos* all just come to me in sequence. My god – the damn thing has worked!

With the barrier of memory out the way, I'm now able to see a more fundamental problem – my delivery is awful, specifically the footwork. I know what I'm meant to be doing – the slides, the little kicks and the shifts in weight that make them possible – but my body just doesn't respond correctly.

Plus the music seems impossibly fast for what I'm trying to fit in – I'm forced to practice out of time as I simply can't keep up. On the occasions I do push myself to go at the right speed, the whole thing collapses in a flustered mess.

This isn't going to work. Doing a routine that's too hard, too fast and too likely to fail isn't brave, it's stupid. And clearly a big part of this is how many routines I'm doing. Why am I even considering the *champeta* if I don't have enough moves? If I don't want to be subjected to the humiliation of qualified praise at the end of my performance – and I really don't – I need to effect some changes, and I need to do it now.

I head to my next urban lesson bearing a non-negotiable list of demands. We need to dance to slower music. We need to simplify the movements. We need to do six dances instead of eight. There. It needed to be said, and I've said it.

Laura just laughs. We don't need to change anything – I just need to keep practising. Oh and we've got plenty of time to do the *champeta*, too.

Some part of me now actively wants me to fail, just to prove myself right. Yet despite this internal sabotage instinct, as little as an hour later I'm left having to concede that I was wrong.

Yes there are plenty of hiccups, but by the end of the session I can actually get through the whole salsa routine from start to finish. And, what's more, it no longer feels like it's too fast: in fact I seem to have mountains of time on my hands when I'm doing the *pasos*. It's hard to believe it's the same dance.

That mixture of practice and rest has worked its magic once again.

Little yellow cars hurtle round the fountain, bottles clank to the ground and people dance around parked-up motorbikes. We're back here again, and I'm talking to some old friends over a soundtrack of trumpets, claves and discordant piano. It's a good night out.

Not everybody is happy with all the conversing I'm doing, however.

"Neil, if you want to chat, go to a café. Here we dance!"

Ha – I'd forgotten about that! No problem – dance avoidance isn't an issue for me anymore.

Not that this means I'm suddenly great at salsa. After all, dancing in nightclubs is very different to doing a pre-prepared routine. I've yet to really get into that instinctive state like I do with merengue, and watching others dance confirms that I'm still lacking – their turns often aren't all that sophisticated but their style is seamless and freeform, devoid of the mechanical repetition and hesitancy that sometimes dogs my own.

I'm not the only person who notices this.

"You dance very symmetrically."

Why, thank you.

But whilst it's a long way up, it's also a long way down –

There are always enough beginners in the dance school doing renditions of the Sailor's Hornpipe to make me feel heartened by the distance I've covered. In the nightclubs it's a similar story: one Colombian woman asks me to help explain to her foreign dance partner that whilst it's great that he can dance so many different *pasos*, it would be even better if he could get them to coincide with the beat.

So I'm doing okay in the salsa stakes, albeit with some room for improvement. But then for me it's not just all about the salsa, anyway, and after all my experiences I crave variety. Fortunately, there are places in Cali where you can get that.

Lasers slice the aniseed nightclub darkness, the air reverberates with brassy horns, metal scrapers and the *THUMP de-THUMP derrr* of drums and abandoned plastic cups roll round on their sides like drunkards. We're at the *crossover* night once again.Around me are the people I came with the first time round; the people I relied on just to know what genres I was listening to.

How things have changed. Now my friends tune in like radios as I share my dance experiences from the coast and the plains, the valleys and the mountains – places they are finally able to go and visit for themselves.

Here are the seats I used to cling to, waiting to see if each song was salsa, then waiting some more because all the girls were now taken. This time round I lead girls off into the carnage all night, knowing that whatever comes on, I can not only identify it – I can dance to it. In fact there's rarely a need to leave the dance floor – I just look around for other friends and we swap partners.

Is this really the same guy?

It's especially the case in the merengue. I whip my partners about and ease them through turns, but also just have outright fun with them – clapping hands together and generally goofing about. *A ratos con elegancia, a otros – loco.* Even the dance mumbling is no longer an issue. I've got enough of a feel for it that I can cope if necessary, and I can lead with enough authority that I rarely have to.

There's not just dancing going on – there's flirting. I seem to be catching the eye of women that had paid little attention to me before. I'm actually dancing in a way that women find attractive – who'd have thought it?

And dancing with a woman can alter my perception of them,

too. Can she have fun and get lost in the moment, or is she forever preoccupied with maintaining her form? Will she humour me if I mess up, or will she just resent me for the experience?

A woman that was barely on my radar before can suddenly have me reassessing her as pretty darned attractive, whilst one I previously admired can just become that aloof one with the awkward arms. It's true that dancing doesn't have to mean anything, but it's also true that chemistry can spark up and break down right there, to the music.

Then something comes on that's the signal for the dance floor to clear – the accordion. Ha! They really don't dance *vallenato* in these parts. But I do. If only there was someone I could share this with.

Fortunately there is – someone I recognise from what seems like such a long time ago.

"You know more dances than me!"

Isabela speaks in such gentle tones that I don't so much hear her words as absorb them. I bring her hands together and lift them oh-so-gently over my head, like I'm presenting myself with a reef. With my hands pressed on her back and hers resting on my neck, we start rotating to the slow strains of accordion, our hips moving in unison.

Dammit, Frank, would you look at me?

A dance from the Dominican Republic is the next to get our attention, under the whisk-like fans of the dance school. Out in the nightclub, the merengue is the icing on the cake, if that makes any sense whatsoever, but back here in the workshop it's the toughest genre so far to choreograph. The reason is simple: it's just far too much fun. I put the same track on over and again, dancing through it with Laura under the pretence that I'm trying things out – even stopping to affect a "hmmm" expression – when the truth is I just want to dance it and dance it some more.

The only problem I have is forgetting to move my hips enough – one of the other dance teachers gets them going again with a nudge when she passes, like a sticking metronome.

The track we've chosen is Mi Niña Bonita (My Pretty Girl) by Venezuelan duo Chino & Nacho – a sickly-sweet but very danceable love song. The genre is actually Latin pop with rhythmic merengue piano rather than full-on example of the genre, but the beat lends itself perfectly to dancing this way and it's a real feel-good number, so why not?

I don't actually understand why merengue dancing isn't a global phenomenon on the scale of salsa. It has many of the same turns but they're done at a much more leisurely pace and the footwork is a cinch by comparison. And once you've got a taste for merengue, you're going to want to try more complex things (cheesecake). It's a gateway drug, and if I ran a dance cartel it would be the main product.

If only the folk dance routine was going so well. For one reason and another, we've fallen a couple of lessons behind schedule and things are looking decidedly tight. With this in mind, the time has come for us to mount up and hit those cattle-laden expanses to the country's East.

Of the three of us, Miguel and I are the experts on this particular genre, so with the harp strumming away in the background we start pitching our differing ideas to each other across the narrow dance floor, like a couple of blokes in a backstreet folkloric face-off.

At one point it's like duelling *zapateos*, with my trump card being the complex Fred Astaire-type one which requires two strikes of the same foot in succession. Miguel christens it *paso* Neil, it being a *joropo paso* that he's never seen before, though *paso* Carlos might be fairer.

However, once I'm paired up with Nanda it's clear that my *joropo* is as rusty as the gate on a long-abandoned ranch. The sounds are so important in *joropo*. My *dan-DAN-tsss paso básico* is just about passable, sounding like a buckled bicycle wheel that keeps catching on the brake shoe. My *desplazamientos*, however, are not. Instead creating a crisp set of slapping and sliding sounds, it's just a mushy mess, like I'm tramping about on the flooded plains. I also have the familiar problem of the footwork collapsing the moment I try and add in the upper body.

It's not the only problem: I don't quite have the feeling quite right, as noted by a friend of Miguel notes who has dropped into the dance school for something or other.

"Always with firm arms."

She explains that it should be like I'm steering cattle by the horns, and that I need to show who's boss (although in these verbal dance exchanges with random passers-by it's rarely ever me).

It can get tiring being the one who is expected to lead all the time. Miguel says there's a dance in La Guajira – the desertified and heavily indigenous region in the far north of the country – where the woman leads. I'd certainly like to see that. In fact I think I'd like to move there.

As the lesson draws to a close, it's clear I'll have something ready for to show on the day, I just don't know quite what. As it stands I'd be just as well hiring a cow and riding that around the dance floor.

"It's a process."

When the weekend arrives, I collapse into it. It's not the physical fatigue – all the practice means I'm feeling fitter than ever – it's my mind. Dance is dominating my life and the pressure is mounting. I don't even feel like I can even go out to escape it, since that would mean even more dancing. Besides, I have to look after myself, so I can ill-afford a late night. Even my meals are timed so I'm neither dancing on empty nor on full.

The focus is necessary given how little time remains – there's only a week to go. In fact I struggle to get my head round it: I'm nowhere near ready, yet in seven days' time I'll have done it. How can that be possible? I can't even fit all the things left to do into my brain at the same time.

All of the dances that I've worked on have problems of one kind of another but the *champeta*, which I haven't even begun yet, is way beyond that. I just laugh when I think about it, in the same way that you'd laugh if you'd forgotten to put your car handbrake on and were watching it disappear over a cliff. And all that's without thinking about the costumes, the narrative or the speech. Damn it – the speech. Every time I think I've thought of all the things I've had to do, something else crops up.

Oh and there's the invitations, of course. I've made a start on this, contacting all my friends via social media, but there's a strange air of non-commitment. The problem – the thing that everybody knows but nobody is saying – is that there's a hugely popular festival celebrating music from the Pacific coast on at the same time. And what I know is that it's too late to change the date. The date of my own event that is – I'm not that arrogant.

Many Colombians would rather say nothing than be

confrontational or hurt someone's feelings. So I know that if they go all quiet, it's probably because there's something they don't want to tell me.

And for the most part, my friends have gone really rather quiet. Some have indicated that they'd like to come to see my show in theory. But I'm not dancing in theory: I'm dancing in Cali, and I'm doing it in one week. Given all the effort I'm putting in, it would be nice if there were people actually there to see me perform. Mind you, I'm not sure which is worse – failing in front of all of my friends, or failing in front of none of them.

Action, I have decided, is the best remedy. As a wise person once said, "Dooo ittt!" And whilst going to the airport and boarding a plane falls firmly in that category, instead I choose to square up to the biggest single problem I currently have: the *champeta*.

But where to begin? One idea floating round in my head is based on Marina's notion that you can dance anything to *champeta*. So how about this? Laura and I are both in little boats – it's a coastal genre, after all – and we paddle towards each other. Then I catch a fish and give it to her. She makes a sandwich out of it, hands it back to me and I eat it.

This would be fine if it wasn't completely ridiculous – I'm just making up a bunch of stuff now and calling it *champeta*. If we're going that we may as well just do the Can-can and appeal to the god of ignorance. Which sounds great now I think of it.

I sit at my desk, working the treadle as I think. There's just so little time. How do I get myself into these situations? I need to try a different tack, so I dig out all the notes I scribbled down at the time, augmenting them with the various bits and pieces still floating around in my head. And I do the fingers-crossed *paso*.

The next day, I talk Laura through my notes and demonstrate a *paso* or two – let's start by seeing what we've got. And the answer is... nowhere near enough for a routine. So Laura employs the power of the internet, opening up her laptop on some chairs at the side of the dance floor. We spend a good while just watching videos of people dancing saucily, occasionally jabbing at the screen when each of us sees something we like. Then we make an attempt at copying them, which, given the subject matter, probably makes us look like a pair of novice soft-porn actors.

None of the moves are completely straightforward, but there's only one that looks like a real problem. It involves the women standing on the man's thighs, with her back to him. He supports her whilst rolling his shoulders and smiling like life's a breeze.

But how did she even get up there? It's not apparent from the video. We commence our own research, using the scientific methodology known as 'trying lots of different stuff'. First Laura tries to climb on to me from the side. It's a disaster. Next she tries to walk backwards on to me. It's a disaster. Finally she tries leaping backwards onto me from in front. It's a disaster, but with a faint glimmer of 'the way forward' about it.

We press ahead with this most likely approach and experience an array of failures: she slips off me; my knees capitulate to gravity; I don't hold her firmly enough and she falls off; I fall over, taking her with me; we fall together in synchronicity. If nothing else, at least we've got a broad repertoire.

I protest to Laura that this is a doomed manoeuvre, but she's having none of it.

"Remember with the salsa?"

I'm not sure I believe it, but I can't flaw her logic.

Perhaps the biggest issue I have with it is the thought of Laura getting hurt due to my own inadequacies. After all, if I fall over, her own chances of staying up there are pretty slim. But this is calmed by the sight of other dancers' failures in the laboratory that is the dance school. People land in the floor in a crumpled heap with reasonable regularity – they just dust themselves down and carry on. So we keep going, making refinements to my posture. We practise it and we keep practising it.

By the end of the lesson, we're experiencing more successes than failures. It's still far from watertight, which is a shame given that getting it wrong means falling into an imaginary sea, but we've got something to work on at least.

Things on the folkloric front are also nearing their conclusion, but the show is now looming and we still haven't even started the cumbia. The good news with this is that Nanda is an accomplished cumbia dancer, and my own skills aren't so bad either. So it's time for our homage to the *sombrero vueltiao*, which we're going to do to El Rey De La Cumbia by Son Cartagena – the same track I learnt to in Barranquilla.

To an *arroyo* of shakers and pinging drum skins, we're straight into it, improvising a routine to the music from nothing. It's ridiculous: within the space of about five minutes – the time it takes to show off some moves and briefly discuss them – we have a working routine.

There is something wrong, however. Yes, I'm shuffling around and waving my hat, and yes she's responding by ruffling her skirt, but somehow it doesn't quite feel right. Wait, I think I know what it is. I switch to the off-beat, like the people clapping at Carnival. It instantly feels better. We're there.

Completing the cumbia choreography means that I've got all eight routines in place. All I need now is a few weeks to iron out all the problems.

I've got two days.

Up in the park children are flying kites – the city finally finds its breath at this time of year – while down on the streets dogs slump behind window bars, occasionally erupting into life if a pedestrian gets too close. Cali is restless.

Coming out my house, I see a woman in front of me, hobbling and glancing back. Something's wrong. She's only wearing one shoe, and the other is lying in the road some distance back. She looks in some distress. I run to help her, and others soon join me.

A local woman comforts her – "*¡Pobrecita!*" (Poor thing!) – whilst I go and retrieve her footwear. It turns out she's just been in a confrontation with a mugger who, from what I can gather, was trying to steal her shoes. We're less than fifty metres from where a *vigilante* usually sits, but apparently even that is too far.

It's not the only reminder I've had in recent days of the realities of life. I was due to have one of my dance lessons in university facilities – so we wouldn't have to share a sound system – but we had to switch the lesson back because a lecturer had been murdered. What's happening? This place is turning crazy.

"I think Neil has finally realised the truth about our country," says Andrés, one of Johana's friends.

With a dubbed version of Black Hawk Down playing out on an old television, Andrés tells me about his time working in an ambulance crew, and how he'd have to deal with serious injuries on a daily basis: stab wounds, machete injuries and so on. He tells me how a British doctor came over and was appalled by what he encountered. He'd never seen that kind of thing before.

I think I'm generally pretty streetwise, but I'd have to tighten my game if I lived here. Everyone in Colombia has a story of a time they were robbed. Marina, for instance, told me about a time a friend lent her a necklace and it was snatched forcibly from her at a coach station, leaving her in tears.

It would be all too easy to become a victim of a *secuestro express* (express kidnapping) or *paseo millonario* (millionaire tour) by getting into the wrong taxi. Plus you have to watch out for people riding pillion on motorbikes as that can be a sign of trouble – the passenger does the dirty work and the driver whisks them both away.

That night, I'm in the safe haven of my bedroom when I hear what sounds for all the world like someone on the roof directly above. There it is again. There's definitely something up there. I throw on some clothes and patter down the stairs in my bare feet and out into the darkness of the rear courtyard.

Up on high, silhouetted against the navy night, I spy a dark shape sticking out. Is that part of the roof? It disappears. I feel my throat tighten. I wait. I wait some more. Nothing happens. It must have been a cat. The tightness in my throat eases and my shoulders drop. This city can't half make you paranoid. Is this how it feels to be Colombian? Always wondering if what you have is about to be taken away?

I'm still ruminating on this when a thud comes from the other side of the high courtyard wall followed by the crunching of feet on gravel, a sound that diminishes as their owner walks away.

With the show closing in, it's time for a dress rehearsal. For the urban dances, this is easy – I'm playing a backpacker, so I just put on my increasingly tatty clothes and I'm good. The rehearsal for the folkloric dances, however, requires a little more effort. In fact it resembles a fight at a jumble sale; Nanda and I throwing clothes skyward between dances in a bid to unite the correct parts of each wardrobe.

The *mapalé* costume isn't quite what I expected, consisting of, amongst other elements, a pair of bloomers. I know it's a sensual dance, but I don't see why that means I have to don Victorian-era women's underwear. Still, at least they kind of blend in, what with them being bright orange. I try them on. I look like a pantomime tree sprite. Thankfully, there is other legwear available. In fact I can wear any leg coverings I like as long as they are brightly-coloured bloomers.

I do have a bigger issue with the costume, though, and that's with the top. Every time I've seen *mapalé* danced it's been bare-chested. Which is fine if, like your average *mapalé* dancer, your muscles are as taut as drum skins, but less so if you're me. If I ever wore a muscle shirt, you'd be right to assume I was being ironic. My skin tone, meanwhile, is best described as moon-kissed. I know it's cowardly and betrays my self-consciousness, but maybe I should just keep the shirt on.

Even having chosen the clothes, there's still the issue of how to change between them. The Buck's Fizz option is a non-starter due to the number of different genres – we can't wear four lots of clothing in one go – so we'll just have to change very quickly between dances. But even that isn't so straightforward as I evidenced when I find myself doing the cumbia in a pair of *cotizas*, and the *mapalé* in a hat. I'm like a learner driver – I keep forgetting to check the mirror.

Props also provide scope for potential disaster, too, given that we've decided to do the cumbia with lit candles. Okay, so it's not exactly Evil Knievel trying to jump Snake River Canyon, but adding fire to a dance definitely ups the stakes, especially given what Juliana told me back in Barranquilla. As if just to increase the chances of conflagration, the show will be the first time I try it with said candles, as they haven't arrived in time for the rehearsal.

However, the costumes and props are all side issues: it's the dances that are the main deal. I've been practising the bachata and salsa routines for long enough that all the initial problems have been laid to rest, but now new problems have started cropping up in their place.

In the bachata, for instance, we've recently starting finishing at different times, for a laugh. And in the salsa I've switched from catching Laura on my hip – a *figura* which I have been doing perfectly well pretty much forever – to trying to catch her in both arms, like a baby. She doesn't try and suckle me, but it's still disconcerting.

The merengue, meanwhile, is so loose in terms of timing that it's touch and go as to whether we'll finish on the right day, let alone the right beat. At least we're likely to get through to the end intact, the same of which can't be said about the *champeta*, which still features the potential for me to incapacitate my partner in front of a live audience.

Time has run out entirely for the *joropo*. Despite adopting Laura's two-pronged approach of faith and hard work I've run out of time to resolve the mushiness and have had to simplify some of the footwork. And for her own part, Nanda is still turning the wrong way at the end of the *guaneña* far too frequently for comfort. The walls echo with raucous laughter every time and, sure, it is funny, but as the big day approaches I'm feeling more and more twitchy.

The cumbia seems solid enough, assuming we can avoid third-degree burns, but perhaps the biggest question mark of all hangs over the *mapalé* – the cymbal-crash ending to the whole show. I've avoided practising the push-up move the whole time for fear of doing myself some damage. I just have to hope that, come the night, the caiman doesn't bite.

We do one last lung-busting run through of the *mapalé* in costume, before coming to a halt. I stand there panting, beat, whilst Nanda collapses in a chair.

"*Poom!*" she says. "*El mapa-poom!*"

"*¡Muestra tu paso!*" says Nanda to a young relative. Show your dance step!

He must only be about five. His feet dart about in a cute, uncontrolled flurry, not unlike my Adam and the Ants routine all those years ago, although something tells me that he won't need to wait until his mid-thirties to learn how to dance properly.

It's the day before the performance, and the city feels swollen with people arrived for the festival. The ethnic mix has shifted noticeably too, with many having come from Buenaventura and all down the coast for this celebration of their music.

I've still not heard back from most of my friends, and I can hardly blame them. If I were them, I'd be going. How could you miss the chance to experience first-hand the marimbas and chanting, and the *currulao* – the one that was suggested to me down in Pasto?

Not everyone is diplomatically avoiding me, though – Nanda has invited me round to her place for lunch, which has a nice touch of 'the condemned man's last meal' about it. We sit at the dining table in her big, open living space eating bright-orange rice with seafood. Nanda's mum has made a huge batch of it to sell down at the festival. Everyone's going to be there.

The door and windows are open, with security bars preventing the entry of anything more than the warm August breeze. Meanwhile, news reports play out in the background of a car bomb in Bogotá, with Santos only having been officially in power for five days.

Despite all the unrest, I just have to keep focussed on my own performance. Tomorrow it's my *sanjuanero* moment, and I get one shot. It all comes down to my performance on the night. That's what people will judge me on, and that will be the difference between receiving unqualified praise, and being told that "it's a process".

I lie in bed under a loose cotton sheet that night, waiting for sleep. I feel edgy, but I don't feel scared. I know I've done everything I can. For the first time since I started preparing, or perhaps for the first time since I came to Colombia, or maybe even the first time in my entire thirty-six years on the planet, I genuinely feel ready to dance.

CHAPTER NINETEEN

Dancing Feat

"*¡Que calor!*" an old woman says to me as I walk to the dance school, as though it isn't hot here every single day. What heat!

My tickets home are booked and my budget has expired. The final deadline is immoveable, and it's today. But doing a show isn't a click of the fingers – it's not the tension and release of injecting heroin in a pub car-park – the build-up is slow. Excruciatingly so.

I've asked for one last quick practice with both Laura and Nanda. When there's a show on, we have to perform across the width of the dance school instead of the length, giving much less space. I want to get familiar with the layout, so when I go out there I feel like I know the space, and also to be sure that the routine will actually fit.

Every single one of the dances has at least one tricky part, and together they form a series of hurdles to be cleared through the night. In the *joropo*, my unfamiliarity with the new space leads to me ending a series of turns with my back to where the audience will be, instead of facing them. Mind you, they're not paying, so they should be grateful for whatever I give them, even if it's just a view of my backside.

In the *champeta*, what should be a reassuring last run-through reveals a new problem: Laura's leap backwards onto my thighs is now failing every single time. We're falling over with the kind of consistency that only dedicated practice could achieve.

"You have to do it more *suave* [gently]," she says, after yet another fall.

The problem is that if I don't bend my knees enough, then she can't stand on my thighs, but if I bend them too much, or I'm leaning fractionally too far forward or back, then we're going over. And my grip on her has to be very firm, as she can't stay up there without it.

We line up again. There's no rush, she tells me, I need to just take my time and get it right. I slow down and ignore the music. She leaps backwards. Her feet land on my taut thighs. They hunt for certainty. My hands grapple then pull hard. I make adjustments of balance, and...

Success!

We do it again and it works again. Two out of two. It's reassuring, but still definitely a toe-on-hat moment.

With the final practice over, we're now into the long, awkward period before the performance itself. There's not really enough time to go home, but not much to occupy myself with, either.

I shower away the practice sweat to make space for the real sweat, then get stuck into the serious business of pottering around. Some of the other dancers are putting chairs out so I help them. We attach balloons to everything in sight – as though we want the whole place to float away – and the venue gradually starts taking on that sense of 'show'.

Then – a commotion. Everyone races outside. Two bare-chested old men are squaring up to each other on the street. For a moment it looks serious, but despite all the posturing, no actual blows are landed. It gradually fizzles out and instead of fighting they walk away.

Everyone else filters back into the dance school, but I don't know what to do with myself, so I just hang about outside. I buy an *arepa* from a nearby stall and just walk around in the vicinity, chewing it and treading the concrete. I feel smothered by the wait; cloaked in a low-level anxiety that persists like the valley heat.

I'm not the only one hanging about. Indeed I'm not the only one taking part on the show – there's also a Japanese guy whose here to do his first *clausura*. He looks a little jittery, so I go up and talk to him. It'll be fine, I tell him. This probably doesn't help him in the slightest but it makes me feel better and that's the important thing.

Actually, it really will be fine - I've seen his salsa routine and it's good; more advanced than mine, in fact. But in a way his very presence is useful to me as it casts me in the role of 'old hand'. Okay, so I've only done one proper *clausura* before, but then someone who has only once leapt out of a plane with a parachute is still infinitely more experienced than someone who hasn't at all. Or is that divide-by-zero-ly more experienced? Perhaps my next journey should be a maths adventure.

"You divide like a twat."

More personnel have arrived in the meantime, Marta amongst them – she sits lapping milk from a saucer at the reception desk. I join her and we discuss the running order. There are various other routines taking place – the kids are up four times, for instance – but one name in particular keeps appearing again and again.

Mine.

To think that the first time round I was mentally quivering at the thought of one appearance, my name cowering, looking for a place to hide. There's definitely nowhere to hide this time – my routines make up nearly half the total on the list. In fact my name pretty much IS the list.

But then I feel differently to the first time. I do feel nervous, but I don't feel scared, and there's a big difference. I'm strolling round the dance school with confidence, like I own the place almost, albeit with slightly less territorial urination. I feel like a cat in state of continual readiness to pounce, begging for a mouse to appear. I feel ready.

It's time to go backstage. As with that first *clausura*, I leave the free world behind knowing that the next time I'm back out, it will be to dance. Behind me are row after row of empty chairs. What if no-one comes? I'm beginning to wish I'd invited every Colombian I've ever met, from the *arepa* vendor on the corner to the bloke who was scaling my house. I head between the screens, my shoes, with their creamy-soft leather and pliant soles, dangling from my fingers.

Behind the scenes, the area is as cramped as ever. I tiptoe between folk sat cross-legged with their make-up boxes and appropriate my own tiny patch of floor, compacts snapping at my heels as I pass.

I'll be starting in my backpacker garb – jeans and a shirt – so what would have been inappropriate at the *clausura* is now fine. I need to remember this in future – if you can't get the clothes, just invent a theme to suit what you have.

"I can't believe you wore dirty overalls to your own wedding."

"Car mechanic theme."

Laura, meanwhile, has put a little more effort in. She's wearing a lemon-yellow top with deep neckline and a black shrug, plus black hot pants, macramé leggings and high heels. Her hair hangs behind her, parted to one side and clipped into place. She has a flash of silver-lilac eye shadow and her upper cheeks sparkle with glitter.

I think men have it quite easy at times.

My costume preparation hasn't been zero, though. The floor can be a little slippy in the academy, so I've been working the suede nap of the soles with a toothbrush in the hope it will give me a bit more traction. I've failed in my attempts to acquire a proper suede brush because no-one in any of the shops knows what the hell I'm talking about.

It's going to be a long show, and I'll need some sustenance, so I've bought some chocolate in lieu of *panela*. Unlike in Pasto, I buy enough for everyone, snapping a couple of big bars up and offering them out to the other dancers. No-one offers me anything back though, so I won't be doing that again.

"Shhhhhh!"

I know what that means, and I'm right. Marta's amplified voice cuts across the chatter – the show has begun. I crouch, hidden from view, and allow Laura to apply some much-needed powder to my nose. No, the other kind.

The first dancers – the kids – troop out, and applause goes up, muffled by the layers of fabric. Well at least there's someone there. Even if it's just a man and his dog then at least he's taught it to clap. Actually, it would be worth holding the show for that alone, as long as he doesn't upstage me by allowing it to dance.

The music begins and cries of excitement go up – the dancing has begun. Or at least I assume so – they could actually be juggling chainsaws for all I know. I tune it out and run through the first few moves in my head, again and again and again. As long as I start okay it should all just flow. If I make a hash of it, however, I could be in for a long night.

Finally ready, Laura and I advance to the free-standing screens – the last protective barrier. I stand hunched to prevent my head showing over the top.

The music ends to a flurry of cheers and whistles, and the children file back past us.

Silence. Then a drum pattern. Deep breath? There's no time.

We head out between the screens. And boom – there's the audience. It's not an amazing crowd, but some people are there and that's a relief.

There's no time to ponder further – we're tied to the music. I sling my backpack against the wall and wander up to Laura, pointing to a page in an open guidebook as the rhythmic clock ticks away. Can she help me with something? She shrugs, takes the guidebook from me and promptly chucks it away.

This is scripted by the way – she's not being surly.

"Here!" she's effectively saying. "I'll show you what Colombia's all about – dance!"

To the sound of plicky-plucky guitar, my hand comes to rest on her shoulder blade. Then away we go, advancing in the basic bachata *paso* with hip *golpe*, while the lead singer sifts through the wreckage of a past relationship. But what the hell's this? I'm slipping like crazy! This is definitely not scripted. Whether it's despite the suede-brushing or because of it, the floor feels like ice.

What we're dancing is not full-on bachata, with all its body sways and sensual interleavings, but a kind of bachata-lite. And it's just as well – it feels like driving on a skid pan, especially when pushing off for the turns. The 'ta-da!' ending can't come soon enough, and thankfully we make it there without either of us careering off into the wall. Laura completes the ending by leaning sideways onto my leg for the final pose.

The crowd fades back into existence. Twenty people. More would have been nice, but given the draw of the festival, I'm profoundly flattered that those twenty have made the choice they did. And they're certainly making themselves heard.

With the audience still bubbling away, the first routine segues into the second. Against a backdrop of clave comes a rhythmic splash of piano chords, asking a question. Laura simultaneously poses me one of her own in the guise of a salsa *paso* and a gesture of the hand. She gets a bachata *paso* and a shrug of the shoulders in response – what is this? Then there's another splash of piano and another dance question from Laura, but I'm still none-the-wiser.

There's only one thing for it – she's going to have to show me. She yanks me off my feet into a dance position. I exaggerate the jolt, whilst trying not to slip onto my backside, and bang – we're hurtling through the land of brass and discordant piano, changing imaginary light bulbs as we go.

Somehow, the speed of the salsa actually makes life easier on the slippy floor. The lift onto my hip, the sequence of turns, the high-speed *patinetas* – they all go cleanly. What was once too fast now feels measured – I even find time to flash a smile to those gathered. Before I know it we're arriving at the end. I drive her feet-first through the gap between my legs, then slide into position to present her in a floor-pose, like it really was an ice dance after all.

Warm applause mixes with the night air. That went well.

Back in the calm melee of backstage, there's no time to relax or reflect: we've got little more than a minute before we're due back out again. I kick off my ice-skates and my jeans in favour of a very welcome pair of beat-up trainers and some shorts. Laura, meanwhile, bares some flesh, slipping into a pink bikini top, but keeps the shrug and leggings.

The idea with the next dance – merengue – is that the same two characters happen upon each other again sometime later. By now, though, the tourist has learnt a thing or two. So much so, in fact, that he's the one proposing the dance.

But Laura and I have a problem. The introductory section – during which this narrative takes place – had been too long. So long, in fact, that the conversation would have gone beyond simple greetings and into questions about each other's family (at which point I'd have got twitchy and started lying about dead relatives). To resolve this, I asked for it to be cut down, but due to some miscommunication the final edit has left us with a paltry two bars.

The instant the poppy merengue starts up, we burst out onto the stage. Despite supposedly not having seen each other for ages, we flash each other the merest of salutations then fling ourselves into a dance together. What can I say – Colombia is a friendly country.

With arms swinging we approach each other from across the stage, but the hurried start means I'm struggling to line up my limbs with the beat. The sloppiness is carried forward, as we meet back to back in a messy hand-clasp, like a pair of docking spacecraft piloted by drunkards.

We revert to a conventional merengue hold, and we're finally able to hit some kind of stride, our hips wagging away like the tails of happy dogs. To the clonking of piano, the singer tells anyone who will listen how he and his special lady are made for each other.

In a few years' time he'll probably be writing a bachata number about her, but for now everything's just great.

On we go, through the sequence of cat's cradle-like entwinements, before sashaying towards the audience clapping hands with each other. My smile is a bit more forced this time round – chiefly because of how hard it is to clap hands whilst dancing and looking a different way. We might as well be riding a pair of motorbikes blindfold along parallel high wires – that's how difficult and dangerous it is.

Into the final clinch we go, finishing the routine in record time – certainly a lot quicker than the song, which saunters in some time after us. Not that anyone seems to notice or care. Laura leans backwards over my knee and watches as the upside-down people make robust hand-sounds.

There's no chance for a respite – the next number is a scant few seconds away. Laura settles herself down on a sarong on an imaginary beach, whilst I slap a straw hat on and wait off-stage in a make-believe boat.

The calypso-like guitar intro is my cue to emerge, paddling along to a slice of classic *champeta* – La Mala Hierba by Nando Hernandez.

I'm just minding my own business, sloshing about in the sea. But what's this? I think I've just spotted the catch of the day! I cast off my fishing line, hook her and reel her back into my arms. It's not really clear if this is part of the same narrative – has the tourist now taken up fishing? – but as long as there's not a Q&A session at the end we should get away with it.

To the sound of sampled DJ scratching, Laura backs into me for a set of conjoined hip rotations. Once upon a time I'd have peeked through my fingers at proximity like this. Now it's just dancing. We circle round together, rolling our hips in time, then break to introduce the people of Cali to the jelly legs and lasso. Great whoops go up – I knew they'd like that.

There's no time to appreciate it, though, as we're lining up for the big one: the one that must have the floor wincing every time we attempt it. I align myself behind Laura and place my hands on her hips. Forget the music. Just get it right. *Suave*. She leaps back towards me and…

…I've got her, my hands gripping her thighs. Boom! I roll my shoulders, leaning to either side of her, smiling like the guy in the video. Yudi would definitely approve. Thankfully Laura's changed her heels for a pair of strappy sandals – it would be cheating if she stayed up there by virtue of having skewered my thighs.

I drop Laura back down to earth in a controlled manner, avoiding the wrecking-ball departure of previous instances. It's plain sailing from here on in – just regular bonkers sauciness. We do a move where I rock forwards and backwards with her between my legs, and another where she crouches down in front of me and I thrust from behind her – which sounds quite raunchy, but is actually just cheeky postcard fun – and that's that.

I beckon her towards me, slap my sun-hat on her head, and we row off towards backstage together, the waves of appreciation lapping up against us as we go.

Sometimes you can be so wrapped up in the tension of doing something that you can forget to actually enjoy it. There's no chance of that tonight – I'm slap-bang in the middle of it and I feel great. The adrenaline is still in my system, and I just want to get out there and dance again. But Marta has chosen this moment for the intermission, leaving me pinging about the place like a top. It takes me some time before I'm calm enough to sit down and reflect.

Everything has gone well, despite the slippy shoes and the sloppy meringue. Nailing that *champeta* – wow, that was a buzz in itself. But I've still got half a show to go, so I can't rest on my laurels. There'd be no room to do that here anyway, short of pinning them to the wall and leaning on them.

Around me are the other dancers – many of them here full-time either as students or teachers. It must be crazy, always preparing for the next show; spending your whole time in a cycle of tension and release.

There is quite a tight-knit feel to the group, perhaps due to the fact that dance schools often tour internationally, giving them a sense of a travelling circus and making dancers amongst the most well-travelled Colombians around. But despite me not being part of that, the feeling I had the first time round – of being a fraud – is a distant memory. I might not be a professional, but I'm the real deal. I belong here just as much as anyone.

Back in the here and now, it's changing time again and not just of clothes, but of personnel: Laura's done for the evening, and in comes Nanda and her cavernous laugh. She's adorned with bright red lipstick, hoop earrings and glitter that bursts open at the corners of her eyes.

It's the cue for me to discard the beachwear and put on the first set of folkloric garments. The clothing for the *guaneña* is refreshingly cool and crisp, like a set of cricket whites. In fact, the first three outfits are all ivory-toned, the main distinguishing feature with this Andean set being the earthy poncho I put on over the top. Then take off again less than a minute later because mountain clothing and Cali evenings don't mix. Thank God we're not taking the layered approach.

The break seems to go on forever, but finally show time comes round again. This time we're first up. On go the final touches – the poncho and the hat (all folkloric dances must include some kind of headwear: it's the law) – and I'm ready to go.

The tiles feel refreshing under my bare feet as we head for the stage. Not cool; but solid and sure, my skin lightly adhering to the surface. Once more I pass between the screens, this time with Nanda. Together we head into what must be the friendliest bear pit in town – we get a round of applause just for having put clothes on.

On this front, I've been outdone once again. Nanda is wearing a white satin blouse with puffed-up cap sleeves and a voluminous black skirt, a knitted shawl cosseting her arms. Her hair is gathered back, re-appearing out front as a friendly pigtail with a royal-blue bow, matching the carnation in her hair, whilst her own little piggies peek out from underneath her dress.

There's no flimsy narrative linking the folk dances – they're all self-contained. The first murmurings of strings swirl about the place like Andean mist, and Nanda and I begin shuffling timidly towards each other from opposite walls.

In come the string bass and panpipes, redolent of mountain passes, hard-working indigenous people and pasty-faced Englishmen, and we hit our full stride, bounding through the sequence of shawl-related capers like the two-handled teapots we are. Nanda smiles at me with total self-assuredness, and I smile back, the tassels on the shawl stroking the floor as we parade it between us.

It's a nice, simple start to the folkloric set, and a world away from the razzamatazz of the urban dances. But we've still got the problem of the hide-and-seek ending. No amount of practice seems to have resolved this – if anything it's been getting worse. That very morning, Nanda had been turning the wrong way with such frequency that I even started calling out "*¡DERECHA!*" (RIGHT!) at the crucial moment. Which might have helped had that been the correct direction.

So it's fair to say we know what's coming. She'll go the wrong way, then correct herself in a fit of giggles. Wait for it... wait for it....

Oh.

Like a true pro, when the time comes Nanda just performs. No-one in the audience has the slightest idea of the sheer quantity of comedic wrong turns that preceded it, but when the moment arrives, she simply gets it right. Damn these professionals. I wrap the shawl about her protectively and the dance draws to its conclusion, amidst a shower of applause that seems at odds with its humble nature.

The moment we're backstage, any semblance of calm is jettisoned along with the outfits, our garments flying about in a hurricane of fabric. Whilst Nanda changes her skirt for a sky blue number with a white lace hem, I make a few changes of my own. The black hat goes, replaced by a marginally larger black hat, whilst the white shirt is replaced by a slightly different white shirt with a mandarin collar.

The outfits are all distinct – this particular one is called a *liqui liqui* – but it would take a connoisseur to tell the difference between them. Still, there's one thing the audience will be sure to notice: the delicious white-and-brown animal-hide *cotizas*. Even if they don't see them, they'll definitely hear them.

It's *joropo* time.

The 'stage' is starting to feel very familiar, as we step out once more, but there's enough tension to keep me on edge. The lights, which felt like headlights in the first *clausura*, now feel like what they're meant to – spotlights.

We take up position, on the edge of the dance floor, hanging about like Villavo does at the edge of the plains. A quick burst of tangled harp sets the tone, and we're away into the sedate *pasaje*, waltzing off into the plains and performing that time-honoured arm-behind-neck movement that's so nearly a headlock. The *joropo*, as I learnt it, is a mentally-and-physically-challenging juggling-act of a dance. Not so this routine – it feels pretty easy given that we've sacrificed the *dan-DAN-tsss* of the *paso básico* to the great God of compromise (whose rituals involve maiming rather than full-on death).

It seemed like the right call at the time, but now I'm out here, doing it, it feels disappointingly understated. This is not the *joropo* I wanted them to see. The crowd, for their part, are as polite and subdued as the dance.

The problem is exacerbated by the fact that I simply can't get any noise out of the floor. I'm spanking the floor once every three beats, just to keep a marker down, but, all I'm getting back is dull thuds. Not only that but the combination of floor and *cotizas* is proving so slippery that I'm like a pond skater once again. Finally the harp can take no more of this restraint – it clears the fence and makes a break for freedom, dragging the tempo up to *recio* as it does so.

About time.

I give a sharp stab of the spurs and we gallop headlong into the rapid-fire footwork of the *metrónomo*. The audience instantly snaps out of its lull. Cheers ring out along with exited clapping. This is the *joropo* I wanted them to see: sparks-flying, hang-on-to-your-hat type stuff.

Now it's time to mete out some real percussive punishment. I attack the ground with all the *berraquera* I can muster, laying down a set of rhythmic *zapateos*. The floor is still about as spankable as a grassy meadow, but the audience are giving me all the acoustic feedback I need. I nail every single one, *paso* Neil included, in a flurry of staccato floor-strikes. This despite me sliding about like someone's emptied a hopper of grain on the floor. Meanwhile, Nanda's skirt darts about, struggling to keep up.

Onwards we surge, and into the *botalón*; a manoeuvre, if I've understood them correctly, is named after a pole that the cowboys used to dance round. Essentially, I just rotate on the spot, pushing Nanda round me in the opposite direction. I arrive at our meeting point later than a Colombian girl on a date, but no matter.

We've got time for one last genteel *figura* or two – passing Nanda behind me; wrapping her up and unwrapping her – then we throw ourselves into the final pose. I stamp on the ground as a final flourish – the most satisfying *zapateo* of them all – and we're done.

Six dances down, two to go. I am really, really enjoying this.

White fabric flies in the breeze like it's on a rotary clothes line, white shirt number two being exchanged for white shirt number three. But this time the garment is rather distinctive, with a gold-embroidered bib. I love this shirt – it's an item of real beauty.

My feet are once again pleasantly sock-liberated, and I've come to see it as the only contact you can really trust. Then there's the hat: the first authentic *sombrero vueltiao* I've encountered in an age. Just seeing it makes me want to balance a can of beer on my head, cultivate a foam beard and make repeated visits to a consulate.

I'm still missing an important item, though – the fire hazard.

One of the dance teachers lights the individual wicks of the tied bundle of candles and hands them to me. I accept them gingerly, like he's just handed me a bundle of lit dynamite sticks. Now that would be a folk dance worth watching. From afar.

Though individually quite weedy, collectively the flames form a single hot-headed dancing spirit that gives off a furious heat. Yet it's a vulnerable creature, prone to dimming with sudden movement, making it a struggle just to keep it lit. Meanwhile, I also have an obligation to try and keep the other dancers in the tight backstage unlit – I imagine Colombians could react quite strongly if I set fire to their children.

There's more to handling cumbia candles than just avoiding the ignition of minors. The dance teacher tells me that the first splash of hot wax on the hand can be surprise enough that you drop the bundle. He suggests I pour a little wax on my candle hand, as I've never called my right hand before, in order to acclimatise.

The time is near, so I tilt the bundle. It scurries onto the soft webbing between my thumb and forefinger. OW. I do it again a second time. Ow. Good tip.

Raucous applause fills the venue. This could be because Nanda has just walked on wearing a white-petal fascinator and an exquisite white-lace *pollera*-style dress with satin bodice. But it could also be because I've followed her on holding some fire.

She stands in a dream-like state centre-stage, whilst I stand in the sidelines holding my *sombrero* – it's a sleeping beauty routine. To a shimmering musical intro, I tip-toe out and gently empty the confetti-like contents of my hat over her from above, like some kind of romantic practical joker.

Roused from her slumber by my magical cellophane, she

comes around just in time for the arrival of the signature *pata-pum pata-pum pata-pum* rhythm. Here comes the *tambor alegre*, here comes the *llamador*, and here's me shuffling towards her with the leg-iron gait; the very same one that none of my own ancestors ever had to master.

I pass the flickering bundle to Nanda as part of our dance flirtation, and we hit the first serious set of turns, poised shoulder-to-shoulder. I've always liked the perpetual falling feeling of these *vueltas*, but this time my mind is on the candles: if they're going to go out, it will be now. We complete the second of the pair of turns and... they live on!

Then Nanda does an innocuous turn and they splutter out, as if just to spite me. It means it doesn't make much sense when I fall to my knees to avoid her waxy swipe in my direction, but no matter: this is a dance that produces its own natural light.

I waft at her hips in the traditional manner and wave my hands in the 'distress call', like someone trapped in a *palco* full of expectant strangers, and before we know it she's back asleep centre stage and we've only got one dance left.

Five minutes.

I never quite believed I would ever do this show, yet five minutes from now it'll all be over. Just one dance separates me and completion, and it's the one I ruled out the first time I saw it. Then tried it just to make sure and ruled it out again. Maybe I'll be ruling it out once more in five minutes time.

On the other side of the divide, the Japanese guy and his dance teacher are getting a lively reception for their salsa routine. They deserve it – I saw what the audience didn't, which is just how much work went into it. As Muhammad Ali said, "The fight is won or lost far away from witnesses – behind the lines, in the gym, and out there on the road, long before I dance under those lights."

On this side, we've got just enough time for our final costume change. Nanda asks me if I want to wear the shirt on the top. So – do I want to hide behind a shirt, or am I going to take a risk and put it out there?

Nanda herself is going for the brave option – a short, stripey dress of lace-edged layers that bares her legs to midway up her thigh.

On go my bloomers and headscarf. The shirt stays on its hanger. And with that, I'm ready for business, albeit a business that employs people who like to tie an item of clothing round their head and pretend to be Rambo. Any business that has a Christmas party, then.

"*Duro amigo, duro,*" one of the dance teachers to me as we wait behind the screen, urging me to give it some stick.

The cheers rebound off the walls as we walk out. It's like they haven't seen a pale, skinny chest before. I feel slightly bashful and find myself acting all kind of "Yeah I know!", even though I'm not quite sure what it is I know. Then the African drum roll begins, and all this changes: my body goes taut and on goes my game face, like a tribal mask. Unless that's an over-simplistic representation of African culture, in which case not like a tribal mask.

Here we go.

It's that slow, intoxicated opening I remember so well from my lessons under the fans with Yudi.

With Nanda spinning about behind me, I roll into action, my skin introduced to the hard surface. Back on my feet, I prowl about, pawing at the floor like a wild animal. A skinny, pale-chested wild animal.

The intro sequence is meant to end with us leaping backwards onto the solid thud of a drumbeat –a clean, crisp ending. But we both jump too early. We land on silence, followed a second later by the *THUD*, like an out-of-sync video.

Bollocks.

"*¡Sigue!*" Esteban would be shouting. Carry on!

The main section kicks in with a torrent of pelted drum skins and suddenly we're thrusting manically: palms, chest and groin.

We switch into something like a frenzied hat-and-cane routine. Here I make a small slip of memory, but Nanda has it right so I take note and self-correct. It's incredible there are still mistakes to make given the number of times I've practised it, but I've come too far to let it throw me.

Next come the adorations. What once seemed impossibly fast – too fast for gravity – now seems pedestrian. It feels like the end scene in the Matrix; appropriate given that 'Neo' is as close as a lot of Colombians can get to saying my name.

Drums plaster the air all around us as the stars come into

alignment for one last move.

I feel drained – so drained – but we're almost there. One last push. I drop to my hands and toes like the men in the square all those months ago, with their impossible dance. I bound along the floor towards Nanda's legs. The hard surface stings my palms. I go through her legs. I come out the other side. I spring to my feet.

I'm good.

Nanda and I reel about, as though under a spell, waiting for the definitive final drum beat. The single moment that marks not only the end of a dance, but the end of a dance journey.

Thud.

Applause.

Thank you and goodnight.

CHAPTER TWENTY

Curtain Call

"*¡Malo! ¡Muy malo!*" Bad! Very Bad!

Isabela always says that when I'm being sarcastic, which means she says it all the time. I can't even remember what prompted it this time. Perhaps I told her I was glad to be leaving.

My other friends also have words for me.

"*Mil disculpas...*" A thousand sorries...

So begins one of a whole host of contrite messages from the friends that didn't make it – mostly because they were down at the festival along with their good intentions. There are no excuses; just open and sincere apologies. This stands to reason – Colombians are amongst the warmest, friendliest people you could ever hope to meet. Just don't hope to meet them on the same evening as a massive party (unless you are also going to that party).

The ne'er-do-wells from the street have also apparently been drawn in by the lure of the festival, as nobody has attached themselves to my dwelling in days. Which is a shame, as a goodbye would have been nice.

As for my own show, all that was left following the *mapalé* was the closing sequence, during which Laura, Marta, Nanda and I all got the opportunity to say lots of complementary things about each other.

My own speech was relatively short. In Colombia, one of the more recent advertising campaigns bore the slogan "*El riesgo es que te quieras quedar.*" (The risk is that you'll want to stay). Referencing this, I announced that "*¡El riesgo es que queiras bailar!*" (The risk is that you'll want to dance). Cheesy? Yes, but they loved it.

Marta presented me with a pair of certificates recording my achievements (there were too many dances to fit on a single certificate). This is great as it means that anytime someone asks if I can dance I can just whip those out, instead of all this 'physically demonstrating it' nonsense.

The defining moment, however, was not what was said, but what wasn't. Because three little words – "*Es un proceso*" (It's a process) – weren't invited to the closing, and their absence meant more than any number of enthusiastic plaudits. Although, let's not kid ourselves – plaudits are pretty great, too.

The show closed with all the performers dancing in front of the audience – the traditional 'Look at us! We're all about the dancing!'-type moment. And this time it was true – we all could, me included. Because I'm not a dance impersonator any more. Or if I am then at least I'm a pretty convincing one.

Colombian goodbyes are long and drawn out, like the love affairs in a Márquez novel, and it took forever to leave the dance academy. I said goodbye to the same people as many as five or six times as we made our way down to the front of the school, mingling, re-mingling and re-re-mingling, before finally emerging into the warm night.

I lay in bed unable to sleep at first, still high on adrenaline. But even that passed, and I slipped into a deep sleep, taking my first true rest – with no commitments to be honoured (or avoided) – in what felt like a long, long time.

Cut to a few days later, and I'm saying goodbye to Isabela. We part with a series of slow kisses, each one seeming to be the last before ending up as merely the precursor to another. In a way it's like it's Colombia I'm kissing goodbye to. Don't tell her that, though – I imagine it's kind of insulting.

I sit in the Bogotá taxi with the cityscape shrinking behind me, accompanied on this final jaunt by the Spanish that has become an everyday part of my life.

We whistle along the concrete-sectioned highway, the radio filling the air with local rhythms. Some songs burst with rapid-fire beat clusters, whilst others are more lilting and gentle. Some sound bouncy and poppy, whilst others are slow and romantic. But this time, not only can I name every type of music coming out of the radio, but I could dance to each of them without a second thought, too.

As the plane taxis down the runway, I bid farewell to the mountains and valleys, plains and coastlines; to the peoples of largely indigenous, African and Spanish descent, and all the colour-bleeds in between; to the amazing cultural heritage, including more dances than a man could learn in his lifetime.

The cloud layer approaches quickly as the aircraft gains altitude, closing behind like a pair of stage curtains. The high-altitude savannah disappears for good, and with it, Colombia.

CHAPTER TWENTY-ONE

Routine

"What were you doing there?" says the taxi driver. "Importing or exporting?"

Eh?

Ha! Oh yeah. I forgot that Colombia is all about cocaine (and kidnapping, and coffee). Thank God I didn't go there – it sounds hellish. Albeit with good coffee.

As it happens, the only time I saw cocaine on the whole trip was in a photograph – two English backpackers in a Bogotá hostel, right at the end of my journey, showed me shots of themselves snorting cocaine off a prostitute's backside.

And now here I am, back in the land of black tarmac, able to spend time with my parents in their pastoral village in Lancashire, despite what I told the men in hammocks in Valledupar.

It's a strange place, this 'England'. You can go to pretty much anywhere you like in the country without having to consider the likelihood of people stealing you and sending you back to your family a piece at a time (if at all).

When you walk through a city centre, the highest probability of mugging comes from the vicious gangs of charity-thugs. People who, rather than saying "give me everything you've got right now" (with the implied threat of violence), prefer to say "give us a small amount on a regular basis" (with the implied threat of guilt). Although the amount of fear they instill in the general populace is roughly similar.

People have this strange habit of only overtaking when they know they can successfully complete the manoeuvre, on roads that don't routinely skirt stunning gorges, pass up through cloud-layers or hug mountainsides.

If you feel breathless it's because you've just done something exhausting: there's no need to factor in that the ground might be two kilometres higher than the sea. Mind you, there's no need to talk to the local people in Spanish, either, but that doesn't stop me occasionally trying.

Everyone respects queues and, bizarrely, they also respect clocks. In fact, a lot of people have the infuriating habit of arriving to meet you at the time you agreed, meaning I go from being someone who's always early to someone who's always late.

Oh, and people like to dance on their own.

"So, can you dance now then?"

It's a good question. In fact it's just about the only question – I'm hearing it all the time now I'm back. I'm not sure how you answer it though.

"Yes, I can – 100%."

It's Christmas, which should be a good time to find out, given all the festivities.

On the streets, in a city in northern England, outside tinselated shops, a glut of accordion players are plying their trade with slow, mournful dirges. I want to rip them out of their hands and show them how to play the instrument properly – don't they know you can squeeze rays of sunshine out of these things? This is despite what a bizarre and appalling sight that would make – especially given that I can't actually play one – and that it would probably just amount to assault and theft.

In Colombia, Cali's annual fair – the Feria de Cali – will be in full swing now. People will be getting carried down Quinta on great waves of salsa; cars will be dancing down the streets in pairs; buildings will be shimmying about exhibiting dizzying displays of footwork.

Back home things are a bit different – here we have piss-ups with tinsel. Sometimes we do it standing up in pubs, and others it's a more formal sit-down affair that involves food. Don't get me wrong – I love the English way of life. It's just that our idea of fun suddenly looks a little one-dimensional.

The one I'm at tonight is an exception, though: a big,

rambling, activity-based event involving about a hundred people in floppy red and white hats. As I stand at the bar chatting to a friend, one of the hosts is making some kind of announcement, and the mention of my name catches my attention.

"Blah blah blah... Neil! ...blah blah blah."

I'm wanted out in front of the gathered throng, apparently, so I join the small group of people who are stood in a line. They have that tenseness about them, like a wall of football players awaiting a free-kick.

"What's this all about?"

"It's a dance competition."

Ha! Brilliant.

It's about now that I realise that I've failed. Specifically it's the moment when Michael Jackson's Billie Jean starts up. I went away with the sole intention of learning how to dance, but the first sign of a well-known bit of music and everything I've learnt is clearly useless.

It was a daft idea, really. Can't dance in country A? Why not go to country B and learn how to dance there? Then come back to country A and adopt a puzzled look. Had I stayed at home studying videos of Justin Timberlake, Robbie Williams – indeed pretty much any pop groover from the last couple of decades – I'd know far more dance moves of relevance to my situation than I do now. Although I'd probably also be in therapy.

I'm about halfway down the running order, the list being a physical one, rather than one taped to a wall. The others before me each get up in turn to perform, but I barely notice them – I'm absorbed in planning. After my introduction people will be expecting something half decent, so I can't just muddle about. If the chosen music was faster I'd do some of my salsa footwork and dazzle through sheer velocity of movement, but the tempo is all wrong for that. Cumbia perhaps? *Guaneña*?

How ridiculous.

Time's up. The dance floor ahead of me is ominously empty; the combined crowd of friends and strangers waiting expectantly. The repeating bassline; the three-chord synth; the man freshly back from a dance adventure.

Here we go. I step forward from the anonymity of the line, and go straight into something halfway between playing the air guitar and the All-Blacks' Haka. It's something I once saw a Scottish friend do, and is just to buy me thinking time. This music is just so slow.

Okay, I've got it

I slip into some reggaeton, throwing my shoulders back, and swaying moodily from side to side. From here, I segue naturally into some reggaeton butt-thrusts. I switch to a kind of slow *mapalé*, thrusting out my flat palms, but with controlled intent, rather than frenetically. Finally I do some salsa footwork, hitting the floor with heel and toe of each foot and crossing over with a cha-cha-cha of the feet. This last one doesn't really fit, and I know it, but I've just got to carry on, and be confident.

Time's up.

I return to the line-up of other dancers to the gratifying sound of applause. Now I can relax and watch the others. Some dude dances with some small shuffly steps, for which he gets practically no applause. It's wrong; unfair – he should be cheered just for getting up there. Another bloke delivers an assured performance of disco moves: shoulder-shimmy to the left and right; falling down to one hand and thrusting his groin; that kind of thing. It's cheesy as heck, but it's meant to be, and he delivers it with great physical confidence.

The contest will be decided by clap volume. One of the hosts reads out the names and the hall reverberates to the sound of applause. One by one we're all clapped. And the winner is....

Disco bloke! And rightly so. I'd have chosen him, too.

Not that everyone agrees.

"You were robbed!" one guy tells me.

Dammit – I knew I should have put my money in my sock.

"You should have won," says another, denying me the ambiguity necessary for a second smartarse comment.

A friend of mine, however, is less complimentary.

"What's all this?" she says, aping my *mapalé*-style hand movements.

I can't mock her own dancing, though, because she didn't do any.

"You should have danced your Latin moves," she says, "then you'd have won."

And there's the irony. Because, outside of the dance porn we consume on the television, dance ability in the UK is judged on how well you do it on your own. In Colombia, whilst they'd surely appreciate a good solo dancer, in a cultural context it would be to miss the point entirely. It would be like saying that someone was good in bed because they were a proficient masturbator.

But then to make it all about dance ability is probably missing the point too. Had this happened a year ago, it's not like I would have got up and danced badly – I just wouldn't have danced at all. I'd have wangled my way out of it. So perhaps I've succeeded after all.

Besides, there are probably more representative places than that to put my new-found skills to the test. Like the indie club I visit with a couple of female friends. Plastic pints are being sloshed about by the youngish clientele, creating sticky patches on the hard floor – there's none of this communal drink-sharing nonsense.

The taller of the two girls drags me off to the dance floor by the hand. Unfortunately, she's very drunk, so we do a good lap and a half of the dance floor, going through the middle and tying a knot in it, before she finally finds a space she's happy with.

People all around us are dancing on their own, in their own made-up style. In many cases this means badly, but then most people are having fun, even if some of them don't look like they're fully aware of their surroundings.

I don't want to just dance 'at' someone any more – it now seems so contrary to everything I've learnt – but nor do I want to dance salsa to the Stone Roses. I've seen this done and it just looks kind of tragic (though *joropo* to the Smiths would be fine). But I'm sure there are things I've learnt that can be abstracted for whatever purpose.

I take my friend's hands and bring her in towards me, reeling her in and unreeling her again. I put her through a few simple turns, all to the music, confident for the first time in my life that I know what I'm doing, and that it won't end up with her lying on the floor in a bundle of knots. Or at least if it does, they'll be of naval quality.

She breaks off to play the temptress, teasing me towards her, then turning her back and walking away, then coming back again. If I had a tie she'd be leading me off by it. The mock-seduction is somewhat tempered by the fact that she's moving like a boat in bad weather, but it's still all good fun.

Something has definitely changed whilst I've been away: dancing has become enjoyable to me. And if there's one reason for this it's because of the connection it allows you to create with another human being. Even if that human being is having problems with basic motor control.

So I guess my skills do translate, though, of course, in England there'll always be occasions when you have to just fit in and dance at people. Some music will be playing and you'll need to do some things with your body, and ideally there'll be some kind of relationship between the two.

At my younger sister's wedding, for instance, where we're all dancing in something akin to a reggaeton circle, except with the Stone Roses in place of Daddy Yankee.

But whilst I don't really have any more new 'moves', I do seem to have more options available to my feet and arms. They just know where to go instinctively. And my hips and shoulders are free to do their own thing, too, rather than being linked stiffly to adjoining body parts like a Thunderbirds puppet. I'm not great at dancing solo, I'm really not, I just feel more comfortable in my own skin; less self-conscious; more willing to just get up and do it.

But that still leaves the question of how other people perceive my dancing. It's a question which two of the bridesmaids come up to me to answer of their own volition, having heard me talking about the genesis of my Colombia trip sometime earlier.

"We've both been watching you dance..."

Go on...

"...and you do not dance like a twat."

It's a low bar, but you've still got to clear it.

There are of course places where my new found Latin sensibilities are better accommodated. The warm-up for the Colombian Salsa class is all too familiar: we all stand on the dance floor in lines, copying the instructor out front. I'm near the back and I can barely see what he's doing.

I'm in salsa hell.

Except for once, it really isn't. All about me, people are bobbing about like accordion-filled crates in the Atlantic, trying to catch a rare glimpse of his footwork. But I don't need to see his feet to copy his steps because I can tell just from his top half what *pasos* he's doing. I collide with the people either side of me, who are out of time and are going left as I'm going right. Others, real first-timers, aren't moving their bodies at all: they're just pointing at stuff with their feet.

"Copy that guy," one girl says, gesturing in my direction. "He knows what he's doing!"

Then we split up into groups and some assistant teacher who has never been to Colombia tries to correct my *paso básico*, which is entertaining if nothing else.

"I bet you showed them a thing or two!" my folks will later suggest.

Ha! No. Well, some of them, maybe. But they're not all amateurs – some of them have been learning for five years or more. I learnt ten dances in a matter of months, so anyone who's has been to salsa classes regularly is going to be a better salsa dancer than me.

But then I'm still improving. And I even occasionally find myself getting 'in the zone', even if it's only for a brief while. In fact, since returning I've discovered that this state of being is a recognised psychological concept. Proposed by psychologist Mihaly Csikszentmihalyi, it's called 'flow', and it occurs when you are immersed in a task which is highly challenging, but which you are equal to.

Mind you, dancing is not just about being in the zone – it's also about self-expression. Something great comes on, a Colombian classic like La Rebelión or Cali Pachanguero, and I get that urge to just… do… something. Only now things are different. Instead of just standing there, barking (or worse – doing the bar-lean dance), I grab someone and get out there. I can channel that buzz right through me, in a way I've never been able to before.

I even have the confidence to start improvising – just trying things out, unsure of whether they'll work out or not.

"I just made that up," I say to one partner. "Could you tell?"

"Yes."

The thing is, I'm not amazing – I'm just okay. But then I'm not doing this to become some dance superstar: I'm doing it because I really enjoy it. I don't need to be frogmarched to the dance floor by angry Caleñas (though I do miss that, now) – I go because I want to.

Not that you could ever mistake this for a Colombian night out. For a start, dance matters are discussed in English, even if that does largely just mean the exchanging of the word "sorry!" every twenty seconds.

Then there are the aspects of proximity. I quickly discover that, in my home country, even a hand on the back can be considered a trifle too sensual. I'd laugh out loud if I hadn't felt exactly the same way myself at one time.

And unlike back in Colombia, the currency here is turns, and lots of them. There are people who know an astonishing variety of moves, and can fill an entire song with *vueltas* without ever repeating themselves. Like Cesar suggested, there are some really good dancers here. Mind you, there are also people who know all the moves but couldn't follow the rhythm if it was a bright red vehicle with 'FOLLOW ME!' painted on the back.

Perhaps it's wrong of me expecting to come back home and still be able to dance like a Colombian. But then maybe I can. Because dancing like a Colombian is about having a desire to dance, to connect, to party; about feeling the rhythm and having a love for the music which you express with your body, and you can take that anywhere.

In a dance school in Cali there's a sign on the wall that says '*no dejamos de bailar porque envejecemos, nos envejecemos porque dejamos de bailar*'. Which means 'We don't die because we get old...' No, that's not it... 'We don't start dancing just because we've stopped dying...' No, wait I've got it: 'We don't stop dancing because we get old – we get old because we stop dancing.'

Fortunately, I have no intention. Of stopping dancing that is – I think my options in terms of the other are quite limited.

And time doesn't spare any of us. Since I came back, a number of Colombian legends have passed away: salsa and *música tropical* singer Joe Arroyo, whose hit La Rebelión I danced to at my show; Diomedes Díaz, who was singing when I entered the stadium in Valledupar; even the beloved Gabo (Gabriel García Márquez).

Colombia itself is still dancing to its own unique rhythm. After I left, Galeras, the volcano that dominates Pasto, erupted on a small scale with no big impact on the town, except that presumably lots of locals now have good photos. No war with Venezuela is imminent, and ties that were broken a month earlier – over Colombia's accusations that their neighbours were aiding rebels – have since resumed.

In the UK things are changing too. A large, predominantly-female portion of the populace has decided to go and learn a variety of Latin American dances via the dance-aerobics craze known as Zumba, as though in a calculated attempt and spiteful attempt to render my mission pointless.

But what about my own plans?

"Will you be opening a dance school then?" I get asked 47 times.

Well, maybe if there's a demand.

"I'm looking to learn a series of dances I can never use anywhere outside of Colombian festivals, all to a fairly mediocre standard."

"You've come to the right place!"

In fact in some ways, things are worse for me than before I went away: anyone who has heard about my trip thinks I must now be some kind of demon on the dance floor. I know how Cesar must feel: people have high expectations that I can't possibly meet. Like the time I win a fancy dress competition and I'm asked – in lieu of doing a speech, and with no time to prepare – to dance like a Colombian. To Bohemian Rhapsody.

But then I've not just learnt how to dance, I've learnt to cope with those awkward way-outside-your-comfort-zone type situations. I'm better than ever at noticing that some part my brain is just scared, and that all I have to do is sigh, laugh, and shake my head, or some weird-looking combination of the three and then give it a go anyway.

I'm also a bit wiser this time, so in the Bohemian Rhapsody situation I grab a female friend from the audience. And the result this time? Rubbish! Ha! I just couldn't get my head round the timing. But even that's not a problem anyway because, well, I hate to say it, but it's a process.

I mean, how could it not be? Complex dances like salsa can take months or even years of perseverance to perform fluently. And then, after all that investment, if you went to a *milonga* (tango club), or even an RnB nightclub, you wouldn't know where to begin. You can't know everything, and even if you suddenly did, like some omniscient dancing smartarse, it would all change again anyway. And maybe that's part of the appeal: you can never learn everything that dance has to offer. The idea I had in my mind all that time ago, that you can learn to dance full stop, was fundamentally flawed.

So, leaving Colombia wasn't the end of the journey – only the start of it. And wherever that journey takes me, dance has already given me so much; unexpected things; things other than just not dancing in a twat-like manner.

For a start, it's turned out to be every bit the alternative to alcohol I'd hoped. I really do now have something to do in the evening other than just the repeated pouring of liquids mouthwards. And whilst it doesn't exactly constitute salacious hedonism in its purest form, it really is a way of letting go, of having that fun and excitement that I craved. It's something to provoke anticipation; to give an evening meaning. Suddenly I've got a reason to go to nightclubs again.

Okay, so when it comes to getting started, the hurdle to be cleared as a non-drinker is still that bit greater, and always will be. But it only takes three or four dances before I'm loosened, and by seven or eight I'm repeating myself and starting fights with strangers. Besides, if I want to see somebody staggering about and vomiting, all I have to do is spin a partner one time too many.

And dance has become a new way of connecting with people wherever it is I am in the world. During my stay in Seville, for instance, I'm invited to join friends at the famous April Fair, where people dress up in finery and make merry in marquee tents, knocking back *rebujitos* (sherry cocktails) and dancing in pairs to the flamenco-like Sevillanas. If you don't drink or dance then you're in for a long night. No problem – I learn the basics from an internet video, and end up staying until all hours dancing with friends and strangers alike.

It's the same in many places I visit. In Croatia, for example, group dance classes turn out to be a great alcohol-free way of meeting locals, as well as of sating my need to be talked at by someone in an unintelligible language. I end up dancing with locals in the *perestil* square of the historic Diocletian's Palace, its ancient stone floor getting polished further by salsa, reggaeton and bachata.

The impact of my journey extends further still. It has given me a pleasure I've never had access to be before, and never even really understood the significance of – that of connecting with someone through dance.

"I know how to hold a woman," as I tell a female friend of mine.

She doesn't reply. This is because she's doubled over with laughter.

But I do. And I know how to turn a woman (no, not like that – I'm not even sure that's possible) and, when I do turn her, I know which hands to hold where, when to let go and how not to end up in a situation that requires the fire service and three tubs of grease to resolve.

Oh, and welcome to the bizarre world of women finding my dancing attractive.

"All the time you were dancing with me, you were seducing me," as one… erm… friend told me.

But then I've developed in many different ways as a result of my journey.

I'm not as stiff-limbed as I used to be. Indeed, suddenly I've got access to things I never used to have. Like hips. On top of that, I feel like I've got more poise, more body confidence, more body awareness. I can stand tall.

But, more generally, I feel like I've found this new joy in my life; a new adventure. Something that I can take with me everywhere and share with people, yet with such depth and variety that no matter how good I get, I'll always be learning.

I love the art of it; the passion; the skill; the joy of self-expression. I love the sociability; the fact that I've learnt this thing where you can communicate with people in a physical way, without babies necessarily appearing nine months later (I've always been terrified of getting pregnant). And I particularly love the way I went away with the hope of ticking off something on a list and came back with a genuine passion.

I've learnt to be patient with myself; to have faith that if I just keep applying myself to something, the ability will just come. And I know what that learning will feel like too: the elation, the despair and the realism. And the not-arsing-to-practice.

I've developed a hunger. Tango! Hip hop! The Macarena! I want to learn anything and everything. It feels like a whole other world has opened up to me – a world very similar to this one except with more leotards.

My respect for other people that can dance has grown – I know all the effort and work that went into even the simplest looking stuff. I know how the simplest looking thing can be incredibly hard, and the hard-looking stuff can be even harder. Except some of the hard-looking things are actually easier than the easy-looking things, and some of the... it doesn't matter.

And then there's the amazing country which I feel privileged to have got such an insight into; one which most of the world still misunderstands, and which has so much more to offer than people realise. Sex with donkeys for a start. I suppose I'd better reluctantly add about the wonderful people, rich culture and breath-taking scenery. Even the food's pretty good, now I think about it.

Despite all my many fears – of looking like an idiot; of failing in front of an audience; of even just going there in the first place – I gave it a go. I went out there and did it. I went to Colombia to learn how to dance like a Colombian, and my life is all the richer as a result.

I still can't do that fucking thing with my shoulders, though.

Mailing List

That's it - you've finished the book.

Hungry for more?

I've got photos, videos and all sorts of other stuff related to Dancing Feat. All the music I mention is in there too – it's pretty much a soundtrack to the whole journey. To gain access, simply sign up to my author mailing list and I'll email you the link immediately.

It also means you'll also be amongst the first to know when I'm bringing a new book out.

SIGN UP HERE:

http://neilbennion.com/dancingfeatsignup

Finally, if you enjoyed this book, and you'd like to help spread the word, then please consider leaving a review on Amazon or Goodreads.

About the Author

Neil Bennion was born in 1974 in Lancashire, England. He's a writer, traveller and mucker-abouter who left a successful career in IT when he realised he much preferred prancing about in foreign countries to discussing technical scope changes. He blogs about travel, productivity and general mucking about at wanderingdesk.com.

Dancing Feat is his first book.

Glossary

Here are some repeated and/or confusingly similar terms that I've used in the book, with (contextual) definitions. The aim is to help you navigate through the book, rather than be a universal guide, so some of the terms may be specific to Colombia, or even to a particular dance teacher I had.

aguardiente: Aniseed flavoured liquor.
arepa: A corn flatbread.
bachata: The fiddly twiddly music from the Dominican Republic with the sensual dance where you intertwine legs. One of the ones I learnt in Pasto.
bailar: To dance.
bambuco: Traditional Andean music and dance genre.
barrio: A neighbourhood.
bullerengue: Fuck knows.
caja: A *vallenato* drum.
calle: A street.
cha-cha-cha: A genre of music and dance whose onomatopoeic name is based on the rhythm. Can also refer to a triple-step of footwork used elsewhere.
champeta: Modern style of music common to the Caribbean coast. The one with all the samples and the saucy dancing that I (kind of) learnt in Cartagena.
clausura: Closing ceremony or graduation show.
coqueta: A flirtatious woman.
cotizas: Flat-soled shoes for dancing *joropo*.
crossover: A music night where they play a mixture of different

genres.

cumbia: Traditional Colombian music with shuffle-gaited dance that has mutated and spread throughout Latin America. The one I learnt in Barranquilla.

currulao: Music and dance of the Pacific coast, with marimbas and handkerchiefs. The one I could have gone to Tumaco to learn.

desplazamientos: Moving about the dance floor whilst performing the basic *joropo* steps.

figura: A fixed sequence of steps.

garabato: A folkloric music and dance ensemble featuring a confrontation with Death. A favourite of Carnival.

golpe: Any kind of blow, strike or accented movement.

guaneña: Traditional Andean music and dance genre. The one I learnt in Pasto.

joropo: Harp-based dance and music from the plains of Colombia and Venezuela. The one I learnt in Villavicencio.

ladron: A thief.

llamador: A small type of drum used in cumbia.

loco: Crazy.

malecón: A waterfront esplanade or promenade.

mapalé: Ridiculously frenetic music and dance style from the Caribbean coast. One of the dances I tried to learn in Cartagena.

merengue: A genre or music from the Dominican Republic whose dance features exaggerated hip movements. The one I learnt in Medellín. It's also the name a variant of *vallenato*.

mestizo: Mixed-race, usually of European and indigenous ancestry.

palco: A viewing stand at a festival.

pasaje: A slow variant of *joropo*.

paseo: A slow variant of *vallenato*.

pasillo: Stately genre of music and dance with a strong European influence.

paso: A dance step i.e. a repeated sequence of movements.

paso básico: The default step for a given dance.

pegado: Dancing so closely that your bodies are pressed (literally 'stuck') together.

peña: A traditional Andean music and dance club.

picó: A speaker stack and DJ set up, typical to the Caribbean coast.

pollera: A folk skirt or dress.

puya: A frenetic variant of cumbia accompanied by the cane flute (naughty oboe), and also a fast variant of *vallenato*.

recio: A fast variant of *joropo*.

reggaeton: Modern bad-boy fusion of dancehall with a load of other things. Has an associated saucy style of dancing, though some just dance in a circle. One of the genres I learnt in Pasto.

ruana: A heavy woollen poncho worn in the Andean regions.

rumba: Known worldwide as an Afro-Cuban genre of music and dance, but in Colombia it simply means a party.

salsa: Oh come on...

sancocho: A soupy stew.

sanjuanero: A specific interpretation of *bambuco*. The one they danced at the festival in Neiva.

sanjuanito: A folkloric Andean dance similar to *guaneña*.

sombrero vueltiao: A wide-brimmed, woven, two-tone hat, common to the Caribbean coast.

suave: Gentle / gently.

tambor: A drum.

vallenato: Ubiquitous, accordion-based folk music from the Caribbean coast. The one I experienced in Valledupar.

verbena: A street party held in the Caribbean coast region. Sometimes spelt *berbena*.

vuelta: A dance turn.

zapateo: Deliberately acoustic footwork, like in *joropo* and flamenco.

zona rosa: The part of town with all the bars and clubs.

Bibliography

I didn't just pull all the factual information in this book out of my backside. Only most of it. This bibliography is not an exhaustive list, but just some useful, selected sources.

Books:

Colombia: Fragmented Land, Divided Society by Frank Safford and Marco Palacios (OUP, 2001) is an excellent all-round guide to the history, from pre-Columbian times to (nearly) the present day.

The Cambridge History of the Native Peoples of the Americas by Frank Salomon, Stuart B. Schwartz (Cambridge University Press, 1999) has yet more historical information whilst **Culture and Customs of Colombia** by Raymond Leslie Williams and Kevin G. Guerrieri (Greenwood, 1999) is about, well, that.

Rivers of Gold: The Rise of the Spanish Empire by Hugh Thomas (Weidenfeld & Nicolson,2003), **Latin American Civilization: History and Society, 1492 to the Present** by Benjamin Keen (Westview Press, 2009) and **The American Indian in Western Legal Thought: The Discourses of Conquest** by Robert A Jr Williams (OUP, 1992) are good sources of information on the madness of the *requerimiento* amongst other things.

Music, Race and Nation: Música Tropical in Colombia by Peter Wade (University of Chicago Press, 2000)) is a brilliant and very readable book on the subject of race, class, music and Colombian identity, especially with reference to the Atlantic coast. The same author has another interesting and related book: **Blackness and Race Mixture: The Dynamics of Racial Identity in**

Colombia (John Hopkins University, 1995).

The City of Musical Memory: Salsa, Record Grooves, and Popular Culture in Cali, Colombia by Lise Waxer (Weslyan University Press, 2002) is another excellent resource, and goes into great detail on Cali's vinyl obsession and how the city became such a big salsa stronghold. For Reggaeton, the book **Reggaeton** by Raquel Rivera, Wayne Marshall and Deborah Pacini Hernandez (Duke University Press, 2009) is a fascinating and diverse collection of essays exploring everything from the roots of the genre to the gender politics. **Culture and Customs of the Dominican Republic** by Isabel Zakrzewski Brown (Westport, 1999), meanwhile, is good source of information on the music and dance of said country.

It's not always easy to find information about the more obscure genres, but the **Bloomsbury Encyclopedia of Popular Music of the World Volume IX** (Bloomsbury Academic, 2014) is so comprehensive that it's almost upsetting. **Music in Latin America and the Caribbean: An Encyclopedic History: Performing the Caribbean Experience Volume 2** by Malena Kuss (University of Texas Press, 2006) isn't bad, either, and has some good stuff on the music and dance of the Atlantic coast. **Musical Imagination: US-Colombian Identity and the Latin Music Boom** by Maria Elena Cepeda (New York: New York University Press, 2010) has some interesting stuff on often overlooked elements such as *rock en Español.* **Living Politics, Making Music: The Writings of Jan Fairley** by Simon Frith, Stan Rijven and Ian Christie (Ashgate, 2014) is a collection of works by the late Jan Fairley – an esteemed musicologist specialising in Latin American genres who died in 2012.

Finding out about specifics of dance steps can also be problematic. **Danzas Colombianas** by Alberto Londoño (Universidad de Antioquia, 1989) is in Spanish but has lots of detailed information on the folkloric dances of Colombia, right down to footwork diagrams. **Social Dance: Steps to Success** by Judy Patterson Wright (Human Kinetics, 2013) is a practical guide to dancing a variety of popular internationally-recognised forms. **The Wicked Waltz and Other Scandalous Dances: Outrage at Couple Dancing in the 19th and Early 20th Centuries** by Mark Knowles (McFarland, 2009), meanwhile, is a good source of dance-related outrage. Of which, it turns out, there is quite a lot.

Websites:

This is a brilliant article on *champeta* and the mobile DJs of Colombia's Atlantic coast (http://bit.ly/1xpTcOv).

There are some good documentaries on *burros*. PBS has one on *biblioburro* (http://to.pbs.org/1vlV6vs), whilst Vice looks at the phenomenon of human-donkey relations (http://bit.ly/1rykzCN).

If you like looking at pictures of accordions used to play *vallenato*, the Hohner website (http://bit.ly/1qCTvwA) is a good place to do it.

Here's a good article by Toby Muse on the subject of the Lost City (http://bit.ly/1wNBilt). And here's one by Richard McColl on the plight of the Nukak people (http://bbc.in/1t2wgxP).

If you want to read more about Mockus and his occasionally hilarious approaches to changing public attitudes then this is a good place: http://bit.ly/1rykRJP

And this is a nice resource on Colombian myths and legends: http://bit.ly/1uN0K9h

Here is a selection of interesting statistics on various subjects: general statistics (http://1.usa.gov/1myuF5S), murder rates (http://bit.ly/1okJLYi), displaced people (http://bit.ly/1wNCcyv), indigenous people (http://bit.ly/ZghDjn) and the civil war (http://bit.ly/Yk1Aj7).

And finally, it's obligatory that you read about Michael Fabricant's unfortunate coffee-whitener misunderstanding (http://bbc.in/1u3dsCT).